HARVARD
HISTORICAL
MONOGRAPHS

L

Published under the direction
of the Department of History
from the income of
The Robert Louis Stroock Fund

Germany and the Diplomacy of the Financial Crisis, *1931*

by EDWARD W. BENNETT

Harvard University Press · Cambridge · 1962

To Sue, Betsy, and Peter

Preface

THE German and American archival records available today are unprecedented in that they give us a full, public view of policies which were pursued within living memory. For the first time, we have records of twentieth century diplomacy which are so complete that significant suppression or omission is almost ruled out. It seems possible to draw from such sources many conclusions which are still applicable today. Some examples, taken from the brief period covered by this study, might be: that new policies must be thoroughly discussed with the other nations concerned before they are publicly announced; that financial experts do not necessarily make good diplomats; that a reportedly adamant internal opposition can be used by a national leader for extracting foreign concessions; that a plausible legal case does not in itself ensure diplomatic success; or that financial pressure used for political ends may be self-defeating. But while I have not hesitated to draw certain conclusions (some of which will doubtless be contested), I would like to suggest that there is another type of conclusion that should not be drawn. No country today is playing the same role it played in 1931. In particular, the West Germany of today cannot properly be identified with the Germany of 1931. Wisdom involves not only the identification of similarities, but also the recognition of differences.

For such conclusions in this study as may go beyond the evidence, I alone am responsible. For assistance in whatever is sound and objective in it, I am indebted to a number of individuals and institutions. Various members of the Harvard History Department were kind enough to read the manuscript and comment on it as it developed from a doctoral dissertation to its present form. I owe particular thanks to Professors Franklin L. Ford, Ernest R. May, and William L. Langer, all of whom did more than their departmental duties required. Professor Langer, especially, performed an act of supererogation in reading the whole manuscript and in making criticisms which were just, encouraging, and indispensable. My mother, my father-in-law, Henry W. Johnstone, and my neighbor Major R. Philip Herget also read all or most of the study, and gave me the reactions of intelligent, nonacademic readers. The resources of the Widener Library, the Library of the University of Michigan, and the Library of Congress were essential for this work. The Yale University Library kindly made available the original manuscript diary of Henry L. Stimson and permitted me to quote extracts therefrom. The Division of Historical Policy Research of the Department of State allowed me to see every official paper conceivably related to my topic, Dr. E. Taylor Parks being particularly helpful. The National Archives and the American Historical Association must be thanked for their activity in making the German Foreign Ministry records accessible to scholars, and I personally am grateful to the Archives staff for their consideration and helpfulness. Dr. Heinrich Brüning graciously granted me an interview in 1951, answering my questions with patience and with a completeness which I can only now—after studying the German Foreign Ministry records—fully appreciate. Herbert Feis was also kind enough to give me oral and written information on certain points. Marilyn K. Fardwell has proved a friend indeed, voluntarily helping to meet typing deadlines on two occasions.

Authors often pay tribute to their spouses, the usual phrase being, "without whose help this book could never have been written." In this case the phrase is literally true. My wife has devoted long hours to typing, copying, and proofreading. More important, she has been a valuable editor and critic. The appearance of this book is our joint accomplishment.

Edward W. Bennett

Arlington, Virginia
December 1961

Contents

*Germany and the Diplomacy
of the Financial Crisis, 1931*

DBFP   E. L. Woodward and Rohan Butler, eds., *Documents on British Foreign Policy* (London, 1946 and continuing).

FRUS   Department of State, *Papers Relating to the Foreign Relations of the United States* (Washington, continuing).

GFMR   German Foreign Ministry Records (microfilmed, copy deposited at the National Archives, Washington).

SDP   State Department Papers (unpublished papers of the Department of State, Washington).

SIA, 1931   Arnold J. Toynbee, *Survey of International Affairs, 1931* (London, 1932).

I

The Impulse Toward Revision

It has always been easy for the West to forget how close Germany came to victory in 1914 and in the spring of 1918. After the Armistice the Allies counted the dead and wondered if the war could have been won more cheaply; the Germans counted the kilometers and knew that they had barely been stopped. While the Allies did win in the field, and not through a stab in the back, the Germans had reason to describe the Versailles Treaty as a *Diktat*, for the peace was not made by negotiation, it was imposed. Whether or not we regard the treaty as just, we must admit that the Germans had no voice in framing it, and we cannot be surprised that they felt no responsibility toward it. Some Germans, like Franz von Papen, were anxious to promote friendship with France or England, and many hoped never to see another war. But those who wanted friendship and peace also wanted "equality" and the revision of the treaty. The makers and leaders of public opinion were often those who had made and led opinion before 1918; there had been no social revolution at home, and there had been no real change in the image of the nation.

Today there are many good Europeans in Germany, and sometimes they seek to trace their roots into the Weimar era. This search for antecedents may do credit to the searchers, but it does not always reflect historical fact. The truth is that the German pan-European movement was feeble, and that Gustav Stresemann was simply a nationalist who recognized the limitations of Germany's postwar position. Recent research has shown that Stresemann never accepted the Versailles settlement, and certainly the permanent officials of the German Foreign Office never accepted it. In the Wilhelmstrasse, the "policy of fulfill-ment" was usually regarded as a tactical expedient.

Foreign observers, such as Raymond Poincaré and the British Ambassador in Berlin, Sir Horace Rumbold, sometimes observed that the Germans seemed to have a regular list or catalogue of grievances.[1] And in fact, in 1927 Chancellor Wilhelm Marx and Stresemann gave the Austrians to understand that there was a regular schedule for revision; the Austrian Vice Chancellor and Foreign Minister, Johann Schober, recalled in 1931 that the order of German foreign policy tasks had been: evacuation of the Rhine, Eastern border, reparations, return of the Saar area, *Anschluss* with Austria.[2] Stresemann may simply have been try-ing to prepare the Austrians for a delay, and in the nature of things this schedule was not a hard and fast one. For one thing, it did not include the right to rearm, certainly a major German aim. But while the order of tasks might be changed, and other ones might be added, there was always a steady pressure for revision. Furthermore, we must bear in mind that this outward pressure was supported by internal pressures. Nationalist senti-ment was an ingredient of social respectability, and although reporting from abroad was still realistic and objective, there was an atmosphere in which ambitious officials thought twice before saying or writing anything suggesting an acceptance of the in-ternational *status quo*.

True, German revisionism was somewhat restrained in the twenties by the power of the Social Democrats, who, despite an

---

[1] *Documents on British Foreign Policy*, ed. E. L. Woodward and Rohan Butler (London, 1946–), Second Series, Vol. I, Nos. 313, 352. This publica-tion is abbreviated hereafter as *DBFP*.

[2] German Foreign Ministry Records (microfilmed, copy deposited in National Archives, Washington, D. C.; henceforth abbreviated as GFMR), Container 2521, Frames E285126, E285138: Note by Dr. Erdmann of the *Kölnischer Zeitung*, June 12, 1931; Dispatch, Clodius to Ministry, June 20, 1931. See also *DBFP*, 2/I, No. 317 (incl. note 5).

interest in such national aims as *Anschluss* and the evacuation of the Rhineland, distrusted the old German ruling classes and cared little for military display and expense. But Socialist participation in the government was one of the depression's first casualties. Germany had enjoyed a fleeting prosperity after the introduction of the Dawes Plan in 1924, but after 1928 the dazzling attractions, and then the collapse, of the New York stock market brought about a decline in the easy lending at high interest which had primed the German pump and overextended the German plant. The market for German exports also shrank, and the rolls of the unemployed grew longer. At the same time that loans became less available, revenues fell, expenditures rose, and the German government had to face the problem of balancing the budget. In particular, the unemployment insurance fund was soon in serious straits. A Keynesian policy of temporary inflation was then unheard of, and in any case, poor credit, the memory of the 1923 inflation, and the requirement that reparations be paid in gold, all made it impossible for Germany to follow such a policy. Rather than agree to a cut in social expenditures, the Socialists, led by Chancellor Hermann Müller, withdrew from the government in March 1930, and Dr. Heinrich Brüning of the Catholic Center Party was called on to form a cabinet. In effect, this meant that conservative, respectable, nationalistic officialdom was in the saddle.

Brüning was an austere bachelor who had succeeded in entering the army in 1915 despite medical disabilities, and he had won the Iron Cross as a *Frontoffizier* in a unit which after the war turned to *Freikorps* activity. Brüning kept his company together through the revolution, but then shed his uniform and went into Centrist politics. He was 46 in 1930, young for a German chancellor, and he had some young conservative friends who were active in politics; he was sometimes described as a leader of the younger, "front-line" generation. But he did not seem young. Although a passionate patriotism lay beneath the surface, and although he had courage and a strong will, he gave the impression, with his bald head, thin lips, and distant manner, of being cold and overly intellectual. Rarely has a man with so little popular appeal risen to the top in a modern state; that he could have risen was in fact a symptom that factors other than the popular will were at work.[3]

The Brüning government was much more than an answer to the budget problem. Brüning's candidacy was urged on President von Hindenburg by General Kurt von Schleicher,[4] who saw in the budget crisis an opportunity to eliminate Socialist influence and bring in a chancellor who would wholeheartedly support the aims of the Ministry of Defense, such as the "pocket battleship" construction program.[5] Hindenburg himself was glad to be rid of the Socialists, and happy to select as chancellor a man with a front-line record. The parties included in Brüning's cabinet did not hold a majority of seats in the Reichstag, and outsiders wondered how Brüning would govern without the support of either the Socialists or the Hugenberg Nationalists. Those who had created the new government were not unduly concerned. The model before their eyes was the Reich of Bismarck and Wilhelm II, with the chancellor responsible to the chief of state rather than to the Reichstag; observers noted similarities between Brüning and the Iron Chancellor.[6] Using Article 48, a chancellor supported by the president could act without awaiting parliamentary sanction, much as under the old system.

Still, the Reichstag ultimately had to approve all emergency

[3] See Karl Dietrich Bracher, *Die Auflösung der Weimarer Republik* (Stuttgart and Düsseldorf, 1957), pp. 307-308; Moritz J. Bonn, *Wandering Scholar* (London, 1949), p. 310; André François-Poncet, *Souvenirs d'une ambassade à Berlin* (Paris, 1946), p. 17.

[4] Otto Meissner, *Staatssekretär unter Ebert-Hindenburg-Hitler* (Hamburg, 1950), p. 188; Lutz, Graf Schwerin von Krosigk, *Es Geschah in Deutschland* (Tübingen and Stuttgart, 1951), p. 117.

[5] See Gordon A. Craig, *The Politics of the Prussian Army, 1640-1945* (New York and Oxford, 1956), pp. 436-438.

[6] Among those who have drawn the Bismarck-Brüning parallel are: Schwerin von Krosigk (*Es Geschah*, pp. 139-140); von Oldenburg-Januschau (*DBFP*, 2/I, No. 349), and Groener (Craig, *Prussian Army*, p. 442). Krosigk compares the position of the other ministers under the presidial regime to that of Bismarck's state secretaries. See also Bracher, *Auflösung*, pp. 341-347.

decrees. Brüning's measures for cutting expenditures and raising revenues met with strong opposition, and when he persisted in issuing decrees, the Reichstag voted, on June 18, 1930, to abrogate them. Instead of resigning, Brüning scheduled new elections for September 14, almost two years before the constitution required them.

This was certainly a rash step, and fatal for German democracy. Conditions within and between the parties made it almost impossible for Brüning (or later, Papen) to benefit from an election. The Catholic vote was inelastic (if we may borrow a term from economics) and the other parties in Brüning's government had no broad popular appeal and had mostly lost their *élan*. Foreign policy was almost the only field in which the government parties could campaign together, and their relatively responsible nationalism was vulnerable to demagogic attack.

THE YOUNG PLAN

A few days after the Chancellor dissolved the Reichstag, the Allies completed their evacuation of the Rhineland. Their departure, years before the term fixed in the Versailles Treaty, was part of a two-sided trade. The other side of the bargain was the Young (or Hague) Agreements, in which Germany formally bound herself to a schedule of reparations payments running until 1982. The Young Plan had been the center of an intense political struggle in Germany, with the Nationalists and Nazis attempting to block its acceptance through a referendum. The reparations problem will be of major importance in this study, and it will be convenient to note here certain aspects of the obligations existing in 1930.

Under the Dawes Plan, reparations payments had been tied to a prosperity index, and had been supervised by the Agent General for Reparations, the American S. Parker Gilbert, whose criticisms of German financial policy aroused resentment, and whose staff was suspected of espionage against German rearmament.[7] But

[7] See GFMR, 2381/E196172-4: Memo from Foreign Ministry (Bülow) to Ministries of Finance and Economics, Oct. 22, 1930.

under the New Plan, as the Young Plan was often called, Germany had full responsibility for her payments, which were fixed according to a schedule. The New Plan foresaw only one contingency in which the payments might be permanently reduced: if there was any reduction in the war debts owed to the United States by the European Allies, reparations would be cut by two thirds (in later stages of the Plan, by all) of that amount. To no one's surprise, the United States turned a deaf ear to this echo of the Balfour Note of 1922, in which Britain had offered to forego all debts and reparations if other nations would do likewise. Americans did not regard reparations, the spoils of victory, as comparable to war debts, money that had been borrowed.

The essential idea in the Young Plan, and the reason for the long fixed schedule of payments, was the desire—so characteristic of the time—to take intergovernmental payments "out of politics" and put them on a commercial basis. Bonds were to be issued which would be sold to the world public and paid off by the German government, the proceeds of sale going to certain of the creditor governments, principally France. The portion of the reparations payments which was eventually to be devoted to the amortization of these bonds was called the "unconditional payments," and Germany was to make them in fair weather or foul. It was realized, however, that circumstances might arise (the experts had a possible shortage of foreign exchange most in mind) in which Germany would be unable to transfer the full amount due; in this event, she could declare a postponement of the transfer of the other part of the scheduled reparations, the "conditional payments."

It was naïve to suppose that a problem like that of reparations could be removed from politics. Indeed, from the French point of view, commercialization was itself expected to serve a very practical political end, in a sense replacing the troops who were leaving the occupied zones. If the German government did not make the unconditional payments, and defaulted on the Young bonds, German private credit would suffer a smashing blow, and German borrowers would be unable to secure loans abroad. Thus commercialization created a new guarantee that reparations would be maintained intact. Actually, only a small part of the unconditional payments was ever commercialized, as the world markets in 1930 were in no condition to absorb large new issues, and the whole system foundered in 1931. But even without the Young bonds, German credit was vulnerable to foreign attack, since the German economy and the German currency itself depended on the maintenance of a high volume of short-term loans from abroad. France, financially strong after Poincaré's devaluation of the franc, was in a position to lend to Germany or to other countries on short term or sight, and then recall her credits at any moment she chose, upsetting the finances of the borrowing country. Many Germans, including Brüning, believed that their financial weakness had been a factor in the Young negotiations in 1929, and that the French had forced the German negotiators to give way by withdrawing credits. Besides, it was difficult to argue that Germany could not pay reparations from her own resources when this had never actually been tried.[8] Politically as well as financially, it seemed imperative to balance the budget and stop the borrowing from abroad, so as to end this vulnerability to foreign pressure.

There was, however, another aspect to the German credit problem, which seems to have been overlooked in the French calculations. Germany was not alone in having a stake in German credit, and if she once began to approach bankruptcy, she might receive financial assistance and political support from her creditors, purely in their own interest. Stresemann had recognized this back in 1925, when he said in a speech: "One must simply have enough debts, one must have so many debts, that the creditor sees his own existence endangered if the debtor collapses . . . These economic matters build bridges of political understanding and of

[8] See Brüning's Oldenburg speech, reported in the *Berliner Tageblatt*, May 11, 1931 (Evening Edition); Hjalmar Schacht, *76 Jahre meines Lebens* (Bad Wöreshofen, 1953), pp. 298–300, and *The End of Reparations* (New York, 1931), pp. 87–94; GFMR, 1683/D786001; 1659/D729026: Cabinet Protocol, Feb. 21, 1931; Memo on Raising Reparations Question, April 9, 1931; *DBFP*, 2/I, No. 341; and *New York Times*, April 28, 1929.

future political support." [9] In effect, he prophesied what happened in 1931.

In order to render the Young Plan more palatable to the German public, those German leaders who bore responsibility for accepting and carrying out the Plan made much of the so-called "alleviations," the emergency rights to suspend payments or to request the Bank for International Settlements (BIS) to convoke a Special Advisory Committee to advise on measures to be taken "in regard to the application of the Plan." (If the Germans declared a suspension of payments, the BIS would automatically summon the Special Advisory Committee.) Actually, although the Germans interpreted the powers of the Committee to include the power to recommend *revision* of the Plan, others held very different views; the French might try instead to use the Committee to re-establish a control commission inside Germany to exact payments. Moreover, the suspension privilege only provided for an early and effective suspension of *transfer*, not of *payment* itself. During the first year of a Young moratorium, Germany was still required to make the monthly conditional payments in marks, although transfers in gold or foreign exchange could be put off for two years. In the second year, fifty per cent or more of the mark payments could also be postponed for one year. But the postponements were so arranged that heavy obligations would accumulate at the end of the second year, and therefore some provision for meeting them would probably be necessary in that year's budget.[10] Thus a Young moratorium could provide no immediate and scarcely any eventual relief for the German government's finances, and this fact undermined the whole German argument for such a moratorium in 1930 and 1931. On the other hand, this same fact might give added impetus to the demand for action outside the framework of the Plan.

[9] Annelise Thimme, *Gustav Stresemann: Eine politische Biographie zur Geschichte der Weimarer Republik* (Hannover and Frankfurt-am-Main, 1957), p. 69.
[10] Great Britain, *Parliamentary Papers*, Command 3343, Report of the Committee of Experts (Young Plan), June 7, 1929, p. 54.

BRÜNING'S CABINET AND THE SEPTEMBER 1930 ELECTIONS

The Foreign Minister, Dr. Julius Curtius, was the only member of Brüning's cabinet who had been closely identified with the Young negotiations. Curtius, a short, well-poised lawyer with a somewhat foxy appearance, was sometimes called *der Young-Plan-Minister* by his numerous enemies. This was rather unfair, since he was revisionist, just as Stresemann, his predecessor and fellow member of the People's Party, had been revisionist. Brüning acknowledged the Young obligation, and deplored the demagogic and irresponsible attacks on the Plan from the extremists, but he hoped that reparations could be revised again before too long. Rather than trying to justify the Young settlement, or even pointing with pride to the evacuation of the Rhineland, members of the cabinet went on during the 1930 election campaign to demand the revision of other parts of the Versailles settlement. Issues raised by them included the Saar, the demilitarization of the Rhineland, and the Polish Corridor. One minister, Gottfried Treviranus, made such a fiery speech against Poland that he provoked an official protest from Warsaw. Curtius also was annoyed at this speech, because it had not been coordinated with the Foreign Office, and because he thought it was too soon to raise this question, and he and Treviranus had heated arguments in the cabinet. Treviranus did explain on the radio that he had had no warlike action in mind, and that his views on the Corridor were identical with Stresemann's, but he then went on to make other aggressive speeches, leading one Social Democratic leader to ask, "Is Dr. Curtius really Minister of Foreign Affairs?" Curtius finally sent Treviranus the following telegram: "Since my return have read with astonishment your latest foreign policy declarations, especially in the *Börsenzeitung*. Consider them inadmissible and out of place. Urgently request you desist from further statements on foreign policy intentions." But Curtius himself took pains to show that he was sufficiently revisionist, telling the cabinet that he had succeeded in interesting the American Ambassador, Frederic M. Sackett, in the Corridor.[11]

---

[11] *DBFP*, 2/I, Nos. 307, 308, 309, 311, 312, 313, 314, 317, 318; Julius Curtius,

In the later stages of the campaign, political attention turned from the Corridor to reparations. Monsignor Kaas, the chairman of Brüning's party, declared: "We realize that no German accepts the Young Plan, and the idea of revision is before our eyes." [12] There were good reasons why reparations revision should move to the head of the list of German objectives. The "tribute payments" were the one item on the national list of grievances that could be regarded as a sufficient cause for the depression, and the fact that the Nazis were in the best position to exploit this argument may help to explain their sudden increase in strength at this time. At the same time, the depression furnished a certain justification for reparations revision, since it could be argued that the Young Plan, framed in the boom conditions of 1928 and 1929, presupposed the existence of a now vanished prosperity. The ink was scarcely dry on the Young agreements, but circumstances had drastically changed.

The world learned the election results on September 15. The National Socialists had increased their strength from 12 to 107 seats. While the radicals of the Right thus rose suddenly to second place among the German parties, the Communists, on the Left, now took third place with 77 seats, a gain of 23. The strongest party, the Social Democrats, lost 10 seats and now had 143 Reichstag representatives. The strongest element in the government, Brüning's own Center Party, placed fourth with a gain of 6 seats, while other government parties, particularly the State Party and the People's Party, lost heavily. The government parties accounted for only 171 out of a total of 577 members.[13] This electoral revolution seems to have been due to the participation of new voters, previously too young or too indifferent to go to the polls, and to the alienation of others from their old bourgeois —or Nationalist—loyalties. With the depression, millions of people

Sechs Jahre Minister der deutschen Republik (Heidelberg, 1948), p. 165; GFMR, 1707/D784627–30, D784797–803; 2382/E196912: Cabinet Protocols, Aug. 8, Sept. 3, 1930; Curtius to Treviranus, Sept. 1, 1930.

[12] *DBFP*, 2/I, Nos. 318, 320.

[13] Statistisches Reichsamt, *Statistisches Jahrbuch für das Deutsche Reich, 1932* (Berlin, 1932), p. 541; *DBFP*, 2/I, No. 321.

lost hope of finding any inspiration, or even place, in the Weimar establishment, and the Nazis and Communists gathered them in. There could hardly have been a more emphatic rejection of Brüning's conservative leadership.

Brüning did not resign, but the election returns increased his dependence on the real supports to his position, Hindenburg and the army. He told the cabinet that he felt they should remain in office: "One could help Germany only through calm and hard work." He and his ministers believed that the first essential was a stern and responsible policy with regard to the budget, and particularly with regard to unemployment insurance.[14] The formation of a majority cabinet was out of the question in any case, and these men believed that Germany needed a government of hard-headed experts. But such a cabinet of *Fachminister* was inevitably one of conservatives, dependent on the support of the President and the Reichswehr. The Reichstag still had to be dealt with, and it was fortunate for Brüning that the Social Democrats, fearing something worse, decided to tolerate his government, making an enabling act possible.

If Brüning was resolved to stay in office, the election none the less had a shock effect, and the cabinet's first reaction was to acknowledge the Nazi gains by adopting a more forceful foreign policy. The German leadership was also anxious to use the voting results to show other countries that concessions to Germany were overdue. Since Curtius was in Geneva at the time, attending a League of Nations Assembly meeting, *Staatssekretär* Bernhard von Bülow, the courtly and prematurely gray young nephew of Wilhelm II's chancellor, and the chief permanent official of the Foreign Ministry, sent him (at 1:15 P.M. on September 15) the following telegram.

Immediate. Confidential for Foreign Minister personally.

Have just come from a discussion with the Chancellor, attended by the Center Party ministers and Treviranus, as well as by Kaas. Dis-

[14] GMFR, 1707/D784833-6: Cabinet Protocol, Sept. 16, 1930. Dietrich (Vice Chancellor and Minister of Finance) mentioned that the last, highly adverse report on tax receipts had been suppressed until after the elections.

cussion was primarily concerned with your speech in the League Assembly. Prelate Kaas is traveling at once by plane to Geneva to discuss with you the Chancellor's wishes in this regard, arriving at 7 o'clock. The intention is to ask you to take a position, in a way acceptable to the Right, with regard to the election results, and to set forth the share of other countries in the guilt for the present situation in Germany. Briefly, this point of view, in the formulation of which I had a part, is as follows:

The Treaty of Versailles was accepted by a scant majority. For ten years this majority has, with great moral sacrifices, followed a policy of understanding, the milestones of which are the tombstones of some of our best leaders, such as Erzberger and Rathenau. From the German side the warning has been made again and again that the situation remains unbearable. Remember Wirth's phrase, "First bread, then reparations" and Kaas's declaration, "The capacity of a people for suffering has its limits." Not enough concern has been devoted to the capacity of a society to live and to the limits of the national ability to assume burdens. For years the German government has vainly striven for more successful results from the policy of understanding. Germany should have been released from political burdens when she entered the League of Nations. Quicker decisions by other countries would have been wiser. Our policy's long-standing poverty in diplomatic successes has brought a reaction, as would naturally have been the necessary result with any other people. The German government is itself, as before, determined to work together with other countries for the reconstruction of Europe. But as has been already stated in the [German] pan-European memorandum, this must take place on the basis of real equality and freedom.

In addition I note that, following the desire of all those who took part [in the meeting], the term "policy of understanding" will have to be avoided. Finally I recommend that on disarmament, only a summary of Henderson's excellent arguments be presented,[15] and that the main emphasis be given to equality of rights in relation to security, that is, on the assimilation of the security requirements of all countries, and therewith the equalization of Germany.[16]

[15] Arthur Henderson had suggested that the powers were pledged to disarm and that the work of disarmament should be speeded up.

[16] GFMR, 1553/D661413-4; an interesting account of the cabinet's reaction was given by Bülow in a letter to Curtius, Sept. 16, 1930 (GFMR,

Curtius has described in his postwar memoirs how Kaas came to Geneva, and he says that Berlin wanted to reverse the whole German foreign policy, and that he refused to do this. He had already drafted his major Assembly speech, and he tells us that he delivered it mainly in the form he had originally planned. But the speech as he describes it followed closely the line laid down in Bülow's telegram.[17] If there was no drastic reversal in Curtius' speech, and no drastic reversal in German policy, it was because the speech and the policy were already nationalist and revisionist before Kaas arrived.

The 1930 elections did not bring a change in the German aim, which had always been to revise the Versailles Treaty. But the elections did dictate that more energy must be brought to bear. On the one side, Brüning felt a need to appease the middle-class voters, who had become impatient with the relative moderation of the old bourgeois parties. This need was expressed quite distinctly in Bülow's telegram. On the other side, the government now relied more heavily than before on Hindenburg and the Reichswehr, both longing for a return to the days of the Empire. A foreign policy success would make their support more secure, and would divert attention from the hardships of deflationary budget policies and of the depression. And there was one important asset at Brüning's disposal: his reputation for being moderate and responsible, largely a result of his financial conservatism, inclined the Western powers to give him help and concessions, lest other elements displace him.[18]

2382/E196938–43). While in Geneva, Curtius had a friendly conversation with Briand, at the end of which Briand proposed a communiqué announcing that "the policy of understanding introduced by him [Briand] and Stresemann must be continued." Curtius was unable to agree, stating that "such a communiqué would, at this time, completely fail to achieve its purpose in Germany" (GFMR, 2382/E196950–1).

[17] Curtius, *Sechs Jahre*, pp. 171–172.

[18] See GFMR, 1776/D808333–4, D808203: Unsigned memos on reparations policy, Dec. 20, 1930; June 18, 1931 [latter possibly by Brüning himself]; Heinrich Brüning, *Die Vereinigten Staaten und Europa* (Stuttgart, 1954), p. 4. Brüning hinted in his Rhein-Ruhr Klub address that he had cultivated internal opposition while chancellor because it encouraged other countries to make concessions to him.

Once before in German history, a conservative chancellor had faced internal opposition and had, by diplomatic successes, overcome it. Could Brüning, with his unpopular economies—like Bismarck, with his unpopular army laws—succeed by means of a popular foreign policy? [19]

[19] Gordon Craig (*From Bismarck to Adenauer: Aspects of German State-craft*, Baltimore, 1958, p. 86) notes that Brüning "decided to rely—as Bismarck had done when he was breaking the opposition of the Prussian parliament in the 1860's—upon victories abroad."

II

Testing the Young Plan

GERMANY was now to suffer a severe strain, brought about by the elections. Even before the voting, rumors that Germany would soon declare a reparations moratorium were affecting Young Loan quotations. The returns themselves brought panic withdrawals of funds from the country, partly by nervous French lenders, and partly by Jewish and liberal Germans. On September 25, Adolf Hitler gave added meaning to the election results by stating, at the trial in Leipzig of three Nazi army officers, that "heads would roll" when his party came to power.[1] Along with the flight of funds, stock quotations fell on the Berlin Börse. The weeks that followed saw the most serious German financial crisis of any period between the spring of 1929 and the summer of 1931, marking a new stage in the world depression.

Since this is a study in international political history, not in economics, no attempt will be made here to analyze this (or the 1931) financial crisis as an economic phenomenon. Suffice it to note that the following June Reichsbank President Hans Luther disclosed at a cabinet meeting that German foreign exchange losses in the period after the 1930 elections had totaled 1.3 billion reichsmarks out of previous holdings of 3.8 billion reichsmarks.[2]

---

[1] *DBFP*, 2/I, Nos. 320, 325; GFMR, 2640/H002819–20; 2384/E198840–2; 4506/K240381–6: Kiep (Washington) to Ministry, Sept. 27, 1930; Rieth (Paris) to Ministry, Sept. 23, 1930; Dispatch, Rieth to Ministry, Oct. 10, 1930. All communications from unpublished sources are telegraphic unless otherwise specified.

[2] GFMR, 1683/D786768: Cabinet Protocol, June 3, 1921. Howard S. Ellis,

For Germany, there was only one compensation for these difficulties: they might lend support to demands for reparations revision.

Insofar as the withdrawals came from abroad, they were mainly recalls of money lent at short term. The great weakness of
Germany in this whole period was not so much that she had
borrowed, as that latterly foreign borrowing had been almost
entirely of the short-term variety, at high interest. Internally,
these short-term funds were used largely for long-term nonliquid
investment; externally they were used to meet reparations charges
and to repay earlier loans. Even when things were calm, the
burden of interest was a heavy one. Should there be some upset,
resulting in a widespread demand for repayment, a general bankruptcy would be inevitable.

In a way, it was largely a question of how long it would be
before the foreign creditors became aware of the danger. Contrary to what one might suppose, it was not at all easy to find
out the volume of international short-term borrowing by Germany. Even though a careful survey was made for the Layton-
Wiggin Committee in 1931, the Germans later revised the
Layton-Wiggin figures upward by fifty per cent. It was not the
custom of the day to make private financial statistics too readily
obtainable, and consequently the danger was not yet widely
recognized in the fall of 1930. French lenders, more than once
burned by their experiences with loans to Russia and elsewhere,
were noted for their timidity, and they were most unwilling to
have any of their money come into Nazi hands; they did most
of their withdrawing during this postelection period. The American and British creditors, who had lent much larger sums, by and
large stolidly left their funds where they were.[3] Neither they nor

_____

"German Exchange Control, 1931–1939," *Quarterly Journal of Economics*,
54:5 (1940, sup.), gives the figure 1.6 billion as estimated loss. The data
given, however, are not sufficient to make possible a strict comparison of the
two figures.

[3] On the basis of figures later published in the Layton-Wiggin Report,
at the end of March 1931 the American short-term involvement in Germany
was in the neighborhood of RM4,000,000,000, with British loans at approxi-

the French really saw how ominous, completely aside from the elections, the situation was.

The Lee, Higginson Loan and Schacht's Tour

The German government does not seem to have feared a final collapse, but the crisis was very unwelcome to it. Despite previous economies, the budget was still unbalanced, owing to the decline in revenue resulting from the depression. The adverse report of income from taxes for August had been kept secret until after the election, but now it was clear that further economies and new taxes would be needed. With the financial situation what it was, the prospects for the German budget were worse than ever. Moreover, in order to repay earlier loans and to tide over until the new measures should be put into effect, the Brüning government was obliged, against its own wishes, to seek yet another loan from abroad. On September 24, the cabinet asked Luther to take up negotiations for an intermediate (literally, a "tiding over") credit of $125,000,000.[4]

Under the circumstances, the most logical place to turn for the money was America. With one exception, the banks in London reportedly took no interest in such a credit, and no approach was made to the French until arrangements were practically concluded. Contrary to what one might expect, the French government had begun immediately after the German elections to consider offering Germany new credits, probably in the hope of gaining better control over German policy in the dangerous period to come, and certainly with the aim of staving off demands for reparations revision. But any loan from France would be subject to various conditions, political as well as financial. Moreover, the French withdrawals actually taking place suggested

---

mately RM2,000,000,000. At that time, 47 per cent of German foreign short-term debt was estimated to be in foreign trade acceptance liabilities, 40 per cent in deposits, etc., payable in foreign currency, and the remainder in reichsmark balances of foreign creditors (*DBFP*, 2/II, Appendix II). For the later German estimate, see *DBFP*, 2/II, No. 278.

[4] GFMR, 1707/D784834–5, D784865, D784990: Cabinet Protocols, Sept. 16, 24, 29, 1930.

that, even with the best will in the world, the French government would not be able to induce French lenders to place their funds in Germany. Luther therefore opened negotiations with the Boston firm of Lee, Higginson and Company.[5] There was a complication, however, even in approaching American lenders. The former President of the Reichsbank, Dr. Hjalmar Schacht, was to land in New York on October 2 for a lecture tour of the United States. Schacht had participated in the Young negotiations, but had been obliged to resign from the presidency of the bank after attempting to reverse certain modifications to the Young Plan already sanctioned by the German government representatives.[6] Actually, he may have desired to conceal his own responsibility in framing the unpopular reparations agreement, for no financial expert was ever more of a politician, or more fascinated by political power. Schacht was now an outspoken advocate of reparations cancellation, and his lectures were to be a series of attacks on reparations, along the line that unless reparations were canceled, the American private loans to Germany could not be repaid.

Schacht was too important and too headstrong a personality to act as a mere propaganda agent of the German government, but his trip had been planned with the government's knowledge and approval.[7] The trip was in the nature of an experiment, to see if America could be induced to intervene. The proposed lectures on the threat to American funds were indeed well calculated to interest Americans in reparations cancellation, and thereby to further revision. They were not, however, exactly appropriate at a moment when Germany was seeking a fresh loan.

[5] GFMR, 1492/D621132–3; 2382/E196948–9; 4506/K240406–7; 4507/K240439: Bülow to Embassy in Washington, Sept. 28, 1930; Memo by Curtius, Sept. 18, 1930; Hoesch to Ministry, Oct. 23, Nov. 10, 1930; *Journal des Débats* (Paris), Oct. 15, 1930 (on absence of British interest).

[6] Julius Curtius, *Sechs Jahre Minister der deutschen Republik* (Heidelberg, 1948), pp. 138–141; Friedrich von Prittwitz und Gaffron, *Zwischen Petersburg und Washington* (München, 1952), pp. 190–191; Hjalmar Schacht, *76 Jahre meines Lebens* (Bad Wöreshofen, 1953), pp. 321–328.

[7] Schacht, *76 Jahre*, p. 343. See also GFMR, 2384/E198835, Bülow to Richthofen (Copenhagen), Nov. 21, 1930.

In his memoirs, Schacht complains that he first heard of the
loan proposal while he was on the boat; had he been consulted,
his personal view would have been that it was better simply to
stop payments than to borrow any more money. When Schacht
landed, his first remarks for the press were framed to support
the loan, but in a speech at the Hotel Astor the next day, he said
flatly that Germany could not pay reparations and that she would
be justified in asking immediately for a moratorium; certainly a
moratorium would be declared some day. On hearing of this,
the German government promptly issued a statement denying
that it would soon seek reparations relief and disclaiming responsibility for Schacht's remarks. This *démenti* in turn aroused
Schacht's anger. According to him, the German government continued to assure him privately that he had its full confidence.
The Chargé d'Affaires in Washington, Otto Kiep, reported to
Berlin that in telephone conversations with Schacht he was doing
his best to stress the risk of damaging German credit while the
loan was pending. For a time Schacht did moderate his tone; at
the Bond Club of New York, on October 9, he assured his audi-
ence that, although he did not believe Germany could pay reparations, all foreign loans, including the Young Bonds, would be
paid.[8]

While in New York, Schacht spoke with George Murnane of
Lee, Higginson. According to Schacht, Murnane asked his opinion of the security of the proposed loan, and the German, after
wrestling with his conscience, told Murnane that he would certainly get his money back, though he might have to wait a while
for some of it. If this report is true, one wonders that the agreement on the loan was concluded at all. Perhaps by this time the
negotiations had gone too far for Murnane to turn back, for on
the evening of October 11, it was announced that the loan arrangements had been concluded, and it later became known that
Lee, Higginson was heading a group of twenty-two American
financial houses in the lending; one Canadian, three Swedish,

[8] GFMR, 1492/D621137, D621140, D621143-4: Kiep to Ministry, Oct. 2, 4,
10, 1930; *New York Times*, Oct. 4, 10, 1930; Schacht, *76 Jahre*, pp. 343, 347.

twenty-three German, and a number of Dutch banks also participated.[9] This was the last great foreign credit that the Weimar Republic was to receive, and those who lent the money soon regretted their action.

DISCUSSION OF REPARATIONS-DEBT REVISION

With Schacht's continuing lectures in America, and a lively public discussion in Germany, where the Reichstag convened on October 13, the reparations question became the center of attention. Certainly the German ministers were thinking more and more of taking action on reparations. In a cabinet meeting on October 4, Curtius had observed that Young Plan revision was coming more quickly than could have been expected, but also that for the time being Germany could not pursue an active revisionist policy, or request a moratorium. Neither the Americans nor the French were "in a position" as yet to make concessions. Brüning said, "Certainly the question of the Young Plan and the question of the inter-Allied debts must come to the fore in the foreseeable future," but added, "at the present moment there was no hope of decisive progress on this question." At another meeting, on October 7, Minister of the Interior Joseph Wirth complained that there had been no success in bringing the government's foreign policy more in tune with the thinking of the German people, and he wondered if it were not possible, without seeking a moratorium, to request a convocation of the Special Advisory Committee of the Bank for International Settlements. Brüning answered that there should be no public declaration on reparations at present: "One could only make internal preparations for a later revision. At present a summoning of the Special Committee would have a devastating effect on our credit." [10]

Probably Brüning was afraid of disturbing the loan negotiations. Five days after the loan was safely in hand, on October 16, the Chancellor made a major Reichstag speech, in which he advanced a new program for further financial reforms, and stated

[9] Schacht, *76 Jahre*, p. 344; *New York Times*, Oct. 12, 13, 1930.
[10] GFMR, 1707/D785029, D785033, D785063: Cabinet Protocols.

that if this program broke down under the continued pressure of crisis at home and abroad, Germany would be forced to resort to those safety devices which were put at her disposal by her existing foreign commitments. Without his mentioning the Young Plan, every informed German knew that these "safety devices" included the possibility of a transfer moratorium and the possibility of summoning the Special Advisory Committee of the BIS. In his speech, while refusing to embark on "a policy of adventures," Brüning stressed the dissatisfaction of Germans with their treatment by other powers, and promised to build up the Reichswehr to the limits allowed by Versailles. It was largely thanks to this speech, together with the realistic decision of the Social Democrats to "tolerate" Brüning's government, that the Reichstag tabled a vote of no confidence and adjourned.[11] With the loan and the Reichstag out of the way, Brüning had passed the first obstacles following the election.

Whatever the feeling was in Germany, the talk of reparations revision came as something of a shock to foreign ears. It was at this time scarcely six months since the Young agreements had gone into operation. In particular, the course of the loan negotiations, Schacht's activities, and Brüning's speech were scarcely soothing to the French. On the day before the agreement with Lee, Higginson was completed, the German government had formally notified the Quai d'Orsay that a loan was being sought. Philippe Berthelot, Secretary-General of the French Foreign Office, had certainly heard before that the Germans were seeking this loan, and not unnaturally, he seems to have supposed that other arrangements had fallen through, and that French participation was now essential for the loan's success; he indicated that he would only be in favor of joining in the credit after some of the proposed financial reforms had been carried out. But then the loan was arranged without French help. On the day after the announcement that the loan had been concluded—also the day

[11] *New York Times*, Oct. 17, 1930; *Deutsche Allgemeine Zeitung* (Berlin), Oct. 17, 1930; S. William Halperin, *Germany Tried Democracy* (New York, 1946), pp. 452–454.

after Nazi riots in Berlin—French state bonds and Bank of France shares fell on the Paris Bourse. On October 15, the *Journal des Débats* declared that the Germans should be made to understand that they could be brought back to the position of 1923 by peaceful means, that is, by the withdrawal of French short-term loans.[12]

While the French were showing bitterness, the Americans seemed to be somewhat caught off balance by Schacht's one-man invasion. When Reichsbank President Luther proposed that he, too, visit the United States, Governor George L. Harrison of the New York Federal Reserve Bank suggested that Luther postpone his trip until it would be "subject to no possible misinterpretation." American officials appeared to be concerned over the growing discussion of reparations and debts, which might have repercussions in Congress, and some apprehension was evident when Schacht visited Washington on October 18. While there, he saw Secretary of State Henry L. Stimson, Chairman of the Federal Reserve Board Eugene Meyer, Secretary of the Treasury Andrew Mellon and his Assistant Secretary, Ogden Mills, and President Herbert Hoover. Meyer and Stimson both shied away from debts and reparations; when Schacht mentioned reparations to Stimson, the Secretary said that that might be a dangerous subject. Schacht reports in his memoirs that he discussed the effects of the "tribute" with Hoover, who showed complete understanding, and Hoover's later comments suggest that Schacht made a good impression; however, the contemporary cable report from the German Embassy says only that Schacht and Hoover had a friendly discussion on economic policy and disarmament.[13]

Schacht's talk with Mellon and Mills seems to have been more

[12] GFMR, 2381/E196193: Memo by Bülow, Oct. 10, 1930; *New York Times*, Oct. 11–15, 1930; *Figaro* (Paris), Oct. 4, 1930; *Journal des Débats* (Paris), Oct. 15, 1930. Press reports from Basel and Paris, possibly inspired, had begun to discuss the prospects of the loan, depicting France as reluctant to give her approval, and representing this approval as essential to the loan's success.

[13] GFMR, 2381/E196150; 1492/D621156–7, D621163–8: Harrison to Luther, Oct. 16, 1930; Bülow to Embassy in Washington, Oct. 18, 1930; Kiep to Ministry, Oct. 20, 21, 1930; Stimson Manuscript Diary (deposited at Yale University Library), Oct. 18, 1930; State Department Papers (unpublished

concrete. Schacht informed the Chargé (who did not accompany him on this call) that the Treasury chiefs had inquired about Germany's ability to pay after the current loan. Apparently Schacht gave a negative answer on reparations, for Mellon went on to ask if, after a two- or three-year moratorium, the normal functioning of the Young Plan could not resume. Mellon also asked if Germany could not take the initiative herself in some such action, but Schacht replied that Germany would then get all the blame. Germany, he pointed out, was not a debtor to the United States government, although she did feel an obligation, in view of American private loans, to keep the United States informed regarding her ability to pay.[14]

This idea of a temporary postponement, which later was to blossom into the Hoover moratorium proposal of June 1931, was apparently being widely discussed at this time. In what may have been a trial balloon, the *New York Times* of October 21 ran a story on the front page, datelined from Paris, to the effect that the United States was considering proposing a five-year moratorium on war debts and reparations. Simultaneously, the newspaper published a denial from Washington that such a proposal had been discussed during Schacht's visit to the capital. Aside from these reports, the world press was now full of rumors about an impending cessation of reparations payments, due to the financial crisis.[15]

---

papers of the Department of State, Washington, henceforth abbreviated as SDP), 862.51/2939: Memo of conversation between Secretary of State and Dr. Schacht, Oct. 18, 1930; Department of State, *Papers Relating to the Foreign Relations of the United States, 1931* (Washington, 1946, henceforth abbreviated as *FRUS, 1931*), vol. I, p. 263; Schacht, *76 Jahre*, p. 348.

[14] GFMR, 1492/D621168-9. The next day Schacht and his wife had lunch with Secretaries Stimson and Mellon, Under Secretary of State Cotton (who died the following spring and was succeeded by William R. Castle), and Governor Harrison. Nothing delicate was discussed during the lunch, but after the others had left, Stimson, Cotton, and Harrison (presumably under the impetus of Schacht's remarks) talked over the need for replacing the credits recently lost by Germany, possibly by hastening repayments from sums held by the Alien Property Custodian (Stimson MS. Diary, Oct. 19, 1930).

[15] *New York Times*, Oct. 20–23, 1930. The moratorium rumor did not appear in all editions.

DIPLOMATIC SOUNDINGS FOR A YOUNG MORATORIUM

In this situation, the German Foreign Office was encouraged to take further soundings. As preparation for a meeting of the Reichstag Foreign Affairs Committee, scheduled for October 29, the Embassies in Washington, Paris, and London were asked to report on the probable reaction of the governments to which they were accredited, should Germany raise the reparations–war debts issue officially, either within or outside the Young framework.[16] The Committee was likely to question Curtius closely, pressing for a more active policy, and the Foreign Minister probably also wanted the information as a guide for future policy. Since the time of the conclusion of the Young agreements, there had been little actual planning and consideration of the next step in reparations, no doubt because, as Curtius said, revision was now coming faster than could have been expected.

The answering report from Paris pointed out that even a Young moratorium would be sharply condemned in France, while a unilateral suspension of payments would lead to demands for reoccupation. If a Special Advisory Committee was convened, the French would seek to use it, not for the revision of the Young agreements as the Germans wanted, but to intervene in Germany and make her capable of paying. From Washington, on the other hand, came word that American financial circles favored liquidating reparations and war debts, and were urging their government to cooperate or even to take the initiative. Conceivably the American government might later, "in a cautious way, enter into negotiations for an earlier liquidation of debts, perhaps in the form of a moratorium, with later lower capitalization," although the American administration was for the time being restrained from acting by the pending congressional elections, and by the session of the lame duck Congress that would follow, as well as by public opposition to any concession on war debts. In England,

[16] GFMR, 2381/E196167: Circular, Oct. 22, 1930. The Rome Embassy was also asked to make a report, but only on whether the Italians were planning to mobilize a part of their reparations receipts (GFMR, 2381/E196171).

there appeared to be considerable resistance to a moratorium or to revision, although this attitude was expected (quite rightly) to change eventually. The report from London stated that although the depression was causing the view to gain ground, even outside financial circles, that revision would soon be necessary, still an immediate move to postpone payment would be a disaster for German credit. It would also be regarded as premature, since neither the Young Plan nor the German financial reforms had yet been given a fair trial, and since America was thought to hold the key to the whole situation.[17]

None of the three reports, from Paris, Washington, or London, supported early action. But two of them held out hope for success later on, with New York and London financial interests urging their governments to act. It was necessary to let the Young Plan lose some of its newness, and to convince the world that Germany had made a real effort to reform her finances and to meet her obligations.

Curtius did not content himself with discreet inquiries; he also received the British, French, and Belgian representatives separately in Berlin on October 27, and in the course of conversation with them he stated that, in view of the deterioration in Germany's financial and economic situation, the German government was obliged, despite the energetic reform of public finances that had been undertaken, to keep in mind the possibility of seeking alleviations under the Young Plan. Moreover, perhaps because Ambassador Pierre de Margerie in Berlin was neither effective nor well informed, Ambassador Leopold von Hoesch in Paris also spoke with Berthelot and Premier André Tardieu in the same sense; Hoesch was said to be the best man in the German diplomatic service, and he could be trusted to give these statements the proper emphasis. Tardieu took a serious view of the possibility of an early Young moratorium declaration, saying that it would have a very bad effect on French opinion, coming only a few months after the Young Plan was signed.[18]

It may be that Curtius' action in interviewing the ambassadors was undertaken mainly so that he could tell the Foreign Affairs Committee he had undertaken it.[19] Essentially he was repeating and amplifying what Brüning had said in his speech on October 16, and he may not have contemplated taking any early action. But his statements suggested that the German government was thinking of seeking a Young moratorium in the not-very-distant future.

THE BRITISH *Démarche* OF DECEMBER 10, 1930

The other governments in question were naturally startled by the way in which Germany was stressing her Young Plan rights. The French and Belgian Ambassadors in London inquired whether the Germans had raised the reparations question with the British, as had been done with their own governments. Even before these inquiries were made, the Foreign Office, under Arthur Henderson and Sir Robert Vansittart, had decided that

---

[18] GFMR, 1554/D666111–7; 2381/196177–81: Memos by Curtius, Oct. 27, 1930; Hoesch to Ministry, Oct. 26, 1930; DBFP, 2/I, Nos. 333, 339; SDP, 462.00R296/3872, 3879: Ambassador in Berlin to Secretary, Nov. 24, 25, 1930. On de Margerie, see GFMR, 1554/D666116 and 2549/E300504: Memo by Curtius, July 25, 1931. The evaluation of Hoesch given above was reported by General Groener—see Reginald H. Phelps, "Aus den Groener Dokumenten," *Deutsche Rundschau*, 76:1015 (1950)—and it is well supported by the files of the *Auswärtiges Amt*. According to Hajo Holborn's "Diplomacy in the Weimar Republic" (in Gordon A. Craig and Felix Gilbert, eds., *The Diplomats*, Princeton, 1953, p. 151), Hoesch had made such an impression as German Chargé d'Affaires in Paris during the Ruhr crisis that Poincaré had requested that he be made ambassador. He was frequently invited by Berlin to give his views on projected actions, and his thoughtful and well-written reports make the best reading of any material in the German documents.

[19] The Committee meetings were important occasions for foreign ministers: Weizsäcker writes that he once heard Stresemann say that when he sat in the League Council meetings at Geneva, he was always thinking about how he was going to justify his actions in the Reichstag Foreign Affairs Committee (Ernst von Weizsäcker, *Erinnerungen*, München, 1950, p. 80). For a specimen Committee resolution, see DBFP, 2/I, No. 335 note 1.

it would be unwise to permit the German Foreign Minister's suggestion of a possible moratorium to pass unchallenged. The Foreign Office was probably influenced in this view by reports from the British Ambassador in Berlin, Sir Horace Rumbold, indicating that on all questions the German government was likely to pursue "a more forward foreign policy" and stating that there were signs that Curtius would "increase the tempo." At the same time, as Henderson informed his ambassador in Paris, Lord Tyrrell, he desired to forestall any proposal for formal or joint representations to the German government by the creditor powers. He therefore sent a memorandum to Rumbold to present "verbally and unofficially" to Curtius.[20] The German documents now reveal that Henderson also sent Rumbold a private letter, stating that the British government sought to support, in France, moderate and conciliatory men like Aristide Briand, the French Foreign Minister; the position of these men, however, depended largely on continued moderation in German policy. Should there be a change in the policy of the German government, England would again be forced more strongly to the side of France. Rumbold was empowered to communicate the substance of this letter to Curtius.[21]

The British memorandum expressed emphatic opposition to any appeal being made to the Young provisions before the financial reforms had been thoroughly tested, and before the German situation became much more serious. It was argued that Germany's difficulties were less than England's, and that, such as they were,

the responsibility for them rests, in different degrees, with Germany, and they cannot be invoked as a ground for revising the annuities which Germany accepted as a complete and final settlement of reparations less than a year ago. It is much more likely that the result of an investigation of the position would be to provoke demands for the

---

[20] See *DBFP*, 2/I, Nos. 308, 309, 311–3, 317, 327, 331–5, 337–9. In his interview with Rumbold on October 27, Curtius also stressed the German interest in disarmament by other nations.

[21] GFMR, 1776/D808339: Memo by Curtius, Dec. 11, 1930.

reimposition of the foreign controls without any reduction of the annuities.

6. In these circumstances there seems to be little prospect of anything but a deadlock arising if the Special Advisory Committee is convened. It appears from the remark made by Dr. Curtius to your Excellency [Rumbold] on the 27th October that the German Government assume that the committee would be entitled to recommend a general revision of the plan. But the actual terms of reference of the committee are to report "What, in their opinion, are the measures that should be taken *in regard to the application of the plan*" (paragraph 121 of the Young plan) [italics in text].

The memorandum argued that unless, as seemed unlikely, the United States granted alleviations in war debts, the other governments would hardly agree to reparations revision. German private credit would be endangered, and an adverse political reaction might be expected in other countries. Henderson's memorandum also pointed out that German "budget difficulties would be unaffected by a moratorium, since even the postponable annuities would continue for at least a year to be paid in Reichsmarks in full." [22] Finally, the memorandum stated:

To sum up, the point of view which I wish your Excellency to put forward in discussing the question with Dr. Curtius is that the convening of the Special Advisory Committee (whether coupled with a moratorium or not) was intended to be resorted to only in case of manifest necessity, and that in the opinion of His Majesty's Government no such necessity can be said at present to exist; that consequently, any such action appears to His Majesty's Government likely to provoke the gravest dangers, without being likely to give Germany the slightest relief; and that if the German Government should decide to adopt such a course, they must expect no support or help from this country in the inevitable difficulties which they will bring upon themselves. [23]

The British memorandum was sent to Berlin by pouch and was

[22] Curtius had told Rumbold on October 27 that a Young moratorium might serve to help German credit, since "the money left in Germany would be used productively and improve her economic situation." See *DBFP*, 2/I, No. 333.

[23] *DBFP*, 2/I, No. 338; GFMR, 1776/D808339–45: Memo by Curtius, Dec. 11, 1930.

not presented to Curtius until December 10. Although the memorandum was "unofficial," the interview was later referred to in the German Foreign Ministry as a *démarche*.[24] If one considers the letter and the memorandum together, the warning was indeed a forceful one. Whatever may be said of later British foreign secretaries, and whatever may be thought of "Uncle Arthur's" self-righteousness and lack of financial knowledge, it cannot be claimed that he failed to take up the cudgels against revisionism.

The summary of Rumbold's presentation written by Curtius, together with other German papers, suggests that the greatest effect was produced by the quotation on the authority of the Special Advisory Committee, and by the expressed view that the Committee would be hamstrung from the start. Curtius denied that on October 27 he had said, as Rumbold had reported, that the Special Advisory Committee could recommend revision. Nevertheless, he apparently had expected revision to result from the Committee's reporting, perhaps because its report would create a political situation favorable to revision. Such a result would not be forthcoming, however, if the British did not support the German position. And Henderson's memorandum and letter made it evident that, at least for the present, the British would not support the Germans, and might well support the French. The Germans were well aware of the endemic rivalry between the British Foreign Office and the Treasury, but at this stage indications were that the Treasury shared the Foreign Office views.[25] Up until this point, the German leaders, perhaps beguiled by their own public statements referring to the "alleviations" in the Young Plan, seem to have assumed that an appeal to the Young clauses could solve their problems. The British memorandum led them to plan their action more carefully.

THE SACKETT-BRÜNING CONFERENCE PROPOSAL

It was becoming more and more apparent that the United States held the key to the situation. The report from Washington had

[24] GFMR, 1659/D728868, D728891, D728898.
[25] GFMR, 1554/D666112; 1776/D808343; 2381/E196187; 1659/D728891-3, D728898-9: Memos by Curtius, Oct. 27, Dec. 11, 1930; Bernstorff to Ministry, Oct. 27, 1930; Memos by Dieckhoff, Jan. 8, 9, 1931.

shown some hopeful signs there. Ambassador Friedrich Wilhelm von Prittwitz und Gaffron later wrote Bülow that Schacht's lectures "did not fail to have an effect," although it seemed to Prittwitz that Schacht had overstressed the German desire to revise the Young Plan, and that he had, against Embassy advice, spoken too many times. "It has been shown by experience [Prittwitz said] that the wrong dosage has a prejudicial effect on any propaganda." Prittwitz believed, however, that Americans approved the realistic policies of the German government, and that Ambassador Sackett had done good work on his last home leave.[26]

True, there were some negative symptoms. The Democratic success in the 1930 congressional elections seriously limited Hoover's ability to take action, should he wish to act. And when Governor Harrison of the New York Federal Reserve Bank visited Berlin in November, he told a group of German bankers and industrialists that nothing could be worse for Germany than the suggestion that she was unwilling or unable to meet any of her obligations. During this visit Harrison talked with *Ministerialdirektor* Karl Ritter, Chief of the Economic Section of the Foreign Ministry. As he emerges from the record, Ritter was an unattractive person, aggressive on most occasions, prone to shift the blame when at fault. But he was one of those men who really make departmental policy, and he was later in charge of economic warfare under Ribbentrop. Ritter found that Harrison shared many of the French and British views on the reparations problem, although he tried to change Harrison's mind. Also in November, Brüning tried to arrange a private and secret meeting with Owen D. Young to exchange ideas, but after some reflection Young decided that such a meeting was impractical and unwise. And as Prittwitz reported, Schacht seemed to some American financial circles, especially bond salesmen, to have been undesirably pessimistic. Although agreement had been reached on the Lee, Higginson loan, American brokers were finding that it was going badly on the American market, and they were said to feel that their share of the credit had, in their respective portfolios, "the weight of a millstone." [27] But the concern of American financiers, indicated by such things as Harrison's remarks to Ritter, was in a different sense an encouraging symptom. Although the financiers might deplore Schacht's teaching methods, his lessons were sinking in. The paradox of Germany in this period was that, the worse economic affairs became, the greater was the prospect for revision.

One potential asset, from the German point of view, was the person of the American Ambassador, Frederic M. Sackett. A former Kentucky Senator and Louisville business leader, Sackett's political outlook seems to have centered around what was for the time an unusually intense preoccupation with the dangers of Communism. Curtius believed that he had Sackett in his vest pocket, and he and Brüning seem to have considered the Ambassador politically naïve. Certainly Sackett was favorably inclined to Germany, although he did not always report as the Germans expected him to. Stimson, who was not infallible, rated Sackett as one of his best ambassadors, and the Secretary also noted in his diary that the Berlin Embassy reports were the best from any of the embassies.[28]

Brüning's opportunity to seek American aid came on December 19, when Sackett met with him to discuss the whole political situation. Brüning began with a description of the German politi-

[27] SDP, 462.00R296/3879: Ambassador in Berlin to Secretary, Nov. 25, 1930; GFMR, 1659/D728788–93; 1492/D621230–1: Memo by Ritter, Nov. 27, 1930; Prittwitz to Ministry, Dec. 4, 1930; Charles G. Dawes, *Journal as Ambassador to Great Britain* (New York, 1939), pp. 256–259.

[28] Stimson MS. Diary, May 4, 1931; Louis P. Lochner, *Herbert Hoover and Germany* (New York, 1960), pp. 76–77. For the German perspective on Sackett: GFMR, 1707/D784628–9; 1493/D621344–8, D621386–8; 1555/D666691–4; 2548/E300246–9. On March 10, 1931, however, after discussing German securities in the U.S. market with the Ambassador, *Staatssekretär* Schäffer wrote: "[The] thoughts of Mr. Sackett are not really so far from reality as they first appeared to us to be" (GFMR, 2375/E192116–121).

cal and economic situation, and argued that Germany would have
been quite stable politically if the international situation had not
led to a feeling of hopelessness, and if the depression had not
created revolutionary currents throughout Europe. Sackett thereupon expressed great concern over the tendency of Soviet policy,
but Brüning did not take this too seriously.

I said [Brüning recorded] that we saw no diplomatic connection
between Russian policy and the Communist movement in Germany,
but that I nevertheless regarded the trend as dangerous in the long
run, in the event that the complicated situation, which arose from the
world economic crisis in connection with the reparations question
and the building up of arms by almost all neighboring lands, progressed
further. The time, then, must come when European politics and the
economic and financial relations of the whole world will have come
to the end of a blind alley, from which no exit can be seen, at least at
present.

Sackett said that it was difficult for President Hoover to act, since
the elections had left him with a veto but with no majority for
constructive action, and Brüning remarked that he knew from his
own experience about opposition to constructive action. Then
Sackett suddenly, and possibly without too much forethought,
asked if Brüning thought that Hoover should convoke an international economic conference. This gave Brüning a perfect opening.

I took up this idea, but in the course of a long conversation I also
sought to show that if this economic conference only dealt with purely
economic questions, and was only attended by economic experts, in all
probability an unsatisfactory outcome must be expected. The difficulty
with all past efforts had been that they had regarded the great related
questions of disarmament, reparations, debt retirement, and international loan requirements as separate matters, leaving them to specialists. We must get away from this method; above all, for me a complete
understanding with France was the truly decisive goal for a pacifica-
tion of the politics of the whole world, but I was afraid that this goal
could not be reached with the necessary speed through direct negotiations with France, due to French internal political factors.

Sackett concurred, but observed that the experts would be unable to agree if they considered all things together.

I said [Brüning continued] I saw the objection, and had not yet had time to think the subject of the negotiations through, but I thought that if President Hoover or the American government would not only get things started, but also take the leadership firmly in hand, results could be reached.

The Ambassador also raised the objection that the war debts were based on the capacity to pay without counting reparations. If war debts were cut, the United States would have to assume responsibility for paying private creditors. The [Allied] countries would have the gift of German reparations, and I pointed out that the money could then be spent on the colossal arms potential of these countries.

I stressed the urgency of the whole proposition, which would not only be very suitable for the talents of the American people, but would also simultaneously deliver the peoples of Europe from a certain dull despair. A bright ray of hope must come, just as in earlier times of psychological depression the peoples had been given the courage for new investments by international agreements. Sackett promised to write a private letter to Hoover at once, and then to talk further with me when we both returned after New Year's.[29]

Brüning's proposal was certainly audacious; these ideas seem to have been an early expression of his "great plan," which he mentioned to the author in 1951, and which has been described in a later context by John Wheeler-Bennett, who was close to and sympathetic with the German Chancellor. To look at the matter cynically, the common denominator of all these questions—reparations, disarmament, loans, debt retirement—was that they represented German desires. It is difficult to see what inducement Brüning was offering in return, aside from his own maintenance in office. Moreover, the suggestion that disarmament should be considered a solution to the economic crisis now seems

---

[29] GFMR, 1776/D808328–31. Years of American exile only confirmed Brüning in his view of American psychology; in his controversial address to the Rhein-Ruhr Klub in 1954, he emphasized that Americans like "great, lasting solutions" (H. Brüning, *Die Vereinigten Staaten und Europa*, Stuttgart, 1954, p. 4).

somewhat ironic, for whatever the moral, political, and long-term economic objections to an arms program may be, such a program has certainly proven to be an effective remedy for deflation. It could be argued that the world would have enjoyed more prosperity (and therefore might ultimately have had more peace) if all the nations in 1930 had been arming to the teeth. But Brüning's program was indeed likely to appeal to American idealism. And in fact, when President Hoover addressed a world congress of economists in May 1931, he took for his theme the association of arms and depression, although he refused, to the disappointment of many, to consider reparations and war debts.[30]

THE GERMAN PLANS FOR REPARATIONS REVISION

In Berlin, the result of Sackett's letter to Hoover was eagerly awaited, and meanwhile, meetings and memoranda discussed the prospects. One memorandum suggested (1) that the domestic weakness of the American, French, and British governments was unfavorable to the revision of the Young Plan, (2) that Americans, Frenchmen, and Englishmen favored financial support of Germany as a means of meeting the financial crisis, and (3) that the Brüning government was regarded as offering a guarantee that bourgeois order would be upheld in Germany. Another paper stated, "It must be very quickly decided how the preliminary financial negotiations in early 1931 are to run." The more hope there was for revision, the more indispensable it seemed.[31]

On December 27 a meeting was held, attended by Brüning, Curtius, and various high officials of the Reichskanzlei and the Foreign Ministry. The participants agreed on the following policy.

If Hoover does not take a completely negative position, the idea of a conference summoned by the United States should be further pur-

[30] Interview with Dr. Brüning, Jan. 31, 1951; John W. Wheeler-Bennett, *The Nemesis of Power: The German Army in Politics, 1918–1945* (London, 1953), pp. 229–230; Arnold J. Toynbee, *Survey of International Affairs, 1931* (London, 1932, henceforth abbreviated as *SIA, 1931*), pp. 46–47.

[31] GFMR, 1776/D808332-4, D808335-7: Unsigned memo, Dec. 20, 1930; Memo by "N," Dec. 20, 1930.

sued. This conference should be attended by heads of governments, not by experts. Also, it should not concern itself primarily with economic or even reparations questions, but should rather have preponderantly a political character, so that the expansion of the Kellogg Pact or the disarmament question would be the most suitable as occasions for its convocation. Naturally, it will emerge in the course of developments that the reparations question, like the question of international war debts, will have to be discussed too.

Hoesch was to assure the French that Germany also wished to pursue the idea of organizing the European economy through Franco-German efforts within the framework of pan-European conversations, and Curtius was to prepare an *aide-mémoire* by January 3 on the proposed "big political conference." It was decided that there would be further discussions after Sackett had received his reply from President Hoover, which was expected around January 13.[32]

Perhaps the best picture of high-level German thinking at this time is provided by a letter *Staatssekretär* Hermann Pünder, permanent chief of the Reichskanzlei under Brüning, sent on January 3, 1931, to *Staatssekretär* von Bülow. Pünder wrote:

I might mention some political thoughts which have arisen in your absence. Don't think that there is any quarrel between our two houses, at least on the important issue. The point of departure for the new deliberations is the Chancellor's firm conviction that the situation on reparations policy will not hold up during the whole year of 1931, either as regards the private economy or as regards government finances. The withdrawal of foreign capital is continuing as before, if not to such an extent as after the Reichstag elections, and it is more and more agreed that the continuing withdrawal of the reparations payments without the leaving of any comparable counter-value inside Germany is not only ruinous in the long run, but indeed must lead to catastrophe very soon.

This was, by and large, the first proposition on which the Chancellor believed himself in agreement with the Foreign Ministry, and indeed also the other offices primarily concerned. The second point is to the

[32] GFMR, 1776/D808318-9.

effect that the possibilities of the Young Plan are actually for us no possibilities at all. To be specific, the Reichsbank, but also, so far as I can see, all the other agencies involved, expect ruinous results from the declaration of a moratorium, without being assured of any significant positive gain, at least for the moment or the near future. And it is further to be feared that, through the Special Advisory Committee, the end of the story might be financial supervision [that is, by the other powers].

Accordingly, after agreement was reached, and, it is to be hoped, will remain reached, on these two points, a third question arose as to the other possibilities. The idea of a political world conference under the leadership of President Hoover was to my knowledge not exactly born in the Wilhelmstrasse. If it should turn out that this course cannot be pursued and that another third proposal must be made, then the Chancellor will certainly be very grateful for any suggestion in this direction. Only it does appear necessary to him *that* another suggestion actually be made, since a vacuum in place of this third (desired) proposition would be scarcely bearable. The idea of the great world conference seems indeed to crop up elsewhere too; in any case a telegram from Ambassador Hoesch about conversations with his British colleague Tyrrell (No. 1161 of 20 December 1930) makes a brief reference to it.

There, I have finished my Latin. I only want once again to make firm our mutual over-all agreement, and not let you think that at our house we have closed minds on the subject of the third proposition. I am ready to talk things over at any time. There is of course no objection if you show these lines, which were not written on orders from the Chancellor, to Herr Curtius.[33]

Bülow had not attended the meeting on December 27, and it appears from this letter that, on resuming his duties, he had found himself unable to share the hopes placed on Sackett's letter to Hoover. His reservations may have arisen from his concern with the Austro-German customs union project, which the Foreign Ministry, under his own and Curtius' leadership, was quietly bringing to fruition. It would be difficult to carry out reparations revision and a customs union simultaneously, and as we shall see,

---

[33] GFMR, 1776/D808311-4. Italics as in original.

the Foreign Ministry was becoming committed to its plans with Vienna.

"Aufgeschoben, aber nicht aufgehoben"

The hopes placed on Sackett's letter to Hoover were doomed to disappointment. It was February 2 before the Ambassador reported to Bülow that the President, in his reply, had in no way taken a position on the question of a conference. Sackett explained that Hoover was fully occupied with internal American affairs, and he modestly added that he did not wish to take up Brüning's valuable time with this message, which he was not inclined to regard as final.[34]

Despite Brüning's desire to avoid a "vacuum" in place of the "third proposition" referred to in Pünder's letter, no one seems to have come forward with a substitute for a Hoover conference. And despite what Pünder wrote to Bülow, the financial and political pressure for reparations revision further decreased, for withdrawals of funds virtually stopped for the time being, while the Nazis and Nationalists made the government's task easier by temporarily boycotting the Reichstag. On January 20, Bülow wrote Ambassador Prittwitz, his personal friend, that there would certainly be no reparations action in February. And on February 21, in the course of a cabinet meeting, Brüning indicated that Germany might pay reparations for a year, or with help, for two years, although these were outside limits; when the reparations crisis came, they must be economically prepared.[35] The reparations issue ceased for an interval openly to engage German diplomacy.

But if they no longer planned an early move on reparations, the Germans did not fold their hands and wait, and they did not forget the importance of America. In an attempt to carry on Schacht's campaign, one Werner Kehl of the Deutsche Bank

[34] GFMR, 1776/D808281. Later, in early March, Sackett also admitted to Rumbold that at the request of the German government he had sounded Hoover on the subject of an international economic conference, but "had met with no response" (*DBFP*, 2/I, No. 354).
[35] GFMR, 2384/E199141; 1683/D786001.

und Diskontogesellschaft, who had just returned from the United States, set forth once more, ostensibly on business, but actually with the aim of presenting American bankers with arguments against reparations.[36] In February, Reichsbank President Luther prepared an eighteen-page letter to Sackett on the German short-term debt and capital shortage problems which argued that the difficulties were insoluble as long as reparations continued; Ambassador Sackett sent copies to the State and Treasury Departments, and Luther himself sent a copy to Governor Harrison—and also two to the German Foreign Ministry. General Hans von Seeckt also took a hand in the proceedings, writing to former Ambassador Alanson B. Houghton and sending a copy of his letter to the Foreign Ministry.[37]

Meanwhile the American banks were growing more and more apprehensive. On January 17, the Chase National Bank, with $190,000,000 lent in Germany, begged off from participating in a new $25,000,000 loan for the Reichsversicherungsanstalt für Angestellte, and suggested that the Germans turn to the Bank for International Settlements. A few days before, the Chairman of the Board of the Chase Bank, Albert H. Wiggin, spoke out in favor of a reconsideration of the reparations question. Owen D. Young told Prittwitz that he now thought that reparations and debts should be reduced 20 per cent, and that he had communicated this view to President Hoover. Officials of Lee, Higginson and Company visiting Berlin in this period were obviously nervous and seeking reassurance. In discussing proposals for the $25,-000,000 loan, they told Sackett it was doubtful that even that amount could be raised. One of them remarked that "the truth was that the short loans to Germany were now in such volume that they could not be called or renewals refused without great

[36] SDP, 862.51/2994: Dispatch, Ambassador in Berlin to Secretary, Jan. 20, 1931. Sackett thought Kehl's first trip had been private, but the German Foreign Ministry had followed it with interest (GFMR, 1659/D728876-7).

[37] SDP, 862.51/3016: Dispatch, Ambassador in Berlin to Secretary, March 25, 1931; GFMR, 1776/D808223-59; 1659/D729038-43: Letter of transmittal and letter from Luther to Sackett, Feb. 27, 1931; Letter of transmittal and letter from Seeckt to Houghton, April 10, 1931.

danger to the financial situation in the United States"; if even 25 per cent of these loans were not renewed, there would be no way for Germany to carry on, as she could neither pay nor borrow elsewhere. Ambassador Sackett was shocked by what he heard, and thought it necessary to warn his government; in Washington, copies of his dispatch were sent to Secretary Mellon and President Hoover. Presumably, then, Hoover became quite aware of the house-of-cards condition of German-American finance.[38]

The September 1930 elections had led the German ministers to look for some means of satisfying, without too much further delay, the desire to revise the Treaty of Versailles. Because of the depression and the publicity which had been given to the reparations issue, this last appeared to be the obvious point for attack. But the German government wished to "negotiate from strength," and had first to secure a foreign credit, and then to try to increase its financial independence by making drastic economies; retrenchment would also help in influencing foreign opinion, which would have to be convinced that Germany had made every effort to pay, and could pay no longer. As part of the preparation of the other nations, and probably also for the sake of appeasing nationalism at home, Curtius warned other governments that an appeal to the Young "alleviations" might be necessary; he was sternly rebuffed by Henderson, who drove home to the Germans the practical uselessness of a Young Plan moratorium. Then Brüning turned his hopes toward a conference under American leadership, but Hoover ignored this proposal. Still, something was accomplished, for the campaign to mobilize American business and financial leaders was succeeding even better than its authors realized.

[38] SDP, 862.51/2898, 2991: Ambassador in Paris to Secretary, Jan. 29, 1931; Dispatch, Ambassador in Berlin to Secretary, Jan. 21, 1931; GFMR, 1659/D728908-9, D728912-3: Prittwitz to Ministry, Jan. 14, 17, 1931. A memorandum warning the British government of the dangerous credit situation was forwarded from Berlin on December 12, 1930 (*DBFP*, 2/I, No. 341). Louis P. Lochner quotes from Sackett's January 1 report, which he apparently found in the Hoover material at Stanford; this seems to confirm that Hoover did indeed receive the report (L. P. Lochner, *Herbert Hoover and Germany*, New York, 1960, p. 115).

III

Berlin and Vienna
Propose a Customs Union

THE POSTPONEMENT of reparations revision was not to mean a relaxation of international tension. Searching for a diplomatic success, the German government now turned its attention to another "foreign policy task," closer relations with Austria. Much ink was spilled between the wars on the question of what to do with the German-speaking remnant of the Austro-Hungarian Empire. It was then widely believed that Austria was unable to survive alone, or was "not viable," and that she would have to be integrated into some larger whole. The two favorite solutions for the Austrian problem were, first, *Anschluss*, or political union with Germany, and second, a Danubian Federation. The latter envisaged the organization of southeast Europe as an economic, if not a unified political, unit, probably under Czech rather than Austrian leadership. In addition, Aristide Briand had proposed an over-all European Union in 1929. Most other nations were cool to Briand's political plans, but there was some interest in economic union, and a Commission of Inquiry for European Union was set up in September 1930 to investigate the possibilities, including those of pacts on a regional scale.

GERMANY AND THE AUSTRIAN PROBLEM

The Austrians themselves generally preferred *Anschluss* as a solution. When the First World War ended, they had immediately indicated their willingness to join with their fellow Germans, under a Berlin government. France, however, had not fought the war to create a bigger Germany, and so Article 88 of the Treaty of St. Germain declared the independence of Austria to be inalienable except with the consent of the League Council; failing that consent, Austria agreed to abstain "from any act which might directly or indirectly or by any means whatever compromise her independence."[1]

Thus immediate *Anschluss* was ruled out, but there were more subtle ways to bring the two countries together. Toward the end of the war, the German and Austrian governments had been studying proposals for a customs union, and the plans—the so-called "Salzburg Agreements"—drawn up in 1918 foreshadowed, in some respects, the proposals published in 1931. Even for economic ties, however, there were legal obstacles. When Austrian bankruptcy led to League intervention and assistance in 1922, a protocol was signed at Geneva, in which Austria not only reaffirmed Article 88, but also agreed to refrain "from any negotiations or from any economic or financial engagement calculated directly or indirectly to compromise [Austrian] independence," and further not to grant "to any State a special regime or exclusive advantages, of a nature to threaten [Austrian economic] independence." The German government convinced itself in 1930–1931 that the Geneva Protocol did not specifically forbid a customs union, but in May 1931 one of the Austrian participants in the 1922 negotiations admitted to the Germans, rather belatedly, that unfortunately the Protocol was indeed intended to prevent any such arrangement.[2]

During the twenties there was some progress toward the adoption of parallel laws and institutions, furthered by various

---

[1] M. Margaret Ball, *Post-War German-Austrian Relations* (Stanford, 1937), pp. 8–25; *SIA, 1931*, p. 297.
[2] Gustav Gratz and Richard Schüller, *Die äussere Wirtschaftspolitik Österreich-Ungarns: Mitteleuropäische Pläne* (Wien, 1925), pp. 93–100; GFMR, 2521/E284833: Dispatch, Rieth to Ministry, May 10, 1931; Julius Curtius, *Sechs Jahre Minister der deutschen Republik* (Heidelberg, 1948), p. 118; *SIA, 1931*, p. 298. The Austrian participant was Richard Schüller.

pan-German organizations such as the Österreichisch-Deutschen Arbeitsgemeinschaft and the Österreichisch-Deutschen Volksbund, and by Dr. Richard Riedl, at one time the Austrian Minister to Berlin, and thereafter the most active proponent of a customs union.[3] Germany interested herself in fostering pro-*Anschluss* attitudes and subsidized various Austrian newspapers, including the *Wiener Neueste Nachrichten*. In the course of such activities, there was a prolonged discussion, in 1928–1929, of the proposal of Dr. Rudolf Sieghart, President of the Boden-Credit-Anstalt, that the Reich government secretly purchase shares in his bank, thus obtaining influence in the Austrian economy. It was probably fortunate for the German government that nothing came of this scheme, for the Boden-Credit-Anstalt was soon found to be in financial difficulties, aggravated by Sieghart's financial incompetence. The cracks were papered over by a forced merger, arranged through Sieghart's political influence, with the famed Creditanstalt für Handel und Gewerbe, like the Boden-Credit-Anstalt a financial remnant of the Dual Monarchy. At one point (in 1929) Sieghart had been suspected of cooperating with the French and the Czechs, but after the loss of his bank, which he blamed largely on the Czech desire to eliminate Austrian influence on their economy, he offered the German Ministry in Vienna the support of his newspaper, the *Neues Wiener Tagblatt*, which had previously been outspokenly anti-German. One is reminded of some of the characters in Graham Greene's *The Third Man*. We do not know, as the Germans did not know, all that was involved in these intrigues, but it appears that Ger-

---

[3] See Ball, *Post-War*, pp. 77–99; GFMR, 2347/E173487–8, E174045–58, E174099: Memo of Riedl-Ritter discussion, June 14, 1928; Letter, Karl Lahm to Dr. Paul Grossmann, Feb. 11, 1930; Memo of conference with Schober, Feb. 24, 1930; *DBFP*, 2/I, No. 22. It was quite conceivable that, while remaining formally independent, Austria and Germany might thus be joined as an economic unit. Indeed, all institutions and laws could be made similar even though technically separate; this process seems to have been the original meaning of the term *Gleichschaltung*. Thus the day might sometime dawn when a short proclamation would be all that was needed for the achievement of an *Anschluss*; perhaps *Anschluss* might even have become superfluous.

man clandestine activities in Vienna were fully matched by those of the Prague government.[4]

While most Austrians favored closer ties with Germany, Vienna did not overlook other possibilities. The Italians had nearly succeeded in forging a link with Austria in 1922, while at one point in the mid-twenties, the Danubian Federation seemed near to realization. The Austrian Foreign Ministry tended to welcome any proposal from any quarter whatever, and the impulse to look in directions other than toward Germany was strengthened by the influence of the legitimist wing of the Christian Socialist Party. This situation gave the Austrians some leverage in Berlin, and early in 1930 German apprehensions were aroused when the Austrian Chancellor, Johann Schober, a bearded former police official and veteran of earlier cabinets, now leader of the Grossdeutsch faction, traveled to Rome to patch up differences over the South Tyrol. The pan-German groups, and elements within the German Foreign Ministry, now urged that, instead of the Austro-German preferential trade treaty which had been considered, a customs union (or *Zollunion*) should be concluded, lest Austria should adopt some other solution.[5] The two governments had discussed the idea before, and Stresemann had reportedly said in 1927 that "the preparatory work for a closer economic connection between the two countries should be taken up at once," but in spite of this, nothing had been done. At the end of 1929 Schober had been invited to visit Berlin in February 1930; spurred by his intervening visit to Rome, the German Foreign Ministry decided to seize this opportunity to revive the customs union idea.[6]

[4] GFMR, 1484/D614640-1; 2347/E173724-5, E173741-4, E173802-83: Dispatch, Lerchenfeld to Ministry, Jan. 31, 1930; Letter, Müller to Curtius, Nov. 9, 1929; Memo, Nov. 15, 1929; Correspondence on proposals of Dr. Sieghart; Walther Federn, "Der Zusammenbruch der österreichischen Kreditanstalt," *Archiv für Sozialwissenschaft und Sozialpolitik*, 67:413-416 (1932).

[5] GFMR, 2347/E173968-71, E174045-9; 2520/E284601-2: Memo, Feb. 1, 1930; Letter, Lahm to Goldman, Feb. 11, 1930; Memo by Ritter, April 15, 1931.

[6] According to Curtius, he and Schober already had a customs union in

The Curtius-Schober Plan for a Customs Union

At the meetings (February 22–24, 1930), Schober and *Sektionschef* Richard Schüller, the head of the Economic Section of the Ballhausplatz, were the first to raise the question of a customs union. It was Curtius, however, who proved to be the strongest advocate of such a union, saying that although the Entente would doubtless object, plans should be prepared to be acted upon when a favorable international situation arose; "My opinion is that, however great the shock might be here and there, the customs union must still be our goal." With regard to the treaty obstacles, Curtius took the view that a customs union which was revocable or limited in duration could not be regarded as compromising Austrian independence: "This of course is not the view of our opponents. But if the legal position is at least doubtful, we can argue for our thesis against the position of our adversaries. Of course, the right moment must be chosen for this battle, and political and diplomatic preparation is also necessary." Schüller had taken part in the Salzburg negotiations, and he suggested reviving certain features of the 1918 proposals, such as the procedures for dividing customs receipts and altering tariffs, and the provision of certain intermediate duties for a transition period. Hermann Müller, at that time still German Chancellor, wound up the discussion by declaring that it was the sense of the meeting that the question of the customs union should be examined.[7]

Despite the warmth of these discussions, there was no immediate action. Two months later a conventional Austro-German trade treaty was signed, without even the preferential tariffs the Austrians wanted. At the end of April 1930, Schober visited

---

the back of their minds when they met at The Hague in January 1930, but the conclusion of the trade treaty seems to have been the only definite item on the program. (See Curtius, *Sechs Jahre*, p. 119; compare GFMR, 1484/D614620–1; 2347/E173970–3, E173988–9.)

[7] See GFMR, 2347/E174086–94, E174098–104. A fuller discussion of the details of Austro-German negotiation prior to March 1931 is given in F. G. Stambrook, "The German-Austrian Customs Union Project of 1931: A Study of German Methods and Motives," *Journal of Central European Affairs*, 21:24–40 (1961).

Paris, where he was warmly received. Immediately after his visit, he sent a reassuring letter to Curtius, reporting that Briand had expressed "complete understanding" for Austria's "especially close relationship with Germany," and had promised to press the Little Entente to aid in maintaining Austrian economic independence. This first report seems to have omitted a key detail, however. A year later, in May 1931 (according to Curtius' recollection of November 1931) Schober informed Curtius that Briand's offer to influence the Little Entente had been in response to a statement by Schober that Austria, having nowhere else to turn, would have to accept an offer of a customs union from Germany.[8] For Schober, there were two, or rather, three directions in which to turn—to Berlin, to Paris, and to Rome—and it seems that he habitually kept three sets of diplomatic accounts. In fairness to him, we should remember that Austria was in a desperate condition economically, and that her leaders felt compelled to exhaust every possibility.

In August, Schober told the German Minister in Vienna, Count Hugo von Lerchenfeld, that "now Germany and Austria must energetically take up the policy of economic union, laid down in Berlin." Curtius states in his memoirs that Austrian and German negotiators did meet during that month, and that following this, he and Schober exchanged reports "on the possibility and basis of a customs union" when they met at the League Assembly meeting in September.[9] In the fall, Schober was replaced as chancellor by the legitimist Carl Vaugoin, whose government was believed to be hostile to such plans. But even so, the Foreign Minister of this government, Monsignor Ignaz Seipel, the Richelieu of the Austrian Republic, spoke in November to Lerchenfeld about Schober's Berlin visit, stated that he was in agreement with the policy laid down at that time, and expressed a strong desire to

[8] *SIA, 1931*, p. 300; GFMR, 1484/D614858–63, D614873; 4631/K281291–3; 3620/K005134: Reichstag Foreign Affairs Committee minutes, June 26, July 11, 1930; Letter, Schober to Curtius, May 14, 1930; Curtius commentary. The latter is contained in a collection of documents which Curtius assembled on the customs union "action" after it failed, adding retrospective comments.

[9] GFMR, 1484/D614896: Letter, Lerchenfeld to Bülow, Aug. 29, 1930; Curtius, *Sechs Jahre*, p. 188.

take up detailed negotiations between the two foreign ministries.[10]

According to Brüning's recollections in 1951, he first heard of the customs union scheme from Bülow during the Reichstag election campaign, and he told Bülow then to lock the plan up where no one could see it; later he gave in to pressure from other ministers and from deputations of Austrians. Otto Meissner says that Curtius talked Brüning into the project. And (admittedly after the event) General Groener wrote in September 1931: "He [Brüning] has no interest in the Vienna affair and just as little in the person of C[urtius]." In short, Brüning was never in full sympathy with the customs union project, which was primarily sponsored by Curtius and Schober. Curtius, in fact, had favored a customs union even when Minister of Economic Affairs, and he says that studies were made by that Ministry as early as 1927.[11]

At the time of Schober's Berlin visit in 1930, both Curtius and *Ministerialdirektor* Karl Ritter had stated that a favorable international situation was necessary before a customs union could actually be launched. Curtius had also spoken of the need for "political and diplomatic preparation." Yet these prerequisites were conspicuously absent when the plan was announced.[12] What did determine the timing of the proposal?

The writer has found no clear evidence of when and how the decision to go ahead was made. It appears that the plan was not

[10] GFMR, 1484/D614908: Letter, Lerchenfeld to Curtius, Nov. 15, 1930. Curtius only says Seipel steered Austria away from Germany into an Italo-Hungarian course (*Sechs Jahre*, p. 189). Few matters in this period have been more misrepresented than Seipel's attitude toward the customs union. See also Paul R. Sweet, "Seipel's Views on Anschluss in 1928: An Unpublished Exchange of Letters," *Journal of Modern History*, 19:320–323 (1947), and Jan Krulis-Randa, *Das deutsch-österreichische Zollunionsplan von 1931* (Zürich, 1955), pp. 75–76.

[11] Interview with Dr. Brüning, Jan. 31, 1951; Otto Meissner, *Staatssekretär unter Ebert-Hindenburg-Hitler* (Hamburg, 1950), p. 198; Reginald H. Phelps, "Aus den Groener Dokumenten," *Deutsche Rundschau*, 76:1016 (1950); Curtius, *Sechs Jahre*, pp. 118–119; GFMR, 2347/E174098: Memo of conference with Schober, Feb. 24, 1930.

[12] Brüning told the author in 1951 that the customs union should of course have been preceded by talks between Hoesch and the French.

generally known in advance to cabinet members or lower-ranking Foreign Ministry officials.[13] Curtius' memoirs state that as soon as Schober returned to office as Austrian Foreign Minister in early December he telephoned Curtius, proposing to continue the customs union negotiations and to "bring them to a conclusion as soon as possible." But since Curtius has tended in his memoirs to minimize his own responsibility, one may wonder if he was not actually the first to reach for the telephone. In any case, Karl Ritter made a secret trip to Vienna early in January, taking with him a German draft of a customs union agreement. Schüller, who had promised to make some technical studies on his side, had nothing to show the visitor, and seemed rather lukewarm on the whole project. Ritter chided him and pointed out to Schober himself that he, Ritter, had done his share, and that Austrian preparations were lagging. Schober told Ritter that the time had now come to proceed actively, but the Austrian Foreign Minister also argued the need for diplomatic preparation, and was not certain whether he could meet Curtius at the January League Council meeting in Geneva.[14] All this was at the very time when Pünder was writing to Bülow to say that something would have to be done on reparations before the end of the new year.

Schober did meet Curtius at Geneva on January 16—two weeks before Sackett reported Hoover's lack of interest in a conference —and Curtius pressed for the Austrian government's comments on the German draft agreement. Curtius suggested to Schober that they should inform their parliaments only after "the conclusion of the government action," and that they should work out later the procedure for informing other countries. Curtius cordially accepted for Brüning and himself a recent invitation from

[13] Weizsäcker, although going to a meeting in Paris, was ignorant of the plan (Ernst Heinrich von Weizsäcker, *Erinnerungen*, München, 1950, p. 86). Probably some cabinet members were informed for the first time on March 16. But Bülow's reported statement to Dr. Bonn (M. J. Bonn, *Wandering Scholar*, London, 1949, p. 316) that he and Brüning were taken by surprise is incredible.

[14] GFMR, 3620/K005109–15: Memo by Ritter, Jan. 7, 1931; Curtius, *Sechs Jahre*, p. 189.

Schober to come to Vienna for a visit, stressing Brüning's desire to come; the date was tentatively set for the end of February. In his own contemporary report, Curtius appeared as the one who was pushing the project along, with Schober cutting a friendly but rather undynamic figure. This report implied that by this time the decision to go ahead with the customs union had definitely been reached. And on January 20, Bülow wrote Prittwitz that a plan existed for a customs union with Austria, one which Czechoslovakia and Hungary might also join. Bülow pointed out that the plan would mean a reshaping of European economic relations and might cause political conflicts, "although we will dress the matter up with a pan-European cloak." But he added that the other powers, primarily France, Italy, and England, would only be approached in May, at the earliest.[15]

Some of the Foreign Ministry papers written after the customs union affair was over show a suspicious sensitivity to the questions of whether Brüning was kept informed, and whether all the diplomatic officials who were consulted approved. At the time Curtius resigned his post, in October 1931, he had copies made of many of the documents related to the customs union project, and he assembled these in a collection, adding some retrospective comments. In one of these comments, Curtius noted in telegraphic style: "*Reichskanzler* informed in January 1931 before my trip to Geneva. Plans for 'Revision' of the Young Plan postponed. Instructions to deny at Geneva rumor that Special Advisory Committee of BIS to be called." Nevertheless, Ritter, after reviewing Curtius' collection, felt it necessary to assert that he and other officials had warned Curtius to inform Brüning before holding his discussion with Schober. Curtius, Ritter noted, had told them "a few days later" that Brüning had been consulted and had approved. It looks as though a complaint had been made that Brüning had not been kept informed.[16]

---

[15] GFMR, 1484/D614923–7; 2384/E199139–40.
[16] GFMR, 3620/K005235: Curtius retrospective comment. The Curtius collection is on GFMR, 3620/K004793–5741. For Ritter's retrospective views: GFMR, 5426/K294597: Feb. 17, 1932.

Again, Curtius noted in his retrospective comments (and also in his memoirs) that he had summoned the German envoys to France, Italy, England, and the Little Entente to Berlin for consultation. None of them, Curtius asserted, had opposed the customs union project; Hoesch, in particular, had warmly approved, regarding the proposal as a means of ending the "stagnation" of Franco-German relations. Ritter added his recollection that, with one minor exception, all the Berlin officials who were informed had also favored the action. But Gerhard Koepke, the chief of the area department concerned (Department II), recalled that he had signed a highly critical memorandum from his department (this memorandum was in fact included in the Curtius collection) and that as far as the envoys were concerned, most of them were only consulted at the last moment, when they could assume that it was no longer a question of "whether," but only a question of "how." Koepke added that several chiefs of mission had said afterward that they had had, from the start, the greatest doubts about the project. Hoesch may have endorsed an economic tie with Austria, but a few days after his consultation he placed on record his view—which he said he had stated while in Berlin—that no prospect existed for a successful discussion with France of *Anschluss*, and that indeed, no German aim could be accomplished without or against France. Far from calling for an end to stagnation, the Ambassador expressed the hope that Germany might be able to continue to follow a policy of "prudence, patience, and discretion." [17]

The evidence suggests that while few officials or diplomats actually spoke beforehand against the project, many had inner doubts. Curtius, Bülow, and Ritter seem to have been the main

[17] GMFR, 3620/K005243; 5426/K294598, K294599–602; 2548/E300320; 4507/K240618, K240625–6: Curtius comment; Ritter comment, Feb. 17, 1932; Koepke comment, Feb. 24, 1932; Hoesch to Ministry, July 11, 1931; Memo by Hoesch, March 6, 1931; Curtius, *Sechs Jahre*, p. 190. Hoesch did later express the view that the customs union had opened French eyes, so that their sterile attitude of promising much and doing nothing had been replaced by a real desire for economic cooperation: see esp. GFMR, 4507/K240778: Dispatch to Ministry, Aug. 21, 1931. Perhaps Curtius was reading these later views back into the March consultation.

proponents.[18] Curtius, perhaps unintentionally, perhaps deliberately, seems to have committed himself first and consulted Brüning and the uninitiated officials afterward. True, the idea of a customs union had been accepted in principle a year before. But Brüning had not been in the cabinet then, and he was primarily interested in the reparations question. We have seen that he expected his officials to suggest some alternative means of revising reparations, should President Hoover fail to respond to Sackett's message. If Brüning and Curtius discussed the customs union before the latter left for Geneva, the discussion was probably highly tentative. But by the end of January, when Curtius returned to Berlin, the Chancellor's hopes for early reparations revision must have dimmed, and we may imagine that Curtius stressed the desire of the Austrians for economic relief in the deepening depression, the moral commitment to them that had developed, and the danger that, as had already happened once, Schober might be swept away and replaced by someone less congenial. Curtius might also have mentioned his own personal need for some kind of political success. It was probably such considerations as these that led Brüning to agree, by early February, to the pursuit of the customs union project at an early date. But despite the warm acceptance by Curtius of Schober's invitation to both German leaders to come to Vienna, Brüning drew the line at this and refused to go along, inventing an excuse for Austrian consumption.[19] Furthermore, Brüning always showed great concern over the problem of timing in German diplomacy, and later he was more anxious than the Foreign Ministry about delays in completing the customs union agreement. It is not unlikely that he made his agreement to pursuing the

---

[18] Bülow had far-reaching hopes that Czechoslovakia would be obliged to join the customs union, and that eventually the new bloc would be in a position to compel Poland to make political concessions (GFMR, 2385/E199512–5).

[19] On date, GFMR, 2375/E192017; 2384/E199058–9, E199170–1: Letter, Bülow to Pünder, Feb. 5, 1931; Letter, Bülow to Hoesch, Feb. 13, 1931; Letter, Bülow to Ritter, Feb. 13, 1931. On Brüning's refusal to go to Vienna, GFMR, 2382/E197113–4: Memo, Bülow to Curtius, Feb. 16, 1931.

project conditional on its rapid execution, so as to get the affair out of the way before the time came to tackle reparations. While Carl von Schubert, the Ambassador to Italy, was in Berlin from March 13 to 15 for consultation on the customs union, Brüning told him that in regard to the Young Plan, "the matter would come to a head as early as May." [20]

THE VIENNA PROTOCOL

Later, when they were being accused of "secret diplomacy," Schober, Hoesch, and Ritter all sought to suggest that the customs union was conceived and planned during the Vienna meetings. Actually, the earlier preparations had been so complete that the negotiators at Vienna could have signed a final treaty; they decided, however, that to avoid giving the impression of a *fait accompli*, it would be best to present the agreed terms to the world as a preliminary protocol, an agreement to enter into negotiations for a treaty along certain designated lines. And a close examination of the protocol shows that it was originally drafted as a treaty; the whole tone is more specific than a mere declaration of intent, and the last article even provides for the details of ratification and denunciation of "the treaty to be concluded." The protocol was distinguished from earlier customs unions by two points: first, the treaty, "destined to mark the beginning of a new order of European economic conditions on lines of regional agreements," was declared open to other states willing to join the group, and second, allowance was made for provisional tariffs between the two countries during a period of adjustment. Incidentally, this agreement was no mere copy of the 1918 proposals, although the provisional tariffs had appeared in the earlier plan.[21]

[20] See GFMR, 4617/K272099, K272118–9; 1683/D786000–2, D786143–5, D786379–80, D786510–11; 2385/E199270: Letters, Pünder to Bülow and Bülow to Pünder, April 30, 1931; Cabinet Protocols, Feb. 21, March 16, April 23, May 27, 1931; Letter, Schubert to Bülow, March 24, 1931. See also *DBFP*, 2/II, No. 34. Schubert had been Bülow's predecessor as *Staatssekretär*.

[21] *DBFP*, 2/II, Nos. 21, 28; GFMR, 1683/D786144; 2520/E284493–4: Cabinet Protocol, March 16, 1931; Circular dispatches, March 18, April 8, 1931. On

Perhaps the negotiators might have considered other less formal and more subtle forms of agreement, if it had not been for two considerations. One was that, in view of the role, real or supposed, of the nineteenth-century *Zollverein* in unifying Germany, and the more recent discussion of an Austro-German *Zollunion* as a step toward *Anschluss*, there were domestic political advantages in announcing the conclusion of a customs union, rather than a mere "trade agreement." [22] The other, more avowable, consideration was the prevalence of the most-favored-nation clause in existing trade treaties. From the economic standpoint, what the Austrians wanted was access to a large foreign market, through arrangements which would exempt them from tariffs levied on others. But such a preferential treatment could not easily be reconciled with the scores of existing bilateral trade agreements, in which the German, Austrian, and other governments had agreed to accord to other nations the same tariffs as those levied on their most-favored fellow nation. As these treaties became widespread, their actual effect was to make all nations equally poorly favored. Most experts conceded, however, that a customs union was an exception to the most-favored-nation rule, on the principle that the parties to a customs union formed, economically speaking, a single country. The Germans and Austrians attempted to claim the privileges of a customs union with regard to the most-favored-nation principle, but at the same

the Salzburg precedent: Gratz and Schüller, *Äussere Wirtschaftspolitik*, pp. 93–100; GFMR, 2519/E283406–22: Memo on Austro-German Conference, June 12, 1918; Henry Cord Meyer, *Mitteleuropa in German Thought and Action* (The Hague, 1955), pp. 285–286.

[22] See Curtius' remarks to the cabinet on March 16–18, below. Berlin noted later that the Austrian press was inclined to avoid using the term *Zollunion*, "in accordance with the Austrian tendency to bring the customs union plan before the European public only gradually and, so to speak, with consideration," while the German government felt obliged to use the term because of the most-favored-nation problem (GFMR, 2520/E284501–2). But Austria had just as much reason as Germany to be concerned with the most-favored-nation problem. If there was a difference in emphasis, it was because the primary goal of each of the partners was different.

time, with an eye to the Geneva Protocol, they had to play down the idea that Austria would thereby lose her economic independence.[23]

PLANNING THE CUSTOMS UNION ANNOUNCEMENT

The need to steer between the Scylla of domestic opinion and of the most-favored-nation clauses and the Charybdis of the Geneva Protocol and of Franco-Czech suspicion made it a very delicate matter to communicate the agreement to other governments. In order to strengthen the impression of Austrian independence, the Germans and Austrians decided that, except in Paris (where Germany would certainly be considered the instigator), the *démarches* in the various capitals should be made first by the Austrian representatives rather than the German. For the sake of appeasing international opinion, they further decided to present the scheme as a contribution to the efforts of the Commission of Inquiry for European Union to implement Briand's pan-European proposals, to "dress the matter up with a pan-European cloak." Moreover, in view of the general concern over the depression, they agreed to describe the new scheme as a "first practical step" in breaking down tariff barriers and reviving world trade. In retrospect, it seems that these elaborate tactics only tended to give an aura of chicanery to the whole enterprise. As Schober said later, they were so anxious to avoid giving offense that they achieved the opposite result.[24]

At Vienna, the announcement of the agreement had been scheduled for the end of April. On March 10, the Germans advanced this date to the week of March 23, in order to precede the Easter vacation, and also to reduce the risk of leakage. We may suspect that Curtius and his officials were also anxious to act before Schober was replaced, or before the Austrians lost

---

[23] Hoesch referred to this dilemma on March 23 as the weak point in the German position (GFMR, 2520/E284393).

[24] GFMR, 2389/E202520-3; 2520/E284258-80: Plans for announcement; Circular dispatch, March 18, 1931; *DBFP*, 2/II, No. 28.

courage, and that Brüning may have objected to a long delay. Another change of schedule soon followed: a meeting of the Organization Committee of the Commission of Inquiry for European Union had been summoned to meet in Paris on March 24, and it seemed unwise to announce the customs union plan during this meeting, perhaps because the meeting was now assuming unexpected importance due to Henderson's decision to attend. So on March 12, the date for the announcement was further advanced to March 21–23. Actually, one government, the Soviet, was officially informed before the announcement. The Treaty of Berlin of 1926 prescribed that its signatories should keep each other *au courant* on important political questions, and consequently Bülow notified the Soviet Ambassador on March 19; the Ambassador answered merely, "Is that all?" and thanked Bülow.[25]

The Austrian cabinet was first informed on March 13, the German cabinet on March 16. Other cabinet meetings followed on the eighteenth and twentieth, and other German political leaders were also notified from the nineteenth to the twenty-first. Curtius described the background of the customs proposal to his fellow ministers:

he stressed that the attitude of the Austrian Federal Government, which at first had been very hesitant, had now become thoroughly and

---

[25] GFMR, 913/384719–20; 2520/E284254, E284255, E284258–80, E284494: Memos by Bülow, March 17, 19, 1931; Curtius to Lerchenfeld, March 10, 1931; Ministry to Lerchenfeld, March 12, 1931; Circular dispatch, March 18, 1931; Circular dispatch, April 8, 1931. The Wilhelmstrasse's instructions and a Ritter comment to a British diplomat (*DBFP*, 2/II, No. 28) claimed that the date for the Organization Committee meeting had been moved up. Stambrook points out ("German-Austrian Customs Union Project," p. 36) that the Germans had actually known in February that the meeting would be in March (GFMR, 3693/K006867), and he therefore concludes that they were "disingenuous" in setting a May date in Vienna and that they were forcing the Austrian hand. It seems more likely, however, that the first change to March 23–28 was made after further reflection in Berlin, and that the slight further advance to the twenty-first was due simply to a belated recognition of the effect of an announcement in the midst of an unexpectedly well-advertised meeting. The actions of bureaucracy seldom result from pure, far-sighted calculation.

actively favorable. Austria had turned away from the idea of the Danubian Economic Federation. This situation must be exploited. Politically, the *Anschluss* was not yet ripe; economically, it could now be decisively furthered, provided that there was a most careful regard for the diplomatic difficulties of such a step.

The Foreign Minister admitted that "Czechoslovakia and France in particular will probably be hostile at first to the Austro-German customs union." However, the Austrian cabinet had already agreed to the proposal, and Germany could not postpone her decision beyond March 18. Moreover, although the plan had been kept secret so far, it was doubtful how long this situation could last, and therefore they should act quickly. At first, the other ministers were highly critical on details of the plan; they probably resented not having been informed sooner and they may have disliked being put under pressure. Ritter endeavored to reassure the ministers, who felt that too much was being conceded to Austria, by saying that "in reality, German preponderance would not be difficult to achieve." In the end, the cabinet members abandoned their resistance to the projected action; it is striking that no one, aside from Curtius, paid any attention to the diplomatic problem. In conclusion, Curtius said:

with these coming agreements, Austria will at first profit more. This was quite in order, however, since the stronger party in such cases must make appropriate concessions to the weaker. [Curtius] recalled that the idea of parity had been very successfully applied in other countries, such as Switzerland and the U.S.A. The political risk with our proposal was considerable. But if one was prepared to take a chance, the present situation was especially favorable. Perhaps the Austro-German step would give the first impulse to a better adjustment of European relations, which was especially desirable following the collapse of the tariff truce negotiations at Geneva. The German action promised to bring beneficial effects in internal politics, too. Other circumstances permitting, a united front might be formed on this question, reaching from the Social Democrats to the National Socialists.

Curtius then added another warning to keep the agreement secret, and the cabinet unanimously approved the proposal.[26]

Later, Brüning and Ritter told members of the British Embassy that leakage had hastened the announcement, and in September 1931 Brüning told the cabinet that disclosures had compromised the whole project at the start. But is doubtful that leakage had much effect on the timing of the announcement, as the date of March 21 to 23 had been fixed by March 12 (because of the Paris meeting), while Curtius told the cabinet on the sixteenth that the negotiations had so far been kept "as good as completely secret." [27]

Nevertheless, a leak did take place somewhere, for on March 18 the Czech Minister in Vienna, Hugo Vavrecka, called on Schober to inquire if a customs union plan was afoot. Schober was reticent, and Vavrecka strongly warned him against making any such agreement with Germany. On March 20, the French government communicated the news of the projected agreement to the British, and proposed that France, Italy, and Czecho-slovakia all carry out separate *démarches* in Vienna before the

[26] Otto Braun, *Von Weimar zu Hitler* (New York, 1940), pp. 345–346; GFMR, 1683/D786143–7, D786167–70, D786206: Cabinet Protocols, March 16, 18, 20, 1931.

[27] *DBFP*, 2/II, Nos. 8, 28; GFMR, 1683/D786144; 1685/D788405: Cabinet Protocols, March 16, Oct. 3, 1931. Actually, Bülow himself revealed the plan to Sir Horace Rumbold on March 13, explaining that at Vienna, Curtius and Schober had discussed, among other things, "the possibility of the creation of a sort of customs union between Austria and Germany." Bülow explained that the "customs union" would not be one in the sense of the old *Zollverein*, as there would still be duties between the two partners. Bülow's own memo on the conversation (dated March 13) states that "the Ambassador showed himself interested, but not disturbed." Probably Bülow decided that this purloined-letter technique was better than a denial which would soon prove to be false; Schober gave a denial to similar inquiries from the Italian Minister in Vienna and thereby created a bad impression later. Bülow's method worked, for Rumbold sent his report by pouch, and it arrived in London on March 18, where it seems to have attracted no particular notice. As the Foreign Office was economizing on cable expenses in this period, practically all of Rumbold's reports were being sent this way (GFMR, 1555/D666573). See GFMR, 1484/D614972–3; *DBFP*, 2/I, No. 358.

public announcement the next day.[28] In this note, the French suggested that the proposed *démarches* "might be attributed to press information appearing in the *Neue Freie Presse* [Vienna] of March 17th," and others, too, have said that the Austrian press prematurely revealed the plan. But although Curtius' visit to Vienna brought a harvest of glowing articles on the theme of brotherly cooperation and closer economic ties, suitable for preparing public opinion, these articles suggested that some kind of agreement would be proposed in the European Commission, but not that there would be an early customs union announcement; moreover, the German press was nearly as informative as the Austrian.[29]

[28] GFMR, 1484/D614976: Memo by Ritter of telephone conversation with Schüller, March 19, 1931; *DBFP*, 2/II, No. 1.

[29] This statement is based on an examination of the *Neue Freie Presse* (Vienna), *Neues Wiener Journal, Frankfurter Zeitung, Berliner Morgenpost, Berliner Tageblatt, Deutsche Allgemeine Zeitung* (Berlin), *Vorwärts* (Berlin), and *Vossische Zeitung* (Berlin) from March 3 to 21. On March 17 the *Neue Freie Presse* (referred to by the French note of March 20) said in its morning edition that the German cabinet had discussed the Vienna talks, which had been "very positive in nature." The conferees had discussed *inter alia* the application of the pan-European idea to Austro-German economic relations. This may also be the grain of fact in Edgar Stern-Rubarth's account (*Drei Männer suchen Europa*, München, 1947, pp. 293-295); most of his story is shown by the German documents to be fictitious. In any case, this *Neue Freie Presse* story appeared to come from a German cabinet leak. Some German party leaders made complaints that the Conti Service (a businessmen's news service associated with Wolff's, the government-controlled wire service) had reported the customs union on March 18, before the cabinet's decision that day (GFMR, 4617/K272071, K272079-80). One newspaper outside Grossdeutschland did foresee what would happen: in the Budapest *Pester Lloyd*, March 6 (A.M.), one Otto Deutsch made an able speculation on the basis of information about the Salzburg agreements and other data. In this connection, the Hungarian Minister in Berlin, when informed on March 20, said he had already concluded that a customs union was impending, and had so informed his government (GFMR, 1484/D614997-8); as later, on the questions of Austrian resolution to continue with the customs union and the Hoover moratorium, the Hungarians displayed their acumen. To show that their plan was really not the bombshell the French said it was, the German Foreign Ministry itself later collected 11 press stories which had hinted at some kind of Austro-German arrangements (GFMR, 2389/E202695-700); none, however, specifically and definitely mentioned

A close scrutiny of the French note of March 20 leads one to believe that the French information actually came from other, more authoritative sources, possibly from persons in or close to the Austrian cabinet. This information may have come from Prague; the inquiry by the Czech Minister on the eighteenth suggests that the Czechs were the first to be informed. The General Director of the French-controlled Zentraleuropäisches Länderbank, a naturalized Frenchman, stated afterward that the Czechs got wind of the Austro-German protocol and informed Paris, and in his memoirs Curtius says that, according to his recollection, there were Viennese indiscretions to the Czechs.[30] But this information could also have come directly to France from Vienna.

THE RESPONSE OF THE FRENCH

So the secret was out. Despite the French proposal, it was much too late by March 20 to try to prevent the announcement. The British Minister in Vienna took no action, and the Italian Minister only asked for information, making no protest. The most dramatic *démarche* was that of the Czech Vavrecka, who declared: "Any country on earth could conclude a customs union, except precisely Austria [*Jedes Land auf der Erde könne eine Zollunion schliessen, nur gerade Österreich nicht*]." The Wilhelmstrasse thought that Paris was trying to build up tension by proposing the four-power diplomatic action and by inspiring a French press story about it, which depicted all of the Allied representatives, including the British, as making a collective *démarche*.[31]

that an Austro-German customs union was on the verge of being concluded. This is not mere quibbling over words; the use of the term "customs union" meant that it was not a question of inconclusive pan-European discussions, but of a definite economic union of the two states, developed bilaterally and implying, through German historical legend and the avowed program of the *Anschluss* movement, a definite step toward political union.

[30] See *DBFP*, 2/II, No. 1; GFMR, 2375/E192458-9: Unsigned memo, forwarded by Schäffer, April 24, 1931; Curtius, *Sechs Jahre*, p. 193.

[31] GFMR, 2520/E284377-9, E284495: Vienna Legation memo, March 24, 1931; Circular dispatch, April 8, 1931.

When Ambassador von Hoesch asked on the twentieth for an interview with Briand the next day, he was told at first that Briand would be too busy, and this caused Berlin to suspect that the French were trying to get the Allied protests in before Austria and Germany could communicate their proposal, in order to make it appear that France was unmasking a secret plot. But to the French, Austro-German guilt was self-evident in any case. The Germans had foreseen French opposition, but its extent exceeded Berlin's expectations. German officials do not seem to have realized the extreme concern their actions could cause abroad. Despite all the efforts to stage the announcement carefully, or perhaps partly because of them, some Frenchmen were reminded of the Agadir crisis. The bugbear of a larger, more populous Germany, the fear of a German *Mitteleuropa,* and the danger of German economic domination—all these strengthened French hostility, and Hoesch, at least, was made to realize that France considered the prevention of the union a vital matter.[32]

Aside from national interests, French internal politics gave added impetus to the hostile reception. Aristide Briand, the French Foreign Minister, usually favored conciliation and concession to Germany, and the German Foreign Ministry recognized this. But Briand, unfortunately, had made a speech in the Chamber of Deputies on March 3, in which he had said, referring to Austria, "I used to be told, 'You are blind. Tomorrow or the day after tomorrow at the latest, the *Anschluss* will be achieved' . . . The danger which could then be considered a danger of war has gradually diminished. If it has not completely disappeared, it is no longer so acute as it was represented to be two years ago. If it had been so imminent as was asserted, it would already have come to pass." Briand's remarks now seemed made to order for his nationalist critics, who also exploited the German government's claim that it was implementing Briand's pan-European

---

[32] GFMR, 1484/D614995: Memo of Bülow-Hoesch telephone conversation, March 20, 1931; Curtius, *Sechs Jahre,* p. 194; *SIA, 1931,* p. 302. Coulondre of the Quai d'Orsay spoke of "the return of Germany to prewar methods" (GFMR, 1659/D729006). See also GFMR, 2520/E284393: Hoesch to Ministry, March 23, 1931, and Bülow's comment on May 6 (*DBFP,* 2/II, No. 34).

ideas. Briand, now on the verge of senility, was hoping to be chosen President of the Republic in the election in May; the customs union scarcely improved his chances. Berthelot was to tell Hoesch that, under the circumstances, Briand was "worse than in a bad temper, he was silent, and well aware of the difficulty of his position." Berthelot added that when he had presented the drafts of strong diplomatic instructions to his chief, Briand had signed them unhesitatingly.[33]

Hoesch succeeded in being received at the Quai d'Orsay on March 21 to announce the project, and when he arrived he saw at once that the question had already been thoroughly discussed there, and that it had caused "great consternation and anger." Briand told Hoesch that, unquestionably, Austria had violated the Geneva Protocol, and he added that "no matter how the agreement was turned or twisted, it represented a preparation for *Anschluss*. Germany could expect no real economic advantage, and this fact emphasized the political character of the agreement." Briand also expressed his resentment at the failure of Curtius to inform him of his activities, as the Germans were always asking the French to do. Hoesch protested that the plan was first developed at the Vienna meetings, and that it was precisely the prior notice that he was giving now. In his report, Hoesch suggested that Berlin maintain that the plan really did first take shape in Vienna, "otherwise complaints of secret action by Germany and Austria may intensify." [34]

Hoesch next spoke with Berthelot. The French Secretary-General began by formally declaring that the French government considered that there had been a clear violation of the obligations (which he read) assumed by Austria in 1922. When Hoesch had presented his "legal, factual, and political arguments," Berthelot answered (in Hoesch's paraphrase), "It might be that by subtle interpretations and careful transpositions we [the Germans] had sought to avoid an obvious violation of obligations assumed.

---

[33] *SIA, 1931*, p. 298; GFMR, 2520/E284395: Hoesch to Ministry, March 23, 1931.

[34] GFMR, 2520/E284311–2; Hoesch to Ministry, March 21, 1931.

Still, a violation of the protocol of 1922 could hardly be denied. France would have to act accordingly, and it would be very desirable if something could still happen on our side to relieve the growing difficulties." After pointing to the problems raised for Briand, Berthelot said that hopes for Franco-German reconciliation were affected, and that all plans for long-term loans (such plans had recently been discussed) were now more or less impossible to carry out. Hoesch's report of Berthelot's statement ended: "Germany's action represented an amazing imprudence [*Unvorsichtigkeit*] and would lead to a stirring up of public opinion and to all kinds of complications. All in all, the incident was extremely regrettable and serious, and well-calculated to injure the development of Franco-German relations." [35]

Curtius took these last words seriously. He told Ambassador de Margerie that if Franco-German relations could be threatened by this agreement, which was within the framework of the treaties, which was an economic necessity for Austria and Germany, and which served the cause of economic reform in Europe, "then thereby an extremely serious situation would be created." However, Curtius was convinced that the specter would vanish after a closer examination of the situation. He claimed that the French had failed to aid understanding, and as a personal message for Briand only, he stated that no one in Germany would understand France's opposing the customs union for no real reason. Curtius added: "Consideration for the Brüning government, for which the Ambassador had found such friendly words, should not be left out of account." [36]

Unfortunately, we are now accustomed to hearing diplomats speak in threatening tones, but in the period between Versailles and Hitler, they rarely accused other countries of "amazing imprudence," and if a foreign minister said that "a very serious

---

[35] GFMR, 2520/E284312–4.
[36] GFMR, 2520/E284359–67: Memo by Curtius, March 3 [*sic:* 23?], 1931. The French Minister in Vienna told his British colleague that Curtius also had refused to suspend negotiations with Austria and "had somewhat acidly remarked to M. de Margerie that negotiations would be opened directly after Easter" (*DBFP*, 2/II, No. 25).

situation would be created," he could expect to produce a real effect. The French press reflected the tone of these official exchanges; on March 23, *Le Temps* stated icily: "None of the explanations with which this Austro-German action might be cloaked has any interest. Only the facts count—facts stated in precise texts." [37]

Curtius seems to have hoped, on the one hand, that French opinion would be somewhat mollified by assertions that Germany was implementing Briand's pan-European plans, and on the other, that France would feel compelled to allow Brüning a diplomatic success to forestall his replacement by radical rightists. He also believed that the customs union proposal would give a "first impulse" to a readjustment of European relations and end the "stagnation" in Franco-German relations—an idea he attributed to Hoesch but evidently shared. Curtius used somewhat the same reasoning (in quite different circumstances) as an earlier chief of the German Foreign Ministry, Alfred von Kiderlen-Wächter, who is reported to have said in 1911: "It is necessary to thump on the table. However, the only object of this is to make the French negotiate." [38] Finally, Curtius thought that Germany could do what she had a legal right to do, regardless of the displeasure of other states. In all these suppositions, however, the German Foreign Minister was mistaken.

HENDERSON'S INTERVENTION

The government in London was not inclined to take the customs union itself too seriously, and although the permanent Under-Secretary, Sir Robert Vansittart, criticized the secrecy of the Austro-German negotiations and warned the Austrian Minister against presenting the world with a *fait accompli*, he did not himself believe that an *Anschluss* would follow in the near future. Vansittart's attitude may have reflected a growing

[37] *Le Temps* (Paris), March 23, 1931. See also *SIA, 1931*, p. 304.
[38] Oscar Freiherr von der Lancken Wakenitz, *Meine dreissig Dienstjahre: 1888–1918* (Berlin, 1931), p. 96, cited by A. J. P. Taylor, *The Struggle for Mastery in Europe, 1848–1918* (Oxford, 1954), pp. 466–467.

coolness in Anglo-French relations, stemming from abortive loan negotiations which took place in January and February. But whatever the view was in Whitehall, Foreign Secretary Henderson, who went to Paris on March 23 for the meeting of the European Commission's Organization Subcommittee, had reasons for raising more strenuous objections. Curtius had predicted that the British might object to the proposal as causing political unrest.[39] His estimate, as far as it concerned Henderson, was correct.

Henderson, as part of his strong interest in disarmament, was particularly anxious at this juncture that France and Italy should complete an agreement limiting naval armaments; it was principally this concern that brought him to Paris. The Franco-Italian agreement, which had seemed near conclusion at the end of February, had foundered early in March when it became known that the French interpreted the draft terms as enabling them to begin new construction in 1935 and 1936. This difficulty cannot properly be blamed on Germany and Austria, since it had arisen before the news of the customs union could be digested, or even apprehended. But now, concern over Austro-German plans would be a further obstacle to any French concessions towards Italy.[40] The naval problem was further aggravated when the German Reichstag voted funds on March 20 for the construction of a second pocket battleship. Together, the new ship and the customs union probably clinched the defeat of Franco-Italian naval disarmament, a cause with which Henderson had thoroughly identified himself.

Aside from these developments, it was especially awkward for Henderson that he had to inform Briand that he had just invited Curtius and Brüning to come for a visit to England. So the Foreign Secretary found himself in a position where he was impelled

[39] *DBFP*, 2/II, Nos. 3, 14, 14 note 2; GFMR, 2520/E284261: Circular dispatch, March 18, 1931.

[40] See *DBFP*, 2/II, No. 15; GFMR, 1555/D666537–8, D666567–8: Letter, Dufour-Féronce to Weizsäcker, March 10, 1931; Neurath to Ministry, March 14, 1931. The first indication of the French claim came on March 2, but it apparently was only confirmed on March 19 (*DBFP*, 2/II, Nos. 324, 326–340; *SIA, 1931*, pp. 269–274).

to intervene in the Franco-German crisis. As we shall see in the next chapter, there was probably a direct connection between the invitation to Brüning and Curtius on the one hand, and Henderson's intervention on the other. It should be added, however, that even if Henderson had not been thwarted and embarrassed by Germany's action, he very likely would have stepped in. Throughout this period, he made himself a mediator between France and Germany, asking the Germans to delay or trim their program, lest the French should adopt a more rigid policy.

Henderson called at the Quai d'Orsay on the morning of March 25 to inform Briand of a message he had sent to the British posts in Berlin and Vienna, and Briand (according to Henderson) said that he was grateful for this action. The message, sent by telephone as well as by telegraph, read as follows:

German (Austrian) Government should be under no misapprehension as to serious misgivings which have been aroused by their action in many countries and in France in particular.

Though there may be two opinions as to the exact conformity of proposed treaty with existing obligations of Austria and, indeed, of Germany, you should make it clear to German (Austrian) Chancellor that state of feeling both in Great Britain and here causes me great concern, and I feel that if nothing is done to calm existing apprehensions the task of those who are anxious that Disarmament Conference should meet under the most favorable conditions will be seriously compromised by any apparent disregard of any treaty obligations by unilateral action.

In this connection the position of M. Briand has become one of great difficulty, and the influence which he has only at great trouble been able to exercise for many years past in controlling more extreme tendencies among his own countrymen will be unquestionably affected. I should regard this as contrary to the interests and the consolidation of peace which I, in concert with the German (Austrian) Government, am anxious to serve.

You should submit these considerations to the German (Austrian) Chancellor with all the emphasis which the circumstances, in my opinion, demand. I appeal to them that before they proceed further opportunity should be given to Council of League of Nations, under whose auspices the protocol of 1922 was negotiated, to assure itself that Treaty is not contrary to the obligations undertaken by Austria by that instrument.

Similar instructions have been sent to His Majesty's Minister at Vienna (His Majesty's Ambassador, Berlin).[41]

Thus Henderson stressed the damage to Briand's position, and proposed a legal review by the League Council. The importance of his message was underlined by the instruction to speak with the chancellors, not the foreign ministers.

On the same day, Henderson discussed the customs union with the German delegate to the Organization Committee, a former *Staatssekretär*, Ernst von Simson. Henderson repeated his phrase about the possibility of there being two opinions on the legality of the proposed treaty, and, after an explanation from Simson, Henderson allowed that he was convinced the draft treaty had nothing to do with *Anschluss*. But he informed Simson of the message he had sent, asked that nothing further be done for the present, and suggested that if the League Council could not find a solution satisfactory to all, there was still the possibility, in a legal question of this kind, of appealing to the Permanent Court of International Justice at The Hague. Despite this reference to the problem as a legal one, Simson gathered from Alexander Cadogan, who was also present, that Henderson was expecting the Council to act, not on the legal basis of the peace treaties or of the 1922 protocol, but rather as a mediator under the general provisions of the League Covenant for settling international disputes. Simson's report to Berlin on this conversation may help to explain the firmness of the German reply which followed, since, for domestic considerations, the last thing the German government wanted was to be publicly hailed before the League Council on a loose, general charge of disturbing international relations. Simson himself told Henderson that, considering the unpopularity of the League in Germany, and the doubts the Germans had of its ability to take a nonpartisan position in such a question, it would be very difficult for Curtius to agree to Henderson's proposal.[42]

Also on the twenty-fifth, Vansittart in London read the text of

[41] *DBFP*, 2/II, Nos. 5, 13.
[42] GFMR, 2520/E284409–10.

Henderson's message to the German Ambassador (and later Foreign Minister), Konstantin von Neurath. The imperturbable Neurath told his government not to take Henderson's message too tragically, and reported that Vansittart would have liked to hold it back, but there had been no possibility of this, since the main part of the message, dealing with the proposed reference to the League Council, was already being published in Paris.[43] Incidentally, in making his proposal public, Henderson eliminated any possible chance of immediate acceptance, since no German government could openly welcome a review of its actions by the League.

Whether through an advance copy of the press report, through Simson, through Neurath, through the Austrians, or (as Sir Horace Rumbold suspected) through a telephone tap, the German government was both forewarned and forearmed when Rumbold presented Henderson's message that evening. After Rumbold had read Henderson's communication and had cited some British and German press criticism of the Austro-German proposal, the German Chancellor read off his reply:

The Austro-German agreement is entirely within the framework of the Geneva Protocol of 4th October, 1922.

Therefore, in our opinion, there is no reason why the Council of the League of Nations should take up the matter. The German and Austrian Governments have nothing to fear if other Governments proceed to an examination of the juridical aspect of the question. The German Government could not admit an examination of the agreement from a political standpoint, as the agreement is of a purely economic character. The negotiations must naturally take their course, and having regard to the numerous technical details which have to be settled, cannot be concluded before two or three months.

Since the protocol could have been a treaty, the statement that

[43] GFMR, 2389/E202658-9, E202681-2: Neurath to Ministry, March 25, 1931 (Nos. 115 and 116). According to Neurath, Vansittart had just finished telling him that neither the Foreign Office nor the Board of Trade had any objection to the substance of the agreement, although the Foreign Office disliked the secrecy in which it had been developed; Sir Robert in consequence was somewhat embarrassed at Henderson's action. That Vansittart did not take the proposal to mean an *Anschluss* is confirmed by *DBFP*, 2/II, No. 14 note 2.

negotiations would continue for several months might be said to represent a concession by the German government. But to the rest of the world, Brüning appeared to be flatly refusing to agree to Henderson's proposal, or to wait upon any outside approval. Sir Horace requested a copy of this statement to avoid any possible misunderstanding, and the text was given to the German press the following morning.[44]

When Brüning went on to comment on his reply, he said that the German government had had no political consideration in mind when it negotiated the agreement. He then added:

Germany had few rights and if she were going to be checked at every turn the position of his government would become untenable. Her right to enter into a Customs Union with Austria could not be disputed. He did not think that M. Briand's position would in fact be really prejudicially affected. If the French were to make a serious *démarche* at Berlin in connection with the proposed Austro-German Customs Union there would be an explosion in this country. The French surely were deeply interested in the stability of the German Government. He did not consider that the French Government had hitherto done anything to help his Government and he made the interesting admission that attempts which he had made to come to an understanding with the French Government had so far led to nothing.

In this way Brüning emphasized that other governments had an interest in supporting him. Rumbold commented that Brüning was absolutely firm throughout the interview and that "I could not shake him in the least . . . [While Brüning was making his comments] I could see that he was imposing considerable restraint on himself, and his language was that of suppressed bitterness." The impression of defiance was strengthened by a speech of Brüning's the same day, in which he stated: "Germany and Austria are in any case resolved to pursue to the end with calm determination the course which they have decided to be the right one in their own interests and in the interests of all." [45]

The Austrian and German Foreign Ministers had coordinated

---

[44] *SIA, 1931*, p. 307; *DBFP*, 2/II, Nos. 7, 17.
[45] *DBFP*, 2/II, Nos. 8, 8 note 1, No. 17; *SIA, 1931*, p. 307.

the replies of their respective governments by telephone, Curtius requesting that Schober's message cover the same ground as the last part of the German reply. Nevertheless, the Austrian statement was somewhat different:

The Austrian Government are of the opinion that the agreement between the Austrian and German Governments is quite in conformity with the Geneva Protocol of 1922.

The Austrian Government, however, do not object to the legal aspect of the agreement being examined by the Governments which signed the Geneva Protocol. To examine the Agreement from a political standpoint should be out of the question, considering its economic character.

The Austrian Government have no intention of making a *fait accompli*.

The last sentence of the Austrian reply was added after Schober's consultation with Curtius, but Schober, with his promise to make no *fait accompli*, avoided making the threat of continued negotiations and eventual bilateral agreement conveyed by the German answer. Moreover, Schober took no position regarding the League Council, and said merely that a political review was unjustified, not that it was inadmissible, as the Germans had argued. In many respects the Austrian answer resembled the German, but the tone of defiance was missing. We may surmise that while the German government, out of regard for nationalist opinion, was phrasing its reply to sound as firm as possible, the Austrian government, aware of its weakness, interested primarily in economic salvation, and ready to entertain counterproposals, was trying to sound conciliatory. Schober falsely told the British Minister in Vienna that he had refused Curtius' request that he make his reply agree with the German reply.[46] Exemplifying the maxim that in diplomacy only the strong can afford to be honest, the Austrians were saying one thing to the Germans and another thing to the other governments. Clearly, there was a tendency on the part of the Austrians to yield.

[46] GFMR, 2389/E202667-8: Note on Curtius-Schober telephone conversation, March 25, 1931; *DBFP*, 2/II, Nos. 9, 10.

Faced with the German reply, Henderson gave more prominence to the idea of taking the matter to The Hague. He sent another message to Berlin on March 26, saying that he had not meant to propose a political examination of the intended treaty, but rather to suggest that the League Council should determine whether the treaty infringed "in any way terms of the financial protocol of 1922." In such a technical question, Henderson continued, the Council would probably seek the opinion of the Hague Court, and he added that he himself would support such a procedure. Henderson again told Briand of the action he was taking, this time before sending his message. Briand replied that he fully agreed, although he suggested that it might be difficult to distinguish between the economic and the political issue, and that in any case the question was one for the League Council to decide. Briand thought that the Austrians were anxious to retreat and that the Germans, too, were not very sure of their ground; he believed that if it was made clear to the Germans that the British and French governments thought the League Council must decide the question, the German government could also be brought around to this view. While not opposing the idea of seeking the legal advice of the Hague Court, Briand evidently preferred to have the League Council settle the question, and as a political, not legal, issue.[47]

Rumbold presented the new message from Henderson to Curtius, urging that surely the German and Austrian governments could suspend their technical discussions until the League Council could examine the legal aspects of the proposed treaty. Curtius consulted with Brüning and then gave Rumbold the following statement:

The German and Austrian Governments, in conformity with their agreement, propose to continue the technical preparation for the conclusion of the definite treaty. These preparations cannot be concluded for two or three months at least. Thus there will be no *fait accompli* before the next meeting of the Council. The German Government, for their part, see no reason to refer the proposed treaty to the League

[47] *DBFP*, 2/II, Nos. 11, 15.

Council, since they are satisfied that it is not contrary to the protocol of 1922. The Powers signatory to the protocol are, of course, at liberty to refer the treaty to the Council, but the German Government must reserve complete liberty of action with regard to any procedure which may be suggested to the Council.

Curtius said nothing about the idea of a review by The Hague, and in fact, a reference to this body was quite unwelcome, since, if nothing else, it would cause even greater delay.[48]

Reporting on this interview, Rumbold called particular attention to the statement that "the German Government must reserve complete liberty of action with regard to any procedure which may be suggested to the Council." He felt that this represented a modification of Brüning's original *non possumus* attitude, and that it, together with other indications, seemed to show that the Germans realized that the customs union would indeed be discussed in the League Council. It now appeared to Sir Horace that no *fait accompli* would take place. Even before receiving Rumbold's dispatch containing these comments, Henderson, in a speech in Parliament on March 30, stated that the German government seemed to him to recognize the propriety of a reference to the Council. There were also statements in press communiqués and in a speech by Curtius that Germany would not avoid a legal discussion of the agreement. The British assumed that the immediate crisis was over.[49]

This conclusion was not without justification. The tone of the second reply to Rumbold, and of the later statements, was certainly more moderate. It was significant that the German government asked the British not to publish the second exchange of notes;[50] a reply intended for publication would presumably have been more rigid. Nevertheless, the Germans did not admit to having modified their position. When Berthelot claimed that

[48] *DBFP*, 2/II, Nos. 12, 17; GFMR, 2520/E284436: Circular, March 28, 1931.

[49] *DBFP*, 2/II, Nos. 17, 20; *SIA, 1931*, pp. 307–309.

[50] *DBFP*, 2/II, No. 12. Henderson, however, disclosed the German reply in the House of Commons (*SIA, 1931*, pp. 307–308).

Curtius, in his speech, had made a concession regarding the possibility of a legal discussion, Hoesch denied this, pointing out that Brüning had told Rumbold from the start that Germany did not fear a *legal* examination of the question.[51] And a Foreign Ministry telegram, for the instruction of Neurath, Hoesch, and Schubert (in Rome), set forth the German position in terms that did not suggest there had been any substantial compromise.

Legalism in the German Customs Union Policy

In this telegram, dated March 28, Curtius welcomed the evidence that the British did not condemn the proposed treaty outright, but he added that Henderson's position could not be regarded as justified; it was not customary for two sovereign states to suspend negotiations and await approval, just because other countries had legal objections and regarded the proposed agreement as politically disturbing. As a minimum, Germany must demand that those objecting state "briefly and clearly [*klipp und klar*]" what concrete points in the proposal were thought to violate the Geneva Protocol. The Reich government asked that the same consideration be given its internal position as had been given Briand's domestic problems. Beneš and the French press had spoken of invoking the general political clauses of the Covenant of the League of Nations, especially Articles 11 and 15,[52] and Germany had therefore specifically rejected any political review: "As soon as the legal question has been settled," the Foreign Minister wrote, "there is no more room for political discussion." The signatories of the Geneva Protocol had a right to bring the matter before the League Council, but the legal question itself was so simple and elementary that if the Council were to take it up, there should be no need for referring the case to The Hague.[53] In this last assertion, Curtius certainly showed confidence in his case. At the conference with Schober in Febru-

---

[51] GFMR, 2520/E284481: Hoesch to Ministry, April 2, 1931.

[52] Article 11 provided that any threat of war or of disturbance to international peace might be brought before the League Assembly or Council. Article 15 provided for the submission of disputes to the League Council.

[53] GFMR, 2520/E284434-7.

ary 1930, Curtius had said that if the legal position was at least doubtful, Germany and Austria could argue for their position against that of their adversaries. Now Curtius no longer recognized any doubt.

It has been plausibly suggested that American diplomacy has suffered from its direction by eminent lawyers, who tend to assume a moral and judicial attitude towards other nations, rather than accepting them as sovereign powers in an unstable world. But the United States was not the only country to employ legal talent in diplomacy; the Wilhelmstrasse, too, tended in this period to approach foreign policy as a legal problem. The difference was that under Dr. Curtius, the viewpoint was not that of the judge, but rather that of the corporation lawyer for a rather aggressive entrepreneur, the type of attorney who points out opportunities lurking in the small print of contracts, or who suggests ways in which the intent of the law may be frustrated, owing to shortcomings in the drafting of the statutes. One can hardly doubt that, as Briand said, there would have been no loan in 1922 if the French had understood the Geneva Protocol as permitting an Austro-German customs union. But by the end of March, even the French began to doubt whether the proposed agreement technically violated the protocol.[54]

In defense of the German attitude, it must be granted that the network of postwar treaties and the politics of Poincaré tended to encourage pettifoggery. From the Germans' point of view, the whole system was rigged against them, and they considered themselves entitled to take advantage of it whenever they could. Moreover, the customs union, reparations revision, and arms equality were regarded by Germans as rightful goals. But if there can be no moral judgments against German legalism, it can still

[54] George F. Kennan, *American Diplomacy, 1900–1950* (Chicago, 1951), pp. 95–101. GFMR, 2521/E284854: Letter, Ritter to Rieth, May 9, 1931; *DBFP*, 2/II, No. 16. Candidates for the German foreign service were required to pass examinations in public and international law, and they were usually recruited from law students, a practice which in Germany tended to ensure that they were conservative as well as legally trained. See Paul Seaburg, *The Wilhelmstrasse* (Berkeley and Los Angeles, 1954), pp. 6–7, 13.

be criticized on grounds of expediency. Just as in the case of the judicial approach of American policy, Curtius, Bülow, and Ritter tended in their concern with the letter of the law to forget the realities of international politics. There was no impartial world judge who could render a verdict of "not guilty," and even if there had been, there was no way to force acceptance of the verdict. As Professor Moritz Bonn has commented, "once more, the German Foreign Office had committed an act of criminal folly by imagining that the world is run on legal subtleties." [55] Events were to show that the members of the Hague Tribunal could not forget their national loyalties, and even if they had, their verdict was not necessarily binding. The French and Czechs were by no means satisfied with a situation in which the Germans were proceeding with negotiation regardless of foreign objections, and they simply did not intend to allow the agreement to be concluded. As the British Ambassador, Lord Tyrrell, reported from Paris, "It should be realized that the French Government are almost certainly determined, whether or not the proposed customs union proves to be in conformity with the letter of the existing obligations of Austria and Germany, to make a most vigorous attempt to secure the abandonment of the policy which it would constitute." [56]

Actually, considering the weakness of Austria, only a moderately vigorous effort by the French was needed. In early April the Austrian government was trying to raise a loan in Paris, even though such a loan, requiring French government sanction, would almost certainly entail political conditions. Indeed, by the morning of April 6, the French had secured a promise from Schober that Austria would not even begin negotiations with Germany until after the League Council meeting. Schober told the French

---

[55] M. J. Bonn, *Wandering Scholar* (London, 1949), p. 315. Oswald Hauser, though generally sympathetic to the customs union, seeing it as a move toward European federation, concedes that Curtius was naïve to think the plan could be justified legally: see "Die Plan einer deutsch-österreichischen Zollunion von 1931 und die europäische Foederation," *Historische Zeitschrift*, 179:91 (1955).
[56] *DBFP*, 2/II, No. 16.

Minister that it did not matter that the Germans refused to make a similar promise, since there could be no treaty until Austria proposed the "intermediate duties." The British Minister in Vienna commented that "Dr. Schober's promise is less valuable than he would like it to appear," since the necessary negotiations between the Austrian government and Austrian industry over temporary, transitional tariffs would in any case last some time. But Schober's promise was even less valuable than that, for, after some hesitation, the Austrians agreed with Ritter two weeks later that negotiations should be continued "unofficially." In practice, however, very little was accomplished beyond extensive discussions of how to present the Austro-German case in Geneva; the Germans wished to hew strictly to the line of legality, while the Austrians wished to stress the economic arguments and to try to win the other countries over.[57]

THE AUSTRO-GERMAN SPLIT OVER ITALY

The basic difference between the Austrian and German aims emerged over the course of the next month in a discussion of policy towards Italy. Italy, with her permanent seat on the League Council, was in a position to cast a deciding vote when the problem of the customs union came before that body, and it was not at all certain which side she would support. Perhaps the danger of *Anschluss* to Italian security would be decisive, but there was also the Italian hostility to France, at this time at a high point due to Rome's belief that France had shown bad faith in the naval disarmament negotiations. If Austria and Germany made the right assurances to Italy and offered her a place in the customs union system, suspicions of *Anschluss* might be dissipated, and Italy's valuable aid enlisted.

This, at least, was the Austrian view, as held by *Sektionschef* Richard Schüller. Schüller believed that the customs union must be broadened and other allies won, and he even suggested that

---

[57] *DBFP*, 2/II, No. 25; GFMR, 2520/E284599, E284686–92; 2521/E284750: Memo by Ritter, April 15, 1931; Dispatch, Rieth to Ministry, May 2, 1931; Drafts for Schober speeches, with comments and rebuttal by Ritter and Schüller. It appears from *SIA, 1931*, p. 311, that the agreement to continue negotiations became public knowledge.

while Austria was proposing another bilateral agreement between herself and Italy, Germany might offer a similar arrangement to France; this should improve the political prospects for the Austro-German project, even if it led to nothing. Schüller thoroughly expounded his ideas to German officials, and particularly to *Ministerialdirektor* Karl Ritter. At one point, he wrote Ritter: "I beg of you, examine these arguments. I see no alternative, since if we simply want to conduct our case as a lawsuit, our prospects are not favorable." The Austrian view was, of course, based on the assumption that the improvement of foreign trade was the essential goal.[58]

German thinking followed different lines. Italy's refusal to honor the Triple Alliance in 1914–15 still rankled in German minds, and Curtius had recently turned aside the suggestions of the Italian Foreign Minister, Dino Grandi, for closer Italo-German cooperation, stating that "formerly people had put the stress on draft treaties and treaty instruments, which then had often failed at the crucial moment." The German image of Italy was colored with contempt, and although Hoesch called attention to the importance of Italian support, Bülow, in a message to Schubert, suggested that when Grandi criticized Austro-German secrecy in planning the customs union, he was only looking for an excuse to justify an adoption of the French position. Germany, Bülow stated, must avoid giving the impression that she was running after the Italians and hoping they would save the project. He also feared that they would demand compensation. He suggested that Ambassador von Schubert merely point out to the Italians that success for the customs union would weaken the Little Entente, and failure would strengthen France.[59]

[58] GFMR, 2520/E284546–51, E284629–30; E284651–61; 2521/E284776–82, E285085–8: Memo by Rieth, April 21, 1931; Rieth to Ministry, April 28, 1931; Letter, [Rieth?] to Bülow, April 25, 1931; Comments on Schober draft speeches, April 26, 28, 1931; Letter, [Rieth?] to Bülow, April 28, 1931.

[59] GFMR, 2385/E199272, E199273; 2520/E284398, E284447–9: Letter, Schubert to Bülow, March 24, 1931; Bülow to Schubert, March 26, 1931; Hoesch to Ministry, March 24, 1931; Bülow to Schubert, March 27, 1931. Schubert complained later that despite Bülow's restrictions, Ritter had told a German official going to Milan to find out what the Italians really wanted: GFMR, 2385/E199642: Letter to Bülow, April 30, 1931.

In further opposition to Schüller's ideas, a German diplomat in Vienna argued that the prospect of an Italo-German bloc would only stiffen French resistance, in fear of an extended *Mitteleuropa*. In writing to Schüller, Ritter maintained that separate Austrian customs unions with Germany and Italy, such as Schüller proposed, would involve impossible technical difficulties owing to differences in the tariff systems and in the internal government monopolies and excise taxes. Although Austria and Germany might, if they included Italy, win her over at Geneva, they would lose the customs union, as they would never arrive at a treaty. But Ritter seems to have regarded another objection as the decisive one:

I am strongly convinced that we will overcome the various opposition views, justified or unjustified, in our two countries. We will be able to remove many anxieties by means of suitable adjustments, and the remainder will be overcome by the striving of the two peoples to come together. If we try to do the same with Italy (and Hungary), then this motivation will be missing, and in all three or four countries so many separate centers of opposition will remain, that in terms of internal politics and parliaments, we will not achieve our goal.[60]

Ritter's argument revealed a sensitive spot. If the Austrians and Germans lost their feeling that the proposed agreement was bringing them closer together, they would cease to support it. If the customs union had been a purely economic plan, then Schüller's ideas would have made sense: the technical problems were not really insurmountable, and on balance it was probably easier to negotiate this type of proposal, because it would arouse less foreign opposition. The real trouble with the Schüller scheme was precisely that it would have removed all the overtones of *Anschluss*.

Although the Austro-German draft provided for bringing in other countries, Berlin showed little interest in enlarging the exclusive circle. The British Commercial Counsellor asked Ritter

[60] GFMR, 2520/E284656–8; 2521/E284777–9: Letter, [Rieth?] to Bülow, April 25, 1931; Comments on draft speech, April 26, 1931.

if Czechoslovakia or other countries had been invited to join, and Ritter answered "with some emphasis" that "the German Government had not approached any country whatsoever"; neither had any other country replied favorably to the original offer to admit other states. Actually, the Czechs had extended feelers in Berlin on March 23, but their approach had been rebuffed. They were thinking of a wider agreement, including France; but Berlin evidently wished to ensure German predominance.[61]

It should be added that Schüller might not have succeeded in winning Italian favor, even if Berlin had agreed with him. By the end of April, Italian officials and Hungarian politicians were concluding that Austria would never see the customs union through. Even Monsignor Ignaz Seipel himself, who surprised Berlin by favoring the customs union project, warned that Curtius must take the lead, since "if ever a modern Austrian sees that a difficulty is cropping up somewhere, he will gladly settle for ten per cent of what has been achieved." [62] The Italian government began to show signs of having decided to oppose the customs union, with rumors suggesting that the Italians were planning an attack through the Allied Control Committee, set up under the 1922 protocol to supervise Austrian finance.[63]

In spite of such indications, and in spite of German pressure, Schüller went to Rome on May 1 and proposed an Austro-Italian agreement similar to the Austro-German one. Possibly there had earlier been more afoot between him and the Italians than he had

[61] *DBFP*, 2/II, No. 28; GFMR, 2520/E284355-8: Memo by Koepke, March 23, 1931. There had been, and continued to be, private negotiations with Beneš through the intermediary of a Dr. Wilhelm Regendanz; Beneš advanced far-reaching suggestions for economic union involving France, and even considered the offer of a loan by a Czech-led consortium. See GFMR, 2375/E192049-57, E192142-53; 2521/E284793.

[62] GFMR, 2520/E284719-20; 2521/E284828-9, E284853: Dispatch, Rieth to Ministry, May 7, 1931; Dispatch, Schoen to Ministry, April 30, 1931; Letter, Rieth to Ritter, May 9, 1931. Seipel also said that failure of the project would be "documented hopelessness."

[63] GFMR, 2520/E284629-30: Rieth to Ministry, April 28, 1931. The rumors were true. On April 29, the Italian Ambassador in London communicated the suggestion of using the Allied Control Committee to the British Foreign Secretary (*DBFP*, 2/II, No. 32).

disclosed to Ritter, for Grandi told Ambassador von Schubert that Italy had planned to extend her influence in Southeast Europe, "especially with Hungary but also with Austria and perhaps also with Yugoslavia." But Schüller now reported to Schubert that he had been curtly informed on May 1 that Italy placed no value on customs union negotiations with Austria. And on the same day, Grandi told the German Ambassador himself "that one could not really expect Italy to join in with [*anschliesse*] our agreement. The affair was now considered everywhere as a first step to *Anschluss*. One could not expect Italy to cooperate in such a policy." Italy had not been won over.[64]

THE QUESTION OF POLITICAL INTENT

Was the German government aiming at *Anschluss?* German records on the preparation and launching of the customs union proposal contain little explicit reference to *Anschluss* as the goal of the program. But after all, the connection between economic and political union was well understood. For responsible circles, there was little point in discussing an annexation which almost all Germans desired, but which could not be realized in the existing circumstances. Action could be taken, however, which would yield immediate political dividends.

Unquestionably, the German leaders were seeking a political success and not just an economic expedient. They hoped that the German public would see the customs union proposal as a step toward *Anschluss*, even while also hoping that non-Germans would see it as a mere trade agreement. Germans and Austrians carefully explained to foreigners why *Anschluss* was not being dreamed of, but significantly, there was no agreement as to what the insurmountable obstacle was supposed to be.[65] The political motivation of the proposal is evident in Curtius' arguments before the cabinet on March 16 and 18, and in the German insistence on

[64] GFMR, 2521/E284914–22, E284973–7: Schubert to Ministry, May 2, 1931 (two telegrams).
[65] See *DBFP*, 2/II, Nos. 3, 22, 34; GFMR, 2520/E284573–6: Schober's remarks recorded by Rieth, April 21, 1931.

describing the proposed arrangement as a customs union while resisting the admission of others, whether Italians or Czechs. And it was not just a matter of winning domestic support. After the beginning of the depression, the Wilhelmstrasse was spurred on by fears that Austria might be obliged to adopt some other alignment, making an ultimate *Anschluss* much more difficult to attain. Curtius believed that Austrian policy, as formulated by Schober, was now less favorable to a Danubian Federation, and the German Foreign Minister wished to strike while the iron was hot.

Furthermore, one leading German official, Bernhard von Bülow, had much more far-reaching aims in mind. Even before he became *Staatssekretär*, he had been interested in economic ties with Austria, regarding them as a modified form of *Anschluss*. We have seen him writing to Prittwitz in January 1931, disclosing that a plan existed for a customs union with Austria, which Czechoslovakia and Hungary might join. On April 19, he wrote to Dr. Walter Koch, Germany's Minister in Prague, affirming that the customs union would be carried through, and predicting that despite the hostile position Eduard Beneš had publicly taken on the customs union, Czechoslovakia would be compelled in a few years "to adhere to it in one way or another." (Bülow's terminology suggests that the Czechs might not have been full partners, and in any case, German supremacy in the union would by this time have been well established.) This in turn, Bülow continued, would lead to the solution of "vital political problems of the Reich," that is, to the questions of the Corridor and the eastern frontiers. "If we should succeed in incorporating Czechoslovakia in our economic bloc, and if in the meantime we should also have established closer economic relations with the Baltic States, then Poland with her unstable economic structure would be exposed to all kinds of dangers: we should have her in a kind of vise which might sooner or later put her in a state of mind to consider further the idea of exchanging political concessions for tangible economic benefits." Koch replied that he doubted that any economic pressure would ever induce the

Czechs to join in a customs union with Germany; he believed that Beneš, who had said Czechoslovakia would resist the customs union "to the point of self-destruction," had meant what he said. Certainly the Czechs had every reason to try to block the project. As Koepke's department had pointed out, the Czechs were bound to regard the customs union as a threat to their independence, since Germany and Austria together could reduce Czech exports by 35 per cent, presenting Prague with the alternatives of bankruptcy or surrender. Bülow's thought should not be regarded as characteristic of the German leadership: for German politicians, the customs union evoked thoughts of eventual *Anschluss*, but hardly of the Corridor. Moreover, influential German agrarian interests, as represented by the Reichs-Landbund under Count Kalckreuth, were stating very clearly that they would not countenance the admission of other countries to the Austro-German union. But Bülow, as chief permanent official of the Foreign Ministry, was exactly the man most responsible for considering the long-term implications of such actions as this.[66]

Most German officials and political leaders did not regard the customs union as a matter of cold calculation; they were emotionally involved. Former allies in peace and war, speaking the same language and sharing much of the same culture, the Austrians were not regarded as aliens. There was a note of shocked surprise from the Germans at Schüller's action in presenting his proposal in Rome despite their disapproval; they had thought that Berlin's judgment would be respected. Later, Ambassador von Hoesch was to write of the customs union as "involving questions of the noblest and, in the last analysis, most promising goals of the German people." Weizsäcker, not an initiate in the planning, comments from a different point of view that the defeat of the plan "was for me a painful experience, not so much because of the

[66] *DBFP*, 2/II, No. 34; GFMR, 2376/E193757-9; 2384/E109139-40; 2385/E199512-5, E199520-2; 3621/K005880-6; 4617/K272059-61, K272089-90: Letter, Bülow to Smend, June 5, 1929; Letter, Bülow to Prittwitz, Jan. 20, 1931; Letter, Bülow to Koch, April 19, 1931; Letter, Koch to Bülow, April 22, 1931; Memo by Koepke, Feb. 21, 1931; Letters, Kalckreuth to Pünder, March 23, April 8, 1931.

sentimental side of the '*Anschluss*,' which never seemed very important to me, but because of the resurrection of the old war-time association of the former allies." Finally, even Brüning, who had no great respect for the plan as such, had difficulty in maintaining his usual calm when Rumbold seemed to suggest that the Western powers might veto this action by German diplomacy; "Germany had few rights and if she were going to be checked at every turn the position of his government would become untenable." [67]

After the announcement and the reaction to it, there was of course more at stake than the Austro-German relationship. It was now a conflict of political power. Brüning had expressed Germany's determination to carry out her plans; France was clearly resolved to prevent this. The customs union was a vital question for Czechoslovakia, and France, aside from her direct concern over increased German strength and increased German militancy, was compelled to support her ally. Prestige was involved on both sides. When Lord Tyrrell reported that France was determined to make a most vigorous attempt to make the Germans and Austrians abandon their policy, Sir Horace Rumbold wrote: "I think it is equally important that it should be realized that the Brüning government will not abandon the proposed customs union with Austria." And when Hoesch talked with Berthelot on April 1, the German Ambassador took occasion to say: "People should not believe that Germany and Austria might be in a position to give up their plans, or to curtail them. Precisely because of the press campaign conducted against us and the pressure being exerted on us, yielding has been made all the more impossible for us." According to Hoesch, "Berthelot received these declarations without making a direct contradiction, but with a very worried expression." [68]

[67] GFMR, 2521/E284974, E285085; 2548/E300320: Schubert to Ministry, May 2, 1930; [Rieth] to Ritter, April 28, 1930; Hoesch to Ministry, July 11, 1931; Weizsäcker, *Erinnerungen*, p. 86; *DBFP*, 2/II, No. 8.

[68] *DBFP*, 2/II, No. 19; GFMR, 2520/E284482: Hoesch to Ministry, April 2, 1931.

IV

The European Triangle

As IN the case of every problem involving German foreign relations in the interwar period, the customs union proposal raised the question of whether or not Britain and France would act in concert. In contrast to their concern over Italy, Berlin and Vienna seem to have given little thought to the question of whether Britain and France might be susceptible to Austro-German influence. In this, the Germans may have missed an opportunity, for in the case of each of the two Western powers, a skillful German approach might have achieved better results. While Berlin and Vienna were drafting elaborate timetables for their formal announcement, they were neglecting any genuine diplomatic preparation. The Wilhelmstrasse seemed almost to prefer regarding London and Paris with suspicion, and while the German Foreign Office would consider overtures from the other powers if they wished to make them, it had no intention of doing anything which might involve a modification of any of Germany's revisionist demands.

BRITAIN, FRANCE, AND DISARMAMENT

It was characteristic of German suspiciousness that Berlin believed, in the period shortly before the customs union, that there might be some new Franco-British understanding. In the message delivered by Rumbold in December 1930, the British Foreign Office seemed to take the French side in reparations, while British views on land disarmament, as expressed in the Preparatory

Disarmament Commission, also seemed to be moving into alignment with French policy. On January 6, an editorial in the London *Times* admonished Germany, in terms recalling Rumbold's *démarche*, not to raise the reparations issue, and concluded by saying: "The looking-glass policy of crying out like the White Queen before feeling the pin-prick is dangerous in the world of real politics, however useful it may appear as a method of stealing the thunder of the National Socialists. Economically it can only help to induce the very crisis which the moratorium is intended to avert, and politically, as the discussions now proceeding between the British and French Treasuries plainly foreshadow, it can only reinforce the solidarity of Germany's creditors."

The German interpretation of this editorial seems to have been different from what its author(s) intended. Instead of concluding that German policy was driving England into the arms of France, German officials inferred that British hostility to Germany was being purchased by French gold. Bertolt Brecht's precept, *"Erst kommt das Fressen, dann kommt die Moral"*—"the gut comes first, then morality"—was only an extreme expression of an outlook shared by many non-Marxist Germans.   When the Paris bank rate was lowered—a move which appeared to Berlin to be contrary to French interests, though highly welcome to London, which was suffering increasingly serious losses of gold and foreign exchange—the Wilhelmstrasse asked its London and Paris embassies to find out what counterconcessions the British were making, suggesting that they might be in naval or land disarmament, or in the field of reparations.[1]

The reports that followed indicated that the French had indeed suggested some kind of counterconcession in the Treasury discussions, but that the British had refused to agree to any such conditions. Governor Clément Moret of the Bank of France told a German informant that the result of the discussions had been

[1] GFMR, 1554/D666379–81: Jan. 13, 1931. Grandi also suspected that the British might be drawn into a position of dependence on France (GFMR, 1554/D666394, D666427: Schubert to Ministry, Jan. 14, 1931; Memo by Curtius, Jan. 25, 1931).

"completely negative"; the British had been too proud (as Moret saw it) to accept a loan offered under "certain conditions and limitations" by France. In London a German contact pointed out that while the French were ready to use the British monetary difficulties as a lever for strengthening the political entente, the British did not intend to mix economic negotiations with politics.[2] And on February 23, the French Secretary-General made some pertinent observations to Ambassador von Hoesch:

Berthelot explained that it was very difficult for the English, with their well-known pride in their hitherto leading position in the world of economics and finance, to enter into financial conversations with France. Even now, the English requests in these conversations are still unacceptable to France. But in view of England's general position, the necessity remains for her to reach certain agreements with France. Britain finds herself in a bad situation. The Empire is falling more and more apart, and in England itself the belief in her own ability to recover is disappearing. The British people also lack courage and the resolve to work.

On my asking [Hoesch continued] whether there were still other subjects of negotiation tied in with the financial discussions between the two countries, Berthelot answered after some hesitation with a definite "Yes," naturally without going into further details.[3]

Other sources also indicated that the talks were proceeding with difficulty.[4] Evidently there was an almost complete failure to reach a financial agreement with London, and we today may suspect that this was exactly because of the introduction of political conditions. Further, if the French introduced political conditions, this may go far to explain the extreme anti-French views held by some British officials in the months that followed. Actually, had the German Foreign Office been inclined to take

[2] GFMR, 1776/D808288-9, D808300-1, D808306-10: Hoesch to Ministry, Jan. 14, 1931; Neurath to Ministry, Jan. 7, 1931 (two telegrams); Hoesch to Ministry, Jan. 6, 1931.

[3] GFMR, 1554/D666472-3: Hoesch to Ministry, Feb. 23, 1931.

[4] GFMR, 1555/D666492: Rieth to Ministry, Feb. 24, 1931. The final British Treasury press communiqué stated that the object of the discussions had been a frank exchange of views, not a definite agreement, and indicated that the French blamed current credit difficulties on the policies of the borrowing countries (London *Times*, Feb. 25, 1931).

sides, it might have sided with France. In the period when the Young Plan was in force, the French and, to a lesser degree, the German foreign offices continually flirted with the idea of a *grand rapprochement*, in which the French longing for security and the German need for capital would somehow be balanced. Berthelot's remarks quoted above may seem surprisingly frank; he was in fact setting the stage for a long conversation on a possible Franco-German understanding.

An Anglo-French exchange of political for financial assistance failed, then, to materialize. The Germans were also unable to find any proof that Britain had induced France to set down limits for her navy in the prospective Franco-Italian naval agreement by promising to oppose land disarmament. In 1928 there had been just such a secret accord, but its disclosure had been too embarrassing to encourage a repetition.[5] When, on February 20, a member of the German Embassy in Paris was bold enough to raise the question with René Massigli, the principal French disarmament negotiator, Massigli acidly observed that the Germans "always thought France wanted a counterconcession in the negotiations. Such a horse trade had not taken place." It was the behavior of the Germans themselves, Massigli said, that had inspired the recent coolness of Lord Robert Cecil, the British delegate in the Preparatory Commission. Arthur Henderson himself categorically denied that there had been any agreement on land disarmament in connection with the Franco-Italian naval disarmament negotiations. And Ambassador von Neurath agreed that there had probably been no British counterpayment to France, remarking, "This leaves the situation unchanged, since England would probably have made concessions to France on land disarmament even before this." [6]

The truth was that British policy was not all of a piece, and

---

[5] See Gordon A. Craig, "The British Foreign Office from Grey to Austen Chamberlain," in G. A. Craig and Felix Gilbert, eds., *The Diplomats* (Princeton, 1953), pp. 44–45. Curtius spoke to Rumbold about this incident on February 24 (GFMR, 1554/D666478); Rumbold glossed over it in his report (*DBFP*, 2/II, No. 351).

[6] GFMR, 1555/D666503–4, D666509, D666528: Rieth to Ministry, Feb. 26, 1931; Schubert to Curtius, Feb. 27, 1931; Neurath to Ministry, March 3, 1931.

that in many questions it was not oriented for or against other powers, but according to what were considered to be the merits of the case. The over-all aim was reconciliation, the restoration of prewar conditions, and the furtherance of trade. If they had thought in terms of the balance of power, most Britons would have considered that France was the weight to be counterbalanced. But instead, most of British opinion put its trust in the League of Nations, and this was especially true within the Labour Party, at this time holding the seals of office. The Foreign Secretary, Arthur Henderson, was particularly devoted to the cause of disarmament, and he praised whoever seemed to him to support it and scolded whoever seemed to him to threaten it, without regard to any such consideration as the alignment of the powers. By the time of the customs union announcement, he had rightly concluded that he was himself the best possible candidate for chairman of the Disarmament Conference;[7] he was in fact the only leading figure in Europe who believed in the Conference. But the pursuit of his honorable ambition may help to explain his constant appearance in the limelight in the spring of 1931. Henderson's interest in disarmament and his hostile reaction to any evidence of German aggressiveness may have gained force from the fact that his eldest son, considered by his brothers "the most gifted of the family and the one most like his father," had been killed in the Battle of the Somme. According to Henderson's biographer, this was the heaviest blow that had ever befallen him.[8] Aside from this, Henderson himself had been personally committed to winning the war, unlike Prime Minister Ramsay MacDonald, who had been a pacifist on principle. This difference in their pasts may help to explain their differing reactions to French and German policies, although Henderson's greater sympathy for the French may also have reflected the influence of the Foreign Office staff.

[7] GFMR, 1555/D666589: Letter, Dufour to Weizsäcker, March 26, 1931; *FRUS, 1931*, I, 492–493.

[8] Mary Agnes Hamilton, *Arthur Henderson* (London, 1938), p. 112. Vansittart, who lost a beloved brother, likewise had personal reasons for his attitude toward Germany.

The German approach to disarmament—that is, that it was an opportunity to eliminate French legal and military superiority—was sometimes hard to reconcile with the Foreign Secretary's ideals. Signs of German impatience led him, on February 12, 1931, to instruct the British Ambassador, Sir Horace Rumbold, to give Curtius a stern warning that the Germans should drop what he regarded as their "somewhat cynical attitude of detachment" on disarmament; they should make a positive contribution, rather than doing nothing and then regarding the failure of others as justification for German rearmament. This warning somewhat resembled that made against launching reparations revision the preceding December, but it was not so well founded, nor so tamely received. On March 18, Curtius gave Rumbold the prepared (though "unofficial") answer of the German government, which stated that it was now the turn of others to make disarmament proposals, and which foresaw a rupture in the coming Disarmament Conference unless the draft convention was modified and the principle of equality recognized. In short, Curtius simply gave more authority to the views against which Henderson had protested.[9]

THE INVITATION TO CHEQUERS

The effect of the exchange just described was mitigated by another British attempt to promote reconciliation and disarmament, Henderson's invitation to Brüning and Curtius to spend a weekend at Chequers, the Prime Minister's ex officio country seat. Alarmed by reports about the German political and economic situation, Henderson had begun to consider whether something could be done to support the existing regime. On February 19, he asked Rumbold to predict whether Brüning could maintain control at home, and also whether Brüning's government might try to win domestic support by taking some

[9] *DBFP*, 2/I, Nos. 348, 356; GFMR, 1555/D666573–6: Memo by Curtius, March 19, 1931. The prepared answer is in GFMR, 1555/D666482. Rumbold diplomatically modified "cynical" to "cold and detached" when he addressed Curtius, but still received a negative response (*DBFP*, 2/I, No. 351).

action in the field of foreign policy. Henderson had also heard that Brüning had discussed with Sackett the idea of convoking an international economic conference, and the British government was very interested in such a meeting, even though prospects seemed poor at the moment.[10]

Rumbold replied on March 4 that the political and economic outlook had improved since the turn of the year, and that the Brüning government would probably maintain its position. He also predicted—wrongly, as it turned out—that no action would be taken in foreign affairs for the sake of winning internal support. He had learned from Sackett that Hoover was not taking up the idea of a general conference, and both Sackett and the Danish Minister to Berlin had suggested that some gesture of recognition by Great Britain would be a great help to Brüning. Most important, Sir Horace also sent a private letter to Henderson, suggesting an invitation to Brüning for an unofficial visit to England, which, besides bringing Germany "out of the cold" and into the disarmament discussions, would "be helpful to [Brüning] in Germany itself. I cannot imagine anything which would more impress and please the Germans than if he were to spend a weekend at Chequers, for instance." [11]

After checking with Ramsay MacDonald, Henderson acted on this proposal and issued an invitation through Ambassador von Neurath on March 14. Rumbold's suggestion can hardly have been the only consideration, for Washington had also suggested that the British might invite the prime ministers or foreign ministers of the principal European powers to London for direct consultation on the main disarmament problems.[12] Moreover, Neurath's report makes it appear that Henderson was anxious to prove that the British policy for the coming Disarmament Con-

[10] *DBFP*, 2/I, No. 350.

[11] *DBFP*, 2/I, Nos. 353, 354. MacDonald later told Stimson that the Foreign Office had opposed the visit to Chequers lest it make trouble with France, giving Stimson "some amusing details of his talks with them" (*FRUS, 1931*, I, 517). If there really was Foreign Office opposition, however, it probably arose after the customs union announcement.

[12] *FRUS, 1931*, I, 491–492.

ference had not been prejudiced by the Franco-Italian naval negotiations. Henderson urged that Curtius come to the Organization Committee meeting in Paris, then added: "In order also to show the world that the British government was far from seeking to build a bloc, they would be very pleased if the Chancellor and Foreign Minister would accept an invitation extended to them for a friendly discussion and visit with the British Prime Minister and Foreign Secretary." Neurath himself strongly endorsed the idea of the visit in his report to Berlin.[13]

Curtius probably had no intention of being in Paris during the week following the customs union announcement, but the invitation to come to England was another matter. He discussed the visit with Rumbold in their conversation on March 18, and although he could not yet set a date, he made it clear that Brüning and he were anxious to accept. As a result, the atmosphere was more harmonious when Curtius proceeded to give Rumbold the German reply on disarmament, already referred to, and Rumbold was able to say simply that this subject could be pursued further when the visit took place.[14] Unquestionably, the British expected, at the time they issued their invitation, that disarmament would be the principal subject of discussion.

What did the French think of this invitation? Two of the published British documents seem to indicate that Henderson informed Briand on March 11, before issuing the invitation, and obtained Briand's approval. But further research shows that Briand was actually told of the invitation only on the morning of the twenty-fifth, at the same time that he was informed of Henderson's first *démarches* on the customs union in Berlin and Vienna.[15] In the light of the coincidence in timing, one cannot

---

[13] GFMR, 1555/D666567: March 14, 1931.

[14] *DBFP*, 2/I, No. 355; GFMR, 1555/D666573.

[15] The two documents in question are *DBFP*, 2/II, No. 40 (April 2) and 2/III, No. 207 (March 25); the reference to "Sir J. Simon" in the heading of the latter is certainly an error. These documents make it appear that Henderson discussed the German visit with Briand at the Quai d'Orsay on "the 11th instant" (No. 207) or "the 11th March" (No. 40). But Henderson answered a question in the House of Commons on March 11 (London

help but suspect that the British *démarches* on the customs union, though justifiable in themselves, were decided on largely in order to soften the impact of the news that Brüning and Curtius had been invited to Chequers. After the customs union announcement, the idea of an Anglo-German tête-à-tête was hardly one to win acclaim in Paris, and as already stated in the last chapter, Henderson's position at the Organization Committee meeting was certainly not an enviable one. But the news of the British *démarches* on the customs union made things much easier, the more so since until the morning of the twenty-fifth the Quai d'Orsay had been in doubt as to whether the British would give them any support on this issue.[16] It is therefore understandable that Briand at first accepted the idea of the invitation, even though he was not enthusiastically in favor of it.

Although Henderson, by asking the German and Austrian governments to desist from negotiation, did much to reassure the French government, his proposals were not, in French eyes, sufficient in themselves. When first informed on March 25, Briand did little but express his gratitude, but some difference in emphasis emerged in his second talk with Henderson on the following day. According to Henderson, Briand "expressed himself as in full agreement," but it is noteworthy that he stressed the League Council, rather than the Hague Court, as the institution which should render a decision.[17] This was logical to the French, who

---

Times, March 12, 1931) and in May Sir Walford Selby told a German diplomat that Henderson had informed Briand of the Chequers meeting while proposing to refer the customs union to the League Council or to the Hague Court (GFMR, 2385/E199370–1: Letter, Dufour to Bülow, May 17, 1931). Also compare the tenor of *DBFP*, 2/II, Nos. 13, 320–322, and 326. A plausible explanation is that the "11th instant" of No. 207 (2/III) was a stenographic error for "11 o'clock in the morning" (see 2/II, No. 13), and that No. 40 (2/II) derives from No. 207: No. 207 still stated that "we had taken" the action of inviting the German leaders; in No. 40 this was edited to make the action a "proposed" one.

[16] SDP, 662.6331/61: Counselor of Embassy in Paris to Secretary, March 25, 1931; GFMR, 2385/E199370–1. Although his position would scarcely have been so bad as Henderson's, Grandi was very glad that he had not gone to Paris (GFMR, 2520/E284403: Schubert to Ministry, March 25, 1931).

[17] *DBFP*, 2/II, No. 15.

did not intend to permit themselves to be fobbed off with the German claims of legality, or satisfied with a possible pro-German decision from the Hague Court. To France, the question was a political one, and could well be decided on a political basis, preferably by the combined action of the Entente powers.

Berthelot outlined his conception of what should be done in a draft memorandum, which the French Chargé d'Affaires in London showed to Henderson on March 30. In it Berthelot proposed that the guarantor states of the Geneva Protocol of 1922 (France, Great Britain, Italy, and Czechoslovakia) should jointly make a formal demand that Austria abstain from further negotiation until the League Council should decide (presumably adversely) on the compatibility of the customs union with the 1922 protocol. As had happened on March 20, when the French suggested that the powers warn the Austrian government not to announce the customs union proposal, the British government did not accept the French suggestion. Henderson now (March 30) replied that he was about to make a parliamentary statement on this subject, and that this statement seemed to him to say "as much as was judicious for the moment about the discontinuance of Austro-German negotiations." Henderson's statement announced his intention of raising the question of the customs union at the next Council meeting, and his readiness to obtain an advisory opinion from the Hague Court. He added that he inferred that the German and Austrian governments would take part in such discussions, and he expressed the earnest hope that Austro-German negotiations would not progress so far "as to prejudice the friendly atmosphere in which matters are normally dealt with by the Council." Henderson told the French Chargé d'Affaires that he did not think it wise even to consider more formal representations until the Austrian and German reaction to this statement was known, and added that he would urge the Italian and Czech governments to adopt the line he was following.[18]

[18] *DBFP*, 2/II, No. 20. On April 1 Berthelot read a paper to Hoesch, which he said he had written himself, and which seems to have been identical

So, once again, French efforts to organize a common front broke down when the British assumed the role of intermediary. If we reflect on the failure of the Anglo-French financial negotiations, the British abstention from the *démarches* proposed on March 20, the difficulties which were arising again at this time over the Franco-Italian naval agreement, the invitation to Brüning and Curtius to come to Chequers, and this last refusal to join in pressing the Austrians to drop negotiations, we must conclude that there was reason for the French to despair of achieving their aims in collaboration with London. If France wished to make sure that the customs union would not be carried out, she would have to rely on her own efforts and perhaps on those of the Czechs.

THE FRENCH ANSWER

Mr. A. J. P. Taylor has commented, in connection with the Spanish succession crisis of 1870: "In these cases, the wise rule is to threaten the weak state, not the strong one." When fighting the customs union, France—wiser in 1931 than in 1870—chose Vienna as the logical point of attack. The Quai d'Orsay began not only to apply pressure, but also to consider what might be done to offer Austria an alternative to the attractions of the Reich. In the course of his conversation with Hoesch on April 1, Berthelot mentioned that France intended to present a far-reaching, over-all plan at Geneva in May. By April 27, the French had disclosed the general nature of their plan to the British government, and the full details were given to the British on May 4. But although Robert Coulondre discussed some of the French ideas with a member of the German Embassy on April 24, and although there were important conversations on May 1 and 2, the French did not give the actual terms to the German government until May 11, probably partly to hinder the Germans in their effort to criticize the plan, and possibly also simply to let them worry a little.[19]

---

with that shown to Henderson on March 30 (GFMR, 2520/E284483: Hoesch to Ministry, April 2, 1931).

[19] A. J. P. Taylor, *The Struggle for Mastery of Europe, 1848–1918* (Ox-

The rather asymmetrical French plan contained four points, three of which—preferential tariffs for the surplus cereals of East European countries, loans for these countries and for Austria under international auspices, and special preferences for Austrian products—bore on Austria and Eastern Europe and to some extent reversed previous French policy, which had been opposed to preferences. But the economic diplomats had argued about preferential tariffs at many a conference, and they were likely to be difficult to bring to life. The loan provision might be applied to Germany as well, but the version of the plan given the German government (unlike that given the British) specified that a precondition was the creation of "an atmosphere of confidence and peace." In specific terms, this seems to have meant that the Germans would be required to abandon revision. As noted earlier, the French had begun to offer new loans after the September 1930 elections, but it was always apparent that political conditions would accompany such loans. In his interview with Hoesch on February 23, 1931, Berthelot had extolled the merits of a comprehensive Franco-German settlement, and various proposals were discussed in the days before the customs union announcement. But as Hoesch pointed out to Berlin, such financial discussions, envisaged as a way around the insoluble political problems, always came at last to grief on just those problems; the French government was always compelled to make assistance conditional on German abandonment of political aims, while the German government could not give up revision.[20]

ford, 2nd ed., 1957), p. 204; GFMR, 2520/E284485, E284636-7; 2521/E284894-905, E284958-60: Hoesch to Ministry, April 2, 24, May 2 (two reports), 1931; *Aide-mémoire* from French Embassy, Berlin, May 11, 1931; *DBFP*, 2/II, No. 31. Word that a plan was in preparation appeared in the French press by April 17 (*Manchester Guardian*, April 18, 1931).

[20] GFMR, 1683/D786462; 2521/E284958-60; 1554/D666473-4; 4507/K140610-11; 2382/E197148: Cabinet Protocol, May 11, 1931; French *aide-mémoire*, May 11, 1931; Hoesch to Ministry, Feb. 24, 1931; Memo by Hoesch, March 6, 1931; Memo by Bülow, March 16, 1931; *DBFP*, 2/II, No. 31. Despite all French conditions, however, the picture of active French hostility given by Curtius in his *Sechs Jahre Minister der deutschen Republik* (Heidelberg, 1948) can only be described as false. For example, Briand did not—as stated in *Sechs Jahre*, pp. 170 and 190—send the François-Poncet group back to

The fourth point in the new French plan, the development of international cartels as a means of making a peaceful division of markets, was more original, and directly concerned Franco-German relations. This was the brain child of André François-Poncet, at this time Under Secretary of State to Premier Pierre Laval, and appears to have owed little or nothing to the French Foreign Ministry. Although François-Poncet all but ignores this proposal in his memoirs of his years in Berlin, the plan probably led to his appointment there, and it should be noted by those who wish to follow the career of Laval, or to trace some of the less publicized antecedents of postwar European planning. The dapper François-Poncet had been a parliamentary spokesman for French industry, and was well acquainted with the business structure of Germany. He had accompanied Briand to Geneva in September 1930, and he seems to have been highly regarded by Laval, who coveted the mantle of Briand, and who was anxious to develop a new policy and to establish a reputation in foreign affairs. What better time for a new departure than at this point, when the customs union had proved the futility of Briand's pan-European ideas?[21]

Cartels (agreements between all the enterprises in particular industries on quotas for production, territories for distribution, and fixed scales for prices) had developed in many countries. In some industries, such as nitrogen and electricity, they were starting to appear on an international level. François-Poncet proposed that the European governments, as a matter of policy, actively support the formation of international cartels, mainly by threaten-

---

Paris in September 1930; instead, he urged Curtius to get in touch with François-Poncet: see GFMR, 2382/E196948-9: Memo by Curtius, Sept. 18, 1930.

[21] André François-Poncet, *Souvenirs d'une ambassade à Berlin* (Paris, 1946), p. 23; Franklin L. Ford, "Three Observers in Berlin: Rumbold, Dodd, and François-Poncet," in Craig and Gilbert, eds., *The Diplomats*, pp. 460–474. On Laval's relation to Briand: GFMR, 2549/E300504: Memo by Curtius, July 25, 1931; François-Poncet, *Ambassade*, p. 20; Alfred Mallet, *Pierre Laval* (2 vols., Paris, 1955), I, 31–33, 43–44.

ing reluctant industries with the removal of protective tariffs. Indeed, he argued that when industries once had been cartelized internationally, it would be possible to eliminate protective tariffs. Only those countries which shared in the industry to be cartelized would be involved in the negotiations for a particular cartel; thus in the case of coal, the cartel would be formed by the coal-mining countries.[22]

A critic of this plan might say that, if it was possible in this manner to eliminate tariffs, this was only because the industries involved would obtain protection without them, through the cartel itself. In these circumstances, the elimination of tariffs seems pointless. As the chief permanent official in the German Ministry of Economic Affairs, Dr. Ernst Trendelenburg, commented, the French basically did not want to improve the European internal division of labor; they only wanted to use cartels to anchor the existing situation.[23] But to François-Poncet, the elimination of tariffs or the furtherance of a more rational division of labor was probably unimportant. It is likely that he only advanced these considerations to meet the claims (at least as dubious) that the customs union was a first step to a general reduction of tariffs in Europe. Insofar as François-Poncet's proposal and the rest of the French counterplan were not simply a tactic to divert or delay the customs union, the idea seems to have been to create a sort of capitalist international, in which French, British, and German industry would be linked together in a way that would tend to preserve the economic—and also the political—*status quo*. In view of the relative financial strength of France at this time, she was likely to take a dominant role in those cartels in which she participated. On the other hand, the popularity of cartels with German industry, and the high state of development they had already reached in Germany, gave some grounds for hoping that the Germans would respond in a favorable way. If the plan could

[22] GFMR, 2520/E284637; 2521/E284896-7: Hoesch to Ministry, April 24, May 2, 1931.
[23] GFMR, 1683/D786489.

be realized, powerful interest groups, instead of aggravating Franco-German competition, would be on the side of Franco-German cooperation.

Franco-German Soundings for a Compromise

An opportunity soon came to test German responsiveness. At the end of April, before the French communicated their plan to the German government, Berlin received reports purporting to describe this plan, and indicating that the French would welcome an opportunity for direct, secret discussions, possibly including other states, before proceeding to fight out the customs union at the Council meeting. One report supposedly stemmed from Beneš, another from François-Poncet. Curtius decided that if these feelers were really being extended with Briand's knowledge, it would be unwise not to respond, especially since there had been no sign that he would see Briand before the public meeting. On the other hand, Curtius did not want to give Briand the impression that there was any weakening in the German resolve to carry out the Austro-German plan. So Hoesch was told on April 30 to find out if Briand in fact stood behind these proposals. If he did, Hoesch could inform him that Curtius would welcome a chance for a private discussion, or for preliminary talks with other powers. Hoesch was to make it clear, however, that there could be no question of substituting negotiation "in a larger circle" for the customs union: "It can only be a matter of finding out if the plans on both sides can be pursued simultaneously, and possibly adapted to each other." We may note that Hoesch himself had suggested on April 14 that although he did not believe France would ever actually enter into a customs union with Germany, it might be good tactics specifically to offer France a place in such an arrangement.[24]

When Hoesch saw Briand on May 1, the French Foreign Minister immediately said that he was in agreement with the suggestion of multilateral talks, although he either would not or could not say much about the French plan. Hoesch, for his part, emphasized that while Germany was ready to carry on negotia-

[24] GFMR, 2521/E284792-9; 4617/K272083-6.

tions with other countries, she would not suspend discussions with Austria, and the conversation ended inconclusively.[25] On the next day, Hoesch had a more extensive discussion with François-Poncet, who spoke for France with the authorization of both Briand and Laval. François-Poncet argued that a defeat of either Germany or France over the customs union would lead to a split of Europe into two camps, with serious consequences in such questions as disarmament. Assuming that Germany was not seeking a political success at the expense of foreign interests, he thought that agreement could be reached; after all, the customs union could not be completed overnight, and it would be necessary to decide which tariffs were to be dropped forthwith, which were to be scaled down, and which were to be retained for the time being in full, "until industrial agreements or the final disposition of those firms condemned to extinction will have made possible the complete elimination of tariff protection." After this hint at some of the problems involved in the customs union, François-Poncet continued: "France wants to suggest the application of the same system to all of Europe, whereby the further pursuit of the Austro-German plan would become superfluous." Having adroitly prepared the ground, he then proceeded to describe his own contribution to the French plan. After explaining the cartelization scheme, François-Poncet said (in Hoesch's paraphrase):

Thus the outcome would be, if in a weakened form, in the direction of the customs union, and Germany might flatter herself that through her initiative, world and especially French opinion was awakened and inspired to make a positive proposal. Germany need not formally give up the customs union. In the last analysis, it would be acceptable if Germany declared that she was provisionally putting off carrying out her plan, in order to see what would result from the pursuit of the French proposals, with the reservation that she might turn back to the Austro-German project if the French ideas proved to be unrealizable. But it is essential that, until then, the further pursuit of the Austro-German plan shall cease.[26]

[25] GFMR, 2521/E284902–4: Hoesch to Ministry, May 2, 1931.
[26] GFMR, 2521/E284894–8: Hoesch to Ministry, May 2, 1931.

François-Poncet was evidently making a supreme effort to interest
the German government in his ideas, and to achieve a positive
compromise solution without resort to coercion.

But as with Briand, Hoesch told François-Poncet repeatedly
that his government was holding fast to the Austro-German
project, and would not be ready even to postpone it, although
Berlin would probably be willing to pursue the French proposals
simultaneously with the Austro-German negotiations. Thus an
impasse was reached, and François-Poncet made it clear that, for
France, no agreement was possible "if Germany continued calmly
to carry on her negotiations with Austria." France would then
have to fight the customs union tooth and nail at Geneva, from
the political and economic as well as from the legal point of view.
The League, he said, "must offer a guarantee that members will
not be left surprised and defenseless in the face of developments
which are likely fundamentally to alter economic and power relationships." At the end, François-Poncet repeated that they were
at a turning point in history; if Germany would accept his proposals, he thought there would be a chance for Franco-German
economic and financial cooperation, apparently referring to the
possibility of French loans.[27]

There was, however, little hope of German acceptance on
these terms. When Bülow sent copies of Hoesch's reports of his
conversations with Briand and François-Poncet to all important
German embassies and legations, his covering letter merely indicated that, in the light of these reports, no prospect existed of a
preliminary, high-level meeting. Bülow told Rumbold that the
French had been sounded "as to the possibility of providing
'cushions' for one another to sit upon at Geneva," and explained
that "these soundings had led to no result." [28] In retrospect, it is
a little hard to see what Curtius had expected as a result of
Hoesch's inquiries: if he really intended to use the Austro-
German proposal to give a "first impulse" to a readjustment of
European relations, then at this point he should have held out

[27] GFMR, 2521/E284898–901: Hoesch to Ministry, May 2, 1931.
[28] GFMR, 2521/E284893: Circular dispatch; *DBFP*, 2/II, No. 34.

some hope to the French that they could purchase a renunciation of the customs union with appropriate counteroffers. Probably he never really intended to barter with the customs union, but merely expected, in regard to France, that if he troubled the waters, the fishing would somehow be better. But Hoesch's interviews with Briand and François-Poncet can only have served to convince Paris that more forceful measures were required.

When the British had examined the French program, they welcomed the offer of a constructive solution, but they had some doubts as to the feasibility of any of the four points, and it seemed to them that the French program, while attractive to Vienna, offered very little to Berlin. This last was Vansittart's immediate reaction when he heard the complete scheme, and the point was stressed again on May 7, when the British comments were presented to Robert Coulondre, the Director of Commercial Relations at the Quai d'Orsay. Coulondre replied that Germany would be offered the cartel scheme and greater facilities for "international finance" and exports to the agrarian countries. To the observation that the proposed assistance in international finance "seemed of a rather nebulous nature," Coulondre answered that

the French Government did not intend to make any definite or precise promises in this connection until they learnt whether the German Government would, in principle, fall in with their scheme. They would not assist the grant of French loans to a Germany which was pursuing a policy economically hostile to France and contrary to the interests of European co-operation . . . The French Government sincerely trusted that the German Government would realize that in the event of their proceeding with the proposals for a customs union with Austria, they would be faced with economic alliances or unions between other countries, which would in all probability close those countries to German goods, leading thus to economic warfare and adding to the distress of Europe and, in particular, of Austria and Germany themselves . . . Germany was a Power of such importance that it was out of the question to bribe her to fall in with the French scheme, and that it was for the German Government either to pursue a policy of general co-operation between the various States of Europe or else to follow one of shortsighted egoism which, whilst perhaps satisfying certain political aspirations, would only accentuate the present economic distress of the continent, and more especially of Germany herself.[29]

Thus, as far as Coulondre was concerned, France had offered Germany a chance to cooperate, and if Germany did not take it, she would have to face the consequences. And indeed, it would have been rather irrelevant to offer further economic inducements to woo the Germans from the customs union, since their interest in the customs union had little economic basis.

THE CREDITANSTALT ANNOUNCEMENT

The increased distress predicted by Coulondre was very soon to manifest itself financially, if not economically. On May 11, the Austrian government announced that the historic Creditanstalt für Handel und Gewerbe, whose balance equalled 60 per cent of that of all other Austrian banks combined, had suffered losses during 1930 of 140,000,000 schillings, as against a capital and reserves of 164,000,000. This did not mean that the bank was closing its doors, for the announcement also stated that the institution was being supported by the Austrian government, with a stock purchase of 100,000,000 schillings; by the Austrian central bank, the Nationalbank, with 30,000,000 schillings; and by the President of the Creditanstalt, Baron Louis de Rothschild (the "Vienna Rothschild"), with a reduction of his stock holdings by 22,500,000 schillings. The truth was that the Creditanstalt was too vital to Austria to be allowed to go into bankruptcy. Moreover, the government shared responsibility for the failure, having among other things practically forced the unfortunate merger with Dr. Rudolf Sieghart's tottering Boden-Credit-Anstalt in 1929.[30]

Was the collapse of the bank brought about, as some have believed, by French intrigue? Was this another, more sinister, way of diverting Austria from the customs union? Since the Creditanstalt losses were suffered before the customs union

---

[29] *DBFP*, 2/II, Nos. 31, 35.

[30] Walther Federn, "Der Zusammenbruch der österreichischen Kreditanstalt," *Archiv für Sozialwissenschaft und Sozialpolitik*, 67:417–418, 420–421 (1932).

was announced, it is hardly plausible to say that France ruined the bank to block the Austro-German project. Moreover, the losses were not due to French withdrawals but to the all-too-real bankruptcy of many Austrian and other East European industries. Indeed, the breakdown of the Creditanstalt could be considered an illustration of Austria's economic weakness and consequent need for a customs union, and this interpretation was in fact immediately advanced in the Vienna press. The argument is a good one, but the idea of French responsibility can hardly be reconciled with it.[31]

Nevertheless, if France did not cause the collapse, it is quite possible that she precipitated the announcement. With financial practices what they were in those days, especially in Central Europe, financiers could often conceal their true predicament for a long time,[32] and the managers of the Creditanstalt had in fact concealed their losses for several months, if not longer. It is difficult to believe that the revelation of the losses at this particular moment, just after the Germans had refused again to suspend negotiations and just before the crucial meeting of the League Council, was only a coincidence.

There were several ways in which France might have brought about the disclosure. First, a study of Austrian banking might easily have suggested to the French that there were possibilities involved in bringing about a disclosure of the Creditanstalt balance sheet. One rumor stated that the announcement became necessary when a new staff expert refused to sign a false statement.[33] This refusal might be credited to genuine scruples; still, it could have been encouraged by interested parties.

[31] Federn, "Zusammenbruch," pp. 404–409; *Neue Freie Presse* (Vienna), May 11, 1931 (A.M.). Ritter also mentioned this idea in one of his memoranda (GFMR, 2521/E285182: June 11, 1931).

[32] See the interesting study of Ivar Kreuger by Robert S. Shaplen (*Kreuger: Genius and Swindler,* New York, 1960). Incidentally, Kreuger was closely associated with Lee, Higginson and Co., and he participated in the Lee, Higginson credit of October 1930.

[33] Federn, "Zusammenbruch," p. 417; P. H. Emden, "Story of the Vienna Creditanstalt," *Menorah Journal,* 28:93 (Jan. 1940); Markas Leser, *La Crise du schilling autrichien et ses causes économiques* (Paris, 1935), p. 85.

Second, France seems to have had influence in the management of the bank. We noted earlier that the German government suspected Dr. Sieghart of being subject to Czech and French influence; in April 1929, it was reported that the French firm, Schneider-Creusot, had bought the Franz-Ferdinand estates with Sieghart's cooperation. Schneider-Creusot was further reported to be interested in the Steyrwerke (which owed the Boden-Credit-Anstalt an amount equal to its entire capital) and also in the Alpin-Montan-Gesellschaft, while Sieghart was unloading Steyr stock in order to buy shares in the French-dominated Länderbank. All this activity reportedly took place shortly after the collapse of Sieghart's negotiations for German support, which suggests that the French may have found his offer more tempting; it provided them with a stake in the Boden-Credit-Anstalt, and hence later in the Creditanstalt. And in fact we learn that in 1931 one of the directors of the Creditanstalt was M. Schneider of Schneider-Creusot. It also became known in 1931 that the Creditanstalt had important shareholdings in two Czech banks, the Böhmische Escomptebank and the Živnostenská Banka. Directors do not always know the true state of the companies they direct, but a well-informed representative of French interests could have forced the announcement of the losses.[34]

Third, the management of the bank may well have made discreet attempts to raise new funds in Paris before throwing in the sponge, and such soundings could have led to a disclosure of the losses. When Curtius was in Vienna, he was approached and asked if it might be possible for the Reichsbank, as had once been proposed to Schacht, to place larger current deposits in the Vienna banks, and especially in the Creditanstalt. Curtius passed this request on to Hans Luther, noting that "the Vienna banks are, as you know, in part oriented toward other money markets, and dependent on them," a situation which might have undesired

---

[34] Federn, "Zusammenbruch," p. 413; GFMR, 2347/E173882–3: Dispatch, Lerchenfeld to Ministry, April 12, 1929; Gustav Stolper, "Wiener Bankkrise," *Der deutsche Volkswirt*, 5:1103 (1931).

consequences. The Creditanstalt management also seems to have attempted to stave off creditors, for according to one story, a director of the bank went to the United States to negotiate with creditors there. Paris, however, was a more likely source for new funds than either Berlin or New York.[35]

The Creditanstalt itself—apart from French influence—had little reason to sympathize with the customs union proposal. The bank stood to suffer further losses on its investments in small Austrian firms unable to compete with German *Konzerne*. It could also look forward to the eventual relegation of Vienna to the status of a provincial capital, at least from the financial point of view, with the major banking business taken over by affiliates of the big German "D" banks: the Deutsche Bank und Diskonto-gesellschaft, the Dresdner Bank, and the Darmstädter und National-albank. As early as March 23, a report from the German Legation in Vienna stated that, while most Austrian businessmen welcomed the customs union, there were also other views: "Reference is also made to the difficulties which must be overcome before the final conclusion of the intended agreement, and therewith mention is made mainly of the two large banks, the Creditanstalt and the Niederösterreichische Escompte-Gesellschaft, which were completely taken by surprise by the agreement and which are involved in precisely those industries which presumably will be most affected by the removal of tariff barriers." [36] Another report from Vienna, dated May 7, said that the opposition of some Austrian industries affected the major banks, "since both are closely intertwined." This report continued, "With certain financial institutions, connections with France and the dependence on

[35] GFMR, 2382/E197214–5: Letter, Curtius to Luther, April 16, 1931; Federn, "Zusammenbruch," p. 417.

[36] GFMR, 2382/E197215–6; 2520/E284416. A more "positive" version of the Vienna report, on E284417–8, omits the reference to the banks. A dispatch from Lerchenfeld of March 28 refers to the opposition of "banking circles" outside Austria, probably meaning primarily the other branches of the Rothschild family, who were believed always to stick together (GFMR, 2520/E284413–4).

French capital play an important role." Creditanstalt stock quotations suggest that rumors had begun to spread about the bank's position several days before the announcement:

May	2	45.55
	6	45.55
	7	45.40
	8	45.20
	9	44.75
	11	43.50
	12	30.00

The Austrian government was told on May 8, and this may have been one source of leakage, affecting the quotations.[37]

The Austrian government's support of the Creditanstalt entailed the raising of another foreign loan, to the amount of 150,000,000 schillings, at a time when the market was already more than saturated with Austrian obligations. Curtius attempted to organize some German assistance, but evidently he could not provide it on the scale required. In these circumstances, the Austrian government turned immediately to the Four-Power Austrian Control Committee, established in 1922. The political implications of this move became apparent during the Geneva meetings a week later, when members of the Control Committee sought to delay approval of the new loan until after the showdown on the customs union in the League Council.[38] Little had Curtius realized, when he initiated the customs union, what an ambush he was walking into.

The British Position on the Customs Union

By early May, the French and Italian governments had taken a stand against the customs union, and ominous clouds were

[37] GMFR, 2520/E284732: Dispatch, Rieth to Ministry, May 7, 1931; Julius Curtius, *Sechs Jahre Minister der deutschen Republik* (Heidelberg, 1948), p. 198. Figures from daily issues of the *Neue Freie Presse* (Vienna).

[38] Federn, "Zusammenbruch," p. 423; GFMR, 2521/E284995, E285181; 2382/E197283–5; 2371/E188655, E188657, E188661; 3620/K005597: Curtius to Ministry, May 16, 1931; Memo by Ritter, June 11, 1931; Memos by Bülow, May 18; May 13, 15, 23, 1931; Curtius to Ministry, May 20, 1931; Curtius, *Sechs Jahre*, pp. 198–199.

gathering on the financial scene. The British, though not sharing the French views, were also taking a position unfavorable to the project. On May 1, Henderson warned Neurath that London might have legal objections, and that in any case, any remnant of tariffs between Germany and Austria would bring a British demand for the same most-favored-nation treatment. The Austro-German proposal threatened to compromise the Disarmament Conference, "and indeed the whole future of European cooperation"; financial confidence had also been upset. Nevertheless, the British sympathized with the Germans and Austrians in their economic difficulties, and Henderson asked if the Germans had some other solution to suggest.[39]

On the other hand, the British cared little for the French alternative, and they did not believe that Germany could accept it. Moreover, the French suggestion of agrarian preferences for Southeast Europe was likely to provoke resistance from overseas wheat-producing countries, including the Canadian and Australian dominions. This last would probably have sufficed in itself to turn the London government against the French plan. And the British also informed Paris, as they had Berlin, that they would claim their most-favored-nation rights to any tariff advantages which might be granted to Austria. Moreover, while they criticized the Germans for disturbing financial confidence, they criticized the French financial proposal as being too abstract and nebulous.[40]

Perhaps one reason for British disapproval was that the Bank of England, under the leadership of its Governor, Montagu Norman, had its own financial plan. The Bank's scheme was to form an international company or bank with a capital of £20,000,000, which would have guaranteed long-term loans to borrowers in financially embarrassed areas, such as Germany, the East European states, and the overseas raw-material-producing countries. This precursor of the World Bank would also, of course, have created better markets for British exports. Unfortunately for the success of this plan, the British themselves could not finance the

[39] *DBFP*, 2/II, No. 29.
[40] *DBFP*, 2/II, No. 36.

project, or even a third of it, and Norman failed to enlist French or American support, even though he made a trip to Washington for this purpose in April.[41]

Henderson's talk with Neurath about the customs union was followed by other discussions in Berlin, in which Rumbold tried to learn what the Germans would do at Geneva. Neither Bülow, who went over Henderson's points with Rumbold, nor Ritter, who discussed them with Thelwall, the Embassy's trade expert, gave any sign of being ready to propose or accept any alternative to their program, and they rigidly held to their legalist position; Bülow said that if the Hague Court raised legal objections, "the German Government would insist on knowing what those objections were in order to be able to meet them." It seemed to Rumbold that Bülow practically admitted that the customs union had been proposed for reasons of internal German politics; according to Bülow's own rather inconsistent report, he told Rumbold:

The German government was also [aside from economic pressures] forced to negotiate for internal political reasons. If one looked at the possible actions in the field of foreign policy—the minorities question, border questions, reparations, etc.—it was apparent that the customs union was by far the least dangerous, besides being an economic and not a political goal. But the ambassador might be sure that internal political motives had not led us to the customs union, it had stemmed exclusively from considerations of economic policy.

In Rumbold's version, Bülow said:

Even when he was a subordinate official at the German Foreign Office he had had some such customs union in mind. On entering office as Secretary of State, he had turned over in his mind the various questions of foreign policy which were of urgent interest to Germany, such as reparations, the eastern frontier and closer economic relations with

[41] *New York Times,* April 10, 15, 22, 1931. According to the *Manchester Guardian,* April 13, 1931, Sir Robert Kindersley of the Bank of England and Sir Charles Addis, at one time British representative with the Reichsbank, were the real authors of the plan. Norman also saw Stimson in New York

Austria, and had come to the conclusion that a customs union with Austria would be the step least likely to provoke opposition on the part of the other powers.

Bülow forgot that, to the British, it was not a question of choosing between actions, but rather of whether any action at all was justified.[42]

THE MEETING OF THE LEAGUE COUNCIL, MAY 1931

Before Curtius left for the League Council meeting in Geneva, the German cabinet held three meetings to discuss the prospects. Curtius tried to present a hopeful picture, even suggesting that a lofty discussion of the usefulness of customs unions might provide an opportunity to bring in reparations. He was obliged to admit, however, that Germany could not refuse a legal review of the customs union proposal, and when Brüning asked him if a reference to the Hague Court would greatly delay the further pursuit of the customs union, he had to say that it would, "since in this case Austria would not wish to pursue genuine negotiations further." It was evident that some of the participants at the meetings, especially Trendelenburg, did not share Curtius' enthusiasm, and he appealed to them not to start off by distrusting the Austrians, or by declaring the prospects for the whole action to be hopeless.

and praised Germany and the customs union; he did not share his government's hesitations on the latter (Stimson MS. Diary, April 1, 8, 1931).

[42] *DBFP*, 2/II, Nos. 29, 34; GFMR, 2521/E284924–8: May 6, 1931. Bülow's quasi-admission is revealing, but his circumstantial account as given by Rumbold is untrue in that it conceals Curtius' role; Curtius, as we have seen, had pushed the customs union in the conference with Schober in February 1930, at a time when Schubert was still the *Staatssekretär*. Bülow's rise may, however, have owed something to the customs union, which he may have discussed with Curtius while still a subordinate official. Curtius says in his memoirs (*Sechs Jahre*, p. 146) that he realized as soon as he entered office that a new *Staatssekretär* was needed; perhaps a suggestion by Schubert at the February 1930 meetings that the Geneva Protocol forbade a customs union contributed to Curtius' dissatisfaction with him (GFMR, 2347/E174087). See also F. G. Stambrook, "The German-Austrian Customs Union Project of 1931: A Study of German Methods and Motives," *Journal of Central European Affairs*, 21:22–23 (1961).

When Trendelenburg suggested that the recent attitude of the Austrian officials was regrettable, Curtius replied "that he could not go to Geneva burdened by doubts; instead he must believe in [the possibility of] his success." Brüning obtained the cabinet's agreement to the plans of the Foreign Minister, and gave Curtius the good wishes of the cabinet in carrying out his difficult task.[43]

On May 13, the election for the French presidency took place, and Briand was defeated by Paul Doumer. Briand remained at the Foreign Ministry, and was therefore able to come to Geneva on the fifteenth, but his defeat, which he may have attributed to the customs union project, probably made him all the more inclined to take a firm line with Curtius and Schober. Laval later told Curtius and Brüning that the customs union had caused Briand's defeat; Curtius retorted that he thought internal French politics were responsible. A sharp decline in Briand's powers became evident over the summer: the most obvious symptom was a growing tendency to fall asleep on any and all occasions. Conceivably, the customs union and the defeat of his candidacy may have hastened his death by depriving the veteran Foreign Minister of his will to live.[44]

The League Council meeting was to begin officially on Monday, May 18, but the Commission of Inquiry for European Union and the Four-Power Austrian Control Committee began their sessions on May 15. On the same day a private discussion took place in Geneva between Briand, Curtius, Henderson, and Grandi; as Grandi had told the German Ambassador, Italy, too, was now opposed to the customs union, so that Germany had no allies. The European Commission, intended to investigate the possibilities for economic union, provided a forum in which the Germans and Austrians could argue their economic case, and Curtius was therefore anxious to have a chance to win support in this

---

[43] GFMR, 1683/D786460-2, D786487-90, D786496-8: Cabinet Protocols, May, 11, 12, 13, 1931.

[44] GFMR, 1683/D786500; 2549/E300506; Cabinet Protocol, May 27, 1931; Memo by Curtius, July 25, 1931. Curtius says that Briand arrived in Geneva exhausted and angry (*Sechs Jahre*, pp. 197–198). Brüning told the writer in 1951 that "Briand had the same disease as Hindenburg."

assembly before the Council convened; he also sought to prevent the Council from considering the customs union until the second day of its deliberations. Briand, on the other hand, wanted the League Council to discuss the customs union first, and to postpone until after that discussion any consideration by the European Commission. The foreign ministers finally agreed that the European Commission might first hold a general discussion—and only that—of customs unions. In return for this somewhat grudging concession, the Austro-German proposal was placed at the beginning of the Council's agenda. When the discussion in the Commission took place, Curtius recommended the development of multilateral customs unions from small, bilateral beginnings, while Briand favored a general agreement, ending his speech by saying, "Whatever systems we may admit, we must not endeavor to do anything that is not permitted by the peace treaties or by international conventions." Schober bravely declared that while Austria would welcome a European customs union, and was ready to negotiate a customs union with any country, she could not afford to wait for schemes to be developed through a series of conferences. The discussion in the European Commission served mainly to outline the rival positions before the main confrontation in the Council meeting.[45]

In Geneva, it was generally expected that the case would go to the Court of International Justice in The Hague. When Schober and Curtius were planning, before the Council meeting, the position they would take, they agreed that Schober would, if asked, promise to make no *fait accompli* before an eventual Hague decision; at the most, according to Curtius, they intended to go no further than to promise there would be no official negotiations before the decision. In other words, they intended to maintain the same position as before, the position Hoesch had maintained with Briand and François-Poncet. Under the rotation system, Curtius was to preside at the Council sessions, and at the meeting on the fifteenth he gave Henderson a free hand in presenting the

[45] GFMR, 2521/E284992–4: Curtius to Ministry, May 16, 1931 (written on May 15); *DBFP*, 2/II, No. 38; *SIA, 1931*, pp. 314–315.

British proposal for a reference to The Hague. In return, Henderson "indicated his intention of sending the draft of his Council speech to Schober and [Curtius] tomorrow [May 16] or Sunday." [46]

Presumably, then, Curtius and Schober saw the speech beforehand. But Henderson told Curtius on May 18, just when the crucial meeting was starting (indeed, after Curtius had taken his seat), that he would be obliged to ask an additional question regarding the further pursuit of negotiations. To his speech he added, "I hope our Austrian colleague will agree that until the Council has taken a decision on the basis of the advisory opinion of the Court, no further progress should be made towards the establishment of the proposed regime." Schober then presented his case, ending by saying that he accepted Henderson's proposal unreservedly, "especially in the sense that nothing will be done to produce a *fait accompli* until the Council has taken a decision on the advisory opinion of the Court." This answer did not rule out further negotiations, however, and "in order that the position may be made absolutely clear," Henderson repeated his question. Schober then said he could certainly give Henderson the assurances he required. Thus the French obtained a new assurance that, as they had desired ever since the Austro-German announcement, negotiations would cease entirely at least until the Council had acted on the basis of a decision from The Hague. Schober had made a real concession, and the Austro-German plans suffered a serious public check. [47]

After the session was over, Curtius asked Henderson to explain his action. Henderson answered that he had had a talk with the French the previous evening, and that they had threatened to publicly humiliate Schober by laying down the most far-reaching conditions, which Schober would probably have had to accept.

---

[46] GFMR, 2521/E284994, E285009; 2382/E197270–5: Curtius to Ministry, May 16, 19, 1931; Memos by Bülow, May 15, 16, 1931; *DBFP*, 2/II, No. 38.

[47] League of Nations, *Official Journal*, XII, No. 7 (July 1931), Minutes of the 63rd Session of the Council (No. 2804), 1068–71. Selby told a German official that Schober had been "generally informed beforehand," and had said he would give the desired assurance (GFMR, 2385/E199368: Letter, Dufour to Bülow, May 17, 1931).

Henderson had only gotten them to give up their plan on condition that he would formulate his question, ask it before Briand spoke, and obtain an immediate response from Schober. Henderson added that the British delegation had settled the form of the question only just before the meeting began.[48]

In a press conference afterward, Schober, encouraged by Curtius, tried to take the sting out of his renunciation. He stated that nothing had changed in Austria's basic position, and that necessarily there would continue to be some interchange of views between German and Austrian officials, if only because they were both to be defendants at The Hague. To Berlin, the German Foreign Minister reported, "In general, the Austrians have resisted all pressure and probing." [49] Curtius was maintaining a brave façade, but the Austrians were unable to lend it much substance.

Schober's concession did not end the tension, for Briand now openly indicated that he would not accept an adverse decision from the Hague Court. When Briand's turn came to speak in the Council, he stated that whatever the Court decided, the Council might still have to review the economic and political aspects of the customs union. Curtius retorted that if the legal question were settled in favor of Germany and Austria, a political treatment of the customs union (that is, a further review by the Council) would not be permissible, and that they would not allow themselves to be treated as disturbers of the peace.[50] The two foreign ministers now confronted each other in open opposition.

In a sense, the problem for France was not so much whether she could block the customs union—there was little doubt, considering Austria's weakness, that she could—as how to block it without evoking too violent a reaction in Germany, thereby ruining any chance of a future understanding. In February Berthelot had frankly told Hoesch that, with Britain losing its former position of power, a weak France of forty million must face the

[48] GFMR, 2521/E285009–10, E285177–8; 1683/D786502: Curtius to Ministry, May 19, 1931; Memo by Ritter, June 11, 1931; Cabinet Protocol, May 27, 1931.
[49] GFMR, 2521/E285010; 1683/D786502.
[50] *SIA, 1931*, p. 317; GFMR, 2521/E285009.

future prospect of standing alone against a prosperous Germany of eighty million, and that the concern of French policy must be to avoid being overwhelmed by Germany—unless a comprehensive agreement could be reached, in which case "the gates would be opened." And Germany, for her part, did not want to go too far toward a rupture with France: Brüning recalled in 1954 that he had always sought economic cooperation with France.[51] True, the customs union proposal had now given a chill to Franco-German relations, and there was always the barrier of irreconcilable aims. But though the two countries were in serious opposition, they each saw the necessity of keeping the conflict within bounds. François-Poncet had been encouraged by Laval to offer his cartel plan, involving close Franco-German cooperation, while Curtius had felt that it would be unwise not to respond to feelers from Briand.

If Franco-German relations were not quite so bad at this time as one might have supposed, Franco-British relations were not quite so good. The French desire to maintain the Versailles system intact, and to enlist British aid in this effort, had through the past decade run counter to the British desire for flexible collective security at minimum cost; now the tension was to be further heightened, not only by British resentment of the French financial ascendancy, sharpened by the financial crisis, but also by French distrust of British intentions with regard to Germany. Henderson's actions, especially his pressure on Schober at the League Council, have tended to obscure these Franco-British differences. But Henderson was exceptional. He placed international cooperation first, recognizing that any unilateral action against the *status quo* was dangerous, and he alone among European diplomats was ready to assume the thankless role of mediator to prevent open controversy. His scene with Schober was his last successful act as director of British foreign policy. Henceforth he would be eclipsed by other, more insular leaders, whose aim was not conciliation but revision.

[51] Curtius, *Sechs Jahre*, p. 16; Brüning, *Die Vereinigten Staaten und Europa* (Stuttgart, 1954), p. 14; GFMR, 1554/D666473-4: Hoesch to Ministry, Feb. 23, 1931.

V

President Hoover Intervenes

ALTHOUGH the appeal to President Hoover for a conference had failed to produce any immediate response, and although the German government, perhaps not entirely by Brüning's design, had committed its diplomatic energies to the Austro-German customs union, reparations revision was not forgotten. The means to revision remained, of course, a problem. The files of the German Foreign Minister's own office contain a twenty-three page memorandum, dated April 9, 1931, which exhaustively analyzed past experience with reparations revision and examined the problems German negotiators would face in seeking further change. This paper indicated that, while further partial revision (like that of the Young Plan itself) might be acceptable if the United States was unready to make a contribution, definitive solutions would depend on American action. And the memorandum concluded: "It would in any case be too bad to take this question up too soon, missing a later, better solution, without achieving the desired effect in terms of internal politics." [1]

THE REVIVAL OF THE REPARATIONS QUESTION

But internal politics would not wait. By mid-April 1931, it was becoming obvious that the deficit for the year just past had been larger than previously expected, and that income would be lower still for the current year. This meant that, to obtain anything approaching a balanced budget, the German people would

[1] GFMR, 1659/D729014–37: Unsigned.

have to make new sacrifices, in the form of further tax increases and cuts in salaries and in unemployment compensation. Even these measures were unlikely to bring about a real balance, and they were sure to meet with strong political opposition, at least unless there was some promise of reparations reduction. Germans of all classes and parties, supported by such authorities as Schacht and Luther, believed that reparations were the root cause of the depression, and it seemed to many of them that their taxes were being increased solely to meet what they considered the unyielding demands of the Allies for "tribute." [2] Resentment against this burden could not be overlooked, even by a presidial government, even if it wished to overlook it; this was a period when every weekend brought its quota of street-fight casualties. On May 10, in a speech during an election campaign in Oldenburg, Brüning warned that there could be no hope of successful revision until the German house was put in order. But this election resulted in the Communists gaining almost 40 per cent and the Nazis 33 per cent over their standings in the September 1930 elections—hardly an indorsement for a policy of political moderation and financial retrenchment.[3]

There was, moreover, a new opportunity for action on reparations presented by the coming meeting at Chequers. Here Brüning and Curtius could speak face-to-face with the British leaders, who might themselves now be interested in sweeping away reparations and war debts. Stories predicting that Germany would seek a moratorium began to appear in the London *Daily Herald* in early May. Since the *Herald* was the official paper of the Labour Party, these stories, which were noted in the German press, suggested that the British government was more or less expecting Brüning and Curtius to raise the issue.[4]

[2] Schacht had just published his book, *Das Ende der Reparationen*, printed in the United States as *The End of Reparations* (New York, 1931). Luther made a major speech on March 1, repeating the ideas expressed in his letter to Sackett and Harrison on Feb. 27, 1931.

[3] *Deutsche Allgemeine Zeitung* (Berlin), May 12, 1931; *Berliner Tageblatt*, May 11 (P.M.), 1931; *DBFP*, 2/II, No. 45.

[4] *Daily Herald* (London), May 7, 8, 26, 28, 1931; *Deutsche Allgemeine Zeitung*, May 1, 8, 21, 27, 29, 31, 1931; *Berliner Tageblatt*, May 3 (A.M.), 6 (P.M.), 22 (P.M.), 26 (P.M.), 28 (P.M.), 29 (P.M.), 1931.

Brüning was preparing for action well before this. When Sackett left on April 23 for home leave in America, the Chancellor took pains to see him before his departure, using the interview to describe the "disastrous financial crisis" developing in Germany. According to the German record, Brüning told the Ambassador that Germany would pay full reparations as long as possible, but added that this might not be feasible over a long period. The German government would spare no pains to balance the budget, but it was very difficult to say whether the German people could accept the sacrifices involved without an early ventilation of the reparations question. Arriving in Washington, Sackett told Stimson that Brüning "doesn't intend to raise the question of reparations until it is absolutely imperative, if possible to avoid it." [5] Brüning's discussion with Sackett suggests that, despite his assurances, the Chancellor was really thinking of raising the reparations question within the next few months. And on the same day he saw Sackett, the Chancellor also met with his ministers to discuss the drafting of a new financial program, to be enacted as an emergency decree. Brüning observed, perhaps with the customs union in mind, that the work of the Reich government "must again be a unified whole." To this end, they would have to discuss the reparations question thoroughly while working out the new budget. Calling for the strictest secrecy on the subject, he said, "The reparations question is today doubtless the gravest problem." [6] Thus Brüning had dropped the *laisser-passer* views he had held in February, and was returning to the ideas expressed in Pünder's letter to Bülow of January 3.

While German officialdom labored over the details of the new budget decree, Brüning met with a select group, including the Foreign Minister, the Minister of Economics, and Reichsbank President Luther, to consider whether the government could

---

[5] *DBFP*, 2/II, No. 43; *Berliner Tageblatt*, April 23 (P.M.), 1931; GFMR, 2375/E192396-8: Memo by Pünder, April 23, 1931; Herbert Hoover, *The Memoirs of Herbert Hoover* (3 vols., New York, 1951-2), III, 64; Stimson Manuscript Diary (Deposited at Yale University Library), May 4, June 2, 1931. Sackett also told Stimson he had engineered the coming meeting at Chequers.

[6] GFMR, 1683/D786379-80: Cabinet Protocol.

carry out the internal financial program without taking up the problem of reparations. The decision was that the government could not. On May 11, the rest of the cabinet learned that the select committee proposed to issue, along with the budget decree, a proclamation setting forth the reasons for the financial measures. The proclamation was to state that the financial measures "could only be seen in an over-all framework, in which the burden of reparations also belonged; the Reich government is in agreement with the overwhelming majority of the German people that the continuation of such reparations burdens is not only unbearable for the German economy, but must also lead to the ruin of the economy of the whole world. The Reich government has, however, still not reached definite conclusions, since it is on the verge of important international discussions on these questions." In passing these proposals on to the cabinet, Brüning indicated his intention of having the actual publication take place while he and Curtius were in England.[7] Essentially, the program thus laid down was the one later followed.

We should note that the German government worked out this basic procedure before the League Council meeting, so that the setback which took place there cannot be held responsible for the resurrection of reparations revision. The plan likewise antedated the Creditanstalt difficulties, and hence was not designed to capitalize on them. Later the Creditanstalt crisis would dangerously amplify the effect of the manifesto, but the German leaders took little account of these developments in their planning. It was internal political pressure and Brüning's will that determined German reparations policy, almost in spite of the diplomatic situation.

THE BEGINNING OF THE 1931 FINANCIAL CRISIS

The nature of the new budget began to leak out in the last week of May, leading to further emphasis on Germany's financial problems and on the need for reparations relief, preferably at

[7] GFMR, 1683/D786471–4: Cabinet memo from Reichskanzlei, May [11?], 1931.

Chequers. The Germans seemed to be making the worst of their situation, and their groans did not go unheard: the foreign creditors began to wonder about the security of their loans. These lenders were already making heavy withdrawals from Austria, where the financial situation itself was grave enough, and whence came reports (as in the *New York Times* of May 19) that France was making financial aid dependent on a surrender of the customs union. Austria reportedly lost $56,000,000 from May 12 to 23; the Bank for International Settlements offered Austria a rediscount credit, but declined to assist with the new issue of three-year Treasury notes. Efforts were made to raise money in London and Berlin, and Curtius told Schober that he hoped to raise 20,000,000 schillings for the purchase of Creditanstalt shares. But the creditors began to have doubts about Germany, too. On May 26, the Berlin Börse took a deep plunge, with foreign exchange rates for dollars and Swiss francs rising sharply. There was a general downward trend in the markets through the following week, including a drop in the Young Loan quotations. These movements were prefaced by the flight of Austrian and German capital, but as time went on, the withdrawal of sight and short-term loans by foreign creditors became more important. There has been some controversy as to who withdrew the fastest, but one thing is clear: America had the most to withdraw.[8]

The *Deutsche Allgemeine Zeitung* advanced the theory that the American creditors had started withdrawing from Germany because they did not know the difference between Austria and the Reich.[9] Judging by the loans they had made, one might indeed suspect that some of the lenders were ignorant of such details. But there were also genuine reasons for the withdrawals from Germany: the budget was unbalanced; budget cuts and higher taxes were foreseen but were unlikely to be effective; the country appeared to be on the brink of political revolution; trade

[8] *Deutsche Allgemeine Zeitung,* May 23, 27, 28, 1931; *Berliner Tageblatt,* May 26 (P.M.), 28 (P.M.), 1931; *New York Times,* May 19, 27–29, June 1–3, 1931; SDP, 863.51/962: Minister in Vienna to Secretary, May 29, 1931: GFMR, 2382/E197283–5: Memo by Bülow, May 18, 1931.
[9] *Deutsche Allgemeine Zeitung,* May 27, June 10, 1931.

and industry seemed to be stagnating; the Germans themselves seemed to have no confidence in their own future. As if to complete the picture, a large and aggressive Stahlhelm rally took place at Breslau on June 1, seeming to portend another world war.[10]

The Gamble with Credit: The German Strategy

Did the German government deliberately further the credit crisis in order to convince the other powers, particularly the United States, that a reparations moratorium was required? The experience of 1923 showed that a German government might be ready to permit or even to contribute to an economic crisis if it would serve a vital national policy. The available documents do not indicate that the German government desired anything like the financial crisis of 1931, but they do show that the American concern over German credit was regarded as something which could be exploited. This attitude naturally meant that there was less anxiety over private credit in the Wilhelmstrasse than on Pennsylvania Avenue. To the German leaders, the private credit problem was only one aspect of an economic crisis brought about by unworkable reparations transfers; with the exception of Luther, they seem at this stage to have simply closed their eyes to the dangers of a credit crisis for Germany herself. They had long planned (witness Hjalmar Schacht) on exploiting Germany's debtor position, and most of them ignored the fact that an avalanche was already starting down the mountain. At the end of May, Karl Ritter told the American Consul at Geneva that Germany intended to cease certain reparations payments in June, July, August, or September, and he calmly speculated on the possible repercussions in the United States and on the attitude of American banks regarding their credits in Germany, especially their short-term credits.[11] Only partially aware of the fragility of

[10] See *DBFP*, 2/II, Nos. 43, 45–47.
[11] SDP, 462.00R296/4127: Memo from Division of Western European Affairs, June 7, 1931 (quoting from report of Consul in Geneva of his discussion with Ritter).

American nerves, Ritter and his chiefs tended to overdo the stimulus.

Cabinet discussions on May 30 and June 3 reveal something of the thinking among German leaders. They recognized that the Young "alleviation" clauses offered no real alleviation, but they intended to use them to raise the reparations issue, and to put the other countries under pressure, expecting that general revision, probably by a conference, would follow. The Vice Chancellor and Minister of Finance, Hermann Dietrich, observed that "in the long run, it will make no difference to the Americans how Germany broaches the reparations question," and he and Brüning agreed that they should ask not only for a summoning of the Special Advisory Committee, but also, simultaneously, for a suspension of transfer, since without the spur of a transfer moratorium, the Committee might simply recommend a loan.[12]

Two contrasting points of view were evident in the cabinet: that of Luther, supported by Trendelenburg; and that of Brüning, supported by most of the ministers and particularly by Wirth and General Wilhelm Groener, who together represented the police and defense forces most concerned over internal security. Luther was certainly in favor of reparations revision, but he thought that the door should not be closed to a suitable loan, and that, because the first step would damage German credit, action should only be taken when success seemed probable. There was still much misunderstanding abroad regarding Germany, but time, Luther stated, was working for the Germans: "It was necessary to await the right moment, when the situation would be ripe for us." Brüning replied that he recognized that it would be desirable "to postpone the decision until the New Year, or even until the summer of 1932, but it would be impossible to hold out so long at home. For reasons of domestic politics, a step had to be taken by the end of June." Luther argued that the Young negotiations in 1929 had come at the wrong time, and said that Germany should learn from this; he again warned against acting before the situation was ripe. But Brüning answered significantly:

[12] GFMR, 1683/D786690-3: Cabinet Protocol.

In America, the nervousness could scarcely be further increased [*In Amerika, könne die Nervösität kaum noch weiter gesteigert werden*]. Soon moratoria for government debts would no longer be unusual. In the next few months moratoria might be expected in various South American countries. Moreover, we must consider the results in internal politics if the present cabinet did not find the right path at once. If a right-wing cabinet followed, it would certainly declare a bombshell moratorium [*Knall-Moratorium*] within four weeks. This would even be necessary if the present cabinet had to count on the support of the Right. Nothing would be achieved thereby with the opposite side. The action would end with an ultimatum from the creditors, and no one in Germany would then be ready to assume responsibility with respect to such an ultimatum.

He also stated that he would accept no partial solution, "since such a solution means nothing but binding ourselves politically for five years." At the June 3 meeting, Dietrich stated that at Chequers they should describe their plight without indicating what they would do, and above all, without renouncing the right to suspend transfer. "After Chequers we must also inform the French that we must and will act and then we must actually take steps. We are taking an action comparable to a declaration of war." Brüning appeared to agree with Dietrich's ideas, saying that he would not discard the weapon of the Young Plan at Chequers.[13]

Brüning's allusion to the possibility of a right-wing cabinet or of his own government turning to the Right for support makes one wonder if President von Hindenburg might have confronted him with the alternatives of replacement by a rightist government, bringing in right-wing support, or taking effective action on reparations. Whether or not this was the case—and we have no proof of such a demand—other reasons suffice to explain Brüning's readiness for action. For one thing, Wirth, the Minister of Interior, believed that the internal situation could not be controlled much longer, and that no dictatorship could explain to

[13] GFMR, 1683/D786693-8, D786766-70: Cabinet Protocols, May 30, June 3, 1931.

the people why further delay on reparations revision was necessary, while General Groener solemnly observed, "With the over-
all situation existing at present, it would be dangerous to let
reparations action wait too long."[14] Brüning could not ignore
these views, especially Groener's. If the army would wait no
longer, Brüning could not wait. And in any case, he had no
desire to wait.

By his talks with the British leaders, and through the manifesto
which had been planned, Brüning could prepare the world for
a reconsideration of the reparations agreements. This technique
was certainly an improvement over the methods used with the
customs union. It was especially important to prepare foreign
opinion in this case because the attitude of the powers in the
Special Advisory Committee would determine whether Germany
emerged with a diplomatic success and lowered payments, or
with a foreign control commission and a ruined currency. It was
essential that the Committee not only "advise on the application
of the Plan," but also bring about a real revision. In preparing to
use the Young "safeguards," Brüning was gambling on the willingness of the other powers, including the United States, to go
beyond those safeguards.[15] If the United States did not take an
interest, the Special Advisory Committee might well cling closely
to the narrow interpretation of the Plan. On the other hand, if
the United States became concerned, more might be done in the
Committee, as the British would then be more likely to favor
revision; the Americans might also join in some other approach,
such as a committee on the Dawes-Young pattern.

[14] GFMR, 1683/D786697-8.
[15] GFMR, 1683/D786773 and 1684/D786774 contain, as an attachment to
the June 3 Cabinet Protocol, an outline for the move the German government might make in requesting a Young moratorium. Aside from appealing
for the maximum relief afforded by the safety clauses, the outline proposed
that an effort be made to determine promptly whether the Special Advisory
Committee could recommend revision. If it could not, a petition should be
made to increase the percentage of the postponed payments or (or possibly
and) the creditor governments should be asked either to grant the Committee further powers or else to call a conference of governments or of
experts.

There has been a long-standing argument between Hoover and American liberals as to whether, after 1930, the depression was intensified and prolonged by European or by American domestic conditions.[16] The problem is largely one of economic interpretation and falls outside the framework of this study. But the material from the German documents suggests that there is also a diplomatic aspect to the problem: in a way and to a degree never realized by Hoover himself, European conditions were indeed a bar to economic recovery. There could hardly be a world recovery when the nation with the most important economy in Europe felt compelled, largely for political reasons, to intensify its deflation, and when it was politically interested in capitalizing on its plight. And if it is true that German revisionist politics significantly deepened the depression, then the depression was not the conclusive demonstration of the economic weakness of capitalism that many Marxists and others have believed it to be.

THE CHEQUERS VISIT, JUNE 5–8, 1931

After the credit crisis in the fall of 1930, Curtius had hinted at a possible use of the Young alleviations, and had been rebuked by Henderson. But, convinced that action was necessary, the German leaders were now determined to exercise their privileges under the Young Plan. Their position was that they were informing the British of their situation and of the steps they might have to take; they were not seeking British assent. The cabinet showed no great confidence, in its discussions, in obtaining a favorable response at Chequers; suggestions for influencing British government opinion, insofar as they were made at all, were along the line of stressing the foreign trade competition resulting from a lowered German standard of living.[17] Ambassador von Neurath reported on June 2 that there was little sign in the London press of what position the British government would take at Chequers, beyond repeated

---

[16] See, for example, Arthur M. Schlesinger, Jr., *The Crisis of the Old Order* (Boston, 1957), pp. 233–234.

[17] See GFMR, 1683/D786693–4, D786772. The latter is from a memorandum by Dietrich, attached to the Cabinet Protocol of June 3.

statements in the *Daily Herald* that England alone could decide nothing, and a general expectation that the Treasury would be averse to any loss of income.[18]

For various reasons, however, the British were inclined to react differently now than at the end of 1930. For one thing, both the Young Plan and German retrenchment had now had a longer trial, and in the interval the German economy had deteriorated further. A recent study even suggests that Brüning's deflationary retrenchment program was deliberately intended to prove to the world that Germany was unable to pay reparations; while this suggestion is an oversimplification, the German economic contractions did help to convince British and other observers that reparations were unworkable.[19] It is likely, however, that London's own immediate problems were the main cause of the change in the British position. At the time Rumbold made his December 1930 *démarche*, the British Treasury stood together with the Foreign Office on reparations. In mid-January, however, a high Treasury official, Sir Frederick Leith-Ross, hinted that he had changed his views and no longer opposed reparations revision as such. It may be that this shift reflected the difficulties which had arisen in the financial negotiations with France. Anyhow, it was no novelty, but a return to normal, if the Treasury now supported action to reduce reparations. The arguments supporting reduction were largely economic, and British government finances and British foreign trade were in a condition, by the spring of 1931, to make economic arguments carry considerable weight. The Macmillan Committee's report showing the unfavorable position of

[18] GFMR, 1659/D729062-3.
[19] See Wolfgang J. Helbich, "Between Stresemann and Hitler: The Foreign Policy of the Brüning Government," *World Politics*, 12:32-39 (1959). In contrast to Helbich's view, Brüning seems, at least until the failure of the reforms became clear in the spring of 1931, to have intended to strengthen Germany's credit in order to be in a strong position in reparations negotiations. The Young "alleviations" provided a means to start reparations negotiations without undergoing an actual collapse, and the Germans were genuinely concerned over how to get their way once the negotiations commenced. That negotiations might be forestalled by a sudden unilateral American action did not occur to them.

British industry and finance was completed in May, though not released until July, and in March the government was obliged by opposition pressure to appoint the May Committee to make recommendations for economy.[20]

But even if they now had more sympathy for the Germans, the British could not put themselves in the position of paying debts without receiving reparations. Reparations and debts, from the British point of view, were one and the same problem, and essentially a problem involving the United States. It may be that this partly explains MacDonald's sudden interest in the visitors; American affairs—which he regarded as his own private diplomatic preserve—were now involved.[21] Chequers was to be MacDonald's conference, not Henderson's, and though Henderson would have liked to discuss disarmament, MacDonald permitted reparations to constitute the whole agenda.

Paul Schmidt, who was still at an early stage in his career as interpreter, has written a vivid description of the hostile Communist and Nazi demonstrations which confronted Brüning and Curtius on their trip to and from England, and of how the shades were drawn in the Chancellor's private car at the station in Hamburg, in an effort to avoid recognition. Brüning and Curtius seem at least to have received a friendly welcome from the British ministers. The visitors, recalling the origin of the invitation, expected that their hosts would want to talk at length about disarmament. This subject was not at the moment very enticing to the Germans, since one obvious (if politically difficult) remedy for Germany's financial problems was to reduce arms expenditures. In spite of the Versailles limitations, the Reichswehr was managing to spend more than three times what the British Army was spending on small arms, and other expenses were almost as heavy. General von Schleicher had pointed out at a cabinet meeting on June 3 that the British might say, "Since you have no

[20] GFMR, 1659/D728910: Neurath to Ministry, Jan. 15, 1931; L. S. Amery, *My Political Life* (3 vols., London, 1955), III, 51–53; Harold Nicolson, *King George the Fifth* (New York, 1953), p. 453.

[21] Compare Henry R. Winkler, "Arthur Henderson," in Gordon A. Craig and Felix Gilbert, eds., *The Diplomats* (Princeton, 1953), p. 321.

money, why won't you join in reducing the [defense] outlays in the budget?" To this question, Schleicher proposed a brusque and evasive answer: "If we have no money for arms, that's nobody's business [*so geht das niemand etwas an*]; we only want equality in principle." Brüning suggested a more diplomatic solution: he intended to meet this problem by saying that he could not agree without consulting the cabinet. The German Foreign Minister was probably as relieved as he was surprised when Henderson asked him on the first evening (June 5) "to give him an opportunity during the visit to talk with me about the disarmament question." Curtius had not thought there would be any doubt about such conversations, but, as he reported, "naturally I immediately agreed, and concealed my astonishment at this request." It appeared to Curtius afterwards that Henderson had realized from the beginning that there would be no thorough discussion of disarmament.[22]

At Chequers the next day (Saturday, June 6), the British invited Brüning to pick his subject, and he plunged directly into reparations. The writer has not found a full record of the Saturday discussions in either the German or the British documents, but it appears that Brüning gave a calm and factual analysis of the German economic and political difficulties, stressing the hardships of the Young Plan, while Curtius described the dangers of internal revolution. The British were sympathetic, but they held that the problem of reparations was really one for France and the United States, the countries that made a net gain on intergovernmental payments. There was evidently some reference to the news that Secretary Stimson was planning a trip to Europe in the cause of disarmament, and apparently there was talk of possibly convincing Stimson of the need for a revision of intergovernmental payments.[23]

[22] Paul Schmidt, *Statist auf diplomatischer Bühne* (Bonn, 1949), pp. 202–203; *DBFP*, 2/II, No. 186; GFMR, 1683/D786770; 1555/D666659: Cabinet Protocol, June 3, 1931; Memo by Curtius, [June] 10, 1931. Curtius did discuss disarmament with Lord Robert Cecil at the German Embassy on June 7 (GFMR, 1555/D666660–2).

[23] GFMR, 1684/D786810: Cabinet Protocol, June 11, 1931; P. Schmidt,

The discussions on Sunday morning were somewhat more formal, with Vansittart, Sir Frederick Leith-Ross of the Treasury, and (latterly) Montagu Norman taking part. For these conversations, the British documents provide a complete record. Early in this meeting, Brüning stated that in the light of the critical situation he had described the day before, he had to consider when he would give the three-month advance warning required for a Young Plan moratorium; Germany would carry on as long as possible, but "he felt that the limit would be reached at the latest in November next." Afterwards, MacDonald seemed to think that this crucial declaration had meant that the prior warning would be given in November, so that the relief would become effective in February 1932. But Brüning certainly intended that the alleviations themselves should begin by November, allowing three months from the time of Stimson's visit in late July. Even this deadline was a shift from that laid down by Brüning in the May 30 cabinet meeting, when he had said that action would have to be taken by the end of June for reasons of internal politics. Evidently Brüning was at this point prepared to brave the internal dangers of a longer delay for the sake of convincing Stimson of the need for action.[24]

Henderson observed that Brüning's declaration was a very serious statement, and characteristically, he suggested that the best course would be to make use of the economic and financial committees which had been set up by the Commission of Inquiry for European Union. Curtius answered that these committees had no authority to consider the reparations problem; the Bank for International Settlements (which would appoint the Special Advisory Committee) was the only body to which this question could be referred. When Vansittart mentioned the subject of long-term credits, and referred to "some actions of the German Government which had not had the effect of encouraging them," Curtius

---

Statist, pp. 206–209; *DBFP*, 2/II, No. 51; *FRUS, 1931*, I, 6–8, 12, 13. Curtius informed Hoesch that MacDonald took the initiative in discussing debts and reparations (GFMR, 2548/E300015).

[24] *DBFP*, 2/II, Nos. 51, 52; *FRUS, 1931*, I, 7, 12; GFMR, 1555/D666655; 1684/D786812; 1683/D786695: Memo by Curtius, June 10, 1931; Cabinet Protocols, May 30, June 11, 1931.

answered that "Germany was long past loans and had neither the desire nor the ability to solve her difficulties in that way." At this point, Governor Norman of the Bank of England arrived.[25]

Affecting a pointed beard and a soft black hat, Norman looked more like an artist—or better, like one of those who prosper on the fringes of art as critics and dealers—than a banker. He was full of that tendency to self-dramatization which Central Europeans call *Temperament*, a term he would have recognized, since he had studied music in Dresden in his youth. Perhaps partly because of this experience, he usually sympathized with German complaints, and he had played an essential role in German stabilization in 1924. He was also an opponent of the system of war debts and reparations.[26] On this occasion, however, Norman emphasized that Austria, not Germany, was the immediate problem: according to Paul Schmidt, he now exclaimed, "Southeast Europe is in flames!" Germany, on the other hand, "had already gone through two or three financial crises which would have been fatal to any other country . . . she might well get through again." Norman predicted that America would not be ready to discuss reparations for at least a year, a forecast which Vansittart extended to two years. Norman, supported by Ramsay MacDonald, also warned against causing any disturbance to credit; "he felt sure that if there were fresh shocks to confidence, the committees [suggested by Henderson] would have not to diagnose the difficulties of Europe, but to conduct a post-mortem on the corpse." [27]

[25] *DBFP*, 2/II, No. 51.

[26] Hjalmar Schacht, *76 Jahre meines Lebens* (Bad Wöreshofen, 1953), pp. 243–253. According to Schacht, Norman's decision to extend a credit in January 1924 appeared largely motivated by a desire to strengthen the Reichsbank against French efforts to establish a separatist currency in the Rhineland; Norman, incidentally, acted as godfather to one of Schacht's grandchildren. Lord Vansittart says Norman was "infatuated by Dr. Schacht" in 1923-4 (*The Mist Procession*, London, 1958, p. 301). To a German diplomat, Norman said that Schacht had certain peculiarities which made him difficult to work with, such as a love of publicity and a tendency, as on his American trip, to make speeches, but it was a joy to talk finance with him. Norman added that he had never disagreed with Schacht on essentials: see GFMR, 2385/E199430: Letter, Dufour to Bülow, Aug. 12, 1931.

[27] *DBFP*, 2/II, No. 51; P. Schmidt, *Statist*, p. 209.

Norman did not know that his warning was already too late. On June 6, after Brüning had telephoned some last-minute changes, the manifesto planned a month before was published in Berlin. In general, it stressed the gloomy side of the picture, emphasizing that this was the last time the German government proposed to tighten the screw for the sake of balancing the budget and paying reparations. The manifesto included the following passage:

We have harnessed all our forces in order to meet our obligations incurred through losing the war and we have had to call on foreign assistance in the widest measure to do this. This is no longer possible. The putting forth of the last power of reserves of the nation entitles the German Government and makes it its duty toward the German people to tell the world: the limits of the privations we have imposed on our people have been reached. The presuppositions upon which the Young Plan came into being have been shown by the course of world development to have been wrong. The alleviations the Young Plan was to bring to the German people, as was the intent of the participants and which at first it gave promise of bringing, have failed to be realized. The government is conscious of the fact that the direly-menaced business and financial situation of the Reich calls imperatively for alleviations of the unbearable reparation obligations. The recovery of the world also depends on it.[28]

Evidently one purpose of this declaration was to appease the demand within Germany, becoming louder due to the sacrifices contained in the new emergency decree, for an active step against reparations. This was the more necessary because an immediate result could scarcely emerge from Chequers. A second purpose was presumably to prepare the rest of the world for Young Plan revision: to win world sympathy and in particular to arouse world concern. But whatever the manifesto was intended to do, its effect on German credit abroad was likely to be disastrous. The British participants at Chequers do not appear to have known of the statement until the end of the Sunday meeting, when three cables arrived from the British Ambassador in Washington, Sir Ronald

---

[28] GFMR, 1683/D786725: Cabinet Protocol, June 6, 1931; *New York Times*, June 7, 1931; compare *FRUS, 1931*, I, 10. The above is the *Times* translation.

Lindsay. One cable repeated an American press summary of the manifesto; the other two indicated that Secretary Stimson was very upset over the German manifesto, and concerned lest something similar might come out of Chequers. As Stimson put it, in his best Dutch-uncle manner, the Chequers conferees "before putting out any further announcement had better know the effect of this one." Lindsay reported:

Secretary of State, who was somewhat agitated, said what United States Government most desired was, of course, that German Government should pursue financial policy hitherto followed of making both ends meet as long as possible without recourse to anything resembling moratorium. President, he said, had been watching whole situation with utmost care, and both he and Administration were most anxious to help in any way possible, though he added it was extremely difficult for them to be helpful now. He was led to fear Chequers Conference might result in some declaration of moratorium, and he hoped at least, if so, the declaration should take the form likely to create least damage to the credit conditions of the world. In particular, he said it should be made clear that the commercial debts were to remain unaffected, and that any moratorium declared in respect of reparations payments would be calculated to increase security of commercial indebtedness; this latter point he made to me twice. He was particularly anxious that these considerations should be before you before any statement is issued by conference.[29]

MacDonald asked Vansittart to read these cables aloud to the assembled group. After they had been read, Brüning expressed surprise at the strong reaction from Stimson, but Norman said that he could well understand the repercussions in America. "It seemed to him [Norman] that this declaration entirely altered the situation. He hoped very much that the German Government had not any more surprises like this to spring during the next few weeks. Dr. Curtius said that there were no more manifestos in preparation." MacDonald then proposed that a communiqué be prepared. There was considerable argument over the text, for the visitors wished the British to make a declaration of their willingness to

[29] *DBFP*, 2/II, Nos. 49, 50.

assist with revision; MacDonald wrote Stimson afterwards that he had been ready to give a private assurance, but not one for publication. The Prime Minister also claimed to have opposed the idea of an appeal to America. The final communiqué, which made no mention of possible aid from either Britain or America, closed by saying:

Special stress was laid by the German Ministers on the difficulties of the existing position in Germany and the need for alleviation.

The British Ministers for their part called attention to the world-wide character of the present depression and its special influence on their own country.

Both parties were agreed that, in addition to efforts and measures of a national character, the revival of confidence and prosperity depended upon international co-operation.

In this spirit both Governments will endeavor to deal with the present crisis in close collaboration with the other governments concerned.[30]

This result was something less than the German nation had hoped for. Brüning made as much as he could of it to his cabinet, and Curtius recorded on June 10:

We have at Chequers brought suit for the "revision" of the Young Plan. Montagu Norman rightly emphasized to MacDonald the significance of the fact that the German Chancellor has informed the Prime Minister of one of the creditor powers about the situation. If we subsequently proceed to take unilateral action, no one can reproach us. The British government and (through the world publicity on the Chequers discussions) the whole world have been informed as to the situation in which Germany finds herself, and on the aims we must pursue.[31]

The record shows that much of the attention of the Chequers conferees was devoted to the possibility of American action, and more was no doubt said about it off the record. This emphasis on

---

[30] *DBFP*, 2/II, No. 51; *FRUS, 1931*, I, 13; GFMR, 1555/D666659–60; 1684/D786810: Memo by Curtius, June 10, 1931; Cabinet Protocol, June 11, 1931.

[31] GFMR, 1684/D786810–11; 1555/D666655.

the United States is likely to have come more from the British side than from the German. In describing the talks in a letter to Stimson, MacDonald wrote: "I said that from my knowledge of both the President and yourself you were fully aware of the situation and would help to ease it if circumstances, political and other, would allow you to do so." [32]

In late July, after Hoover had intervened, Curtius reported a conversation with Montagu Norman, including an interesting claim, not elsewhere confirmed, about German prognostications at Chequers:

Against [Norman's] pessimism, which now once again was coloring all his views, I made the point that not he, but we, had been right at Chequers. He had maintained again and again that in no circumstances could either President Hoover or the United States take any part in European affairs before 1933. Against this, we had taken the view that Hoover, in his own interest and in the interest of the American people, could not help but come quickly to the aid of Europe. He confirmed in a friendly way that this was correct. [33]

But this was after the event, and it does not say that independent American action was expected. On June 11 Brüning was telling his cabinet that the Young mechanism, inadequate as it was, was the only available way to bring about revision. At that time his reason for awaiting Stimson's visit was that the other European countries wished to let the Germans appear to the United States as disturbers of the peace. Allowing for the likelihood that Brüning was trying to play the sober, tough-minded *Realpolitiker*, the evidence still indicates that the German leaders were expecting no American help until after the Young apparatus had been set in motion. Presumably the recollection of Hoover's complete lack of interest in January made Brüning chary of expecting action from Washington. There is something rather uncanny about the way the German leaders steadily pursued their own plans through

<hr/>

[32] *FRUS, 1931*, I, 13.
[33] GFMR, 1660/D729634: Memo by Curtius, July 24, 1931. On June 10, Curtius noted only that Norman was pessimistic: GFMR, 5385/K513281–2.

the first three weeks in June, incurious about what was developing elsewhere.

WASHINGTON TAKES INTEREST

Hoover's views, however, had changed. As Secretary Stimson told the British Ambassador, Sir Ronald Lindsay, the President had been watching the situation, "and both he and Administration were most anxious to help in any way possible." According to the account of Under Secretary William R. Castle, given later to a *New York Times* correspondent, Hoover had been watching developments in Europe even before Sackett reported to him on May 6; by May 1, the President had the idea very strongly in mind that something had to be done to improve the economic situation, which was, he felt, going from bad to worse. The conference of the International Chamber of Commerce, held in Washington from May 4 to 7, must have given further impetus and direction to Hoover's thoughts. True, his own speech to the delegates stressed the importance of arms as a cause of the depression, and American influence was brought to bear to prevent a strong resolution on reparations and debts. But the German delegates did their utmost to gain publicity for the German point of view, which was also reported privately to the President. Hoover's memoirs state that on May 11 he asked Secretaries Stimson and Mellon to study some method of relieving the pressure by a relaxation of reparations and war debts, and that the two secretaries were unable to make any suggestion.[34]

Hoover had developed at least some kind of proposal by May 20, when he and Stimson discussed a possible statement. He was worried about attacks on United States tariff and war debt policies, and Stimson's diary adds, "On the question of debts, my position was that that would be a very important statement for him to make, if he ever made it; that people would probably be

---

[34] *New York Times* (Richard V. Oulahan), July 8, 1931; GFMR, 1493/D621333-4: Prittwitz to Ministry, May 11, 1931; *SIA, 1931*, pp. 46–47; Hoover, *Memoirs*, III, 63–64; Louis P. Lochner, *Herbert Hoover and Germany* (New York, 1960), p. 84.

glad to have it made, but that it was so sensational that it ought not to be shot off unless he was sure that he could back it up; that I wasn't at all sure that we could back it up politically." [35] Stimson referred to Hoover's statement only as "that" in his own diary: he dictated each day's entry and may have feared a leakage by a secretary. The caution shown by this omission and by Stimson's own recorded attitude lend support to Hoover's statement that Stimson and Mellon had been unable to suggest anything. But Stimson was soon to take another attitude.

Up until the last week in May, the European financial illness, though grave, hardly seemed to require emergency treatment. Sackett had stressed to Hoover the seriousness of the German situation, but the Ambassador had not expected a political or economic crisis in Germany before autumn. The American Chargé d'Affaires in Berlin, George Gordon, reported hearing on high authority that "the cool heads" in the German government believed it unwise to press for revision in 1931. At this stage, President Hoover, who, if anything, tended to overestimate the importance of publicity and propaganda, may have been looking mainly for some dramatic action to check the loss of confidence at home without violating his *laissez-faire*, individualist principles. He was not restrained by reverence for the peace settlements or by regard for French interests; on March 30 he had expressed to Stimson his approval of the customs union, "and [Stimson records] he made such a vigorous argument against the Versailles Treaty which had set up these separate little countries that I said to him, 'Evidently you don't approve of the Versailles Treaty.' He replied, 'Of course I don't, I never did.' " His suspicion of the French, probably stemming from earlier experiences in the war and after, and soon to be further nourished, was quite unconcealed. [36] It is

[35] Stimson MS. Diary, May 20, 1931.

[36] Hoover, *Memoirs*, III, 64; SDP, 462.00R296/3941; Chargé in Berlin to Secretary, May 4, 1931; Stimson MS. Diary, March 30, 1931. On June 11, Hoover told Emil Ludwig, in connection with disarmament, that "our French friends" needed to get a stronger taste of depression (GFMR, 1555/D666666: Leitner to Ministry, June 11, 1931). On earlier experiences, see Herbert Hoover, *The Ordeal of Woodrow Wilson* (New York, 1958), esp. chap. 11.

doubtful, however, that he would have proceeded much further, had there not now come a sudden skid downhill.

The atmosphere in New York was uneasy; the fall in the stock market during May was the heaviest in eight months. Hoover blamed the decline in Wall Street prices on liquidation by European holders of American securities, and no doubt there was some of this. There was also some flight of capital from Europe, which was largely deposited or lent at short term, creating a threat of withdrawal.[37] But contrary to the impression fostered in Hoover's memoirs, the immediate problem was American funds in Austria and Germany, not European "hot money" in the United States. As we have seen, the Creditanstalt difficulties had started a flood of withdrawals of short-term funds. A frightened Schober talked to the American Minister on May 26, asking if the State Department could influence American bankers not to withdraw their credits to the Creditanstalt, amounting to $23,000,000. The American Minister replied that any such efforts by the State Department might have the opposite effect to that intended, and Schober then withdrew his request.[38]

May 27 seems to have marked a turning point for the Department of State. Governor Harrison of the New York Federal Reserve Bank telephoned Secretary Stimson, calling his attention to the dangerous situation in Austria, and communicating Wall Street's fear that, to judge by the sudden drop in German exchange rates the day before, the dangerous financial situation in Austria was spreading to other countries. If Austrian finances failed, Germany would have further cause to seek a postponement of reparations payments. On top of this, "there were rumors that France had forced the situation in order to make Germany ask for loans," and thereby to force a renunciation of the customs union. Stimson recorded officially:

I first asked Harrison who in Washington knew about this matter.

[37] *New York Times*, June 2, 1931; Hoover, *Memoirs*, III, 63, 65–67.
[38] Julius Curtius, *Sechs Jahre Minister der deutschen Republik* (Heidelberg, 1948), p. 199; SDP, 863.51/960: Minister in Vienna to Secretary, May 26, 1931.

He said Eugene Meyer knew about it, and I asked him [?] whether he had any suggested remedy. He said that he had nothing for the immediate emergency—nothing except rather drastic general suggestions which he could not discuss over the telephone.

I then called up the President and told him of this. He said that he had been following the trouble in Austria for several days. I told him we had received a confirmation of this from our Minister in Austria. He said that it was believed that a part of the recent liquidation on our stock market had come from the unloading of securities from Austria due to this situation.[39]

Stimson also reported Harrison's phone call in his diary, with the observation, "These are all rumors, and nobody knows how true they are." It appears, however, that Harrison's call brought about a change in Stimson's outlook. He sent Hoover a letter containing the substance of Schober's remarks to the American Minister in Vienna, and he asked the Minister to keep him informed. Henceforth, reports from Berlin and Vienna were forwarded to the President and to Under Secretary of the Treasury Ogden Mills. And, perhaps not surprisingly, a memorandum appeared on June 4, intended to show that the State Department had long been considering the possibility of a reduction or cessation of reparations payments, "such as is currently expected from the Anglo-German conversations at Chequers."[40]

On June 2 and 3 Hoover discussed the European situation with Sackett, Charles G. Dawes, and Hugh Gibson; Dawes and Gibson were the American representatives at London and Brussels. Sackett suggested adjusting the Young Plan to the fall in commodity prices, and Hoover pointed out to Stimson afterward the dangers involved in thus opening the door to all kinds of de-

[39] *FRUS, 1931*, I, 1–2.
[40] Stimson MS. Diary, May 27, 1931; *FRUS, 1931*, I, 2–5; SDP, 863.51/960, 961: Minister in Vienna to Secretary, May 26, 27, 1931; Secretary to President, May 27, 28, 1931; 462.00R296/3945, 3946, 3948, 5027: Secretary to Chargé in Berlin, May 29, June 2, 1931; Secretary to Chargé in London, June 4, 1931; Memo from Division of Western European Affairs, June 4, 1931. SDP, 462.00R296/3945, –6, and –8 include, besides the documents published in *FRUS*, record that these documents were forwarded as described.

mands.[41] But three days later the President swung strongly toward taking action. He and the State Department had considered the idea of a conference, but Hoover now decided in favor of making a direct proposal to the other powers of a one- or two-year moratorium on both war debts and reparations: the world would later call it the "Hoover moratorium." He outlined this plan to Stimson, Mellon, and Mills on June 5. Stimson and Mills reacted favorably; Mellon was more hesitant. According to Dawes, Mellon's face, like those of all the business leaders he saw in New York, was by this time "sicklied o'er with the pale cast of thought." [42]

There was nothing very novel about the idea of such a moratorium; the now hesitant Mellon had himself discussed it with Schacht in October, and the *New York Times* had made a front-page story out of rumors on the subject. The German reports show that the idea of an American proposal for the reduction or suspension of debts and reparations had been a favorite suggestion in New York financial circles, apparently because it was the procedure most likely to benefit German credit.[43] This may have been the "drastic" suggestion that Harrison (or Eugene Meyer?) could not discuss on the telephone. The question arises, to what extent was Hoover influenced by anxiety over the large New York banks?

Hoover maintains in his memoirs that he was motivated at this time by concern for the international economy (more specifically, for the erratic movement of European capital), for world peace, and for democratic government in Germany, and he says that he only learned of the loans of the New York banks in July, well after the moratorium announcement.[44] It is interesting to compare

[41] *New York Times* (Richard V. Oulahan), July 7, 1931; Charles G. Dawes, *Journal as Ambassador to Great Britain* (New York, 1939), p. 349; Stimson MS. Diary, June 2, 1931.

[42] *New York Times* (Richard V. Oulahan), July 7, 1931; SDP, 462.00R-296/5027; Hoover, *Memoirs*, III, 67–68; Dawes, *Journal as Ambassador*, p. 349.

[43] GFMR, 1492/D621170–1, D621180; 1776/D808335; 1659/D728909; 1493/D621339.

[44] Hoover, *Memoirs*, III, 62–70, 73–74.

the contemporary evidence of Dawes's diary with Hoover's latter-day version. On June 18, Dawes noted on his talk with Hoover on the sixteenth, when the President was expecting a collapse of Austria:

If the Austrian bank failed, it was expected that the Reichsbank would be compelled to take a moratorium. This would precipitate a world crisis, affecting our own country materially, as the New York banks alone were reported to have $500,000,000 of German acceptances.

The New York bankers had been phoning Hoover . . . requesting governmental assistance in the European difficulty. In this situation, as generally outlined, Hoover was considering what he could do to relieve it. His present thought was to suggest a reparations moratorium all around for one or two years, funding the payment due to the United States for that time.

And on July 3, Dawes commented, in connection with his expectation that agreement was about to be reached with France: "If so, it makes a great American achievement. It demonstrates, too, how entirely self-interest determines the attitude of nations in real emergency. What first moved Hoover to immediate action was the fear of the collapse of the Reichsbank and of German credit, which would affect adversely the immense American holdings in German securities, especially in short term German bank credits, about $500,000,000 of which were held by the New York banks." [45]

And there are other grounds for believing that Hoover was quite conscious of the short-term loans. Sackett probably discussed the short-term debt problem in his June 2 talks with the President, since he stressed it to Stimson that day; in any case, Sackett had sent a dispatch on the subject back on January 21, and this had been forwarded to Hoover. We can also recall how a "somewhat agitated" Stimson had repeatedly emphasized the credit problem when discussing the German manifesto with Ambassador Lindsay on June 6. More direct evidence comes from Stimson's diary,

[45] Dawes, *Journal as Ambassador*, pp. 351, 356.

which records that on June 11 the President, when hesitating to take action, told Stimson he had heard that the short-term situation was not really as bad as he had previously thought. Finally, Louis P. Lochner, Hoover's most recent defender, discloses (probably inadvertently) that Senator Dwight Morrow informed the President that leading New York bankers were panicky.[46] In the light of all this, and considering Hoover's familiarity with international trade and finance, it is simply impossible to believe the explanation he gives in his memoirs.

It would be a mistake, however, to build a conspiracy thesis on this foundation. The President, disillusioned by his experiences in 1932 and 1933, seems to have despaired of gaining credence for his true motives. For Dawes, the hard-boiled Chicago banker, probably overstressed the President's concern for the banks in his July 3 entry, although that concern certainly existed. Herbert Feis maintains that Hoover was the last man to let himself be dictated to by New York bankers, and Hoover's memoirs show that his antipathies included a dislike of Eastern finance.[47] It seems apparent that Hoover did not act for the sake of the officers of Lee, Higginson, The Guaranty Trust Company, and "The Chase," but because, among other things, the collapse of these banks would have been for the United States comparable to what the collapse of the Creditanstalt was for Austria. We should remember, too, that Hoover had been considering making some move on debts and reparations even before the Creditanstalt crisis became acute. To Hoover, the most important argument for the moratorium proposal was probably the hope of achieving a psychological victory over the depression. Nevertheless, the choice of method—a unilateral declaration—was also influenced by a desire to avoid a world conference which would consider debts and reparations together, and by a fear that the Germans, if left to act for themselves, would hopelessly damage their own credit, in which the United States had so large a stake.

[46] SDP, 862.51/2991: Ambassador in Berlin to Secretary, Jan. 21, 1931, including appended notes; Stimson MS. Diary, June 2, 11, 1931; Lochner, *Hoover and Germany*, p. 87.

[47] Conversation with Herbert Feis, Oct. 3, 1951; Hoover, *Memoirs*, III, 78.

Stimson's diary report of the June 5 discussion gives us an insight into the motives behind the proposal:

He [Hoover] laid before us a very serious situation which he feared would come out of the German situation and laid before us a plan which he had in mind. It involved a bold, emphatic proposition to assume leadership himself, and I, myself, felt more glad than I could say that he was at least turning that way. Mellon was conservative about it and held back and questioned whether it was necessary. Ogden Mills raised the point, and it was probably well taken, that the President's power to do what he proposed to do were [*sic*] limited by some of the former agreements, so that he could not do all that he expected. I took the position that the matter was one of psychology and credit, and that the points to be studied were how far and in what direction the proposed action would influence public opinion here and abroad and what effect it would have upon credit here and abroad. After the conference, which lasted better than an hour, we all three started to go out of the room, but the President called me back. From the fact that he had had Mellon come in from the Cabinet Room with Mills and I had come in from the Secretary's Room, I rather gathered that he had foreseen this. He then told me some further facts which he had not told the others, telling me that he was leaving Mellon to find out for himself and that he thought it would be quite a shock to him. He and I then had further talk about the matter and he gave some interesting, most interesting, views on the Great War and its prolongation by the lack of initiative on the part of the people concerned. He told me that he always believed in going out to meet a situation rather than to let it come and commented on Mellon's habit of doing the other thing. Altogether it was one of the most satisfactory talks I have had with him for a long time. Whether or not his position proves feasible, I am very glad that his mind is turning that way and I am still more glad of his confidence in me and my judgment which the whole of the events of the afternoon showed.

The "very serious situation" Hoover feared was presumably the collapse of German credit and the resulting blow to American finance and the American economy. Hoover's comparison with the First World War shows his estimate of the seriousness of the situation; he repeats the parallel in his memoirs, where he compares the customs union announcement with the assassination of Franz Ferdinand at Sarajevo.[48]

THE IMPACT OF CHEQUERS ON WASHINGTON

It was at this juncture that the Chequers conference intervened, and the Germans published their manifesto. The American Embassy in Berlin had reported fully on the campaign against reparations, and one cable, sent on June 3, had said, "Events here are moving very rapidly (the situation, for instance, has changed materially since Friday last) and it appears from here that (if the phrase may be used) the buck is rapidly being passed to us, and the moment when the German Government will take definite steps toward the revision of reparations is approaching rapidly also." Washington was awaiting the results of the Chequers meeting with considerable nervousness when the United Press report of the manifesto came out, making it appear that the Germans had practically declared a moratorium. According to Stimson, Mills exclaimed that this was "a facer, a bombshell," while "the President was very much upset, of course, for it seemed to knock all our plans into a cocked hat." On June 9, Stimson castigated the UP at a press conference for what he had now come to consider an exaggerated story.[49] We must bear in mind that, from the outside, it appeared that Germany might very well simply break off payments rather than declare a Young moratorium; either way, a deadly blow would be dealt her credit.

Although Brüning and Curtius had heard Vansittart read Lindsay's messages, they do not seem to have fully comprehended the significance of Stimson's statements to Lindsay. But the British leaders, who could study Lindsay's telegrams at their leisure, realized that something was afoot, and Ramsay MacDonald proceeded to do what he could to influence the American government. His aim, of course, was to increase the American interest in

---

[48] Stimson MS. Diary, June 5, 1931; Hoover, *Memoirs*, III, 62.

[49] *FRUS, 1931*, I, 5; Stimson MS. Diary, June 6, 1931; *DBFP*, 2/II, Nos. 49, 50; GFMR, 1493/D621339: Leitner to Ministry, June 9, 1931. The full UP story appeared in the New York *World-Telegram*, June 6, 1931, and the UP's translation was the one, apparently, that Lindsay sent to London.

doing something about war debts and reparations. Without informing the Foreign Office, the Prime Minister gave Ray Atherton, the American Chargé d'Affaires, a long description of the Chequers meeting, and he immediately followed this up with a personal letter to Stimson. MacDonald told Atherton he had taken special pains at Chequers to explain that England would at this time be entirely unwilling to broach any question of "reparations debts" to the United States. But he also stated that there was a danger both of revolution in Germany and of French domination in Europe, and in the letter to Stimson he wrote, "These men are facing a very awful situation and anything which any of us can do to help them discreetly really ought to be done." MacDonald clearly wrote the letter to calm the fears of immediate moratorium which Stimson had expressed to Lindsay, and at the same time to prepare Stimson for a discussion of reparations on his trip. In his diary, Stimson commented that it was "an admirable letter, fairminded in its spirit and perfectly frank with us, a model of what relations should be between two foreign offices"—Stimson did not realize that the British Foreign Office was ignorant of the message.[50] Another British leader, Montagu Norman, was to play an even larger role in influencing American policy. At this stage he was still more concerned over Austria than Germany, but he cabled Governor Harrison, reporting on the Chequers conference and suggesting that the real danger would appear after the Berlin statement sank in. Harrison relayed the contents of this message to Stimson on June 8.[51]

When Brüning and Curtius journeyed back to Germany, they boarded the *Europa* at Southampton and found Ambassador Sackett on board, returning from New York. In his memoirs, Curtius says that Sackett told them "something would happen." This Delphic utterance did not appear in Curtius' contemporary memorandum, which depicted Sackett as saying that although the

---

[50] *FRUS, 1931*, I, 6–8, 11–14; Stimson MS. Diary, June 9, 1931; *DBFP*, 2/II, No. 51, note 2.

[51] SDP, 462.00R296/3956½. On Norman's activity, see also *FRUS, 1931*, I, 19–20; SDP, 462.00R296/3956, 4039; 863.51/968½, 969½: Memos of phone calls from Governor of New York Federal Reserve Bank.

situation (in Washington) had altered in favor of the German standpoint, "America could not help directly." Sackett's personal opinion, as then recorded by Curtius, was that Germany might declare a moratorium without damaging her credit *if* (and he stressed this) she declared that she wanted to preserve her capital, so as not to endanger her private creditors. Sackett gave the Germans no indication that Hoover was considering taking steps on his own; instead, he rather encouraged them to act.[52] In contrast to this, Sackett's report to Washington, which he did not send until three days later, shows signs of having been carefully calculated to provoke an American action. The Ambassador cabled that Brüning and Curtius had told him they expected to have several weeks before they would be forced to take steps, and that they intended to make no move until Stimson's visit to Berlin. Sackett estimated, however, that developments in the three days since their conversation had so clouded the situation that the Germans might now have to act at an earlier date. He stated that Brüning and Curtius appreciated the need to safeguard credit, but also felt an urgent need to act, and that they were convinced of the need for revision instead of a mere moratorium, in order to get "an adjustment to suit present depressed conditions." According to the Curtius memorandum, both these latter points, credit and the need for going beyond a moratorium, had actually been raised and emphasized by Sackett himself. But by attributing these views to Curtius and Brüning, Sackett made it appear that the Germans were at once considerate of American interests and also dangerously close to a unilateral moratorium. His report was forwarded to the White House on June 15.[53]

THE GERMAN CRISIS INTENSIFIES

It was true that, as Sackett reported, the German financial and political situation was growing uglier. After Chequers, and doubt-

[52] Curtius, *Sechs Jahre,* p. 216; GFMR, 1493/D621346–7: Memo by Curtius, June 10, 1931.
[53] SDP, 462.00R296/3971: Ambassador in Berlin to Secretary, June 13, 1931; GFMR, 1493/D621346–7.

less largely because of the manifesto, withdrawals of foreign exchange grew heavier and German security quotations dropped further. The government was seeking a RM250,000,000 credit from the large German banks to bridge the gap between receipts and expenses in the old budget. This operation, which would normally have offered no difficulty, seemed in danger of failing. The German banks were losing confidence in the ability of the government to meet future obligations, and the government considered negotiating a loan from France. Most serious, groups hostile to the government demanded that the Reichstag should be convened, in order to force a modification of the emergency decree and the adoption of a more radical reparations policy.[54] On the morning of June 11, Brüning told the cabinet: "For the calm continuation of an appropriate foreign policy, it was absolutely necessary to avoid a convening of the Reichstag or of its Main Committee. The cabinet must be agreed to resign in case the Reichstag was convened. And in that case, he himself, the Chancellor, would not take part in the formation of another cabinet." Brüning declared that he would inform the Reichstag parties that a summoning of the Reichstag or of its Budget Committee, or the declaration of a moratorium before Stimson's visit, was unacceptable to the cabinet. But that very evening, a meeting of the German People's Party decided to vote for a summoning of the Reichstag, thereby bringing about a full-fledged political crisis.[55] The financial repercussions were soon obvious enough. On June 11 the demand for foreign currency in Berlin was RM80,000,000, and the next day it rose to over RM150,000,000. Two days later the Reichsbank raised its discount rate from 5 per cent to 7 per cent and let it be known that if this type of action was ineffective, it would impose credit restrictions, controlling and reducing all lending. Such action would have a crippling effect on the German economy and would probably end all prospects for the

[54] *New York Times*, June 8, 10–13, 1931; GFMR, 1684/D786814; 2548/E300024–6: Cabinet Protocol, June 11, 1931; Ministry to Embassy in Paris, June 14, 1931; *DBFP*, 2/II, Nos. 53, 54.
[55] GFMR, 1684/D786812–4: Cabinet Protocol; *DBFP*, 2/II, No. 53.

RM250,000,000 credit for the Reich government.[56] These developments would greatly increase the pressure, both on the German
government and on Germany's creditors, to suspend reparations
payments.

Meanwhile, the German government continued to spin out its
diplomatic program, ignorant of what was going on in Washington. On June 11, as we have seen, Brüning insisted to his cabinet
that it was necessary to await Stimson's visit to avoid the stigma
of disturbing the peace.[57] But already the German leaders were
thinking of bowing to—or exploiting—the domestic clamor. On
June 8, Bülow wrote to Hoesch that he was forwarding a memorandum on reparations.

> As you will see from it, we intend—forced by our internal difficulties
> in raising money, and by internal political pressure—to open the repara-
> tions question. We wish above all to get a breathing space of about
> three years, that is, a long holiday on all international payments arising
> from the war. We wish to use the Young moratorium as a means of
> bringing pressure [*Als Druckmittel wollen wir das Young-Moratorium
> benutzen*], being firmly resolved to proceed to a Young moratorium
> if we cannot get something better. The opposing side apparently hopes
> to divert us onto the path of [contracting] new loans; we reject these
> as unhealthy for our economy and finance, even if they are not tied
> in with political conditions.

On the thirteenth Curtius sent a long telegram to Ambassador
von Hoesch, giving instructions for the next step in German
diplomacy, a formal warning to France that payments could not
be continued. This message strongly suggested that Berlin would
request a moratorium before Stimson's arrival. Curtius pointed out
that, even if the British had made no concrete commitment at
Chequers, reparations had now been brought to the attention of
world opinion and no diplomatic complications had resulted, so
that a critical hurdle had been passed. "Now it is a question

---

[56] *New York Times*, June 13, 14, 1931; *DBFP*, 2/II, Nos. 54, 55; GFMR,
2548/E300025 and 1684/D786819: Cabinet Protocol, June 15, 1931; Stimson
MS. Diary, June 12, 1931.

[57] GFMR, 1684/D786813: Cabinet Protocol, June 11, 1931.

[Curtius wrote] of continuing what we have started, of not letting the public discussion die down, and of pushing forward our diplomatic program. We would consider it a mistake if we were to await Henderson's initiative or his visit in Berlin or the arrival of the American Secretary of State, Stimson. The various cabinets and public opinion would have calmed down meanwhile, and would then have to be aroused all over again." A previous promise to inform Briand about the Chequers conference offered an opportunity for taking the next step. Hoesch was instructed to report to Briand on the talks with the British, and to add that Germany was ready to conduct the same kind of discussion with other creditor governments. Then Hoesch was to describe the intensification of the financial crisis in the last few days, and he was to declare that, in the light of this, the existing reparations situation could no longer be maintained. He was also to inform the French that the German government would be obliged to take decisive steps on reparations "in the immediate future [*in allernächster Zeit*]," and declare a Young moratorium. Curtius recognized that a Young moratorium would only provide relief after eighteen months, but he did not want Hoesch to suggest any alternative procedure; if made at this time, such suggestions would be promptly rejected and would then be unavailable later.[58]

The French had been watching the trend of events with some concern; they apparently had received no information on the Chequers conversations, and they realized that the financial crisis was likely to be a pretext for a moratorium, which they feared would not be within the limits of the Young Plan. On the thirteenth, Pierre-Etienne Flandin, the Minister of Finance, had a sympathetic talk with a German banker about the perils of the financial situation. Perhaps it was this discussion that caused the Quai d'Orsay to tell the British Ambassador, Lord Tyrrell, that they had privately received the "somewhat alarming news" that if the crisis continued, a suspension of payments might become necessary; they wished to know if the British government had

[58] GFMR, 2548/E300015–22.

received confirmation of this. As we shall see, they received a most emphatic reply.[59]

Hoesch was at first unable to see Briand, and to avoid delay, he saw Berthelot on June 15, making the explanation and declaration prescribed by Curtius. Berthelot's chief reaction seemed to be relief that the Germans were planning to act within the Young Plan framework. Hoesch did see Briand the next day, and Flandin on the seventeenth. Berthelot, Briand, and Flandin all showed understanding, but Briand asked if a moratorium declaration, with its inability to bring immediate relief, and its probable effect on German credit, might not do more harm than good, while Flandin, besides mentioning the credit danger, remarked that Germany was getting further and further away from the idea of attracting capital by creating an atmosphere of confidence. Hoesch replied that, in any case, French capital had not been forthcoming.[60]

Meanwhile, from across the Atlantic, bankers and government officials watched the German financial and political crisis with consternation. Hoover, alarmed at his own temerity, had begun to back away from action. On June 8 he was concerned over the danger of European entanglements, and three days later he was saying that he had inside information that the short-term problem was not really so bad, after all. This did not square with Ogden Mills's Federal Reserve data; Mills, at first cautious, had now become the stoutest advocate of announcing a moratorium, preferably for two years. On the twelfth, Montagu Norman cabled Harrison that the Reichsbank was on the verge of credit restrictions, and that the German political situation was worse than ever. The idea of sending Harrison over to examine the situation was considered and then abandoned.[61] From Washington, the German financial and political structure seemed to be falling apart.

[59] SDP, 840.50/121; 862.51/3045: Memo of conversation between French Ambassador and Secretary, June 4, 1931; Memo of conversation between Under Secretary and member of French Embassy, June 8, 1931; GFMR, 2548/E300024: Ministry to Embassy in Paris, June 14, 1931; *DBFP*, 2/II, No. 55 note 1.

[60] GFMR, 1776/D808215-6: Hoesch to Ministry, June 17, 1931.

[61] Stimson MS. Diary, June 5, 8, 11, 12, 1931.

Mills had been impressed by MacDonald's letter to Stimson, and in view of the now critical situation, he proposed that Secretary Stimson call MacDonald on the transatlantic telephone and learn his views on Hoover's moratorium idea. Stimson accordingly put in a call at 5:45 A.M. on June 13 and informed MacDonald in general terms of what was afoot. It is not surprising that Hoover was annoyed when he heard of the call, and he was particularly fearful lest the British begin discussions with the French; Hoover had not even made up his own mind as yet. MacDonald phoned back in the evening to say that Norman was all in favor of the proposed action, and Stimson, alarmed by Hoover's reaction, stressed that MacDonald should not approach any other nation; apparently the Secretary said that if any soundings were to be made, the United States would make them herself. Perhaps because of the poor connection, MacDonald seems to have gathered from this that the American government had in fact decided to go ahead, and was about to approach France. This misunderstanding was unfortunate, but not too serious. The significant thing was that Stimson had gone so far as to inform the British Prime Minister about the scheme the American government was still considering.[62] While this was going on in secret, a statement made by Under Secretary of State William R. Castle, also on the night of the thirteenth, attracted public attention: Castle said that the United States might alter its views on war debts in the event of a serious crisis, although he added that such a crisis did not then exist. According to Stimson's diary, this aroused a furor, and the Secretary had difficulty in persuading Hoover, for Castle's own sake, not to repudiate the statement.[63]

Stimson's telephone call and Castle's statement made it clear to London that a long-awaited opportunity had arrived. From this point forward the London government put aside all hesitations and devoted itself to an attempt to achieve a major revision of

[62] Stimson MS. Diary, June 12, 13, 1931; *FRUS, 1931*, I, 16–19.
[63] *New York Times*, June 14, 1931; Stimson MS. Diary, June 15, 1931. Apparently Castle and others had been making similar statements for several days (see GFMR, 1493/D621349). It seems, however, that June 13 was the date when this calculated leakage first received widespread attention.

reparations and debts. The following message was sent to Paris on June 15, and a copy was sent to Stimson by Ambassador Lindsay:

There is no doubt that the situation in Germany is exceedingly critical. It is in fact more critical than at any time during the past six years. During the past few days, and in part at least for psychological reasons, the situation has rapidly deteriorated and has now become gravely alarming. Reichsbank has lost over £30,000,000 during past ten days, mainly due to withdrawals of foreign money. If movement extends to German capital it may involve collapse of mark, with disastrous consequences not only to Germany but to Austria and Hungary. As you know, the Reichsbank on Saturday raised its discount rate by 2 per cent., and it is hoped that this may have a steadying effect. But as the movement is due to political rather than financial causes, the increase of the bank rate may be ineffective. The political difficulties of the Brüning Cabinet, or any delay in settling the Austrian bank trouble, may in any case be sufficient to neutralize the effect of the increased bank rate. On the other hand, if, as of course, we hope, the Brüning Government can survive their present political difficulties, and the Austrian trouble is cleared up, an easing of the financial situation may be hoped for. We are aware that there has been an improvement in the situation today, but financial circles here still feel deepest apprehension. The key to the situation seems to rest with the United States and France. We should, of course, be prepared to join in any action that might be deemed salutary, but it would seem best for the first move for joint action to come from those chiefly interested, and it is no use disguising our fear that if confidence is not speedily restored we may be faced not merely with a complete cessation of reparation payments, but with a financial collapse in Germany and Austria, involving serious risk of political and social trouble in those countries and consequent repercussions on the rest of Europe. We hope the situation is fully realized by the French Government.[64]

This statement was a far cry from the suggestions made at Chequers that it would be necessary to wait until after the 1932 presidential elections. The British were now not even ready to

---

[64] *DBFP,* 2/II, No. 55; *FRUS, 1931,* I, 22.

wait for Stimson's visit; they were calling for action within a matter of days, even hours.

THE CLIMAX OF THE AUSTRIAN CRISIS

While Brüning's government had been proceeding step by step toward a Young moratorium, and Hoover's administration had been contemplating a proposal for a moratorium on all inter-governmental payments, Paris had been maturing its plans to force an Austrian renunciation of the customs union. During Hoesch's interviews with Briand and Flandin, warning them of the imminence of a Young moratorium, the French Ministers asked the Ambassador several times if he did not have a declaration to make with regard to Austria. "In answer to my astonished question," Hoesch reported, "as to what kind of a declaration he expected of me, [Briand] finally let it be understood, in halting words, that it had been hoped here that Germany and Austria would declare their readiness to abandon the plan for a customs union in the interests of fulfilling Austria's desire for credit." Hoesch told both Briand and Flandin that he knew nothing of any such declaration, and that, considering that the Hague Court was examining the legal side of the matter, such a renunciation seemed to him unlikely.[65]

The question of the loan to Austria, totaling 150,000,000 schillings, had now come to a head. Despite the rumor that France would impose political conditions on any assistance she might grant, the Austrian government had been led to hope that, without any retreat, it would still obtain half the sum in France; various other countries were expected to furnish the other half. The Austrian Minister in Paris was told that the French government would influence the banks in favor of the loan, provided that Austria would "fully appreciate this French procedure and not permit any difficulties to arise later"; when the Minister asked what this reservation meant, he was told that it was expected "that Austria will not by any later actions make difficulties for the

---

[65] GFMR, 2521/E285132-3: Hoesch to Ministry, June 17, 1931.

placing of the treasury certificates." On this basis, Schober assumed that French credit had not been made subject to political conditions.[66]

This French explanation seems to have been deliberately intended to lead the Austrians on; similar statements were made in July to the Germans, when, as Paul Schmidt observes, Laval and Flandin "skillfully glossed over their conditions." [67] And after all, political recalcitrance on the part of Vienna might prejudice the sale of the certificates on the Paris market. Days went by, and no agreement was reached. On June 10, Laval remarked to Hoesch that if he made funds available to Austria he would face great difficulties with his parliament and public opinion—unless there was some counterpayment. A government guarantee of the past foreign debts of the Creditanstalt was probably a precondition for any foreign assistance, French or other, and so, despite the objections of the Minister of the Interior, Franz Winkler, a guarantee agreement was signed in the early morning of the sixteenth (according to the *Berliner Tageblatt*, at 4:00 A.M., after all-night negotiations). Later in the morning, as a stipulation for floating half of the treasury certificates, the French demanded the abandonment of the customs union and agreement that the League Council should investigate the situation; the Austrian government would agree in advance to accept the Council's recommendations. These conditions were secret, but Austria was further asked to agree that they might be published whenever France desired. Schober afterwards told the American Minister that he was given three hours to accept or decline this ultimatum.[68]

Although the Austrians later stated that these were conditions

---

[66] GFMR, 2521/E285120–1: Hoesch to Ministry, June 11, 1931; *New York Times*, June 14, 1931.

[67] Schmidt, *Statist*, p. 219.

[68] GFMR, 2521/E285119: Hoesch to Ministry, June 11, 1931; SDP, 863.51/70: Minister in Vienna to Secretary, June 18, 1931; *FRUS, 1931*, I, 23; London *Times*, June 16, 17, 1931; *Berliner Tageblatt*, June 17 (A.M.), 1931; *Neue Freie Presse* (Vienna), June 17 (A.M.), 1931. For French acknowledgments that the demand was made, see *FRUS, 1931*, I, 25; *DBFP*, 2/II, No. 76.

which no Austrian government could accept, Vienna would probably have surrendered had it not been for the prospect of help
from Montagu Norman. On the same day, "in time for the latest
papers," Norman advanced a short-term (seven-day) Bank of
England credit of 150,000,000 schillings, the amount of the whole
new treasury certificate issue, to the Austrian central bank, intending to tide the Austrians over until the certificates could be
floated. To increase the day's excitement, the Austrian Minister
of Interior resigned at 1:00 P.M. in protest against the guarantee
of foreign debts and in consequence, the cabinet was obliged to
submit its collective resignation in the late afternoon. It is likely
that Norman decided to make his advance before he knew of these
last developments. In any case, the London *Times* showed confidence that the guarantee would be honored by any succeeding
government, and in fact, a new cabinet, formed on the twenty-
first, and retaining Schober as Foreign Minister, ultimately accepted the guarantee obligation.[69]

Norman's action was probably the result of a whole complex
of motives. For one thing, he apparently believed that aid had to
be given quickly, "by Thursday" (June 18), or there would be a
complete moratorium in Austria; Britain was a leading creditor of
Austria's and was therefore directly interested in stemming the
tide of disaster there. For another thing, Norman was outraged
at the attempt of France to impose political conditions—a feeling
shared by both British and American leaders. From this point of
view, the Bank of England advance was an act of chivalry as well
as a display of financial leadership by what was still regarded as
the world's greatest central bank. Finally, Governor Norman may
have desired to demonstrate the seriousness of the crisis to the

---

[69] *Berliner Tageblatt*, June 17 (A.M.), 1931; *Neue Freie Presse*, June 17
(A.M.), 1931; London *Times*, June 17, 1931; SDP, 863.51/968½, 970, 973:
Memo of phone conversation between Governor of New York Federal
Reserve Bank and Governor of Bank of England, June 16, 1931; Minister in
Vienna to Secretary, June 18, 1931; Memo of conversation between Secretary
and British Ambassador, June 18, 1931; Walther Federn, "Der Zusammen-
bruch der österreichischen Kreditanstalt," *Archiv für Sozialwissenschaft und
Sozialpolitik*, 67:424-425 (1932).

governments involved, and to point to the need for some corresponding action on their part; to some extent, his action on behalf
of Austrian finance gave him a license to urge the governments to
act on reparations and war debts.[70] The credit to Austria did
temporarily save the Austrian government, but it also contributed
to the Bank of England's own problems at the end of the summer.
We may well imagine that this assistance did nothing to endear
Norman or the British to the French. Moreover, London's urgent
message of the fifteenth, stating that the German situation was
exceedingly critical and that the key to the situation seemed to
rest with the United States and France, probably struck Paris as
an attempt to launch a revision of the whole reparations structure
for the sake of British financial interests. New points of friction
were thus arising between Britain and France.

Relief came on June 16 for the German government as well as
for the Austrian. After lengthy negotiations, Brüning induced the
People's Party to reverse its decision to call the Reichstag, and he
appeased the other parties. To judge by statements from the
leader of the People's Party, Eduard Dingeldey, which appeared
in the *Deutsche Allgemeine Zeitung,* Brüning may have purchased
acquiescence with a promise to invoke a Young moratorium at an
early date, or at least to do so before imposing credit restrictions.
Certainly by this time there was little question of awaiting Stimson's arrival. During the crisis, the presidential *Staatssekretär,* Otto
Meissner, told the ministers that if they resigned, Hindenburg
would invite other party leaders to form a cabinet based on a
Reichstag majority; such attempts would presumably fail, and
then Hindenburg would probably call on Brüning to form another
minority government. Thus, despite Brüning's statement earlier
that he would not share in another cabinet, the end result would
very likely have been another Brüning cabinet. Considering the
financial situation, however, it was well that the need for these

[70] See SDP, 863.51/969½, 968½; 462.00R296/4040: Memos of phone calls
between Governor of Bank of England and Governor of New York Federal
Reserve Bank, June 15, 16, 18, 1931; *FRUS, 1931,* I, 21, 23, 26–27; *SIA,
1931,* p. 210.

expedients did not arise. The loss of gold and foreign exchange began to slacken a little, presumably in response to Norman's credit and the ending of the German political crisis, and on June 17 withdrawals of gold and exchange from Germany fell to RM29,000,000 from over RM50,000,000 the previous day; nevertheless, RM250,000,000 had been lost since the political crisis arose on June 12.[71]

MAINTAINING THE MOMENTUM

One might now have thought that the need for a moratorium had become somewhat less immediate. This was the opinion of the British Chargé d'Affaires in Berlin, Basil Newton, who wired to London on June 19: "It is not easy to understand how a sudden declaration of a moratorium could be genuinely necessitated by present financial crisis, which, primarily affecting commercial and private credit, has been of an immediately urgent nature, and might now, in the absence of future shocks, be expected to abate rather than increase in severity, particularly in view of the settlement of the political crisis and temporary rescue of the Kreditanstalt by the Bank of England." But others wished to exploit the opportunity. The occasion for Newton's comment was a report (dated June 18) of an interview between the British Embassy's financial expert, Colonel J. W. F. Thelwall, and Karl Ritter, which recorded Ritter's opinion that the

German Government may feel itself compelled to declare a moratorium in the course of the next few days. Cabinet has not yet taken a decision to this effect, and had hoped to defer action at least until after the visit of American Secretary of State. Effect of financial crisis had, however, been so grave that even Dr. Luther, who had hitherto opposed a moratorium, had changed his views and felt he could hold out no longer.

It was above all things necessary to secure effective discussion of Germany's difficulties at a very early date. It would be useless for American Secretary of State to visit Europe and receive different

[71] GFMR, 1684/D786826: Cabinet Protocol, June 16, 1931; *Deutsche Allgemeine Zeitung*, June 18, 1931; *New York Times*, June 17, 18, 1931.

impressions in each capital. Speech of Mr. Castle seemed an invitation to take action.

Ritter indicated that Germany would have welcomed discussion with other countries, but the French had issued no invitation so far, and "the only thing likely to bring about a useful discussion would be declaration of a moratorium." When Thelwall protested that German credit would be damaged, Ritter observed that further withdrawals would occur anyway, and that uncertainty was more damaging than an actual moratorium declaration, which he did not think would make the credit situation in Germany and Southeast Europe any worse than it would be otherwise.[72]

Ritter was doubtless trying to produce an effect, but in the light of the instructions Curtius sent to Hoesch on June 13, it seems that a declaration of a moratorium within a few days was indeed a distinct possibility. An unsigned memorandum in the Chancellor's "Revision Policy" file, dated "early June 18" (and from internal evidence possibly written by Brüning himself), indicated that "the most urgent question is whether, in the next hours or days, we should declare a postponement or not." Many officials had been urging an early move; against their arguments, the memorandum suggested that it would be unwise to request a moratorium until the Reichsbank had accumulated a greater reserve of credits, and until creditors could be assured that the appeal to "the legal potentialities of the Young Plan" was being accompanied by appropriate diplomatic soundings and preparations. This paper also suggested that an approach through Montagu Norman would be the best channel for explaining to the British why it was no longer possible to wait for Stimson's visit; even the author of the memorandum would not wait that long.[73] The German leaders had no intention of letting reparations be forgotten again.

Some authorities in London, despite Newton's own doubts, also wished to maintain the pressure. Norman became very upset when

---

[72] *DBFP*, 2/II, Nos. 60, 61.
[73] See GFMR, 1776/D808196–204 for the whole memorandum.

he learned, on June 16, that Gates McGarrah of the Bank for International Settlements had cabled Harrison that the Reichsbank claimed to have the financial situation in hand. Norman told Harrison that he had different information from the same Reichsbank source, and insisted that Harrison must believe him and not McGarrah; he said he was in daily contact with the Reichsbank and was giving Harrison an absolutely uncolored version of the facts. Despite the improvement after the sixteenth, Norman was still very pessimistic about the Austrian, German, and European situation on the eighteenth, and he told Secretary Mellon, who had arrived in England, that he was extremely apprehensive about the position of the Reichsbank and conditions in Germany. Mellon cabled Washington that the British, apparently meaning MacDonald and Henderson as well as Norman, feared that a debacle in Austria or in Germany would "lead to chaos economically and politically not only in those countries but spreading to Rumania, Hungary and other Eastern European countries as well." [74]

In Washington, too, efforts were made to conceal any improvement. The President's advisers were having a trying time in the face of his indecision. On June 12, Hoover seemed to be more impressed with the difficulties than ever, and Stimson's telephone calls with MacDonald, together with Castle's statement, made him even more inclined to draw back. It is not surprising, therefore, to find Stimson noting in his diary on June 16, after seeing Mills, "We think there is a respite, but that the President must not be allowed to think that the crisis is over." Hoover had gone, as Mills put it, "out West," dedicating Harding's tomb at Marion, Ohio, making a speech to a group of Republican editors at Indianapolis, and taking part in Lincoln ceremonies at Springfield, Illinois. Stimson called Hoover, at the moment (June 16) passing through Columbus, Ohio, and told him that the situation was better because of Norman's advance to Austria, but that this was only a

[74] SDP, 863.51/969½, 968½: Cable from President of Bank for International Settlements, June 15, 1931; Memo of phone conversation between Governor of Bank of England and Governor of New York Federal Reserve Bank, June 16, 1931; *FRUS, 1931*, I, 24.

breathing spell. By this time, Owen D. Young, S. Parker Gilbert, Governor Harrison, Eugene Meyer, and Senator Morrow had pronounced in favor of the proposed plan, and while traveling with Hoover from Marion to Springfield, Dawes added his approval, recommending, as did some others, that the proposed moratorium should be for two years rather than one. Thus there was an imposing array of leaders prodding Hoover into action.[75]

GERMANY AND FRANCE IN THE DARK

Berlin's preoccupation with its own plans continued until the Hoover proposal actually came. There was some intelligence on American intentions, but it was passed over because it did not fit in with the prevailing line of thought. In January, Owen D. Young had suggested to Prittwitz that if Germany felt compelled to appeal to the Young Plan, Hoover should be secretly informed first, so that he might have a last chance to take the initiative. Prittwitz reported this to Bülow at the time and in May he repeated Young's suggestion that Hoover be forewarned. But Bülow seems to have missed the point about giving Hoover a chance to act, since in forwarding Young's suggestion to the Ministry of Finance, he added only the comment, "I care very little for acts of courtesy which take place in secret." On June 16, the Hungarian Minister in Berlin had told Bülow that his colleague in Washington, who had contact with wealthy society circles, had heard that Hoover was very impressed with the European financial crisis and was ready to take action to help, by offering a moratorium or otherwise. Bülow promised to inform Curtius and Brüning of this, and perhaps Ritter knew of this story when he spoke to Thelwall. Rumors of a non-Young moratorium also appeared in the press, and no doubt elsewhere. Nevertheless, the anonymous memorandum of "early June 18," already mentioned, assumed throughout that, sooner or later, Germany would take

[75] Stimson MS. Diary, June 5, 8, 11, 12–14, 16; Dawes, *Journal as Ambassador*, p. 350; *FRUS, 1931*, I, 19–20. The hostile but surprisingly well-informed book by Drew Pearson and Robert S. Allen, *The Washington Merry-Go-Round* (Garden City, N.Y., 1931), p. 77, says Hoover was pushed into the moratorium by Young, Stimson, Dawes, Morrow, and Mellon.

the initiative, or rather, pursue the initiative already taken at Chequers and by Hoesch, by formally requesting a Young moratorium. Schubert and Hoesch went to Berlin for consultation on June 17, probably to prepare for such action.[76] Just prior to Hoover's announcement, on June 19 or 20, the German government decided on an early declaration of a Young moratorium— that is, around July 1.[77] The Chancellor and his fellows were planning to act themselves when Hoover took them by surprise. Like other German leaders on other historic occasions, Brüning may have been unable in the last analysis to believe that the United States could have any significant influence on European events.

Until June 18, the French were just as unaware of Hoover's thinking as the Germans. Discussion on June 4 and 11 between Secretary Stimson and the French Ambassador, Paul Claudel, about Germany had been academic, not to say philosophical. And after Hoover's reaction to Stimson's telephone call to MacDonald, the Secretary became even more cautious; on the fifteenth, while in this mood, he sent a cable to Ambassador Walter Edge in Paris, alluding to the "false rumors" which had appeared, and stating that, although a reparations-debt moratorium plan was being considered, the United States would not act unless European countries, particularly France, were willing to take similar action. Edge was told that he could explain this situation if he were questioned by Briand or other members of the French government, but he was not to initiate any discussions. Edge interpreted these instructions too cautiously, and although he had a long talk with Briand on June 17, mostly about Hoesch's warning to the French of an impending Young moratorium, he did not mention the

[76] GFMR, 2384/E199145; 2385/E199570–2; 1493/D621354: Letters, Prittwitz to Bülow, Jan. 19 and May 11, 1931; Memo by Bülow, June 16, 1931; *DBFP*, 2/II, No. 61; *New York Times*, June 4–10, 13, 16, 18, 1931; *Evening Star* (Washington), June 17, 1931. These sources also referred to Prittwitz as being summoned to Berlin, but he was already there on leave (GFMR, 2379/E194713–4).

[77] GFMR, 2548/E300060–1; 1684/D786784; 4078/L051201: Hoesch to Ministry, June 23, 1931; Cabinet Protocol, June 23, 1931; Circular dispatch, July 31, 1931.

scheme under consideration in Washington.[78] On the eighteenth, Stimson himself finally carried out the approach he had suggested to Edge.

Hoover had no desire to consult the French, and indeed, one of his chief objections to Stimson's notifying MacDonald had been that it might lead to Franco-British talks. But Stimson and Mills recognized the importance of making soundings. They had advised consulting other governments on June 12, and although Hoover had frowned on their approach to MacDonald, Mills told Stimson on the sixteenth that they should sound out France as soon as Hoover had dealt with the opposition in the United States. On the eighteenth the chance came to inform the French Ambassador. During a call on the Secretary of State, Claudel raised the subject of the German financial crisis, mentioning that the New York bankers thought something should be done. The discussion that followed was a curious piece of shadowboxing. Stimson pointed out that difficulties were involved, both for America and for France. "Nobody," he said, "could help unless France helped." Claudel asked if this meant that the United States would help if France did. Stimson replied that he could not speak on that subject with authority, but he could assure Claudel that unless France helped, the United States would not. Claudel said that these were weighty words, and Stimson agreed; evidently they were thinking of the implication that American help was a possibility. Stimson went on to say that there was doubt as to whether a Young moratorium would give Germany sufficient relief, and continued:

"The least objectionable plan which I have read would seem to be the plan of giving time on the part of everybody for one or two years; that might give relief, but it must be on the part of everybody, and not on the part of America alone; that no plan which would

[78] SDP, 840.50/121; 462.00R296/3986: Memo of conversation between French Ambassador and Secretary, June 4, 1931; Ambassador in Paris to Secretary, June 17, 1931; *FRUS, 1931*, I, 20. According to Edge's later recollection, he first heard of the moratorium on Sunday, June 21 (Walter Edge, *Jerseyman's Journal*, Princeton, 1948, p. 191). It is possible, judging by his report of June 17, that he did not comprehend the significance of Stimson's message. See also SDP, 462.00R296/4361.

propose that America should give up her debt receipts and leave France and England free to hold on to their receipts from Germany would have any chance of acceptance by this Government." He [Claudel] asked, "Do you mean the move must come from France?" I said, "Yes, we shall certainly make no move or consent to any move until we are certain what France's attitude is."

Stimson went on to explain, using a chart, what receipts the various governments would be expected to forego. At the end of the discussion, Stimson repeated that he could not say that this plan would be accepted by the American government, but he was sure that America would not be willing to make the only sacrifice. Claudel's personal reaction to the plan was highly favorable.[79]

Thus, although Stimson disclosed the plan to Claudel on Thursday, June 18, he definitely told the Ambassador that there would be no action until the French government had agreed. And this was what Claudel reported. Hoesch informed Berlin on June 24, on the basis of a talk with Briand, that "Ambassador Claudel had reported on his conversation of last Friday [Thursday?] with Stimson, [that] the American government planned a common action of the most interested powers, France and America, to bring relief to the world. The circumstance that the American government, without further bothering with France and without awaiting the French reply, then proceeded to act independently and unexpectedly, is regarded in Paris as a brutal lack of consideration [*wird als brutale Rücksichtslösigkeit aufgefasst*]."[80] Hoesch's report speaks for itself.

MELLON'S INVESTIGATION

The arrival of Secretary Mellon in England on June 16 marked the beginning of the crucial stage in American intervention, as far as diplomacy had a bearing on the question. Mellon's trip had

---

[79] Stimson MS. Diary, June 12, 13, 1931; *FRUS, 1931*, I, 27–28.

[80] GFMR, 2548/E300082: Hoesch to Ministry, June 24, 1931. Claudel may in fact have reported his Friday conversation as foreshadowing a joint Franco-American action. He would hardly have drawn this conclusion, however, if it had not been for the Thursday conversation. See *FRUS, 1931*, I, 28–29 for Stimson's record of the Friday conversation.

been planned as a vacation and as a chance to see his son at Cambridge, but Hoover had suggested before he left that he might report on conditions in Europe. Awaiting him was a cable from Ogden Mills, reporting that the situation appeared from Washington to have become more serious, and that Young, Gilbert, and Harrison were all in favor of proceeding with the plan. Hoover, however, was postponing action until he had consulted opposition leaders in Congress and until he could hear from Mellon. Thus, part of the responsibility for a decision was placed in Mellon's hands.[81]

The Secretary of the Treasury saw MacDonald and Henderson on June 17 and 18, and Governor Norman on June 18. MacDonald and Henderson strongly criticized the French, while Norman, who was, as we have seen, very pessimistic, was convinced that without his advance there would have been a "complete collapse in the Austrian situation." Mellon also asked a French friend, Robert Lacour-Gayet of the Bank of France, to come to London. The result was not encouraging: Lacour-Gayet stated that Laval's cabinet had been unanimous for placing the French political conditions before the Austrians,[82] and he told Mellon the French government was inclined to resist any movement on the part of Germany to obtain relief. Mellon apparently did not discuss the American plan with Lacour-Gayet. But the French difficulty (Mellon's report continued) was outweighed by another consideration. As Lacour-Gayet had remarked, there was the possibility that Germany would take some action on her own behalf. Mellon did not know of Ritter's statements to Newton, but there were other signs that the German government seriously intended to act on reparations: the Reichsbank's situation was precarious, and Foreign Secretary Henderson told Mellon that the Germans had warned the French and Italian governments that they would have to seek relief under the Young Plan.

In the light of this situation, Secretary Mellon advised Hoover,

[81] *FRUS, 1931*, I, 19–20; *New York Times* (Richard V. Oulahan), July 7, 1931; Drew Pearson and Constantine Brown, *The American Diplomatic Game* (Garden City, N.Y., 1935), pp. 214–215.

[82] Norman later told the Germans the French cabinet had *not* been unanimous (GFMR, 2548/E300042: Bernstorff to Ministry, June 21, 1931).

Stimson, and Mills that he thought the President would be justified in proposing a postponement of payments. "The French, without payment from Germany, will undoubtedly refuse to continue payments under their agreement, and other countries will, it is most likely, follow that course, so that in any event it seems likely payments to us will cease for a time." Possibly at Norman's suggestion, Mellon urged at least a two-year moratorium, with the amounts due in that period to be paid after the final Young Plan payments, and he suggested that it was essential to sound the French on any proposal considered, as "they may not be in a frame of mind to cooperate." Unless there was grave danger, however, he thought there was no need for action before Secretary Stimson arrived in Europe (that is, about July 8).[83]

Although Hoover, in his memoirs, is somewhat scornful of Mellon's change of mind, the Secretary's recommendations probably influenced the President's final decision, and in view of Mellon's role in concluding the war debt agreements, his acceptance of the moratorium plan had some political importance. Hoover had now (June 18) returned to Washington, and Stimson records that when he and Mills went to urge the plan to Hoover on the evening of June 18, apparently after Mellon's call, "the President was tired and . . . he went through all the blackest surmises . . . It was like sitting in a bath of ink to sit in his room"; Stimson thought, however, that Hoover was "moving at last." Hoover's biggest problem now was getting Congressional consent. He had been consulting congressmen and senators during his trip, and during the night and the next morning he attempted to line up as many additional supporters as possible.[84]

HOOVER GOES AHEAD

On June 19, cables arrived from Sackett and Edge, indicating that Germany would probably act before Stimson's arrival in

---

[83] *FRUS, 1931*, I, 24–26; Norman told the Germans he had urged a longer term, tied in with a clearing up of European political relations (GFMR, 2548/E300040: Bernstorff to Ministry, June 21, 1931).

[84] Stimson MS. Diary, June 18, 19, 1931; H. L. Stimson and McGeorge Bundy, *On Active Service in Peace and War* (New York, 1948), p. 205; Hoover, *Memoirs*, III, 68.

Europe. But at noon, before he could even have heard of these reports, Hoover told Stimson to inform the representatives of the powers of the intended action. At about 4:00 P.M. Hoover made a preliminary announcement to the press that he was conferring with political leaders about possible action to promote economic recovery, especially in Germany.[85]

Mellon had recommended a moratorium, but he had not recommended spreading the news the next day. Even the Berlin and Paris cables just cited did not justify such haste. The truth is that the timing of Hoover's announcement was determined by domestic factors. The President had attempted to see or reach by telephone as many political leaders as possible. He had reason to take such soundings, for Congress had always supervised war debt negotiations, and the 1930 elections had produced a Democratic House and a Senate in which administration control would at best be nominal. The response was favorable and it was this that made him feel able to go ahead. But such discussions were fatal to the secrecy of the plan. There was bound to be a leak to the press and, according to Hoover, it came when Senator William H. King of Utah gave reporters a "garbled and antagonistic version" of the plan. King was not the only source of leakage, although he may have been the most hostile. At all events, Hoover felt obliged to come out and issue his own statement, lest the whole effect be ruined. In his memoirs, Hoover states that he had to choose between displeasing governments by not giving them a few days' notice, and having the proposal discussed by their peoples in a garbled and destructive form; he implies that between these alternatives there was only one possible course.[86] But MacDonald had been given notice. And even if Hoover's alternatives were the only ones, it is not perhaps so certain that he made the best choice.

On the afternoon of June 19, Stimson began summoning the ambassadors of the interested countries to give them official

[85] SDP, 462.00R296/3993, 3995, 4130: Ambassador in Berlin to Secretary, June 19, 1931; Ambassador in Paris to Secretary, June 19, 1931; Memo of press conference held by Secretary of State, 4:30 P.M., June 19, 1931; Stimson MS. Diary, June 19, 1931; *New York Times*, June 20, 1931.

[86] Hoover, *Memoirs*, III, 69–70.

notification. He saw Claudel first, and thus was able, when the Ambassador asked, to tell him that France was the first country to which he had made the announcement. But shortly after that interview was over, MacDonald telephoned Stimson, who told him of the decision and asked him to help in exerting pressure on Paris. The diplomatic representatives of Germany, Great Britain, Italy, and Austria were also informed on June 19; Belgian, Yugoslav, Rumanian, and Greek diplomats were informed the next day.[87]

On the morning of June 20, an attempt was made to stage an appeal for help from President von Hindenburg, to which Hoover's final announcement would supposedly be a reply. As the problem was put in the instructions to Ambassador Sackett, "The average American has no tangible evidence at the present time of such a critical situation, and he is inclined to think that the bankers, for their own purposes, have raised a mere scare." But on the same morning, the *New York Times*, on the basis of the preliminary announcement, leaks, and other indications, was able to publish substantially the full story, and the Washington *Star* in the afternoon came out with what the administration considered a garbled account. By evening, Hoover felt that he had to give the full announcement to the press.[88] Although Brüning gladly cooperated in getting out a document for Hindenburg's signature, it arrived too late to be used, and besides, its tone was so full of despair that Washington felt its publication might limit the psychological benefits of Hoover's proposal. Even so, the existence of Hindenburg's message soon became known. Hoover also made efforts through Dawes and Mellon to gain the support of Colonel Robert R. McCormick and William Randolph Hearst. Although McCormick was in Ontario, Dawes got the *Tribune* staff in Chicago to promise to withhold editorial comment, but Mellon

[87] *FRUS, 1931*, I, 28–30, 31, incl. footnote 36; Stimson MS. Diary, June 19, 1931.

[88] *FRUS, 1931*, I, 32; Stimson MS. Diary, June 19, 20, 1931; *New York Times*, June 20, 1931; *Evening Star* (Washington), June 20, 1931. Actually, the *Star's* story had little of substance (assuming all editions had the same story) beyond suggesting that a moratorium seemed the most likely alternative. It hardly justified Hoover's haste.

failed to win over Hearst, who was touring in Wales, and the Hearst press denounced Hoover's action and urged the re-election of Coolidge in 1932.[89]

President Hoover issued the formal announcement of his proposal on the evening of June 20. The essential part of the statement read as follows:

The American Government proposes the postponement during one year of all payments on intergovernmental debts, reparations and relief debts, both principal and interest, of course not including obligations of governments held by private parties. Subject to confirmation by Congress, the American Government will postpone all payments upon the debts of foreign governments to the American Government payable during the fiscal year beginning July 1 next, conditional on a like postponement for one year of all payments on intergovernmental debts owing the important creditor powers.

The statement listed congressmen who had given their approval, explained how the action would help combat the depression, recognized the authority of Congress in this field, and denied that war debts had any relation to reparations, which were repeatedly described as a purely European problem. But despite this elaborate disclaimer, the American government was involved, heavily involved, in the reparations question.[90]

The moratorium proposal had not been adequately discussed with the French. Nevertheless, it did not come any too soon. On June 19 the demand for foreign exchange in Berlin rose again to RM70,000,000. Early on the twentieth, the Reichsbank decided to apply credit restrictions—although the application was later modified because of the news from Washington.[91] With credit restric-

---

[89] Stimson MS. Diary, June 21, 1931; *FRUS, 1931*, I, 32–33, 35–42; Dawes, *Journal as Ambassador,* p. 352; SDP, 462.00R296/3996, 4018: Secretary to London Embassy, June 19, 1931; Chargé in London to Secretary, June 20, 1931; *Chicago Herald and Examiner,* June 23, 1931. Anyone interested in the details concerning the Hindenburg message should also see the unpublished papers of the State Department, esp. 462.00R296/4057, and the German Foreign Ministry records, esp. 1493/D621369, D621373, D621375–6.

[90] *FRUS, 1931*, I, 33–35.

[91] GFMR, 1684/D786782–3: Cabinet Protocol, June 23, 1931.

tions, the German government would have little left to lose, financially, if it sought a Young moratorium at an early date, and such restrictions would intensify the domestic pressure for a moratorium; as already noted, there may in fact have been a promise that credit restrictions would be followed by a moratorium. As we have also seen, the Hoover proposal arrived after the government had already decided to declare a postponement of payments. Hoover's proposal forestalled by only a few days the much-feared German declaration.

The American government has not often attempted to elaborate so rapidly a new program where no policy, or an opposed policy, had existed before. In proposing his moratorium, Hoover was suddenly casting aside the national inhibitions of eleven years and his own settled convictions. He apparently acted because he wished to restore confidence and because he thought inaction would lead to a financial disaster spreading from New York to the whole country. Considering the haste involved, the scope of the new policy, and the rather ambiguous and unacknowledgeable motives behind it, there was probably bound to be difficulty in carrying out Hoover's program. The feature which led to French resistance is fairly obvious: Paris was not consulted, even though its political and financial interest was directly affected. And even in the case of Germany, difficulties arose due to discrepancies between Hoover's and Brüning's aims. Brüning wanted not only to cast off reparations, but also to win a political success. It was German politics, more than the impossibility of paying reparations, that spurred him to pursue his plan of revision via a Young moratorium. While the manipulation of American interest in German finance had, as hoped, brought Hoover onto the scene, his arrival as *deus ex machina* was not appropriate to Teutonic drama, and it did not leave much of a role for the German heroes in their struggle with the dragon, Tribute.

VI

Efforts to Obtain a Quid Pro Quo

PRESIDENT Hoover had feared that the American press and public would be halfhearted about his proposal, but for once in his presidential career, he was to have a pleasant surprise: the American reaction was overwhelmingly in favor of the moratorium. The stock market rose sharply and businessmen, professors, and congressmen issued statements of approval. With the exception of the Hearst papers, almost the entire press came out in support. The *Chicago Tribune*, which did not refrain from comment after all, assessed the proposal as a good one, as long as it was understood that this was not to lead to a debt cancellation. Probably the main reason for the favorable response was that Hoover at last appeared to be taking action against the depression.[1]

EUROPEAN REACTIONS TO THE HOOVER PROPOSAL

Not so surprisingly, the German reaction was also mainly enthusiastic. Only Nazi, Nationalist, and Communist papers were critical, while the Börse gained strength and the loss of foreign exchange declined.[2] The German governmental leaders were sincerely grateful in their conversations with Ambassador Sackett.

---

[1] *FRUS, 1931*, I, 38; *New York Times*, June 21–23, 1931 (reviewed press comment); *Chicago Tribune*, June 22, 1931.

[2] SDP, 462.00R296/4070: Ambassador in Berlin to Secretary, June 24, 1931; *New York Times*, June 21, 23, 1931; *DBFP*, 2/II, Nos. 71, 71 note 1; *SIA, 1931*, p. 74. On June 23, German foreign exchange quotations were the highest since May 26.

Sackett reported: "I saw the Chancellor and explained the purpose that I had in view. He exhibited great appreciation as well as relief from the severe strain as soon as I delivered my message." On Sunday afternoon Sackett went to a luncheon at the Chancellor's residence, in honor of Sir Walter Layton, editor of the *Economist*, and attended by twenty-eight prominent persons in the German government; "The tone of the entire group was most optimistic and eulogistic of President Hoover and congratulatory for themselves." For some weeks, almost every contact between American and German officials was prefaced or concluded by a German statement of thanks. If the German leaders regretted not having a chance to play a more active role, they concealed their regret.[3]

The authorities in London were also very pleased, and readily accepted the proposed moratorium, assuming that what was involved was an over-all postponement of all governmental payments for a year. Although the top British officials had known of the plan, it still seemed amazing to them that it had actually come to life. Sir Robert Vansittart spoke to the Belgian Chargé d'Affaires in London as follows: "For years everybody had been saying that no solution of the tangle was possible because the key was in American hands and the Americans would not move. Now the unexpected had happened and had happened with unhoped-for rapidity. Our general view was that it was up to everybody concerned to collaborate with the utmost goodwill and to put no obstacles in the way of a step which the United States had so often been blamed for not taking." It was evident from Vansittart's statements to the Belgian Chargé and also to the French Ambassador that he saw in Hoover's proposal not just a one-year suspension, but a long-awaited step toward ending reparations and war debts entirely. This was, of course, a major goal of British policy, as expressed in the Balfour Note of 1922.[4]

Some people in the United States and Britain hoped that

---

[3] *FRUS, 1931*, I, 39–40; GFMR, 1493/D621363–4, D621392–3: Leitner to Ministry, June 19, 24, 1931; SDP, 462.00R296/5028: Conversation between Secretary and German Chargé, June 23, 1931. Brüning had probably received the information from his Washington Embassy before Sackett called, but this does not seem to have diminished his enthusiasm.

[4] *DBFP*, 2/II, Nos. 75, 76, 80; *FRUS, 1931*, I, 204–206.

Hoover's action would bring about a new era in international relations, and a return of prosperity. But so much could not be accomplished in one act. The bitterness from the war still remained and the American private loans were still unrecovered. Perhaps the United States could have helped solve the world's problems, but constant participation and an assumption of responsibility would have been necessary. The world had asked for bread and had received the Smoot-Hawley Tariff. Unfortunately, in terms of diplomacy, Hoover's proposal probably did more harm than good: it made the French government feel threatened, overborne, and hence defensive, while Germany was encouraged to refuse any counterconcessions, since they now appeared unnecessary. Unilateral bombshell proposals like Hoover's have perhaps about the same relation to international politics as a new insecticide or epizootic disease has to the balance of natural life.

Some of the first signs of difficulty came from Italy. The usually inspired press reacted by stating that although the Fascist government would be glad to accept the proposal, it had reason to ask Germany in return to give up the customs union, which, while supposedly economic, would actually disturb the European political order. On the morning of June 22, Foreign Minister Dino Grandi told the American Ambassador, John W. Garrett, that Italy was inclined to help Germany, but would not help her to extend her dominion over Austria. In reply, Stimson sent a strongly worded telegram to Garrett, stressing that President Hoover and the congressional leaders who had been consulted would find any introduction of political conditions completely unacceptable, and the Italian Ambassador in Washington also sent his government a warning against trying to impose conditions. Before Stimson's cable reached Rome, Mussolini had already made his official reply, cordially accepting the plan and adding that later on he would convey to the American government some observations "concerning an application at once equitable and practical, as is certainly within the intention of President Hoover, of the happy initiative of the American government." Perhaps these observations were originally intended to concern the customs union, but they were never forwarded, and Stimson's message was also withheld on later instructions. Grandi subsequently told the British Ambassador that "somewhat misleading information" had been given to the Italian press, and he assured Garrett that Italy had in fact made a full and cordial acceptance, not limited by any political reservations. To the German Ambassador, Grandi admitted that, unfortunately, there had been a slip-up, which he blamed on the mistaken guidance his press chief had given the newspapers, and the Italian Foreign Minister denied that the Italian government had ever considered making agreement conditional on a surrender of the customs union. In Berlin, however, the Italian Ambassador disclosed the whole story to Bülow, who was grateful for this indication that the Americans would take a strong line with the French.[5]

It was the French reaction that was not only the most important but also the most hostile. France was the other great creditor, with net receipts for the coming year scheduled at $79,000,000, about the same influx per capita as the American. A telegram from Ambassador von Hoesch of June 24 reported the atmosphere at a British reception, where he spoke to various French politicians and also to Lord Tyrrell:

Total impression was one of extraordinarily great agitation, illhumor, and nervousness. It is hard, unless one lives in this atmosphere, to conceive of the state of mind in which the French political world has been placed by Hoover's initiative. From a practical standpoint, France sees what she regards as her absolutely sacred right to her unconditional reparations claim placed in question. She is indignant that this holy claim should be placed in parallel with American debt collection. She is dumbfounded that the unconditional annuities, supposedly settled beyond question only a year ago, should already be stripped of their special nimbus. In terms of opinion, moreover, France feels the American action to be an unheard-of presumption and an

[5] *Il Giornale d'Italia* (Rome) (Virginio Gayda), June 23, 1931; *FRUS, 1931*, I, 219–225; *DBFP*, 2/II, Nos. 77, 78, 82; Stimson Manuscript Diary (Deposited at Yale University Library), June 23, 1931; GFMR, 913/384330–1; 1555/D666714: Memo by Bülow, June 25, 1931; Schubert to Ministry, July 14, 1931.

unprecedented encroachment on French rights, in which connection the real motive for the American action is assumed to be the pure self-interest of America in saving its large volume of endangered credits in Germany.

Hoesch went on to describe the anger over the lack of prior diplomatic consultation, and the resentment over two American memoranda, which tried to demonstrate that France would profit more by accepting the plan. "Still greater [Hoesch continued] is the bitterness over an ultimatum-like demand from America that the positions of the governments involved will have to be made known within this week, in addition to which a further American pronouncement has come that the American proposal may only be accepted or rejected en bloc, and that no consideration will be given to counterproposals." A French observer told Hoesch that there had not been such excitement in the French Parliament since the Armistice. Hoesch thought it was uncertain whether the French cabinet would survive.[6]

There was reason for French anger. In the first place, the manner of notification was, to say the least, unfortunate. As Ambassador Claudel had correctly reported from his interview on June 18, Stimson had indicated that no action would be taken without the agreement of France. Then, on the very next day, the Ambassador was informed that the American government was going ahead; on the day following that, the final announcement was made. There were rumors in the French press and elsewhere that the Americans had concerted not only with the British but also with the Germans.[7] As a highly interested party to the Young Plan, France strongly resented the lack of genuine consultation with her. She was even more incensed when Washington tried to use threats.

Second, the American proposal was regarded as a danger to the

---

[6] GFMR, 2548/E300081–4. See also SDP, 462.00R296/4068: Ambassador in Paris to Secretary, June 23, 1931 (16 pp.); Walter Edge, *Jerseyman's Journal* (Princeton, 1948), pp. 191–195. It appears from Edge's memoirs that he greatly minimized the actual French reaction in his reports to Washington.

[7] GFMR, 2548/E300060: Hoesch to Ministry, June 23, 1931; *FRUS, 1931,* I, 44.

Young Plan and to the continuation of reparations. Englishmen and Americans might argue that, without Hoover's proposal, reparations would cease temporarily anyhow, but the French kept asking how payments could possibly be resumed at the end of the holiday year. Once reparations were eliminated from the German budget, they said, no German government would ever be in a political position to put them back in again. The Young Plan, the object of years of negotiation, provided for a partial moratorium, with safeguards against any lasting interruption of payments. Why depart from that plan?[8]

In the third place, to get down to tangible matters, the beneficiaries of the Hoover proposal were the German government and American and British private interests. No one benefited in France—neither the government nor private individuals. After the withdrawals following the September 1930 elections, little in the way of French funds was left in Germany, so that there was no such concern over German credit in Paris as there was in New York or London. There was, on the other hand, concern for reparations receipts. While arguing that reparations would stop anyhow, Americans added that the Hoover proposal saved the French from their war debt charges and from their obligation, laid down in the Young Plan for the eventuality of a transfer moratorium on conditional payments, to establish a guarantee fund of $106,000,000. (From this fund the other reparations creditors were supposed to be given advances to tide them over until the conditional payments which were held up could be transferred; the guarantee fund was a compensation to the other creditors for their relatively small share of unconditional payments.) Americans argued that together, the French debts and the guarantee fund amounted to more than twice the French receipts from unconditional reparations—and the Germans might not pay them, either. But the French public had by no means adjusted to the idea that there had to be any loss at all.[9]

[8] SDP, 462.00R296/4207: Ambassador in Paris to Acting Secretary, June 30, 1931; *FRUS, 1931,* I, 56, 90–91, 116–117; *DBFP,* 2/II, Nos. 76, 88, 100, 179.
[9] *FRUS, 1931,* I, 115–117; *DBFP,* 2/II, Nos. 123, 168, 179.

Finally, the French Parliament was in session, and the Center and Right sections of the Chamber of Deputies, where Pierre Laval's cabinet might normally hope to find a majority, were precisely the sections least likely to accept the idea of a moratorium. Briand later told Hoesch that no French cabinet could have survived if it had simply accepted the Hoover moratorium as proposed.[10] Here again, as with the other powers, diplomacy seems to have been subordinate to the domestic position of the government. Behind all these reasons was a feeling that Germany had somehow circumvented the Versailles order and stolen a march on France. If reparations went, what would go next? What check would there be on the potent and populous Reich?

But despite all their objections, the French did not reject the Hoover proposal outright. The French cabinet realized that under this plan France would lose less than with a German Young moratorium, and the Minister of Finance, Pierre-Etienne Flandin, pointed this out in the Chamber of Deputies. More important, France did not wish to be isolated and face the opposition of other powers on this and other issues as well. The Laval Ministry therefore adopted the policy of driving a hard bargain, thereby satisfying (and outlasting) the French Parliament and salvaging as much as possible of the Young Plan. The French reply to Hoover's proposal was handed over to Ambassador Edge on the afternoon of June 24, but Berthelot had mentioned its essential provision to the American Ambassador as early as the twenty-second. This main provision was that Germany should continue to pay the unconditional payments to the Bank for International Settlements (BIS) as she would have under a Young moratorium; France, however, would forego her immediate receipts by placing the amount of the unconditional payments at the disposal of the BIS for reloan in Central Europe.[11] The fact that the Quai d'Orsay was able to develop its plan so rapidly suggests that something similar must have been under consideration beforehand, perhaps for the eventuality of a German moratorium proposal. But this

[10] GFMR, 2548/E300087: Hoesch to Ministry, June 25, 1931.
[11] *FRUS, 1931*, I, 47–49, 58–59, 63–64, 82–83.

reloan scheme had a family relationship with an old French idea: to restrain Germany by placing her under a financial obligation.

The French reloan idea did not, in itself, necessarily involve a major departure from the substance of the Hoover moratorium, for Germany could get back most if not all of the unconditional payments. Although this embellishment proposed by the French spoiled the psychological effect of the Hoover proposal, led to complications with other countries, and annoyed the President, and although MacDonald informed Stimson that he had secretly learned that the French had a more acceptable alternative ready in case this reply was rejected, the American government soon agreed to accept a payment-and-repayment device for the sake of an early agreement.[12] But aside from this token payment of unconditional reparations, there were certain practical ways in which the French proposals would prevent Germany from receiving all the benefits Hoover had intended. Under them:

1) The money advanced back to Germany by the BIS was to be made available to France again at the end of the holiday year, so that Germany would then have to be ready both to repay and to resume normal payments. The French may have calculated that another loan would then be necessary; the negotiations for it would give new opportunities for political pressure on Germany. Their avowed reason, however, was that they might have to make guarantee fund payments under the Young Plan.

2) On the grounds that it was German private credit that was the immediate problem, the reloan was not to go to the German government but to German private interests. The idea here was probably to ensure that the German budget would continue to provide for reparations, with no chance for an increase in arms expenditures.

3) Payments in kind were to continue, being counted as part of the unconditional reparations, but this part was not to be re-

---

[12] *FRUS, 1931*, I, 60–62, 65–69, 74–82; Stimson MS. Diary, July 24, 25, 1931; SDP, 462.00R296/4110: Chargé in London to Secretary and Secretary to Ambassador in Paris, June 25, 1931; 462.00R296/4139: Memo of Paris-Washington telephone conversation, June 26, 1931.

loaned to Germany. The German government would still have been obliged to find money to pay the German producers.

4) The BIS was to make part of the reloan, not to Germany, but to other countries in Central Europe, "and especially those in which the suspension of the Young Plan during one year might create financial or economic disturbance"—that is, to France's Eastern allies, and particularly Yugoslavia, in whose budget reparations played a big role. French influence in the BIS was strong, and might divert a large share of the reloan to Eastern countries which were allies of hers, but enemies of Germany.

5) Precautions were to be taken against the use of the relief afforded for noneconomic purposes (read "arms") or for the financing of dumping operations. This implied that the Germans would be required to give guarantees before the French would assent to Hoover's proposal.[13]

The first four points represented proposals to alter the Hoover plan at the expense of Germany and certainly affected her interests, but France and the United States could if necessary discuss these points without German participation. The Reich had no actual right to the Hoover year, and the creditors, France and the United States, were the powers whose decision was final. But the fifth point, on the use of the Hoover benefits, did require an explicit commitment from Germany, and it was quite conceivable that she might wish to be heard on all these points. Thus, while the French and American governments could if necessary settle most of the questions raised by the French reply between them, the French counterproposals also implied German participation in the negotiations; certainly the French wanted the Germans to participate.

THE FRANCO-AMERICAN NEGOTIATIONS

Having brought itself to the point of sacrificing war debts, and having issued its evangelist message to the world, the United States government was determined to see its proposal succeed. Secretary Mellon arrived in Paris, and he and Ambassador Edge

[13] For the full French proposal: *FRUS, 1931*, I, 62–65 and 70–71.

began ten days of intense and difficult negotiations, trying to get the French to come into line with the spirit of Hoover's proposal before its psychological benefits were lost.[14]

The negotiators on both sides underwent a grueling test: the French ministers were simultaneously sitting through all-night sessions in Parliament, while the Americans, using cables and telephone to communicate across the Atlantic, were working both Washington and Paris hours; those in Washington were also suffering through a non–air-conditioned heat wave. The American government's diplomatic team was formed *ad hoc;* its members, except for Hoover and the aged Mellon, lacked experience in major negotiation with foreign countries, and they had to learn the unfamiliar details of the complicated Young agreements. Every point had to be cleared with Washington, for Hoover kept all decisions in his own hands.

The American reliance on the new transatlantic radio-telephone was more than incidentally important. Voices often faded, and although Hoover recalls that special devices protected the security of the conversations, Sackett, at least, did not regard his conversations as secure.[15] On the other hand, the telephone could be and was used to communicate without leaving an official record, and some things were said that were not meant to be recorded in Washington. It should also be noted that telephone conversations did not give the participants time to grasp each other's ideas and to clearly formulate their own. Significantly, Hoover's use of the phone for diplomacy in June and July 1931 has not been imitated since on the same scale, although this has been partly because the development of air travel has made it unnecessary to rely on the persons who happen to be on the spot.

[14] These negotiations are covered in *FRUS, 1931,* I, 42–162.

[15] Herbert Hoover, *The Memoirs of Herbert Hoover* (3 vols., New York, 1951–2), III, 71; *FRUS, 1931,* I, 111–112: see footnote 34 below. But State Department ciphers were not secure, either: see Herbert O. Yardley, *The American Black Chamber* (New York, 1931), pp. 351–367, 373. German and British diplomats called the attention of their governments to the unorthodox communications being used (*DBFP,* 2/II, No. 109, note italics; GFMR, 2548/E300159: Leitner to Ministry, June 29, 1931).

The main stages of Franco-American negotiation were:

1) June 24–June 27: The United States accepted the device of having Germany technically pay unconditional reparations while receiving all or most of them back as a reloan.

2) June 28–July 2: After some delay, while the French government wound up its parliamentary session, the negotiators reached agreement on the length of time for the repayment of the sums due from Germany (both conditional and unconditional). They also agreed that France's Eastern allies would be offered a loan, rather than part of the German unconditional payment. And the question of the guarantee fund was left to be settled between France and the European powers benefiting from the fund; in practice, this settled the question in the way the French desired, since once the rest of the arrangements had gone into operation, it was too late for effective protest on this point.

3) July 3–July 6: There followed a debate on whether or not reparations in kind should be disposed of in accordance with the spirit of Hoover's plan. Final agreement was reached on terms drafted by the French, which appeared to meet the American requirement of suspending intergovernmental payments. The Hoover moratorium went into effect.

If we consider the discussions (as the French did) as bargaining between two powers, each holding good cards and very different views, the negotiations went very rapidly. If we consider the discussions (as the Americans did) as arrangements for accepting a new political gospel, they dragged interminably. The weakness in the American position was the need for a speedy decision on something resembling the original offer, before financial panic returned. Washington repeatedly considered the idea of a different approach, that of making arrangements with each of the powers separately, but never adopted it, probably because of the risk involved and the likelihood of further delay. Moreover, Mellon told Premier Laval that this move was being considered. Such action would presumably have hit the French at their own weak point, their fear of being utterly isolated; yet agreement was reached only after Washington made it quite clear that all threat of separate arrangements was being dropped. This suggests that one of the biggest obstacles to agreement was the French feeling that they were being presented with a series of ultimatums. Hoesch's comments on the Paris atmosphere lend support to this conclusion. Hoover and Ogden Mills seemed at times to forget the difference between firmness and dictation, and did not always recognize the genuine importance of national pride—or "face"—in international relations. France had not sent Germany a threat over the customs union; she did not intend to submit to one herself. Considering the chasm that separated the American and French outlooks, it is amazing that agreement was reached on July 6.

When agreement was finally reached, Mills, Castle, and Herbert Feis, the Economic Adviser to the State Department, are said to have made a congratulatory call at the French Embassy, on whose extraterritorial precincts Ambassador Claudel ordered a bottle of champagne and proposed the following prophetic toast: "To the crisis we have just avoided and to the catastrophe which will follow." And in fact, the German financial crisis, which had been reversed for a few days, was by this time returning with renewed vigor. On June 25, the Bank of England, the Bank of France, the New York Federal Reserve Bank, and the Bank for International Settlements had united in extending rediscount credits of RM400,000,000; this type of international assistance was customarily given when central banks were in difficulties. But by June 30, RM280,000,000 of the credit were reportedly gone. According to another source, foreign withdrawals of funds began again on July 1.[16] It was clear all along that unless the powers promptly accepted the Hoover plan, the financial crisis would return more violently than before. Yet in spite of this danger, the German government displayed an astonishing *sang froid* during the Paris negotiations; American resentment over this seeming unwillingness to make a "positive contribution" to the success of the Hoover proposal almost equalled French resentment over Germany's

---

[16] Drew Pearson and Constantine Brown, *The American Diplomatic Game* (Garden City, N.Y., 1935), p. 232; *New York Times*, June 26, July 2, 1931; *SIA, 1931*, p. 78.

escape from reparations. Despite Hoover's reservations, the permanent modification of reparations was now almost a foregone conclusion. But it was not so certain that Germany could succeed in evading any contributions or concessions in return. This question absorbed much of the energy of German diplomacy for the rest of the summer; although the sacrifice of the customs union was finally necessary, the revision movement remained unchecked.

Proposals for a French "Chequers"

France was the first to try to extract counterconcessions from Germany, partly with an eye to public opinion, but not, in the last analysis, with a view merely to scoring points. Berthelot had told Hoesch back on February 23 that what was really wanted was to reach a comprehensive Franco-German agreement. Premier Pierre Laval, who now began to replace Briand as the director of French foreign affairs, seems to have been confident that he could achieve results in direct Franco-German discussions; indeed, he apparently never lost this belief.[17] Naturally, France wanted an agreement that would buttress the *status quo*. This would, of course, require a reversal in the whole German position, and it was to the end of reversing Germany policy that schemes such as François-Poncet's cartel proposals were directed. It was with this same purpose in mind that the French leaders now began to think of exploiting their bargaining position in a direct meeting with Brüning and Curtius.

Before Hoover announced his plan, the German leaders had been very interested in the idea of a "Chequers" with the French; apparently they wanted to work out the problems involved in a Young moratorium, such as the question of the authority of the Special Advisory Committee. At Chequers itself, Brüning related that Briand had made and then withdrawn a proposal for a meeting in early May. In a letter of June 9, Bülow asked Hoesch to consider the possibility of a high-level Franco-German meeting on

[17] GFMR, 1554/D666473–4: Hoesch to Ministry, Feb. 23, 1931; André François-Poncet, *Souvenirs d'une ambassade à Berlin* (Paris, 1946), pp. 20–21, 25.

neutral territory, and told him not to discourage any French proposals on these lines, no matter on what level they might be made. When Curtius told Hoesch on June 13 to declare that a moratorium was impending, he also instructed the Ambassador to say that he and Brüning were ready for the same type of discussion "with other creditor governments" as had been held at Chequers. A few days later, Ritter complained to a British diplomat that no invitation for discussion had come from France. Then, on June 19, hearing of an unofficial inquiry, supposedly originating with Laval, as to whether the German leaders would attend a French "Chequers," Berlin sent word that such an invitation would be immediately and gladly accepted. It turned out, however, that this feeler had not actually originated with the French Premier; Laval expressed interest when he heard the German response, but failed to suggest a meeting.[18]

The Hoover moratorium, however, changed the situation. After the American proposal was made, the Germans had no further interest in a Young moratorium, while the French, for their part, now discovered that they had something to bargain with, that is, their own assent to Hoover's plan. Now it was the French who became the more interested in a conference, with the Germans much less so than before.

As early as June 22 an unofficial emissary, the Paris representative of Lee, Higginson and Company, arrived in Berlin with a message alleged to be from two highly placed Frenchmen, René Massigli and Emile Moreau, asking Chancellor Brüning to recognize publicly the French point of view, and to declare his desire to come to Paris.[19] This request may have helped to induce Brün-

---

[18] *DBFP*, 2/II, Nos. 51, 60; GFMR, 2385/E199485-8, 2548/E300015-23, E300059; 1657/D729196-7: Letter, Bülow to Hoesch, June 9, 1931; Curtius to Hoesch, June 13, 1931; Memo by Planck, June 19, 1931; Memo of telephone conversation with Hoesch, June 23, 1931. Brüning told the author in 1951 that in June a meeting with Laval had fallen through, after the Germans had already arranged for their special train; perhaps this June 19 inquiry was the occasion.

[19] GFMR, 1659/D729164-74: Curtius to Hoesch, June 22, 1931; Courtney notes.

ing to express, in a radio address on June 23, his readiness to engage in "straightforward discussion" with the French government. In his broadcast, the Chancellor described the German financial difficulties and explained to his German listeners why the Hoover proposal did not permit any softening of the austerities of the new emergency decree. Then, after asking for moderation in all German utterances, Brüning proceeded to stress the importance of Franco-German relations, proposing that the two countries overcome the past and turn to the future:

> The German Government for its part will not spare good will. When once agreement has been reached regarding the holiday year, all the more easily will it be possible to pave the way for peaceful collaboration of both countries by means of a straightforward discussion. I would welcome it if an opportunity presented itself for such a preliminary discussion, as the recent meeting in Chequers paved the way for a discussion between Germany and England. The tasks confronting Germany and France are too big and too urgent for both countries that it should not be possible to find a common ground, in confidential and unreserved exchange of views, from which the solution of these tasks could be attacked with prospects of success.[20]

Presumably Brüning meant that he would welcome a French "Chequers" *after* the French had accepted the Hoover moratorium, but in Paris his words had the effect of encouraging hopes for a meeting *before* France came to terms with the Americans. On the evening of June 23, Hoesch, with the approval of Brüning and Curtius, had cautioned Briand that it would not be safe for the German leaders to leave their posts in Berlin until the final acceptance of the Hoover moratorium, and also that settlement of the question seemed necessary for the creation of a proper atmosphere. On the twenty-fifth, after the broadcast, and after the French had sent their reply to Hoover, Briand had another long talk with Hoesch, but the Ambassador repeated that although Brüning had indicated the basic German willingness for a meeting,

---

[20] *FRUS, 1931*, I, 51–54. The original German is also not completely clear as to the necessity of Franco-American agreement before the "preliminary discussion."

it could not take place "until the completion of the Hoover arrangements had brought the necessary calm and stability to German affairs." In spite of his own arguments for an early meeting, Briand realized that the Germans were in a strong position, and at one point he candidly admitted to Hoesch that the German position "was indeed so good tactically that he also could only advise [them] to remain passive." [21]

Some American officials also hoped at first that the Germans would come to Paris. On June 26, the reparations expert at the United States Embassy in Paris gave a member of the German Embassy staff his personal advice that the Germans should participate in the negotiations, and drew such a somber picture of the chances for a complete Hoover moratorium that Hoesch now telephoned Berlin for instructions. Should Germany (Hoesch asked) enter the negotiations at this point, or only when a Franco-American agreement had been reached? [22]

Berlin's answer has not come to light, but evidently Hoesch was told to stand pat. On the next evening, Laval, Briand, and François-Poncet made another, more serious attempt to move the Germans from their position. The French were so confident that a group of reporters was assembled outside the room to receive the announcement of the visit. To Hoesch, Laval argued that his cabinet's precarious political position could only be saved if the German ministers came to Paris as quickly as possible. In reply to Hoesch's question as to what was so urgently in need of negotiation, Laval referred to a passage in the French reply to the United States which asked for assurances that the sums made available to Germany would only be used for economic purposes, with dumping excluded. Briand suggested that the Germans might refrain from building the second pocket battleship, Cruiser B, in which case the French would not construct a 23,000-ton warship they

---

[21] GFMR, 2548/E300058, E300086–92: Hoesch to Ministry, June 23, 25, 1931.

[22] *FRUS, 1931*, I, 49–50, 60; Stimson MS. Diary, June 25, 1931; SDP, 462.00R296/5030, 4206: Memo of conversation between Acting Secretary and German Chargé, June 26, 1931; Secretary to Acting Secretary, June 30, 1931 (radiogram); GFMR, 2548/E300120–1: Memo by Bülow, June 26, 1931.

were planning to build, and Laval finally mentioned the customs union cautiously and fleetingly, "which," Hoesch reported, "I excluded with a wave of the hand." Hoesch explained that Brüning had wanted a visit like Chequers, a discussion between equals of current problems, but the German ministers would not come at a time when, because the Hoover moratorium problem was still unsettled, their position would be prejudiced and they might be asked to make political concessions. Hoesch added that the French should also realize that the Germans themselves would have many demands to make, and that it would be necessary to work out the agenda carefully beforehand. Laval dropped the idea of an immediate visit, and suggested that he might negotiate with Hoesch himself. Again Hoesch asked what they would negotiate, and again the French expressed their ideas. The Ambassador finally said, speaking personally, that he thought it possible that Germany might give an assurance that the sums saved by the Hoover plan would only be used for economic purposes; he knew of no German dumping activities. This seemed to the French to offer a possible way out, but there still remained the problem of what to tell the waiting reporters. Laval wished to announce that an invitation had been formally issued, but he was dissuaded by Hoesch's suggestion that there might be an embarrassing delay in fixing the date.[23]

For practical purposes, this meeting settled the question of a visit before a French acceptance: the Germans were not coming. But it did not seem to rule out the possibility of a German political concession. Hoesch himself had suggested the possibility of one German contribution, an assurance that the benefits of the Hoover plan would only be used for economic ends—that is, not for armaments. After much difficulty, such a declaration was later published, but it was obtained by the United States, not by France.

Proposals for "Voluntary Contributions"

On June 27, a few hours before the French effort to bring the Germans to Paris failed, Arthur Henderson took up the idea of

[23] GFMR, 2548/E300104-9: Hoesch to Ministry, June 27, 1931; SDP, 462.00R296/4177: Ambassador in Paris to Acting Secretary, June 28, 1931.

seeking concessions, of a voluntary nature, from Berlin. Brüning's radio speech had been a gesture of sorts, but it had not really offered anything tangible. Henderson appears to have been inspired in part by a suggestion from Dino Grandi that, while Italy was not trying to impose conditions, Hoover's offer had so strengthened the Germans that it would be a graceful act on Germany's part to proceed no further with the customs union project. No doubt another consideration in Henderson's mind was the hope that Germany, by making a concession, might induce a less intransigent state of mind in Paris, hastening French acceptance of the American moratorium proposal. Finally, as when he proposed the Chequers meeting, Henderson wished to bring about a general calming of the European scene, this time by eliminating two of the problems that had tended to keep the powers at loggerheads. Perhaps, since America had set an example, other countries might be swept along in a tide of generosity.[24]

The British Foreign Secretary sent a cable to Sir Ronald Lindsay in Washington, referring to the Italian views and suggesting that while Britain, like America, opposed the political exploitation of the Hoover proposal, feeling was growing that Germany was receiving all and giving nothing. In return for what she was gaining by the moratorium, Germany might voluntarily "contribute something to [the] restoration of international confidence." Possible German contributions included cutting the swollen military budget, which might well include an end to pocket battleship construction, and dropping the customs union. In regard to the second, "His Majesty's Government have adopted an impartial attitude," but Germany might give up the project without a humiliating renunciation "as a token of the immense service which Mr. Hoover has rendered her, and of her desire to collaborate in and carry forward the gesture of appeasement." And he also asked that there should be no reduction in the total financial yield of the recent emergency decree.[25]

Secretary Stimson had by this time departed for Italy, but on June 27 Ambassador Lindsay presented Henderson's message to

[24] *DBFP*, 2/II, Nos. 82, 118.
[25] *DBFP*, 2/II, No. 87.

the Acting Secretary of State, William R. Castle, and asked if the American government would be willing to take steps to help gain concessions. But Hoover and Castle were afraid that any American political action would cause Congress to refuse to approve the moratorium, and at first Castle could only agree to instruct Sackett "not to discourage any action" the Germans "might wish to take." [26] This was certainly being optimistic; the Germans hoped that the French would accept the Hoover plan, but they had little faith in the influence of generous gestures,[27] and the Brüning government, which was trying to solve its domestic problems by winning diplomatic successes, was hardly ready to volunteer a concession, least of all on a question (like naval construction) of interest to Hindenburg and the Reichswehr.

After a little reflection, Hoover and Castle had second thoughts. After all, they were anxious to get a French acceptance, and Congress need not be told every detail of what went on. So on the following day Castle informed Sackett by telephone that "so far as the new German battleship was concerned, we did not really consider that a political question"; it belonged in the realm of disarmament, which apparently was not, to Castle, a political matter. Sackett was to emphasize to Brüning "that it would be disastrous if the Americans should get the idea that with the money we gave up Germany was increasing its armament," and Castle himself spoke to the German Chargé in this sense.[28] Thus the American administration was advancing rapidly from moral exhortation into power politics.

Various diplomatic approaches followed on June 30, but without much promise of success. Henderson spoke to Neurath about the desirability of abandoning plans for the customs union, delaying cruiser construction, and discouraging Stahlhelm demonstra-

---

[26] *DBFP*, 2/II, No. 89; *FRUS, 1931*, I, 84–85.

[27] Brüning's attitude is illustrated by his statement to the author, in criticizing Curtius for joining Austria in surrendering the customs union in September, that in politics one should always get something in return when giving something up.

[28] *FRUS, 1931*, I, 97–98; GFMR, 2548/E300159–60: Leitner to Ministry, June 29, 1931.

tions, but Neurath did not take him very seriously, reporting, "In general, he was all the old Party Secretary." On instructions from London, the British Chargé in Berlin, Basil Newton, raised the question of the customs union, but Curtius declined to make any comment, while managing to indicate that any comment he might have made would have been unfavorable. Sackett observed to Castle that the British suggestion had been so weak that the Germans had simply brushed it aside, but the American Ambassador did not really earn any laurels, either. According to the German record, it was Brüning who raised the question of political concessions with Sackett, and the Ambassador answered that he didn't know about the customs union, but only about the cruiser, which his government hoped would be dropped. Curtius told Sackett that, for three reasons, cruiser construction could not be curtailed: the existing ships were so old that their replacement was unavoidable; the German government could accept no reduction below the meager navy allowed by Versailles; and any such reduction would cause President von Hindenburg to resign, as he took a deep personal interest in the battleship question.[29]

Castle was indignant at this response, particularly regarding Hindenburg. On July 1, Ambassador Lindsay reported:

United States Ambassador in Berlin spoke to Minister for Foreign Affairs about German battleship and was told it was particularly difficult to postpone its construction because aged Reichspräsident had it very much at heart. This made Acting Secretary very angry, and he sent some very stiff instructions to United States Ambassador *by telephone* to put pressure on the German Government, who must understand that they cannot possibly expect to receive all benefits of the President's scheme without contributing towards securing its accomplishment.[30]

The Acting Secretary also sent a cable on July 1, addressed to

[29] GFMR, 1660/D729396; 2548/E300143, E300162–7: Memo by [Curtius], July 1, 1931; Neurath to Ministry, June 30, 1931; Memo by Bülow, July 1, 1931; *DBFP*, 2/II, Nos. 93, 98, 105, 106; *FRUS, 1931*, I, 110, 111; SDP, 462.00R296/4207: Ambassador in Paris to Acting Secretary, June 30, 1931.
[30] *DBFP*, 2/II, No. 109. Italics in text.

Ambassador Sackett personally, stating that the feelings of an individual (Hindenburg was not mentioned by name) should not be brought in as an argument for a decision; he was sure that "the individual in question" was too patriotic not to act for the clear benefit of his country. Castle stated that he wanted Sackett to raise the question again as vigorously as he could, as a German statement might be decisive for success or failure. But Castle also took pains to write on the cable form, "No distribution"; he did not want any word of his message to leak out in Washington.[31]

Even aside from the question of political gestures, Stimson and Castle were dissatisfied with Berlin's demeanor, owing to their impression that the Germans were contributing little but criticism to the Franco-American negotiations. In a wireless message to Stimson's ship on June 27, Castle reported that Brüning had found any reloan to French allies unacceptable, had rejected the idea of paying marks to the Bank for International Settlements, and had felt it politically impossible to make any reaffirmation of the Young Plan. Thus the German position, as Castle understood it, was highly negative. In reply, Stimson suggested telling Sackett that Brüning's remarks were not helpful, and that Brüning should be warned lest the responsibility for nonacceptance shift from the French to him. In noting Castle's and Stimson's impatience, we must bear in mind that the Franco-American negotiations were progressing very slowly, at least from the American point of view; on June 29 the two sides were still far from agreement, particularly on the method of repayment and on the related question of the French obligation to put up a guarantee fund. It was still not settled that all the reloan should go to Germany or to the Reichsbahn rather than to truly private interests.[32] There was no

---

[31] SDP, 462.00R296/4360A: Acting Secretary to Ambassador in Berlin, July 1, 1931.

[32] *FRUS, 1931*, I, 83, 105–108; SDP, 462.00R296/4174: Secretary to Acting Secretary, June 28, 1931. The Reichsbahn, or German railway system, had been converted into a private corporation as part of the Dawes Plan payment system. But it worked hand in glove with the government, which appointed the directors, and when the Franco-American compromise went into operation, the German government actually paid the unconditional reparations directly to the Reichsbahn rather than to the BIS; in effect, the government paid the money to itself.

Franco-American meeting on the thirtieth because the French cabinet was involved in winding up the session of the French Parliament; and it was on this day of suspense that the Germans disclosed their objections to renouncing the cruiser.

BERLIN AND THE PARIS NEGOTIATIONS

While taking no official responsibility in the Paris negotiations, the German government followed closely what was going on, and the German and American reparations experts in Paris constantly compared notes. Thus Germany could attempt to adapt her policy to the state of the Franco-American bargaining. In response to urging from Paris and Berlin, Brüning did suggest on June 30 that ordinary unsecured bonds, repayable from 1933 to 1958, might be issued for the direct payment of the unconditional annuity. This would, he told Sackett, make a repayment scheme unnecessary, and the bonds would give France something "in hand," which she could use to meet her obligation under the guarantee fund.[33] This German bond plan was never considered in Paris, where the negotiators had already agreed on the French payment-and-re-payment principle; it did, however, represent an offer of sorts.

After Brüning had described this plan to Sackett, the Ambassador asked, on instruction, what the German government would do if the Paris negotiations broke down. Brüning answered that Germany would announce the following day her intention of declaring a moratorium, effective July 14. She would try to pay the monthly installment of the unconditional payment due July 15, and later unconditional payments, but it was doubtful whether it would be possible to raise the money or the foreign exchange in time.[34] Such a declaration would have gone beyond the Young moratorium that had been planned up until June 20, as there would

---

[33] GFMR, 2548/E300165-6: Memo by Bülow, July 1, 1931; *FRUS, 1931*, I, 111–112; SDP, 462.00R296/4178: Ambassador in Berlin to Acting Secretary, June 27, 1931.

[34] *FRUS, 1931*, I, 112. Sackett sent this information in a cable, "as I do not think it should be sent on the telephone." Washington informed Mellon and Edge as early as June 27 that this would probably be the German response (*FRUS, 1931*, I, 90), and a member of the German Embassy had predicted it to the Americans on June 29 (GFMR, 2548/E300130-1).

have been no three-month delay, and as there apparently would have been a suspension of payment, not just of transfer, on conditional reparations. Only the payment of unconditional reparations would distinguish such action from plain default, and the unconditional payments might also be dropped in the end. Brüning was not merely uttering a threat; by this time, it really would have been impossible to continue conditional payments, for political and also for financial reasons. At the same time, Brüning no doubt hoped that his statement would hasten a Franco-American agreement. Indeed, the German idea of the way to put the Hoover moratorium across was more along the lines Luther had recommended to Sackett on June 28: the Reichsbank President had held that, from his experience with the French, an absolutely firm stand by the United States for total suspension of payments would be effective.[35]

The Germans soon had another reason for standing firm: they found out that a failure of the Paris negotiations would probably not entail the loss of the Hoover benefits. Early on July 1, their Chargé in Washington reported that Hoover was considering repeating his offer separately to each of the countries involved. If this had been done, the French would have had to choose between either accepting or being liable for their war debts without receiving reparations. Furthermore, the United States reportedly intended to lend the war debt payments she received from France to the German government. As the Germans would, at the most, pay no more than the unconditional payments, and as France would be obliged to pay the guarantee fund, intransigence on the part of the French would leave them with a financial loss. Even more serious for France, she would also be isolated politically. But Germany would not have considered this eventuality too tragic.[36]

[35] SDP, 462.00R296/4186: Ambassador in Berlin to Acting Secretary, June 28, 1931. Luther backed down a little when Sackett asked him if he would, as President of the Reichsbank, advise such a stand and take the consequences if the French refused to yield.

[36] GFMR, 2548/E300169: Leitner to Ministry, July 1, 1931 (received 9:55 A.M.). Mills had described the plan in a talk to the Overseas Writers'

This plan for repeating the proposal to each power separately had been outlined to Ambassador Claudel in Washington as early as June 27. When, on the twenty-ninth, Laval asked flatly what would happen if France could not accept the Hoover moratorium, Mellon replied by describing the new plan to him "as a frank answer to Laval's question and not in the nature of a threat." On June 30, Castle, in a telephone call, described the plan to Sackett and told him that Hoover wished to get Germany's reaction to it. Sackett was enough of a bargainer to ignore Hoover's wish and hold his tongue, but in Washington, Ogden Mills told newspapermen about the proposed new approach, and on July 1 the story began to appear in the press, notably in the London *Daily Herald*. This led Sackett to complain that his efforts to obtain a concession on naval construction were being undercut, and he asked to be informed before the proposal was communicated to governments other than the French.[37]

But Edge and Mellon were already informing Hoesch; in fact, they made two statements of some importance to the German government. In the first place, having received warnings from Castle against any French attempt to extract concessions, they told Hoesch that America had no interest in the political aims of France, and that they had little hope that any positive results would ensue from a new public declaration by the German government, in view of the lack of French response to Brüning's

---

Club on June 30; naturally as a result there were also press reports. France could of course have defaulted, as she did in 1932. But as Edouard Herriot pointed out then, default was a dubious policy for a country whose whole position depended on the sanctity of contracts.

[37] *FRUS, 1931*, I, 109, 112; GFMR, 2548/E300169–77: Leitner to Ministry, July 1, 1931 (two cables); SDP, 462.00R296/4219: Ambassador in Berlin to Acting Secretary, July 1, 1931; *Daily Herald* (London), July 1, 1931. The timing of the *Herald*'s story (reprinted in a Berlin newspaper by noon) and its content suggest that it did not stem from Mills's statements the night before, but from British official inspiration; Lindsay had been told of the idea on June 29 (*DBFP*, 2/II, No. 95). The *Herald* appeared to be a vehicle for inspired stories on other occasions as well. Castle informed Sackett that no suggestions of the new plan had been made to Italy, England, or Germany (which was formally true), and Sackett was told that he should issue a *démenti* (SDP, 462.00R296/4219: July 1, 1931).

radio speech. In the second place, Mellon and Edge expressed their fear that, in response to a new American memorandum, the French would simply shrug their shoulders and say that they could not depart from their previous position. These garrulous Americans went on to tell Hoesch that, if negotiations were broken off, the plan would still be offered to other countries, leaving France out, although there was much reluctance to isolate France. Thus the Germans were discouraged from offering any new declaration, and the reports of the idea of reoffering the plan to individual countries were confirmed—excepting that France might not even receive another invitation.[38]

To sum up, Castle had now reached a state of exasperation in which his first suggestions that Sackett recommend gestures were turning into orders that Sackett obtain concessions. But the German government, which in any case could no longer pay reparations in full, had no intention of offering any gesture of appeasement, not believing in the efficacy of such action, and probably not daring to consider it. Besides, the Berlin government now learned that there was no American interest in the French political aims; Mellon and Edge failed even to respond when Hoesch mentioned the rumors of disarmament proposals.[39] Finally, it appeared that if the Paris negotiations fell through, Germany would still receive the benefits of the Hoover proposal, as the offer would be repeated individually and separately to each power, and, if France were still adamant, her debt payments would probably be lent to Germany. All in all, there was little chance of a German contribution.

BRÜNING'S SECRET CONCESSION

The French, as we have seen, were trying to induce the Germans to give up Cruiser B, the second pocket battleship, by offering to forego the construction of a 23,000-ton ship themselves. This offer was perhaps not all it appeared to be, since the plan to build this

---

[38] GFMR, 2548/E300180–1, E300186–7: Memos by [Bülow] and Curtius, July 1, 1931; *FRUS, 1931*, I, 93–94, 97.
[39] GFMR, 2548/E300187: Memo by Curtius, July 1, 1931.

French ship had only been announced in May, and since it was doubtful that the French Parliament, which was currently debating the question, would ultimately vote funds for its construction. The construction of Cruiser B, on the other hand, had already begun. But although Hoesch did not warm to the French suggestion, which Briand made to him on June 27 and again on June 29, Laval told Mellon and Edge that the offer would be aired in the French Senate. This last information was cabled from Paris to Washington and from there on to Sackett in the vague form that Germany should "halt its construction of ships of the *Deutschland* type," with no specific reference to Cruiser B. Castle's relay of the message to Sackett ended, "I trust that for their part the German Government will deem it possible to answer [the French] by renouncing such construction"; this sounded like merely a pious hope. Yet, according to the German record, when Sackett repeated the French proposal in Berlin on July 1, he asked specifically that Germany give up Cruiser B.[40] Evidently he was getting other, more detailed instructions, probably by telephone.

By July 2 Sackett had had time to assimilate Castle's telephone and cable messages ordering him to raise the question of naval construction as vigorously as he could. The Ambassador saw Curtius in the morning and Brüning in the evening in what were the crucial German-American meetings on the subject of the pocket battleships. In the case of the conversation with Curtius, the German record shows that Sackett argued again, with more determination than before, that the construction of the second pocket battleship, Crusier B, should be stopped. To show the need for some such gesture, he described the delicate state of the Paris negotiations. When Curtius said that there would be extraordinary difficulties in halting work on the second cruiser, Sackett interrupted to say, probably with Hindenburg in mind, that difficulties could easily be overcome when it was "a question of higher political goals." Curtius protested that he was just in the process of explaining the political difficulties: there was Hinden-

[40] GFMR, 2548/E300137, E300178: Hoesch to Ministry, June 29, 1931; Memo by [Bülow], July 1, 1931; *FRUS, 1931,* I, 108–109, 111.

burg's attitude, there was the internal political fight which had taken place earlier over the ship, and above all, there was the disillusion which the army and navy would feel. Replacement construction was urgently needed in order, within the limits of Versailles, to make "our little fleet" capable of defense. It would be insupportable for the navy to reduce even below the Versailles limits, and it was very hard to understand such a proposal, coming as it did before the Disarmament Conference. Sackett seemed to be impressed by these arguments, but insisted again on the importance of the "great goal," hoping that Hindenburg could make the sacrifice. And Sackett added that the British government supported the American views.[41]

When Sackett saw Brüning and Bülow in the evening, the Chancellor began with a justification (which Sackett reported at length) of his reluctance to make the desired gestures. First, Brüning described the seriousness of the financial conditions in Germany, informing Sackett of the impending bankruptcies of the Nordwolle firm of Bremen and of the Darmstädter und Nationalbank. Then he went on to point out the internal dangers that would result from these catastrophies, stating frankly that he had to rely on the army, which might have to be called on in a matter of days. Brüning then argued the impossibility of offending public and military opinion at this juncture:

> Brüning was convinced that any public statement made by the Government which implied any renunciation of the meager rights granted by the Treaty of Versailles to Germany to build cruisers as replacements for the over-age ships which are now part of the German Navy, would have so great a "symbolic" meaning for the German nation that it would revive all the antagonisms and passions which had been allayed with some difficulty last spring at the time of the Reichstag debates on the subject. Even though this is principally a naval question, the younger army officers in particular would view this as so great a renunciation of the interests of the armed forces of Germany that the loyalty of the army would be heavily jeopardized. Brüning feels that notwithstanding the desperate financial condition

[41] GFMR, 2548/E300220–2: Memo by Curtius, July 3, 1931.

of the country it is his obligation to safeguard the one arm of defense that is available for his use in controlling imminent disturbances, and that he has neither the strength nor the ability to risk sacrificing that protection—an eventuality which he knows, from his acquaintance with the serious internal political situation, would result if he issued a statement such as you feel should be made.

Brüning added that he was sure Hindenburg also believed that the armed forces were the sole support of the state in the circumstances, but Sackett, perhaps to avoid another flare-up from Castle, did not report this.[42]

Nowhere in Sackett's cabled report did he mention exactly what he had asked the Germans to renounce. According to Bülow's record, however, he was quite specific. He repeated the full request he had stated in the morning: "Naturally [Sackett reportedly said] Cruiser A, now launched, might be completed, but the construction of Cruiser B should be stopped during the holiday year, and an assurance given that there would be no increase in the army budget." [43] Brüning's recorded reply was that it was impossible to stop work at Kiel on Cruiser B during the holiday year. "The only concession that he might make might be that Cruiser C should not be started according to plan, and money should not be laid aside for it in the budget." Bülow says that Sackett thought a confidential declaration on this, together with a public declaration that there would be no budget increase, might perhaps satisfy his government. "It was agreed that a statement from the Chancellor would be sent to Washington that night, but no arrangements were made for its publication and the Chancellor expressly forbade any publication of the renunciation of the construction of Cruiser C." [44]

According to the German record, then, Brüning refused to surrender Cruiser B, but he did privately concede that Cruiser C would not be started. It is not hard to guess the explanation for

[42] *FRUS, 1931*, I, 130–131; GFMR, 2548/E300195: Memo by Bülow, July 2, 1931.

[43] GFMR, 2548/E300196.

[44] GFMR, 2548/E300196–7: Memo by Bülow, July 2, 1931. The substance of this was sent to the Washington Embassy (GFMR, 1555/D666682).

the difference in Brüning's positions on the two cruisers. If work ceased at Kiel on Cruiser B, it could not remain a secret very long. On the other hand, Cruiser C had not yet been voted, the Reichstag would not meet for several months, and when it met, it would be easy to avoid bringing the third cruiser to a vote. The gesture confirms that Brüning was ready to make private concessions, but would not make any public renunciation, or offer any private assurance that might become public knowledge. Of course, aside from the publicity problem, a promise not to proceed with a third ship which had not even been voted (and would in fact be difficult to get voted) was easier to make than an offer to halt work on a second ship already on the ways.

Sackett's cable said nothing of the specific concessions which had been discussed, and it made no reference to the private assurance that the third ship would not be undertaken. The cable only reported, as the fruit of Sackett's representations: "Brüning tells me that it is not at all his intention to use any of the money which accrues to Germany as a result of the moratorium year for increasing the annual military and naval appropriations over and above the appropriations which have already been made for this year."

Two hours after this interview, Sackett cabled the following draft statement, which Bülow had brought to him from Brüning:

"In view of the fears which have sprung up in some circles that the amounts released in the German budget by the relief from reparation payments might be used to increase armaments, I declare that an increase in the appropriation for the army and navy during the holiday year has never been contemplated nor will it take place. The aggregate alleviations accruing to Germany from the Hoover Plan are required and will be used in their entirety to cover the deficits in revenue which are to be expected, to consolidate financial conditions, and to save German economic life."

And Sackett described the German reluctance to have this statement appear, saying, "It seems to me that this view, along with the nature of the statement itself, brings out sharply the state of mind of the Government and the Chancellor and their extreme hesitation about taking the step which you have requested. In consideration of all the above circumstances may I have your instructions?" Certainly Brüning could not have asked for a more sympathetic exposition of his point of view than that given by the American Ambassador; without openly saying so, Sackett evidently agreed that it was necessary to let Brüning have his way, in order to avoid his overthrow by the radical opposition.[45]

There is a striking contrast between the German records of these discussions and what is contained in the State Department files. Sackett, in his cables, referred only in the vaguest terms to what he was asking the Germans to concede; he did not even specify which battleships were discussed. That specific ships *were* discussed is shown not only by the German records, but also by a report from Newton to London. And the British and German documents indicate that there were many telephone conversations between Castle and Sackett which went unrecorded, or whose records were never logged into the State Department files. The American policy of relatively early documentary publication and public access to the archives may have the drawback of increasing the temptation to keep sensitive documents out of the general archives. But in the case of Sackett and Castle, the main reason for concealment was no doubt the fear that, as Castle put it, "Congress might not support the President if they felt that this [Hoover's] plan was being used to bring political pressure to bear." All the discussion of Cruiser B and Cruiser C would have caused a volcanic eruption had it reached the ears of Senator William E. Borah, Chairman of the Senate Foreign Relations Committee. Castle apparently did not trust the discretion of the State Department staff.[46]

---

[45] *FRUS, 1931*, I, 131–132.

[46] A fuller discussion of these conversations is contained in the author's unpublished dissertation (Harvard, 1960), "The Diplomacy of the Financial Crisis: The Relations of Germany with the Western Powers, September 1930–September 1931," pp. 298–311. Newton's and Lindsay's reports (*DBFP*, 2/II, Nos. 109, 120) are especially to be noted. For references to concern over congressional reaction, see esp. SDP, 462.00R296/4139, 5034: Memos of telephone conversations with Paris and Berlin Embassies, June 24, 27, 1931; Stimson MS. Diary, June 24, 1931; *FRUS, 1931*, I, 74. Despite Castle's

Sackett did at least attempt to induce Brüning to make a significant concession; to judge by what Newton reported, Sackett may even have gone beyond his latest instructions when talking with Brüning. But the Germans could not fail to note the discrepancies between what was asked by Sackett and what they heard from Paris and Washington; they could not fail to realize that if they ignored the proposal for concessions on Cruiser B, nothing would happen. If they really wished to stop the American pressure, all they had to do was to leak it to the press. When Brüning's statement finally came out, the Germans did in fact publish a few discreet hints, and the American part of the campaign to halt work on Cruiser B abruptly ceased.[47] Both sides had reason to conceal the nature of the negotiations from the public, but the Germans had the advantage that they could reveal some of what Sackett was doing without giving away their own hand.

---

and Sackett's precautions, there was some leakage: see Pearson and Brown, *American Diplomatic Game*, pp. 229–230. It is possible that Sackett did not report the German secret concession on Cruiser C, even by telephone, even to Castle. On July 18, when it was obvious that Brüning and Curtius would shortly be seeing Stimson in Paris and London, as well as in Berlin, Sackett casually reported, in the midst of a cable "For the President and Acting Secretary," that Brüning "has confided that he does not intend to lay down any new pocket battleship [i.e., Cruiser C] during the holiday year although he did not see how he could consent to publish the fact and I believe that if pressed the German Government will hold up construction on pocket battleship B during the coming year." Sackett added that the cabinet had seemed greatly chastened in the last few days, and were ready to make "reasonable concessions"; he wished to press this view for what it might be worth in the forthcoming discussions (SDP, 462.00R296/4593). When Curtius and Stimson did discuss Cruiser C in London on July 21, George Gordon, Sackett's Counselor of Embassy and chief lieutenant, was present and dictated our record of the meeting, according to which Curtius remarked: "Dr. Brüning moreover had stated to Mr. Sackett that during the Hoover holiday year the German Government would not commence the construction of pocket battleship C or appropriate further sums for the construction of B." Gordon added the following parenthetical comment: "(I may note here that Dr. Brüning did make the first of these statements to Mr. Sackett, but not the second, though we had reported to the Department that we thought the Germans would agree to that point if pressed.)" (SDP, 462.00R296/4671½). One wonders whether either of these points was reported before July 18.

[47] See *DBFP*, 2/II, Nos. 146, 165.

ISSUING BRÜNING'S STATEMENT

In Paris, negotiations did not go badly on July 2. That night a message was sent from Washington to Berlin, stating that a Franco-American agreement might be reached, if at all, within two days, and also that Sackett should try to arrange for a new expression of German appreciation. At this point, what was wanted was a strong German endorsement of the prospective Franco-American agreement; a German rejection or halfhearted acceptance would lead to criticism from Congress and an intensification of the financial crisis. But by July 4 it seemed to Washington that agreement with the French was still far away, after all, and Sackett was obliged to ask that Brüning's draft statement be published immediately, preferably with the addition that no new construction would be undertaken during the Hoover year. Curtius argued that the French were now following their well-known tactic of "struggling and haggling" after fundamental agreement had been reached, and that it was impossible for the Chancellor to make a statement to influence the Paris negotiations one day, and then to congratulate the negotiators the next. After Curtius had conjured up other obstacles, Sackett relented and said that he would consult his government before pressing further for a declaration. Curtius hinted that Sackett's requests had been inspired by the French government, and Sackett assured the Foreign Minister that the political wishes which he "had only presented very reluctantly, did not derive from a French initiative, but on the contrary sprang exclusively from the desires of President Hoover himself." [48]

Washington, however, now wanted more than ever to publish a statement. Once again, on July 5, Sackett told the Germans he had received orders to secure the issuance of Brüning's July 2 statement "at least in its original form, but preferably extended (meaning: by the renunciation of the construction of Cruiser C during the holiday year) . . . Hoover knew that this would make a very

---

[48] *FRUS, 1931*, I, 129; SDP, 462.00R296/4260: Acting Secretary to Ambassador in Berlin, July 3, 1931; GFMR, 1555/D666691-4: Memo by Curtius, July 4, 1931.

strong impression in Paris and he hoped that thereby a satisfactory solution would be brought about." [49] Very reluctantly, Chancellor Brüning agreed to the publication of the July 2 statement; he could not agree to any public declaration on Cruiser C, although he repeated for President Hoover the assurance that the third cruiser would not in fact be started during the moratorium year. It was agreed that the statement should be released in Washington, and Sackett assured the Germans that, in regard to disarmament, they "could be sure that President Hoover had this very much at heart, and that he would not leave [them] in the lurch. This subject should be discussed with Secretary Stimson when he comes." Brüning expressed a fear that the French might now increase their demands. The Ambassador, on his side, would not admit that Hoover had made any political conditions: "He considered the Chancellor's declaration as a voluntary gesture. In general, during this whole course of negotiations, America had permitted no political demands, as his own instructions confirmed." [50] The Chancellor told Sackett that German information from Paris showed that both parties had now spoken their last word, and he thought it unlikely that the French would make a concession which would enable the President to accept their proposals. Sackett, on the other hand, argued that success was very probable. "At this [the German record continues], the Chancellor declared that President Hoover was assuming a heavy responsibility. The Ambassador assured him that we could count on America, and that if the expected success failed to materialize, we could be supported by Hoover's strong right arm." [51] Brüning described this discussion to the German cabinet in the following terms:

The Chancellor declared that he had indicated to the American Ambassador the delicacy of this American step [the publication of Brüning's statement], having regard to the German internal situation

---

[49] The parenthesis is in the original German document.
[50] This passage is heavily underlined and marked in Koepke's file copy.
[51] SDP, 462.00R296/4263: Acting Secretary to Ambassador in Berlin, July 4, 1931; GFMR, 2548/E300246–9: Memo by Bülow, July 5, 1931.

and German disarmament policy, and in this connection he had called attention to the fact that President Hoover was hereby taking a great responsibility upon himself. Thereupon Sackett answered that President Hoover realized this; Germany could count on the aid of America, which would also intervene most decisively against further political demands on Germany.

One wonders how much of these commitments was ever known to President Hoover. In any case, the statement was released that evening (July 5).[52]

FURTHER DISCUSSION ON THE CUSTOMS UNION

There was also the other proposed "voluntary gesture," a renunciation of the customs union. Newton saw Curtius on July 2, and the Chargé and the Foreign Minister discussed this subject, as well as that of pocket battleship construction. According to Newton's version, he stated that he understood the American government shared the British views on the customs union. Curtius, on the other hand, did not record that Newton made any such allusion to American views. Actually, Newton reported on this part of his talk with Curtius only on the evening of July 3, after he had received a stern message from his Foreign Secretary, ending with: "I shall be glad to know whether you see any prospect of inducing German Government to consult United States Ambassador on the subject [of the customs union] and whether you propose to press German Government for an answer to your own representations." To judge by Curtius' account, Newton, in his reply to Henderson, somewhat exaggerated the forcefulness of his suggestions to the German Foreign Minister. At all events, Curtius declined to make a renunciation of the customs union: the Hague Court was considering it, the Economic Committee of the European Commission had now taken up the matter, and various people, especially Sir Walter Layton, had declared in favor of customs unions.[53]

[52] GFMR, 1684/D786863; 2548/E300249. The former of these references is to the Cabinet Protocol, July 6, 1931.

[53] *DBFP*, 2/II, Nos. 113, 124; GFMR, 2548/E300226: Memo by Curtius, July 3, 1931.

After Newton's failure to make any headway, the best remaining hope of getting a customs union renunciation lay in persuading Washington to order Sackett to tackle the matter. Both Henderson and Newton now turned their energies in this direction, seeking both through the American Embassy in Berlin and through Washington to have Sackett authorized to raise the question of the Austro-German agreement. Later, on July 4, Newton reported that in view of favorable news from Paris, the American Ambassador was refraining for the present from making any suggestion on the customs union to Washington. Newton added that "a day or two ago" Sackett had "half suggested" that his authority to discuss the customs union might be further extended; Sackett may have told Newton this, and he may have said something in one of his own unrecorded telephone conversations, but we have no American evidence. If the American Ambassador said anything to Washington, it is likely that it was indeed no more than half a suggestion, for the truth is that the British and Americans were each willing to let the other take up the burden.[54]

Back on June 28, and again on July 1, Sackett actually had strongly urged that the British could suggest an explicit, clear-cut compromise, whereby the German government would renounce the customs union in return for an unconditional French acceptance of the Hoover scheme. Washington and London apparently failed to pursue this idea, presumably because such an open bargain, like the original suggestions made in the Italian press, made the involvement of Hoover's offer with European political pressures too obvious. Acting Secretary Castle clearly stated this objection on July 6 when Ambassador Lindsay conveyed the British desire that Sackett take the initiative on the customs union question. According to Lindsay, Castle "expressed considerable annoyance at German refusal to help, but also emphasized acute difficulties to the United States Administration if the German Government, to defend itself against criticism at home, announced that it had acted under pressure from United States Government." Lindsay added that Castle had telephoned Sackett, "authorizing

[54] *DBFP*, 2/II, Nos. 124, 128, 131.

him to seek to draw German Minister of Foreign Affairs on to ground which would enable him to state United States views about customs union": another instance of Castle's use of the telephone. But there is no indication that Sackett took action, and with the end of the Franco-American negotiations, there was less prospect than ever of a German response.[55]

As we have seen, the American and British diplomats felt obliged to maintain the fiction that, with regard to the cruisers and the customs union, they were merely proposing that the Germans make a voluntary contribution to better understanding. Although this fiction was stretched rather thin at times, these two Western powers always drew back from making a direct demand. Even in France, where public opinion might have supported such action, the government hesitated to demand concessions from the Germans. In these circumstances, Berlin did not have too much difficulty in evading any real contribution. Curtius, in discussing the possibility of a concession on the customs union in his memoirs, has observed: "There existed at the moment no reason at all for any kind of advance offer. Against the fear of diplomatic compulsion later we set down the consideration that we ourselves were not the petitioners for the moratorium plan, but rather could and must leave it to the Americans to push it through against French opposition. But making things easier for the Americans by a 'contribution to over-all conciliation' was unnecessary; when we declined to make such a contribution they did not press further." [56] Curtius here forgets that the American government actually sought more than once to get a German "contribution," although his forgetfulness may itself be a comment on the weakness of the American pressure. But the main thing to note is the shortsighted attitude Curtius reveals on the question of making a concession; the Creditanstalt difficulties had already made the prospects for the customs union very dark, and in two months,

[55] SDP, 462.00R296/4186: Ambassador in Berlin to Acting Secretary, June 28, 1931; *FRUS, 1931*, I, 110; *DBFP*, 2/II, No. 146.
[56] Julius Curtius, *Sechs Jahre Minister der deutschen Republik* (Heidelberg, 1948), pp. 201–202.

indeed, Curtius and Schober were forced to renounce it. A public postponement of Cruiser C could have been justified on financial grounds, and would at least have met with Socialist approval. By itself, a voluntary contribution would perhaps have been a naïve gesture, but if Curtius and Brüning had been as interested in German prosperity as they were in appeasing German nationalism, they might have offered something to France in return for a prompt acceptance of the Hoover moratorium. Granted that Hoover's action had its origins in the short-term commitments of American banks and that there was more than a little hypocrisy in the Anglo-American appeals for political generosity from Germany, still, President Hoover showed courage in taking action, and he was largely motivated by a desire to pull the world out of depression and to lessen international friction. In contrast, the narrow type of nationalism displayed by the Weimar leaders could never lift the German people out of the rut of suspicion and self-pity.

The Influence of the German Attitude on Paris

We do not know whether the Franco-American negotiations were prolonged by French hopes of a German change of policy. Certainly there were other difficulties, and the delay from July 3 to 6 was technically due to the fact that, after Mellon had won French agreement to a ten-year repayment period by retreating on reparations in kind, Washington refused to authorize his retreat, which involved a departure from the spirit of the Hoover proposal, the principle that there should be no actual intergovernmental payments. When agreement was finally reached on July 6, it followed the publication of Brüning's statement, but it also followed a dropping of threats by Washington, and a French agreement that, on reparations in kind, a committee should "reconcile the material necessities with the spirit of President Hoover's proposal." [57]

Yet France was acutely interested in the Anglo-American efforts to gain concessions. The French repeated their need for German

[57] *FRUS, 1931*, I, 135–162.

assurances when they put forward a detailed draft agreement on July 4, and significantly, the need was mentioned yet again in the last paragraph of the French-drafted final agreement: "France reserves the right to request of the German Government assurances concerning the utilization for exclusively economic purposes of the sums freed to the Reich budget." This implied that Brüning's July 2 statement, published on the fifth, was insufficient. And in fact Laval told Hoesch on July 8 that it was still not certain that the French government could declare itself satisfied with Brüning's statement.[58]

Whatever it might declare, the French cabinet was certainly not satisfied. France still wanted a guarantee of the *status quo*. On July 7, Lord Tyrrell in Paris telegraphed to London:

> I venture again to emphasize the extent to which, as far as France is concerned, the whole politico-economic situation in Europe is conditioned by the necessity of a clear understanding of permanent German intentions . . . Enlightened economic and political opinion in France tacitly realizes the inevitable fact of German economic predominance in Europe, but unless Germany will abandon her ceaseless demands for changes in political conditions which are not in themselves obstacles to economic progress, France will not supply money which is spent by Germany on an economic equipment out of all proportion to markets restricted by political insecurity.[59]

Tyrrell sent this telegram in connection with the return, with increased violence, of financial crisis in Germany, and in the belief that Germany would now seek a loan. The German government had refused to make a concession to hasten French acceptance of the Hoover moratorium; would it make concessions to get financial assistance, to save the Germany currency?

[58] *FRUS, 1931*, I, 143, 162; GFMR, 2548/E300296: Hoesch to Ministry, July 8, 1931.
[59] *DBFP*, 2/II, No. 158.

VII

The Crisis Out of Control

THE Wilhelmstrasse had now obtained, through Hoover's action, the desired breakthrough in reparations, and the one-year moratorium had begun. The problem now was how to hold on to what had been gained, without suffering an equivalent loss in another area. The German leaders began to think less about how to attain a diplomatic success, and to worry more about the financial repercussions of the actions already taken. They could let further reparations discussion wait a bit; diplomatically speaking, they had already progressed farther than they could have expected. But the crisis continued to develop, and not merely from its own momentum. It appeared to British financial circles that the Hoover moratorium offered an opportunity to end or drastically curtail reparations and war debts in the immediate future, thus removing an incubus from international, and especially British, trade, and dispelling a danger to the pound sterling. On the other hand, if this opportunity were not seized, Britain would have to reduce her commitments and adjust herself to a world of economic nationalism; as matters stood, this readjustment could not be postponed much longer. There was a British as well as a German revisionism, for if the Wilhelmstrasse longed to regain its prewar political power, the City of London wanted—more justifiably and more urgently—a return to prewar trade and finance. During the rest of the summer of 1931, the impulse for revision would come, not from Berlin, but from London. And like German revisionism, British revisionism intensified the financial difficulties.

TREASURY VERSUS FOREIGN OFFICE

From Henderson's activities in seeking renunciations of the customs union and of pocket battleship construction, one might have supposed that the main aim of British policy was simply to safeguard the European *status quo* and to accommodate French desires. Yet this supposition would have been mistaken, since in the crisis of 1931 other British leaders contributed as much as Brüning and Hoover to making the French fearful for their security. Actually, there were two British foreign policies, and they were, more often than not, in conflict. As happens so often in the politics of modern nations, these policies were those supported by rival bureaucratic organizations, with little or no relation to the programs ostensibly pursued by the British political parties. The rival organizations in this case were the Foreign Office and the Treasury, the latter being closely linked with the Bank of England, and usually closer to the ear of the Prime Minister.[1] The Foreign Office, faithful to the tradition of Sir Eyre Crowe, usually tended to support the Entente with France, even though refusing to join in the French security system, while the Treasury, headed by the cold, intransigent Philip Snowden and following the ideas of leading British economists and of the City, wished to end reparations and war debts, or failing that, to secure as large a share as possible against the claims of the French government. Treasury officials pushed their policy in ignorance of long-term British political interests, while the Foreign Office, deprived by Treasury economy measures of an adequate economic staff, was unable either to make its ideas prevail or to adapt them to the needs of the current situation.[2]

---

[1] For a description of the Foreign Office–Treasury rivalry from the Foreign Office point of view, see Sir Walford Selby, *Diplomatic Twilight, 1930–1940* (London, 1953), pp. 1–6, and Frank Ashton-Gwatkin, "Thoughts on the Foreign Office," *Contemporary Review*, 188:374–378 (Dec. 1955).

[2] Sir Victor Wellesley laments the lack of coordination between British finance and diplomacy, and as an example states that Norman's Creditanstalt credit was against the interests of British diplomacy. German finance and diplomacy (he says) were, by contrast, well coordinated (*Diplomacy in Fetters,* London, 1944, pp. 90–91).

For a happy moment in the winter of 1930–1931, Foreign Office and Treasury policy had coincided, both departments agreeing that it was too soon to undertake a revision of the Young Plan. But Treasury views soon began to change again, while after Chequers, and with the announcement of the Hoover moratorium, Montagu Norman, whose vivid imagination served to supplement and direct Snowden's essentially orthodox and negative mind, began to see new horizons and indeed to hope that Hoover's proposal could be extended into an immediate and permanent cancellation of all intergovernmental payments. As we have seen, Norman tended to sympathize with Germany, and in April 1931 he was backing a project for long-term loans to Germany and other financially embarrassed countries in Eastern Europe and South America. While expounding this plan in the United States, Norman met Secretary Stimson and expressed to him the view that Britain and Germany were in similar straits, both suffering from a flight of capital, although the flight of funds from Germany at that time appeared to be temporarily checked. "He then [Stimson recorded] made quite a eulogy of Germany saying she was one country whose policy had been directed with manly courage, and he spoke very highly of Brüning. He spoke of Germany's employment policy and how they had got it to a point now where the members of the employed class were ashamed not to be employed. They were ashamed to rest upon the dole, in other words, because the pressure of their associates who furnished the dole was so strong." In retrospect, Norman's views on the dole are as interesting as his views on Brüning. He went on to praise the customs union scheme, considering it sound economics, while he regarded French encirclement policies as based on false economics.[3]

But Norman was not interested in German chestnuts only, he had his own to extricate. The Bank of England's loan scheme was directed at maintaining the solvency of the countries that had previously borrowed from England, and since he now proposed to

[3] Stimson Manuscript Diary (Deposited at Yale University Library), April 1, 8, 1931.

make but a small British contribution, it might be described as a plan to unload what had become a burden onto others. This was one of a number of reasons why this long-term loan plan never made any progress. Norman was also uttering a *cri de coeur* when he associated England with Germany as a country suffering from capital flight. There had long been a drain of funds from London, stemming basically from the unfortunate decision in 1925 to return the pound to its prewar level, and this tendency was aggravated by the opinion of conservatives everywhere that the Labour government lacked the will to truly balance the budget. We have already seen how negotiations to check the drain were undertaken with France in January, only to end inconclusively. Matters were coming to a head in the summer of 1931, and the Macmillan and May Reports, showing that Britain's long- and short-term financial prospects were poor, were about to be published. Norman was unwilling to abandon the gold standard, and the Labour ministers were unwilling to make cuts in the dole. In such circumstances it was natural to blame the foreigner, in this case the Frenchman, for it was the French who were the largest holders of claims against British funds. Perhaps there were other specific reasons, arising from French demands made during the Franco-British financial negotiations, but the threats that French withdrawals might force Britain off gold or oblige her to reduce the dole were enough in themselves to make the French unpopular in many British circles.

London and the Paris Negotiations

French popularity in London sank even deeper during the Paris negotiations with Mellon and Edge. Like the American administration, the British government had hoped that the Hoover moratorium would open a new era of peace and prosperity. The efforts of the Foreign Office to get the German government to make a "voluntary contribution" represented an attempt to develop a new political atmosphere. Others began to hope for another radical change, a final sweeping away of the factors upsetting the balance of trade and making the maintenance of a gold standard impossible, and they believed that the first of these factors was the postwar system of intergovernmental payments. They regarded Hoover's proposal as a start in the right direction, but now, before the scheme was even launched, the French were trying to bolster up the Young Plan, with special reference to their own privileged position in relation to unconditional reparations. All the old animosities which had flourished during the Young Plan negotiations in 1929 now flared up again.

Even before the Hoover announcement, Vansittart had read to the American Chargé a memorandum, probably of Treasury origin, pointing out that the French would "probably exhibit a very strong tendency to bargain for a continuation of the unconditional annuities." The memorandum argued that a concession on this point would be fatal, since other countries would then seek exceptions as well, German payments would not be sufficiently reduced, and a precedent would be established for suspending war debts while insisting on the payment of reparations.[4] In the matter of unconditional payments, the unknown author of this memorandum proved to be an excellent prophet.

During its negotiations with France, the American government asked for British suggestions, and accordingly, a number of Treasury memoranda and messages inspired by Treasury thinking were sent to Washington and Paris. The first of these, commenting on the French note of June 24, contained the following passages:

French reservation about payment of unconditional annuities seems to the Treasury radically to alter proposal of President Hoover, which His Majesty's Government accepted and have offered to carry into effect.

If Germany has to pay unconditional annuities, in any form, she will *not* obtain the relief required for the situation and the effect in Berlin will be very dangerous. The fact of the case is that Germany

[4] *FRUS, 1931*, I, 17. It might be added that Vansittart, although earlier a career diplomat and later intensely pro-French, had at this time only just emerged from a stint as Principal Private Secretary to Baldwin and Mac-Donald, and was appointed by the latter to his post in the Foreign Office (Lord Vansittart, *The Mist Procession*, London, 1958, p. 394); he did not always typify the Foreign Office outlook.

cannot pay. London is financing the Reichsbank and must withdraw money if the complete suspension of reparation payments is not accepted unreservedly.

In view of Treasury, the French proposal that the payments should be lent by the Bank for International Settlements to Germany or other countries is no good. In so far as money is lent to other countries, obviously Germany gets no relief at all. If it is re-lent to Germany, Germany only gets a short-term credit, and she will have to pay at the end of the year *both* the postponed payments *and* the full payment for next year, which is obviously impossible. France will therefore have Germany at her mercy . . .

The only certain way to save the situation is to get the French to accept the President's proposal for suspension of all German payments for one year . . .

The only effective course is to tackle the difficulty made by the French firmly and at once, and get it over.[5]

Even Hoover did not state his views so strongly.

The guarantee fund question was a particularly sore point with the British Treasury, which had seen the French corner the lion's share of the unconditional payments at The Hague, exceeding the over-all percentage of reparations allotted them at Spa in July 1920; the British now found the French maintaining the inviolability of these unconditional payments, while trying to evade or at least reduce their own related obligation to compensate the other powers, through the guarantee fund, for their losses due to the suspension of conditional payments. The guarantee fund had been a *quid pro quo* for the disproportionate French share of unconditional reparations, and it should have worked in effect as a redistribution of unconditional payments in the direction of the Spa percentages. But openly to redistribute the unconditional payments, as the British now suggested, would have involved a reversal of the Young provisions and a public surrender of the

---

[5] *DBFP*, 2/II, No. 88 (emphasis in original); also *FRUS, 1931*, I, 95. Where this cable suggested that at the end of the Hoover year Germany would have to make "the full payment for next year," it was misleading. Full *scale* payments would have been resumed, but payments were made once a month, not once a year.

French position of priority; it was not surprising that the French government rejected this proposition when London made it later.[6]

On July 6, toward the end of the Paris negotiations, Sir Ronald Lindsay "uttered a strong protest" to Mills and Castle:

I said that His Majesty's Government had accepted the President's scheme on the supposition that it was a simple plan involving postponement of annuities due this year to next year and so on to the end. On this assumption His Majesty's Government have cordially accepted it, had set to work to make it a success, and had committed themselves to first steps for its execution. They were now confronted with something completely different, which not only introduced great complications, but also affected their interest in very material manner. This declaration caused, I think, some disquietude. Mr. Castle indicated that he entirely agreed with its reasonableness. Mr. Mills then said it seemed to him that even if United States Government could come to terms with French Government the discussions would have to begin all over again with His Majesty's Government. He asked whether my protest was official. I said that I had no instructions to make any official protest or to predicate the action which His Majesty's Government would take, but that these were views which were being expressed to Mr. Mellon, and I was able to express them to State Department also. Mr. Mills said he thought that they should have been expressed earlier.[7]

Mills's patience had worn very thin by this time, so that his comment is understandable, but the fact was that the British Treasury's objections had been frequently and forcefully expressed. On one occasion, Hoover had reacted by saying that he wished the British would "express their views with equal directness to French Government," but after Sir Frederick Leith-Ross of the British Treasury had advocated the simple postponement of all payments to a representative of the French Treasury, the British learned that the American government had already accepted the principle that, instead of postponement, the unconditional payment should be repaid with interest in twenty-five years. Leith-Ross did not give up, however, and on July 3 he was still telling Lord Tyrrell (by telephone) that Hoover's plan must be accepted in its entirety, that the French must be forced to accept it.[8]

THE FIRST CONFERENCE PROPOSAL

On June 29, alongside the idea of repeating Hoover's offer to the various countries separately, Castle mentioned to Lindsay that an alternative procedure might be to let Europe work out its own solution to the problem. Spurred by a second request from Hoover that London bring pressure on the French, the British government took Castle's suggestion for a European solution as an invitation to propose a conference of the powers, with American representation, to be held on the next weekend in London.[9] Probably Castle's statement to Lindsay, and Hoover's urgent request, only served as convenient pretexts for an action which London was considering taking anyway. Conferences were a favorite device of MacDonald's; he liked the éclat of leading a conference, and to do him justice, he made a genuinely good chairman. At such a meeting (he probably reasoned) Germany might make a contribution to political tranquillity without compulsion from France, while France might surrender her claim to reparations, in accordance with the original Hoover proposal; if possible, the Hoover one-year moratorium should be made permanent. London may also have wished to ensure against an American return to isolation.

The London government began by directing its proposal of a conference to the French and Americans; other notifications might have followed, but these two powers begged off. According to Lord Tyrrell's report to London, the French government "received the proposal . . . with great interest and gratification," but the French ministers could not leave Paris when they were about

---

[8] SDP, 462.00R296/5045, 4259: Memo of conversation with British Ambassador, June 29, 1931; Ambassador in Paris to Acting Secretary, July 3, 1931; *DBFP*, 2/II, Nos. 92, 100, 101.

[9] SDP, 462.00R296/5045: Memo of conversation with British Ambassador, July 29, 1931; *DBFP*, 2/II, Nos. 95, 102 note 1, 103, 116.

to conclude their parliamentary session; the French had suggested to him that the problem might be solved by having the weekend meeting in Paris instead. Actually, as Tyrrell privately told Edge, Briand had positively refused the invitation; to go, the old man had said, "would be to give the impression in France that he was going to London to get instructions." [10] A meeting in Paris instead would indeed have suited the French leaders, for whom it would have been a way of getting Brüning to come for a discussion of political concessions. But London wanted a British-led conference for British goals, not a French-led conference for French goals.

In Washington, meanwhile, Ambassador Lindsay had been deprecating the idea of a European conference, and he reported that Hoover was returning to his scheme of a separate approach to each power. The conference proposal went out from London before this news was considered, but the idea of separate approaches was also quite acceptable to the Foreign Office. When he learned of the conference proposal, Castle telephoned Henderson "and told him I thought it was important that our negotiations should be buttoned up before there is any conference in London, but that it would be very much worthwhile for the others to get together in London afterwards. He more or less agreed with me." To Lindsay, it was explained that although the administration favored the idea of a London conference, things were looking quite encouraging in Paris, and the next meeting with the French might produce a "definitely favorable result." So the weekend conference did not take place.[11]

Nor was Hoover's offer repeated separately; the Americans could not quite bring themselves to take this "leap in the dark," as Castle once described it. Contrary to what Hoover says in his memoirs, it appears from contemporary records that in the final stages of the Paris negotiations Washington withdrew the threat of carrying out the plan without France and told Mellon and Edge that previous instructions were modified:

[10] *DBFP*, 2/II, No. 112; *FRUS, 1931*, I, 122.
[11] *DBFP*, 2/II, Nos. 102, 107, 110; *FRUS, 1931*, I, 122; SDP, 462.00R-296/5048: Memo of conversation between Acting Secretary and British Ambassador, July 1, 1931.

Our intention is to keep the original proposal of the President open to the nations of the world because, as developments have occurred, we believe it unwise to make the President's second offer [the approach to the powers individually], with which you are already acquainted. It is our belief that the original proposal is more apt to be successful and will be plainer and more understandable to the world in general if it is maintained in its original form and if the French Government is obliged to make a choice and accept the consequences thereof. The American Government has no threats to offer in this connection. Our impression is that France is making no effort to solve the problem but is trying to prevent acceptance of the proposal and to make it appear that we are responsible for its failure by building up a fog of technical details. In case tonight's proposal is rejected by the French, we will continue to express the hope that in the end they will fall in line and in the meantime we will await developments.[12]

Far from coercing the French into agreement, the administration in Washington, worn out with ten days of frustration, and alarmed by the renewal of the financial crisis in Germany, seems now to have been on the point of giving up. The American quandary was reflected in Lindsay's reports, especially that of his discussion with Castle and Mills on the morning of July 6, already mentioned, in which he made his protest against the departure from the original Hoover proposal. After he had registered this protest (and Mills had protested against it), Lindsay reported further:

A long discussion followed as to any possible alternative procedure. Although they [Castle and Mills] began by telling us that President had decided that, in view of the acute situation in Germany, it would be impossible for him now to proceed with any alternative plan, nevertheless they discussed possible alternatives, namely, 1) to declare that offer was still open, and that, as difficulties had arisen in Europe as to its execution, they would leave it to the European Powers to settle all outstanding questions; 2) to restate the offer separately and individually to each Power . . . I tried to elicit what Mr. Mills and

[12] Herbert Hoover, *The Memoirs of Herbert Hoover* (3 vols., New York, 1951–1952)), II, 72 (compare SDP, 462.00R296/4459½: Letter from Acting Secretary to Secretary, July 14, 1931); *FRUS, 1931*, I, 155–156 (sent 10 P.M., July 5).

Mr. Castle would do next, but did not succeed. I imagine they will have to consult with the President. They promised to send for me when they had anything further to communicate.[13]

Early the same morning a French memorandum came in from Edge indicating that France was still unwilling to have the arrangements for payments in kind settled in accordance with the Hoover spirit.[14] By noon, Hoover seems to have despaired of any decision being reached in Paris, while there was also the problem of the British attitude as pointed up by Lindsay's protest.

But Henderson's earlier proposal of a conference offered a solution. At 12:30 P.M. Washington time, Castle telephoned the Foreign Office in London to say that the French government would probably not accept the latest American proposal, and that Hoover therefore wanted Henderson to call an immediate meeting of the heads of states, as had been considered the week before. The junior Foreign Office official with whom Castle was speaking was better informed on events in Paris, and he asked if it made any difference about the advance announcement of what was happening there. Castle answered that although another meeting was scheduled, he did not think agreement would be reached, and even if it were, a meeting in London would be very helpful. The Foreign Office official promised Castle to pass Hoover's message to Henderson at once, and said that London would let Castle know the next morning the British decision on summoning a conference.[15]

At about 8:30 P.M. Paris time (2:30 P.M. in Washington) the final French counterproposal was given to Mellon and Edge, who

---

[13] *DBFP*, 2/II, No. 144.

[14] *FRUS, 1931*, I, 157–159, received 12:47 A.M. That telegram No. 411 on p. 160, received at 10:47 A.M., would actually have been in Hoover's or Castle's hands by noon is doubtful; in any case it was not entirely reassuring.

[15] SDP, 462.00R296/5053: Memo of conversation between Acting Secretary and Foreign Office official, July 6, 1931. Castle's transatlantic phone call included some discussion of the relative merits of London and Paris as the scene for a meeting; both speakers thought London preferable, Castle saying that "the atmosphere" in London was "different." Havas was reporting that the French government intended to convoke a conference in Paris (*DBFP*, 2/II, No. 141), but the French proposal failed to materialize after all.

then consulted Hoover by telephone and were able to report his agreement to the French at 10 P.M. Paris time (Washington: 4 P.M.).[16] At 6:33 P.M. (Washington) a telegram left the British Embassy in Washington for London, reporting the Franco-American agreement, but still bearing the request that Whitehall summon a conference:

> Acting Secretary of State has telephoned to say that French and American negotiators have today reached agreement in Paris. He could not give me details of agreement, but he says that French have agreed that any committee of experts called to settle them must act within spirit of President's proposal.
>
> He urges very strongly now that His Majesty's Government shall immediately summon a conference to carry settlement further. President thinks this action may have considerable effect in supporting German credit, and hopes it may be taken without any delay. He even hopes that you may act without consideration of terms of agreement now reached in Paris. Moreover, French Prime Minister hinted to Mr. Mellon that conference might be called in Paris. United States Administration feel strongly that London would be by far the better place in every respect, and hopes that you will forestall French Government in issuing invitations.[17]

Hoover never reconciled himself to the French modifications, and it appears from Lindsay's telegram that he accepted the final French terms with some reluctance and with the hope of later revision. He presumably reasoned that, considering the German financial situation, it was better to overlook details and come to an agreement. He could hope that matters might be put right in London.[18]

---

[16] *FRUS, 1931,* I, 161.

[17] *DBFP,* 2/II, No. 147. The time given was that when the telegram, enciphered, left the Embassy. It would have been drafted some time before, and probably represents Castle's very first impulse. Lindsay may have somewhat exaggerated the strength of the American desire for a conference in London after agreement was reached in Paris; later he gave a misleading impression of the kind of conference desired. But there is other evidence that Hoover hoped the British might succeed in scrapping the agreement: see *FRUS, 1931,* I, 164–165, 169–171.

[18] This interpretation of Hoover's attitude is also supported by the message

The British government apparently took a graver view of the problem. The Franco-American agreement itself foresaw a meeting of experts, and there were signs that France would propose holding this meeting in Paris. In order to safeguard its own interests, and also in response to President Hoover's request, the London government, early on July 7, issued its own invitation to a conference. The invitation proposed that the experts should meet on July 13, with their responsible ministers meeting a week later, since there were issues involved "of considerable magnitude." [19]

We need not trace the details of the French and British diplomatic exchanges that followed during the next four days.[20] The French wished to delay any meeting of the experts until July 17; they evidently expected that the Germans would by then have gone through the motions of paying a month's installment of unconditional reparations, due on the fifteenth, thus confirming the French modifications to the Hoover plan by established usage. After that, it would in practice be too late to return to the original Hoover proposal, or to contest the French interpretation of the guarantee fund liability.[21] The idea of a general conference of ministers held little attraction for the French, although there was still some interest in having Brüning come to Paris. The French position was characterized by their first reply, which stated that they considered that the object of any meeting "would be to adapt the Hoover proposal to the Young Plan," thus relegating the Hoover principle to second place.

---

asking Hugh Gibson to represent American interests at the Experts' Conference (see *FRUS, 1931*, I, 164–165, also 169–171). It appears that Hoover hoped that Gibson, whom he knew personally and trusted, might encourage the British to secure some improvements in the June 6 agreement. However, Castle's diary (as reported by Robert H. Ferrell, *American Diplomacy in the Great Depression*, New Haven, 1957, p. 115) recorded that the agreement was "all right, really a paraphrase of our memorandum of the night before. We almost hugged each other and all . . . congratulated the President."

[19] See *DBFP*, 2/II, Nos. 141, 148, 149.

[20] For details, see *DBFP*, 2/II, Nos. 149, 166–168, 171, 174–177, 179, 190; *FRUS, 1931*, I, 165–168.

[21] Laval realized that Germany would not make any real payment: see GFMR, 2548/E300302: Hoesch to Ministry, July 8, 1931.

The British, on the other hand, took the view that the object of the conference was "to consider and recommend the measures necessary to give effect to President Hoover's proposal." They wished to scrap the Franco-American agreement and start afresh, particularly in the matter of the guarantee fund. They wanted an experts' conference at an early date and a conference of ministers shortly thereafter. The British ultimately went ahead with a final invitation for the experts to meet in London on July 17, professing to assume that Franco-British differences could be settled by that date. The differences were not settled, but all the powers invited accepted, and the experts, including French representatives and an American observer, did meet as scheduled.[22]

The differences between the British and French went beyond the details of the unconditional payments and the guarantee fund. The British Treasury and the Bank of England wanted not only to overthrow the Franco-American agreement, but also to revise the Hague Agreements, or even to end reparations completely.[23] The French may not have known this at first, but they knew enough to make them apprehensive. Berthelot sent Lord Tyrrell a letter which included the following (as summarized by Tyrrell):

French have gained impression from messages from London that His Majesty's Government intend to reject Franco-American agreement and demand application of Hoover plan in its entirety. French do not see that their proposals for guarantee fund imply any fresh burden for British Exchequer; and if their impression of British attitude is correct, "failure" of the experts' meeting "is certain, and it would be useless for us to go to London." M. Berthelot is the more anxious as to situation in that he "knows from authoritative source that British Treasury acted constantly on Washington during Paris negotiations and preached an uncompromising attitude and worked against the unconditional and [*sic*] reparations."[24]

[22] Since by that time a conference of ministers had been arranged to meet on the twentieth, no important business was transacted until July 24.
[23] See especially *DBFP*, 2/II, Nos. 123, 168; *FRUS, 1931*, I, 256, 262; also GFMR, 2548/E300326-7: Hoesch to Ministry, July 11, 1931; SDP, 462.00R-296/4400: Consul in Basel to Acting Secretary, July 11, 1931.
[24] *DBFP*, 2/II, No. 166.

We must bear in mind that to the British, the French had just been coercing Austria and frustrating Hoover's proposal, while to the French, that proposal, so unwelcome, seemed to have stemmed at least in part from the Chequers meetings. The question of the guarantee fund had little immediate practical significance, but the air was now saturated with suspicion, while the whole future of war debts and reparations stood in question in the background.

GERMANY TAKES ALARM

Under other circumstances this quarrel between the French and the British Treasury might have been just what the Wilhelmstrasse wanted, but this was not now the case. Although not informed officially, the Germans had on July 2 gotten wind of the original British conference proposal; on July 3 they learned of its withdrawal. When the plan was revived on July 7 and announced in Parliament, Karl Ritter telephoned Ambassador von Neurath and told him that, after expressing German gratitude for the British role in supporting the Hoover plan, he should take the opportunity to say that the German government was very disturbed over the conference proposal. What Berlin wanted was a small, quiet meeting of experts in some lesser city, such as Basel.[25]

Considering what we know of the British motives in wanting a conference, this German reaction may seem somewhat surprising; it might appear that Germany could only have gained from meetings calculated to eliminate the French modifications to the Hoover moratorium proposal. After all, the Germans had been hoping for a conference before the Hoover announcement. But for one thing, it probably appeared to Berlin that a conference might turn out to be the occasion for new pressure to abandon Cruiser B and the customs union. Such suspicions would have gained strength in the next few days, when a press campaign developed in the London *Times,* the London *Daily Herald,* and the *Manchester Guardian,* urging that Germany make voluntary

[25] GFMR, 913/384856; 2548/E300193, E300274: Memo by Bülow, July 3, 1931; Memo by Wiehl, July 2, 1931; Memo [by Ritter], July 7, 1931.

renunciations on these points. On July 9, Neurath reported that he had protested to Henderson, but had only drawn from the Foreign Secretary an indication that he intended to pursue these questions when he visited Berlin later in the month. Moreover, although the German government wanted MacDonald and Henderson to be received by President von Hindenburg on Monday, July 20, Henderson explained that he had arranged with Briand that he would leave Berlin on the twentieth for Paris, where they would weigh the results of Henderson's discussions with the Germans. This was hardly reassuring. And although the American government was making no further moves to evoke concessions (partly because the German government was making public hints at the assurances Sackett had given on July 5), it and the British Treasury might support France and the British Foreign Office on concessions in a conference in order to gain other points.[26]

More important, the German government had finally become genuinely alarmed at the development of the financial crisis. When the Franco-American agreement was reached on July 6, the German government feared, as the now more cautious Ritter put it to Neurath, that "the urgently-needed calm" would not come if a big conference now assembled in London, with new tensions and delays; financial confidence would not be restored. Curtius repeated similar views to Sackett on July 9, even making the interesting objection that a conference of ministers would raise political problems, perhaps including the whole question of the Young Plan.[27] The real difficulty seems to have been that a major conference, attended by ministers, would suggest to everyone that the Hoover plan was still not being applied. This would mean a loss of any remaining psychological benefits, and although the German government had been rather insensitive to this considera-

[26] *DBFP*, 2/II, Nos. 165, 172, 178; GFMR, 1555/D666706: Neurath to Ministry, July 9, 1931; London *Times*, July 9, 1931; London *Daily Herald*, July 9, 1931; *Manchester Guardian*, July 13, 1931; *Berliner Tageblatt*, July 6, 1931 (P.M.).

[27] GFMR, 2548/E300374; SDP, 462.00R296/4345; Ambassador in Berlin to Acting Secretary, July 9, 1931.

tion before, it was very conscious of it now, for the crisis had entered a new phase. The Hoover moratorium had been delayed too long, and could not now restore calm.

Up until the beginning of July, the chief problem had been the withdrawal of foreign short-term loans. Now a domestic crisis was added, similar in some respects to that which occurred in the United States in early 1933. On July 3 the failure of the Norddeutsche Wollkämmerei (North German Wool Combing Corporation), or Nordwolle, became publicly known; as we have seen, Brüning had informed Sackett about this danger the previous evening. As Brüning had also told Sackett, two of the largest German banks were thereby endangered, since Nordwolle owed the Darmstädter und Nationalbank (or Danat Bank) RM35,000,000 and the Dresdner Bank RM25,000,000. In consequence, there was a run on these and other banks, and also a German flight from the mark, while the freezing of some assets led to a scramble for others—and often to the discovery that they were frozen, too.[28] These developments brought the crisis closer to home for the Berlin government. It was one thing to keep calm and cool when German foreign credit was suffering; it was another thing to maintain composure when the country was entering into financial panic itself, and especially when it had the inflationary memories and political actualities that Germany had.

Dietrich had said that, in launching reparations revision, the German government was taking an action comparable to a declaration of war, and the developments that followed the German manifesto of June 6 did indeed resemble a war in their effects on German policy. Sober statesmen have observed that the trouble with a war is that its outcome cannot be predicted, and the same would seem to be true of a financial crisis. Like others before him, Brüning discovered that he had underestimated the risks and hardships involved in a forward policy. And now, to meet these difficulties, the state was forced to extend its activity, to become more *dirigiste* and more vigilant against subversion—to enter a state of siege.

[28] See *FRUS, 1931,* I, 130; *SIA, 1931,* p. 213.

Aside from the general political dangers which now arose as major bank failures and corporation bankruptcies were added to an unstable internal situation, many of the threatened failures created special political problems for the Reich government, forcing it to intervene, to the further detriment of its budget. In one case, the Reichswehr had secretly invested money in machinery at the Borsig-Tegel factory in Berlin as part of its clandestine industrial mobilization plan. General von Schleicher argued that Borsig must be saved from bankruptcy, lest the previous investment be lost, and the Reich be obliged to start over with another plant; it was essential, he said, to have one source of arms at a safe distance from France. Moreover, any Borsig bankruptcy proceedings would cause embarrassment for the Junkers aircraft firm, which owed money to Borsig. Another case was that of the Mechernich lead mines and refinery near the western border; they had been subsidized as early as 1928, partly because it would have been difficult to find other employment for people in the area, and partly because of the adverse effects a shutdown would have on German propaganda in nearby Eupen-Malmédy and in the Saar. Then there was the appalling problem of the Rheinische Landesbank, reportedly in a worse condition than Nordwolle, having borrowed at short term from abroad and then having lent heavily to the over-indebted Rhenish local governments; this was a case for the Reichsbank, which was asked to put up RM28,000,000 to meet the most pressing demands. The cabinet discussed whether or not to aid Nordwolle itself, but since much of the funds raised would have gone to satisfy foreign—including Czech—creditors, any government aid given would have had to be camouflaged, and the sums were too large for this to be feasible.[29]

The question of priority for foreign versus domestic creditors arose on all sides; for the sake of German credit it was desirable for the government to pay off the foreign creditors of the bankrupt institutions, but on the other hand, domestic political considerations demanded that German creditors, especially small

[29] GFMR, 1684/D786794–808, D786864–8, D786874–5, D786885–8, D786895–6, D786913–4, D786922: Cabinet Protocols, July 4, 6 (2), 7, 8, 9, 1931.

depositors in banks, should be satisfied first. The foreign versus domestic argument also arose in the charges and countercharges as to whether foreign institutions were still to blame for the drain of credits, or whether transfers by German nationals were now more important. On July 6, Sackett reported hearing that the Guaranty Trust Company of New York had given notice to the large Berlin banks that they were withdrawing credits; this action would probably have set off withdrawals by the other large New York banks, turning the situation into chaos. Two days later Castle cabled back that according to Governor Harrison, the main New York banks, including the Guaranty Trust, were definitely not withdrawing credits; Guaranty Trust had even increased its credits to Germany since June 21. Moreover, Harrison was said to believe that the main part of the withdrawals were being made by the Germans themselves. Perhaps the Guaranty Trust withdrawal had indeed been planned, but was then reversed through Harrison's influence.[30] During the next two weeks, the American line continued to be that German capital flight and withdrawals by other countries were responsible, while the Germans pointed an accusing finger at their foreign creditors. Actually, it appears that a large share of the blame (if a bank can be blamed for trying to protect its interests) belonged to the banks of smaller countries, such as those of Switzerland, Sweden, Belgium, and the Netherlands, and also to the smaller American and British banks, which were not under the direct influence of Harrison or Norman.[31]

Wherever the responsibility may have lain, the loss of short-term credits went beyond anything Germany had experienced in the spring of 1929 or the fall of 1930. The rediscount credit of

[30] SDP, 462.00R296/4290: Ambassador in Berlin to Acting Secretary, July 6, 1931; Acting Secretary to Ambassador in Berlin, July 8, 1931. New York bankers reportedly said on July 10 that the New York Federal Reserve Bank had required them to promise to leave their credits in Germany as a prior condition for its participation in the June 25 credit (*New York Times*, July 11, 1931).

[31] Willard Hurst, "Holland, Switzerland and Belgium and the English Gold Crisis," *Journal of Political Economy*, 40:638–660 (1932); note esp. p. 652. See also *DBFP*, 2/II, Appendix I: Remarks by Brüning (pp. 440–441) and Snowden (p. 451).

$100,000,000, which the other central banks had granted on June 25 and which was due to be repaid on July 16, had been practically exhausted. Every transfer of funds abroad meant a call on the meager supply of German gold or foreign assets, and the Reichsbank's holdings of these were the basis for the German currency. If losses continued, the cover for the Reichsbank note issue would fall below the legal minimum laid down in the Young Plan and in German law. It would be difficult to obtain sanction for lowering the minimum legal coverage, and more important, a lowering of coverage would mean inflation. After the experience of 1923, inflation was the bugbear of Germany, and any return to it might well precipitate a political revolution.[32]

LUTHER'S TRIP TO LONDON AND PARIS

In an effort to re-establish confidence, President Luther of the Reichsbank revived the dormant Gold Discount Bank, which had been established under the Dawes Plan, and which had at its disposal an unused foreign credit of $50,000,000. By July 7, Luther had also organized a group of German banking and industrial leaders who guaranteed RM500,000,000 to pay, if need be, any debts of the Gold Discount Bank. It was hoped that, armed with this guarantee, the Gold Discount Bank would enjoy public confidence at home and abroad; if anyone was fearful about the money he had lent in Germany, the debt to him could be assumed by the Gold Discount Bank, and the funds would then remain in the country. Or in other words, the Gold Discount Bank would receive credit from abroad, and would give credit to other German borrowers. As Luther explained it to the cabinet, the aim was similar to that of the Rentenmark device that ended inflation in 1923, that is, to create confidence by providing a sort of mortgage on the national capital.[33]

The revival of the Gold Discount Bank was not intended merely

[32] See *DBFP*, 2/II, Nos. 177, 180, 184 (includes 8-page memo by Rowe-Dutton and Thelwall), 185; *New York Times*, July 1, 11, 1931.

[33] SDP, 462.00R296/4336, 4473: Ambassador in Berlin to Acting Secretary, July 8, 1931; Memo from Economic Adviser to Acting Secretary, July 7, 1931; *DBFP*, 2/II, No. 180; GFMR, 1684/D786890-5: Cabinet Proctocol, July 8, 1931.

to stabilize the existing situation. For that purpose, Reichsbank action, through credit restrictions and a temporary (if somewhat illegal) moratorium on payments, might have been sufficient. Instead—and this is very important to understanding Brüning's actions in the two weeks following—it was hoped that with the Gold Discount Bank, large new foreign credits could be arranged. The guarantee was announced through the device of publishing a letter from some of the prominent bankers and industrialists involved. This letter ended: "This guarantee on our part can, however, only become effective if the Reichsbank succeeds in securing for us, in cooperation with foreign central banks, the necessary assistance for the German economic system and for German credit with the help of foreign banks. We trust that the steps necessary to realize this project may immediately be put in hand." [34]

Luther may or may not have shared in drafting this letter himself, but in any case he must have approved its publication. By the inclusion of the paragraph just quoted, the Reichsbank chief was publicly committed to seeking new credits abroad. Presumably the statement was intended to bring pressure on the other central banks to meet German demands; as with the June 6 manifesto, if not quite so obviously, the Germans were serving notice that failure to meet their wishes would mean disaster—and they were thereby making disaster all the more certain if the failure took place.

To give the forcing play more force, Luther arranged a hasty and highly publicized trip to London and Paris. For the first leg of the journey, on the way to London on July 9, Luther traveled by air, then a highly unconventional mode of transportation, the use of which seemed to emphasize his desperation. But Luther's pilgrimage failed to produce a large new advance, or even to secure conclusively a renewal of the $100,000,000 credit due on July 16. He originally intended to go from Paris to Basel for a meeting of the directors of the Bank for International Settlements, but developments in Germany and his own experiences in Paris

[34] *DBFP*, 2/II, No. 180.

led him to fly directly back to Berlin, possibly a wiser but certainly not a quieter man. No effort was made to conceal or minimize his failure.

In England, Norman and Luther conferred mainly while on the boat train from London to Dover. Norman stated that the Bank of England was too deeply involved in Austria and Hungary to provide further assistance, and he also suggested that the Reichsbank might do more on its own behalf. The Bank of England was indeed over-extended, but Luther got the impression that Norman's chief grounds for holding back were political: Norman considered that the Franco-American agreement was "in no way a fulfillment of the Hoover Plan." And although the Reich government was politically obligated to pay unconditional reparations on July 15, he held that the Reichsbank was not entitled to use the $100,000,000 rediscount credit, in which the Bank of England had participated, for this purpose. In an account which may be compared with such historical curiosa as the Kaiser's story of his meeting with Nicky at Björkö, or Ciano's of his discussions with Ribbentrop, Luther reported some of Norman's other views:

Norman continued to hold that the situation was basically the same as before the Hoover proposal, only made worse by the passing of time and the further weakening of Germany. He admitted that he had had confidence in the Hoover proposal and therefore, early on Monday, June 22, he had urged the Reichsbank to relax its [credit] restrictions as far as possible. The new Gold Discount Bank proposal represented Germany's supreme effort and was good, but could not succeed because political calm was lacking, and nothing that the Reichsbank or the cooperation of the central banks could accomplish would help. He recommended that as banker of the Reich, I should tell the Reich government that the withdrawal of foreign exchange could only be mastered through negotiations between the governments, because only in that way could confidence be re-established. While I was alone with him in Dover, he told me for my private information that he had talked with his government last night and had established that its views were in agreement [with his]. I thereupon questioned him directly: "Then the British government would not be surprised if the German government, describing the position of the

German economy and the Reichsbank, addressed it on the subject of a credit for Germany?" Norman answered that the British government would conceal the fact that it was not surprised, but it was now expecting some such action. Other states were in the same position . . . Norman is completely clear on the importance of the Brüning government for keeping things stable, to which I had occasion to refer at an earlier stage of the conversation.

Norman obviously was not clear as to what should happen if no central bank credit came into existence or if instead of that the German government took action with a request for credit from the other governments. On the one hand he said that in such a situation the governments must be ready to act in a few hours. On the other hand, he expressed the idea that one of the participating governments [France] would probably only be brought over to the right point of view if the crisis became still greater. I then described with the greatest seriousness the danger of letting a crisis grow worse and worse, because then one could not be sure of avoiding the really critical stage. When the conversation then came to the question of whether all governments, or rather all parliaments, really had the desire and the ability in any case to avoid the worst, Norman emphasized strongly that the British government was at all events ready to help. In general, I had the impression that Great Britain would like to take the direction of affairs tightly into her own hands. On the significance of the holiday year if established in the pure Hoover spirit, in relation to which Norman, as already mentioned, considered the French additions a basic alteration, he made the usual comment that provision must be made for the future during that year. If the central banks were now to give a credit, then it would happen in the bargain that reparations would be paid from this credit, which was by all means to be avoided.[35]

Thus Norman (1) proposed to prevent the use for reparations payments of credits extended by the three Western central banks; (2) urged that the governments intervene, asserting (probably falsely) that his own was prepared to do so; and (3) entertained the idea of bringing the French to reason by letting the situation

[35] GFMR, 1660/D729417; 2548/E300306–9: Neurath to Ministry, July 2, 1931; Luther and Hoesch to Brüning and Dreyse (Vice President of the Reichsbank), July 10, 1931 (written July 9).

deteriorate still further. Irresponsible and inexperienced in diplomacy, Norman promised everything and nothing. It was a basic postulate in this period, especially in London and Washington, that central banks must be independent of governmental control; perhaps some thought might have been given to defending the governments against the central banks. The Populist charges against the "international bankers" were not entirely without foundation. Norman's conversation with Luther was particularly mischievous because, while Norman was interested in governmental action to bring about the permanent elimination of reparations, Luther's report encouraged Berlin to hope that governmental action might secure a rediscount credit for Germany.

We may suppose that when Luther reached Paris, Hoesch listened attentively. The Ambassador commented, on the eleventh:

Luther's conversation with Montague [*sic*] Norman does not very clearly indicate what Norman and the British government are really after. I have no doubt that the British wish to help Germany in her need. But with Norman personally, his wish to bring France to reason and his anger over French resistance to the Hoover Plan certainly play a great role. If he declares that the holiday in its present form is a complete distortion of the Hoover Plan and makes the whole plan ineffective, and if at the same time he maintains that the crisis in Germany must get still worse, in order to bring everyone to reason on the subject of the German burden, then it seems to me that these methods for bringing France to terms are rather dangerous for us. On the whole, I fail to find in Luther's discussion with Norman any clarity on the question as to how Norman and the British really picture the further development.[36]

After sending this apt warning, Hoesch had lunch with the British Ambassador, Lord Tyrrell, who confirmed, from his own somewhat Francophile point of view, the tendency of Norman's policy. According to Hoesch's report of Tyrrell's remarks:

Under the spiritual leadership of Snowden and Montagu Norman, the British have intended, with the proposal for summoning the Experts' Conference in London, to overthrow the Paris settlement as

[36] GFMR, 2548/E300317–8: Hoesch to Brüning and Bülow, July 11, 1931.

far as possible and return to the original Hoover proposal. In the London Conference of Ministers, also proposed, Snowden and Norman are said to desire that the reparation and debts questions be attacked in their totality, and so far as possible carried to a new solution. The French have got wind of the threatening danger, and only Tyrrell's persuasion induced them to agree to the London Experts' Conference, while they have made all reserves regarding a Conference of Ministers. Subsequently they have also attached conditions to their acceptance of the Experts' Conference. Tyrrell disapproves of the British plans mentioned above because he is convinced, probably rightly, that there is no prospect of success in connection with France. He has repeatedly informed London that the French government can in no case depart from the Paris moratorium settlement, for the simple reason that this would be suicide for it.

In relation to Norman's special viewpoint, Tyrrell further confirms that, in keeping with Norman's whole mental orientation, which leads him to seek ideal solutions in spite of all obstacles, he now wants, so to speak, to go "all out"; for this reason he also prefers, instead of plugging gaps, to let the situation in Germany become still more critical. Thereby, and especially in relation to France, the preconditions would be created for a real relief of Germany and the world.

Tyrrell seemed pleased to hear from Hoesch that the German objections to a conference of ministers had been brought to the attention of the Foreign Office.[37]

The French, for their part, were priming themselves to receive the German traveler. Thanks to a French study on German clandestine rearmament, written with the use of the records of the *Deuxième Bureau*, we have for once a document from French archives, a letter of July 10 from André Maginot, the Minister of War, presumably to either Laval or Briand:

The exaggerated expenses of Germany for the Reichswehr represent only the financial aspect of a military policy involving numerous and flagrant breaches in the Treaty of Versailles, especially in the fields of matériel and armaments.

In view of the conversations which you may have with the German Ambassador, I believe that I should call your attention to the very

[37] GFMR, 2548/E300326–8: Hoesch to Ministry, July 11, 1931.

serious infractions which can be charged against Germany since the departure of the military experts from Berlin . . .

These breaches are to be added to those which the military experts pointed out in their final report and which the Conference of Ambassadors brought to the knowledge of the Council of the League of Nations on March 16, 1931.[38]

They clearly prove that the German command, while refusing to keep its army within the role assigned to it by the Treaty of Versailles, i.e., the maintenance of internal order and the policing of the frontiers, tends to make of it the cadre of a modern army capable of waging war beyond the frontiers of the Reich.

In these circumstances, I consider that the negotiations under way offer an occasion to clearly point out to Germany the grave breaches which she has already committed in the spirit and letter of the Versailles Treaty.

And on this basis, from the financial viewpoint now under discussion, we would be justified in obtaining from her a promise to bring her expenses strictly into line with the military statute which she has committed herself to uphold.[39]

We have seen French policy mainly through the mirror of German, British, or American reporting, and as expressed by the mediating personalities of Briand, Laval, and Berthelot. Maginot's letter reminds us that there were still Frenchmen in prominent positions who wanted to hold to the letter of Versailles, who thought that the Germans could and should, for example, be obliged to limit their army to a police function. Berthelot had warned Hoesch that some cabinet members were much less moderate than the Premier,[40] and Maginot's letter shows how true this was.

Luther's own discussions in Paris on July 10 were with Flandin and Moret, the Governor of the Bank of France. The French agreed to extend the existing credit, due on July 16, for ninety

[38] See *DBFP*, 2/I, No. 357.

[39] Georges Castellan, *Le Réarmament clandestin du Reich, 1930–1935* (Paris, 1954), Annex I, p. 536; the addressee of the letter is not given by Castellan. It is unfortunate from the point of view of the present study that this book does not describe French naval attaché reports on the cruisers.

[40] GFMR, 2548/E300297–8: Hoesch to Ministry, July 8, 1931.

days, but refused to grant a large new credit until certain other matters had been settled. After commenting on the lack of clarity in Norman's views (see above), Hoesch continued his July 11 report as follows:

In contrast, the result of Luther's Paris discussions with Moret and Flandin is in no way lacking in clarity. As was to be foreseen, and as was simply inevitable, considering the whole situation, the French make the granting of further credits dependent on an improvement in Franco-German relations, in other words, on German political concessions. This development is so natural in international life, especially between two countries with so many points of difference, that one cannot develop moral indignation about it.[41]

After Luther returned home, the press was informed in Berlin that the French had made additional assistance conditional on a suspension of the pocket battleship program, the abandonment of the customs union, further German credit restrictions, the inauguration of measures to prevent the flight of capital, and an "Eastern Locarno," that is, a renunciation of any intention of regaining Danzig and the Polish Corridor. The French protested in Washington and New York, and also with Hoesch, that they had made no political demands of Luther, and they regretted that Germany had thus made a public issue of concessions, making it much more difficult to concede anything.[42] As Berthelot put it to Hoesch:

France had still not really laid down any preconditions. It was simply a matter of having Berlin create an atmosphere which would make possible measures of assistance on the part of France. One should find something which could be publicly declared. Perhaps the Reich government could still say that at a moment when it was necessary to turn to the whole world for help, further stringent economies would be made in the Reich budget. These measures would also affect defense

[41] GFMR, 2548/E300318.
[42] *New York Times*, July 11, 12, 1931; *SIA, 1931*, p. 83; *FRUS, 1931*, I, 251; GFMR, 2548/E300338: Leitner to Ministry, July 12, 1931; SDP, 462.00R296/5055: Memo from Division of Western European Affairs, July 11, 1931.

appropriations, and among other things the construction of the cruiser would be halted for the time being. Berthelot added that such a declaration by the Reich government did not have to be addressed to France, it would be much more appropriate if it was given to America.[43]

Perhaps the French made no direct, official demands to Luther, who was not technically an agent of the German government, but they apparently told him, as Hoesch reported at the time, that there was no hope of French help unless there was an improvement in Franco-German relations. We can guess that Flandin and Moret then went to explain the sort of thing which would improve the relationship; this was what Laval did later when Brüning came to Paris. For all practical purposes, we may take it that the French stated their conditions; what annoyed them was that Luther had characteristically burned his bridges by letting these conditions be published.

THE GERMAN GOVERNMENT'S APPEAL FOR HELP

The British and French financial leaders had refused to grant the large new credit sought by Luther. Now the German government itself, probably influenced by Norman's statement that the British government was expecting it to make an appeal, entered into the efforts to obtain financial assistance. This was a reflection of German desperation, for a disclosure that the government was seeking a loan was very undesirable. During the weeks that followed some hints emerged of this activity, but it was never admitted, it was hidden even from the cabinet, and it is still denied in postwar memoirs.[44]

Luther did not venture to fly to the United States, but as soon as the results of his discussions in London and Paris were known,

[43] GFMR, 2548/E300331: Memo on telephone call from Hoesch, July 12, 1931. See also SDP, 462.00R296/4410: Ambasasdor in Paris to Acting Secretary, July 11, 1931, for Riesser's version, according to which the French proposed a political holiday and the dropping of the customs union.

[44] GFMR, 1684/D787114–8, D787120: Cabinet Protocol, July 25, 1931; Paul Schmidt, *Statist auf diplomatischer Bühne* (Bonn, 1949), pp. 218–219; Julius Curtius, *Sechs Jahre Minister der deutschen Republik* (Heidelberg, 1948), pp. 219–220.

even before he had finished his Paris discussions, the government and the Reichsbank took the matter of a loan up with Sackett. The Ambassador was asked to come to the Wilhelmstrasse on the afternoon of Friday, July 10, where he saw Bülow and Brüning, and that evening Bülow called at the Embassy in the company of *Staatssekretär* Hans Schäffer of the Finance Ministry and Vice President Friedrich Wilhelm Dreyse of the Reichsbank. The Germans described Luther's failure, and alleged that both France and Britain were trying to use Germany's difficulties to extort political concessions; Bülow seems to have deliberately exaggerated the degree of pressure, misquoting Norman and emphasizing French demands. The financial experts predicted that the crisis would culminate on Monday (July 13) in the exhaustion of Reichsbank resources, the closing of banks, an inability to meet payrolls, general panic, and probably revolution. There was no time for arranging a long-term loan. Two main points emerge from the discussions. In the first place, the Germans hoped that they could again mobilize the sympathy and interest of the American government. Governor Harrison was known to be skeptical about aiding Germany, blaming her difficulties on the flight of German funds. But Berlin hoped to get Hoover and the State Department to use their influence to make the Federal Reserve authorities take the initiative in obtaining for Germany the large rediscount credit Luther had been seeking, winning over the Banks of England and France and perhaps the Bank for International Settlements. In the second place, the Germans now hinted that they could discuss concessions, that for example the customs union might be made more comprehensive after the Hague Tribunal had made its decision, and that the cruiser (that is, Cruiser B) might be taken up at the coming Disarmament Conference. "The only thing impossible," Bülow said, "was a one-sided political sacrifice by Germany." The concessions thus foreshadowed were more apparent than real, and seem to have been mentioned largely to impress Sackett, but it was a measure of the seriousness of the situation that there should be any talk of concessions at all. The chief difficulty, Bülow stated, was that the French required a "spectacular" concession to show their public, rather than an eventual real concession which might be easier for the German government to make.[45]

Leaving no avenues unexplored, on Saturday, July 11, the German government repeated its appeal for financial help in a circular telegram to Washington, London, Rome, and Paris, instructing its envoys to make *démarches* at each of the Western capitals. The Washington Embassy was further ordered to inform Eugene Meyer, Chairman of the Federal Reserve Board, while Consul General Kiep in New York was told to approach Parker Gilbert and, "if possible," J. P. Morgan.[46] But the Americans were slow in responding, first, because Hoover and Castle had gone to spend the weekend away from Washington heat at the President's camp on the Rapidan, and second, because the American government was reluctant to urge any action on the Federal Reserve officials. The substance of Sackett's cable was telephoned to Governor Harrison on Saturday morning (July 11), but Harrison thought no action was possible until the British and French acted, and also that there was no reason for advancing American money while German money was fleeing the Fatherland. Eugene Meyer, when finally tracked down at Mount Kisco by Consul General Kiep, was polite but noncommittal; Meyer was much more caustic when interviewed by a State Department official on Monday, indicating that the crisis was purely a banking one in which American action was entirely up to the discretion of the Federal Reserve, and that the Germans were to blame for their difficulties and should find their own way out. Kiep never did gain access to the presence of J. P. Morgan, and had to content himself with sending Morgan a memorandum and explaining the situation to Parker Gilbert, Morgan's lieutenant.[47] After a hectic Sunday,

[45] SDP, 462.00R296/4398: Ambassador in Berlin to Acting Secretary, July 11, 1931; GFMR, 2548/E300348-50, E300315: Memos by Bülow, July 10, 11, 1931.

[46] GFMR, 1660/D729524-6. Otto Kiep had left the Embassy to become Consul General in New York in March, 1931.

[47] *FRUS, 1931*, I, 250-251; GFMR, 2548/E300337-8, E300341-5: Leitner to Ministry, July 12, 1931; Kiep to Ministry, July 12, 1931 (two messages); SDP, 462.00R296/4626: Memo by Economic Adviser, July 13, 1931.

during which Kiep was in frequent communication with Harrison and Luther, the American authorities began to take the position that Germany should first undertake credit restrictions and halt, possibly by voluntary means but if necessary through government action, the flight of German funds. Harrison believed that the best course for Luther to follow would be to present a concrete proposal to the heads of the various central banks, who had assembled in Basel for the BIS meeting. In spite of all the efforts of the Germans, they obtained no definite commitment, and in fact a decision was reached in New York on Sunday night that the Federal Reserve banks could take no initiative.[48]

The appeal for American help was not confined to the foregoing. Secretary Stimson had now arrived in Rome and on Monday evening, July 13, he received Ambassador von Schubert, along with the British and French Ambassadors. Stimson inquired about the situation in Germany, and Schubert proceeded to give what the British Ambassador described afterwards as a "piteous account" of the crisis, by then far worse than it had been on Sunday. Stimson informed Schubert that he had no knowledge of the current negotiations, although he understood that the Federal Reserve Bank (not further clarified) had decided on comprehensive credit assistance for Germany.[49]

In his easy-going way, Ambassador von Neurath managed to see Henderson only on Monday morning; Neurath's outstanding quality was always that he was (in a later idiom) "unflappable." Although Neurath left an *aide-mémoire*, repeating the main part of Saturday's circular telegram, the discussion revolved mainly around the question of German concessions and the coming British visit, not the financial crisis. According to Neurath, Henderson

---

[48] GFMR, 2548/E300329–30, E300340–5: Kiep to Ministry, July 12, 1931 (three messages); *FRUS, 1931*, I, 250–254; SDP, 462.00R296/4626: Memo by Economic Adviser, July 13, 1931. Kiep reported Harrison and Gilbert as stating they had received no specific information that Sackett had transmitted a proposal for a new credit. But the State Department record, published and unpublished, shows that Harrison, at least, had been told by Washington of the German request.

[49] GFMR, 1660/D729543–5: Schubert to Ministry, July 14, 1931; *DBFP*, 2/II, No. 192.

was very concerned over the reception he would get in Germany, confessing that he had expected that Neurath was coming to call the visit off, to which Neurath replied "that while I could not deny that the atmosphere was less favorable, I would consider the abandonment of the visit a mistake. I could well imagine that perhaps at the present moment he could, after talking again with Paris, do something effective for removing Franco-German tension." Neurath's account made it appear that he had put Henderson in his place, but some officials in Berlin may have wondered if, in the existing situation, it would not have been more appropriate to have dwelt more on the need for the large new credit. On that subject, the Ambassador only reported that "Mr. Henderson did not take a position on the credit we requested." But even if Neurath had pressed for an answer, he would have met with a refusal. On Monday morning Henderson informed the French, in line with what Norman had told Luther, that "from the financial point of view, London had done its part in financing both Germany and Austria, and there was no further financial help which could be made from here." [50]

Laval was also away from his capital, but Hoesch managed to forward the German entreaty to him Saturday night, and through the intervention of Berthelot, he succeeded in getting the Premier to return to Paris for an interview on Sunday evening. Hoesch gave Laval a full description of the situation, including developments since Saturday, but Laval proved to be quite well informed already. The swarthy *Auvergnat* had some qualities, and among them was a keen sense of the possible, a readiness to face the facts of a situation; perhaps this partly explains his later collaboration. Hoesch reported:

[50] Lutz, Graf Schwerin von Krosigk, *Es Geschah in Deutschland* (Tübingen and Stuttgart, 1951), p. 310; *DBFP*, 2/II, No. 185, including note 1; GFMR, 2548/E300357–8: Neurath to Ministry, July 13, 1931. The words "this morning" (when Neurath finally saw Henderson) are underlined on the German Foreign Office file copy, apparently indicating the raising of someone's eyebrows over Neurath's late action. He had, of course, the English weekend to contend with. Henderson's account of the meeting does not support Neurath's picture of the latter's triumph.

[Laval] made no mention at all of political concessions, but rather observed that he would only be able to mention political desires when he was in a position at the same time to offer me a sure prospect of assistance. In general, he continued, the question of political concessions, which had never been formally demanded by France, had been overtaken by events. He also recognized that the making of political declarations under the force of pressure from the financial situation must lead to the fall of the German government. In view of Germany's situation, it seemed to him that the questions of cruiser construction and of the Austro-German customs union had little present reality. All that belonged to the past, just as the Hoover Plan was also already behind us; he sees very clearly that at the present moment everything comes down to one question: whether Germany can be saved and how.

Laval agreed that they "had come to a decisive point in world history" and said that he would have to consult his fellow cabinet members. Hoesch volunteered that Germany would be ready to discuss political questions in a calmer atmosphere, provided one-sided concessions were not required, and hinted that the German ministers would be ready to discuss such matters when they visited Paris early in August. He also mentioned that the German government did not intend to lay down Cruiser C in the next year, and that, in view of the coming Disarmament Conference, the construction of this ship might never take place. Laval seemed, nevertheless, to be more interested in concentrating on the financial crisis. All in all, if Laval did not promise anything, he displayed a moderation and understanding which were, for a man in his position, quite remarkable. And he declined to demand concessions—at least, until he had a definite proposal to make.[51]

The Appeal to the Bank for International Settlements

One wonders if Laval, when he was carrying out the demands of the Nazi conquerors, ever reflected back on this incident and on the change in relative positions. The Germans were certainly

---

[51] GFMR, 1660/D729537–40: Hoesch to Curtius and Bülow, July 13, 1931. See also SDP, 462.00R296/4432: Ambassador in Paris to Acting Secretary, July 12, 1931.

far from victory in 1931. The cabinet in Berlin spent the Sunday in continuous session, mainly on the immediate problem of what should be done the next day about opening the Danat and Dresdner Banks. The ministers decided that on Monday, while the Danat Bank might close its doors, the other banks could and should at first remain open; all banks were later closed on Tuesday and Wednesday. The foreign exchange and stock markets were to be closed on Monday and Tuesday; the latter was not to reopen for nearly two months.[52] After prolonged argument, the cabinet agreed in the small hours of Monday morning on an emergency decree for posting outside the locked doors of the Danat Bank's branches; the main provision of the decree was a guarantee by the government of the bank's deposits.[53]

It was during this period that the German presidential dictatorship passed the point of no return. Efforts to win popular support through foreign policy had failed, and instead, foreign policy itself had precipitated a financial upheaval. The closing of the banks and the effort to check foreign exchange withdrawals entailed the issuance of a whole series of measures and decrees, "which," as Rumbold reported, "have brought business to a standstill, have interfered with liberty to travel, practically destroyed the freedom of the press and have set up a sort of inquisition into people's private affairs." [54] Many of the restrictions which shocked Rumbold have since become unpleasantly familiar (as, for example, in Attlee's Britain), but they have usually been legitimized by national elections and conducted under the banner of some popular national goal. Brüning's restrictions, however, were directed by an unpopular government, apparently toward an unpopular goal, the cutting of wages and prices. He appeared to be trying to use the methods of modern bureaucracy to enforce the austerities of Victorian "hard times." Thus the last hopes of win-

---

[52] *SIA, 1931*, p. 222. The British sterling crisis provided a welcome pretext for closing it again (*DBFP*, 2/II, Nos. 252, 265).

[53] GFMR, 1684/D786972–80: Cabinet Protocol, July 12, 1931. The Dresdner Bank was found to be in slightly better condition than the Danat, and its weakness was more or less successfully concealed from the public.

[54] *DBFP*, 2/II, No. 225.

ning popularity waned, while the running of the country became an enormous administrative task. Many decisions were taken from legislators and private interests and irrevocably centralized in the Reich ministries. Involuntarily, Brüning created the framework for totalitarianism; a popular leader with popular symbols could easily complete the transition.

A symptom of the general evolution was the fleeting reappearance of Dr. Schacht, who soon would openly commit himself to the enemies of the republic. Statements in his new book, *The End of Reparations*, had aroused extreme resentment in the cabinet, which had gone to the length of publishing an official rebuttal, but now the ministers swallowed their pride and asked for Schacht's advice, which he gave with his customary assurance. He argued that the government should only guarantee deposits up to a low limit of RM10,000–30,000. This would keep the government commitment within reasonable bounds, help the small depositors, and leave the big accounts, largely foreign, to go through the wringer. It was also the easy, irresponsible answer. The cabinet, presumably because it wished to secure a new rediscount credit from abroad, did not adopt this policy.[55] But word that Schacht was advising the cabinet spread rapidly, partly thanks to Schacht's own efforts. The wizard of German finance saw Sackett on Monday, when, after criticizing what he considered to be the "half-baked" ideas of the cabinet, and accusing the Reichsbank management of falsifying its accounts, he declared significantly that the only political solution for Germany was a directorate of five business leaders. On July 24, Sir Horace Rumbold reported that small but widening circles felt that if only Schacht could overcome his unpopularity abroad, especially in the United States, and also at home with the Social Democrats, he "might yet be the man to save Germany." Schacht was not in fact entirely unpopular

[55] Julius Curtius, *Der Young Plan* (Stuttgart, 1950), pp. 8–9; Schacht, *76 Jahre*, pp. 361–362. Schacht's version, challenged by Krosigk (*Es Geschah*, pp. 128–129), is confirmed by the cabinet meeting records, which also support Schacht's statement that Brüning wanted him to take on the responsibility of liquidating the Danat Bank (GFMR, 1684/D786976–7, D786980–2, D786882). Schacht declined (*76 Jahre*, pp. 362–363).

in America. Prittwitz says that American bankers considered their German colleague too emotional, but Schacht was on good terms with Owen D. Young, and on July 15 President Hoover, in the course of a telephone conversation with Stimson, said that he thought Luther was "a distinct loss" and that the situation would be greatly improved if Schacht replaced him. Hoover's opinion, which he said was also the opinion of "American and British bankers," could have originated with Montagu Norman.[56]

On Monday, July 13, while the doors of the Danat Bank remained closed, the German leaders anxiously turned their attention to Basel, where the banking leaders of Europe were attending the BIS Directors' meeting. Luther had been obliged to remain in Berlin on Sunday for the deliberations there, but after that, he dashed off in order to reach Basel before the meeting broke up:[57] perhaps there would be a chance to obtain help. And Governor Harrison had strongly recommended that Luther present a plan to the BIS meeting.

But as it turned out, the result of the BIS conference seemed to justify the suspicion with which the Germans customarily regarded this institution. The communiqué stated:

The Directors took notice of the statement presented by Luther on the situation in Germany and on the satisfactory character of her economic and budget position in spite of the crisis brought about by the withdrawals of short-term capital from Germany. The German Government having approached the various governments with a view to obtaining financial assistance on their respective markets, the Board,

---

[56] SDP, 462.00R296/4456; 862.51/3139: Ambassador in Paris to Acting Secretary, July 13, 1931; Chargé in Paris to Acting Secretary, July 24, 1931; *DBFP*, 2/II, Nos. 188, 225; *FRUS, 1931*, I, 263; Friedrich von Prittwitz und Gaffron, *Zwischen Petersburg und Washington* (München, 1952), p. 190. Apparently at Brüning's instigation, the Berlin representative of General Electric sent cables to Young on the crisis, originally to correct Schacht's report that the German government could and should undertake further retrenchment. Brüning was also interested in explaining why French conditions could not be met, and in getting Young's support for an American loan (GFMR, 913/384895; 1776/D808135-40).

[57] GFMR, 1684/D786972, D786978, D787013: Cabinet Protocols, July 12, 13, 1931; *FRUS, 1931*, I, 254.

being convinced of the necessity for such assistance under present circumstances, declares that it is prepared to collaborate therein and to strengthen the American assistance by all means at the disposal of the Central Banks. In the meantime the Board authorized the President in agreements with the other institutions concerned, to renew its participation in the rediscount credit previously accorded to the Reichsbank.[58]

Although Luther's activities had been public enough before this, they had supposedly been on behalf of the Reichsbank and the Gold Discount Bank; the German government's appeal had been secret. The statement that the German government was seeking help was quite embarrassing, in view of past pronouncements by Schacht and by Brüning himself against further government borrowing, and also in view of the widespread belief that such a loan could only be had in exchange for political concessions. Berlin telephoned Luther to try to get the reference to the government's appeal deleted, but the communiqué had already been released. The BIS also seemed to be trying to cast off onto the governments part of the responsibility for making a loan, and in general, the wording of the statement was not very fortunate.[59]

But the reality was worse than the communiqué. As Luther put it when telephoning Berlin, BIS assistance was "completely ruled out." The British were too short of foreign exchange to help, and the French were only interested in discussing a long-term loan, which could be tied up with long-term German political commitments. The French bankers, with this in mind, and the British, under Norman's guidance, agreed for very different reasons that the difficulties of Germany were too much for the central banks, and must be handled by the governments. According to the American Consul in Basel, H. Merle Cochran, the British representatives talked "in favor of letting circumstances force a complete revision of existing agreements even including Versailles Treaty." [60]

[58] *FRUS, 1931*, I, 255.
[59] GFMR, 1684/D787000–1, D787007–9: Cabinet Protocols, July 13, 1931.
[60] GFMR, 1684/D787000–2, D787007–9: Cabinet Protocols, July 13, 1931;

Back in the first days of June, the Germans had been ready to manipulate the financial situation for political purposes. Now, when they wanted to deal with a more serious crisis in purely financial terms, they discovered that others wanted to engage in further political manipulation. Norman was playing with the idea of using the crisis to force the revision he and the British Treasury thought necessary. And although Laval seemed reasonable, signs were multiplying that France would seek to use Germany's financial distress to commit her to the *status quo*. German hopes for financial salvation depended mainly on the United States, but the American administration, and even more, the American bankers (who this time would have to carry the burden themselves) were more cautious than before, no longer hoping for a psychological revolution. There were as many opposing aims as there were countries, and there was no Bismarck or Talleyrand in sight to conceive and carry through a solution. Hoover had the impulse to lead, but not the necessary tact and skill. Laval's advisers had at least the conception of a European order, but France was the most lonely power of all.

No one can say that the men involved were unaware of the seriousness of the situation. One is tempted to think now that they were overconscious of it; Hoover's comparisons with 1914, the warnings to Sackett of possible revolution, Laval's and Hoesch's agreement that they had reached "a decisive point in world history"—all this seems overdrawn. Civilization did not end after all. Yet Laval and Hoesch may have been right, if not quite in the way they supposed. This was the time when the world depression was changing from a mere cyclical adjustment to the apparent failure of a whole system. Andreas Predöhl, a German economist, has noted in an able essay that when the Darmstädter und Nationalbank failed, "German economic policy, with its liberal [that is, classical] methods, was at an end." He adds that the British departure from gold in September 1931 was, for the world

---

SDP, 462.00R296/4469, 4506: Ambassador in Berlin to Acting Secretary, July 14, 1931; Consul in Basel to Acting Secretary, July 15, 1931; *FRUS*, *1931*, I, 255.

economy, more significant: "This is the decisive turning point." At any rate, the two cases were closely linked, in time and in the logic of events. Predöhl notes that, although the gold standard remained economic orthodoxy through the Second World War, it has never been restored. It was supposed to end crises automatically, but proved unable to do this in the face of reparations and debts—as well as of higher tariffs, bars to migration, and rigidities in wages and prices.[61]

The gold standard had much more than monetary significance. If it was to operate, capital had to move freely without any governmental restraint. Under the gold standard, when a country did not pay its way in the world with goods and services, it would be obliged to export capital; the resulting scarcity of capital would cause a rise in interest rates; this would force a reduction of prices and wages; and as goods became cheaper, it would become possible to sell them in foreign and domestic markets, restoring the balance. Moreover, during the period of falling prices, the less efficient producers would go to the wall, thus reducing the total volume of goods and bringing an end to overproduction. The theory of the gold standard assumed that, in the event of overproduction or an excess of imports, prices would and should fall, wages would and should be cut, inefficient companies would and should be allowed to go bankrupt, and unemployment would and should temporarily increase. In theory, capitalists would suffer along with workers, but in practice, the maintenance of classical principles encouraged and required a rather ruthless attitude toward the "lower classes." There was also fear in class and nationality relations, as shown in the General Strike of 1926 or in the Sacco-Vanzetti case. Norman's views on unemployment—that the workers should be ashamed to be on the dole, that they were guilty—was a rationalization, psychologically required by his support of the gold standard; he resembled the colonialist of the late period who mutters into his pink gin, "You can't trust the natives." There may be no sounder basis for inhumanity, no more

[61] Andreas Predöhl, "Die Epochenbedeutung der Weltwirtschaftskrise von 1929 bis 1931," *Vierteljahrshefte für Zeitgeschichte*, 1:97–118 (1953).

fertile inspiration for false suspicions, than a well-developed body of social doctrine.

When the classical theory failed in its automatic operation, economic—and consequently political—alternatives were made explicit, and conscious decisions had to be made. This was usually done by extending bureaucratic powers. Another result, as Predöhl points out, was to give state boundaries fundamental importance. The economy became more an extension of the national state, more political. Under such conditions, the state tends to become a "Behemoth" and as Franz Neumann has described, this is what happened in Germany. But a third result was the end of a major source of class friction and fear. It may be that in the long run the beneficial effects of this last change will prove to outweigh the immediate adverse effects of the other changes. Autarchy seems already to be declining, and bureaucracy loses some of its onerous character when it ceases to be recruited on a class basis. Besides, as in the case of the Foreign Office and the Treasury, bureaucratic rule is by no means necessarily monolithic or lacking in checks and balances.

VIII

The Paris Meetings and the London Conference

THE Germans had by now taken their plea for a new rediscount credit to the major central banks, the major governments, and to the BIS, and they still did not have any definite commitment for assistance. Developments on Monday, July 13, made it imperative to close all banks on Tuesday, but some kind of partial opening was going to be necessary on Thursday, so that the week's wages and salaries could be paid. All the German bankers consulted agreed that they must have a moratorium on payments abroad. The cover for the note circulation was falling below forty per cent, and the Reichsbank was on the verge of raising the discount rate to the appalling figure of ten per cent. It seemed that a general moratorium might be inevitable; if it came, however, it would strangle what was left of German trade and destroy completely what remained of German credit.[1]

GERMAN PLANS FOR A CONFERENCE IN PARIS

Brüning was economically orthodox, and he was very anxious to avoid such action. There were still some unexhausted expedients, and a new plan was now devised to obtain the foreign credit. On July 14, Bülow telegraphed to Hoesch that Berlin was considering the idea of calling off the British visit, scheduled for the weekend

---

[1] GFMR, 1684/D787019–21: Cabinet Protocol, July 14, 1931; *SIA, 1931,* pp. 84–85; *FRUS, 1931,* I, 254.

of July 19 in return for Chequers, and instead of that, proposing to the French that Brüning make his long-discussed trip to Paris around the eighteenth or nineteenth. Stimson and Henderson were to be in Paris just before that, discussing disarmament, and if they were present, it would be possible for the Germans to avoid dealing alone, in their weakened condition, with the French. The sympathetic attitude shown by Laval in his discussion with Hoesch seems to have helped to evoke this scheme. Aside from the consideration of trying to make the Paris visit under the best possible conditions, it was thought that it might be possible at one stroke to get the British and French to make a definite financial commitment, clarifying the foggy hints in the BIS communiqué.

Bülow anticipated a general discussion, following which a communiqué might say, in his classic phraseology, "that these discussions had led to a far-reaching clarification of the respective viewpoints, that many (not specified) misunderstandings had been removed, and that for certain problems at issue, certain paths were envisaged for further negotiation." Bülow explained that in regard to this last, he personally thought that perhaps the cruiser question might be handled in connection with the Disarmament Conference; that the customs union could be dropped if the Hague Tribunal decided against it, or its expansion or modification could be discussed with the French and others if the Tribunal ruled in favor of it; finally, that Germany might bind herself by signing, for three years only, the League General Act, which provided for the arbitration of international disputes, and to which Germany had hitherto refused to subscribe because, as Bülow put it, it "excludes in practice any real pursuit of revision." If the French government was strong enough to be satisfied with such inconclusive results, then a conference was worth while; if the French would have to have concrete political successes, then it was not. Hoesch was asked to give his personal opinion, without approaching the French.[2]

In his reply to Bülow that same night, Hoesch pointed out that French help or leadership might fail to materialize, even if the

[2] GFMR, 1555/D666708–10: July 14, 1931.

Chancellor himself offered concessions, because the ending of the negotiations with Mellon and Edge and the state of German finances now made a Franco-German discussion much less attractive to the French. Nevertheless, Hoesch favored the proposed multilateral meeting. It was no longer a question of bringing about an improvement in Franco-German relations, "which under the circumstances would necessarily have lacked a real foundation," but rather of "whether, through the common exertions of the leading powers, help can still be given to Germany." Clearly, Hoesch agreed with Bülow's suggestion, not for the sake of holding the long-planned Franco-German meeting, or attaining a sudden reconciliation, but because he hoped that the new rediscount credit might thereby be secured. Neither Bülow nor Hoesch made any suggestion that such a conference could serve as an occasion for the permanent revision of reparations or of the Versailles Treaty. On the face of it, such revision could scarcely be undertaken in Paris, and the Germans were quite aware that their position was that of a supplicant. It is worth remembering that the German government was thus the first to conceive the idea of a multilateral meeting in Paris, since the British and Brüning allowed the American government to get the impression that this was purely a French scheme.[3]

HOOVER AGAIN SUGGESTS A LONDON CONFERENCE

The BIS meeting, which helped to call forth this German plan, evoked quite a different proposal from the United States. Because the bankers at Basel had recommended that the governments take up the German problem, and because there seemed to be a tendency to place on the United States an unsought responsibility for saving German credit, Hoover proceeded on July 14 to urge the

[3] GFMR, 1660/D729550–4: July 14, 1931; SDP, 462.00R296/4577, 4578: Ambassador in Berlin to Acting Secretary, July 17, 1931; Chargé in London to Acting Secretary, July 17, 1931. Hoesch also wondered if the meetings should be held outside Paris, to avoid undesirable demonstrations. The fact that the meetings did take place in Paris probably explains why, when the French later made their return visit, the German government felt compelled to shoulder the more difficult task of preventing demonstrations in Berlin.

British to call a conference of ministers in London at the earliest possible date, preferably by the next weekend. Washington defined the purposes of the conference as trying "to smooth out the differences between Germany and France which make practically impossible any solution of the present difficulties," and as drawing up "a permanent and far reaching plan on the relief of Germany for the consideration of the bankers." These statements of aim were certainly not very specific; it would seem that at this point there was no clear idea of just how France and Germany were to be reconciled, or of whether the plan for relief should include a foreign loan. But in the President's mind, this was definitely not to be a conference such as Norman wanted, making far-reaching changes involving, among others things, war debts, but only a meeting "for the sole purpose of dealing with the present emergency." [4]

As on certain other occasions in his career, Lindsay did not clearly and unmistakably report an American divergence from his own government's point of view. He cabled London:

Acting Secretary of State told me today that at meeting of Bank for International Settlements it was felt that matter had gone beyond the powers of central banks and that Governments must take situation in hand. The Governor of the Bank of England seems to favor immediate calling of conference of heads of Governments to deal with the situation on broadest lines, contemplating even revision of Treaty of Versailles.

View of the United States Government is that meeting of such a conference at the earliest possible moment is indeed now most desirable, but they think though the widest issues may have to be raised eventually it is important that conference itself should have only limited object, namely, that of dealing with immediate crisis. They would warmly support summons of conference, preferably this week and at London, for this purpose, and Secretary of State would represent them at it. At the same time they perfectly recognize that the conference would have to deal with political questions. If you concur in these views they would leave it to you to decide what Governments

[4] *FRUS, 1931*, I, 256–257.

should be invited and all other details, which you only can appreciate. (Repeated to Paris.)[5]

If examined by someone like Snowden or Norman, this message would have given the impression that while the Americans were hesitant, they would not really be too sorry to see the major political problems taken up. This had certainly been the sense of Lindsay's July 6 message, sent immediately after the Franco-American agreement was reached. The Foreign Office, on the other hand, could read into this new cable the possibility of discussing the customs union and Cruiser B. Accordingly, the government in London had no difficulty in taking up Hoover's suggestion. The desire on the part of the Treasury and the Bank of England for an immediate meeting was enhanced by the fact that there had lately been an increasing withdrawal of foreign funds, especially French, from London; if this continued, Britain would soon be in the same predicament as Germany. Suspicions arose that this withdrawal of funds was politically motivated and aimed at overcoming British resistance to the Franco-American agreement and to French policies in Central Europe.[6]

[5] *DBFP*, 2/II, No. 191. For other misleading reports by Lindsay, see *DBFP*, 2/III, Nos. 2, 3, 8; William L. Langer and S. Everett Gleason, *The Challenge to Isolation, 1937–1940* (New York, 1952), p. 28.

[6] In this case the truth on French financial diplomacy is difficult to gauge. Brüning had no doubt (when questioned by the author in 1951) that the French had exerted financial pressure on London for political purposes. This was also Castle's belief, expressed to Claudel (SDP, 462.00R296/5064: Memo by Acting Secretary, July 23, 1931). It seems significant that, as reported in the *Vierteljahrsheft zur Konjunkturforschung*, 6 (1931), II, pt. A, p. 13, a drop in British gold holdings in Paris began abruptly on July 6; this was the very time when Franco-British political differences became inflamed. British pride and tact may well have led to the concealing of evidence on this point. Yet, there were plenty of purely financial reasons for withdrawals. In a reply to a telegram from London on the withdrawals, Tyrrell sent a message describing some of these financial motives, especially the desire for liquidity due to losses in Germany, Austria, and Hungary (*DBFP*, 2/II, No. 207). Tyrrell stressed the withdrawals by smaller European countries, and this explanation is supported by Willard Hurst, "Holland, Switzerland and Belgium and the English Gold Crisis of 1931," *Journal of Political Economy*, 40:638–660 (1932). The French had no scruples about making withdrawals for political purposes—see Appendix I—but in this case such a policy would

The American proposal marked the beginning of a week of frenzied negotiations and jockeyings for place among the powers, resulting in the mutual frustration of almost all their aims. If none of the governments, excepting perhaps the American, could get its own way, at least they were able to block each other's path. And where American aims succeeded, it was because they represented little but resignation, the least common denominator. When all was over, the situation had changed, but to no one's advantage. The Germans failed to get a credit, the French failed to get concessions, the British Treasury failed to get permanent revision, and, one might add, the American lenders failed to get their money back.

HENDERSON IN PARIS

The first problem to be dealt with was that of the location and sequence of meetings. Henderson arrived in Paris on Tuesday, July 14, ostensibly to discuss disarmament, and that evening he received Lindsay's telegram, quoted above. He and MacDonald were due to visit Berlin the following weekend, and they had to consider whether they should hold to that plan, summoning the conference of ministers in London after that, or postpone the Berlin trip until after the conference. When they discussed the situation by telephone on the morning of the fifteenth, MacDonald was in favor of postponing the trip, but Henderson reserved his opinion until he had seen the French.[7] If Henderson had not made up his mind before, the French seem to have made it up for him when he saw them later in the morning. Not surprisingly, they were somewhat cool to the idea of a conference of ministers in London, and they argued that it was necessary to obtain more

---

have endangered French funds. Whatever they did in July, they certainly supported London in August and September, and they suffered heavy losses when Britain went off gold. The French financial relation to London resembled the American financial relation to Germany. The pressure that was probably used in the negotiations in February, of making a new loan dependent on certain conditions, was a different and safer tactic.

[7] To judge by *DBFP*, 2/II, No. 194 and GFMR, 2548/E300405: Hoesch to Ministry, July 16, 1931. *DBFP*, 2/II, No. 193, written five days later, tells a different story.

information on conditions in Germany before deciding on financial assistance or on holding a conference. Their nominees for gathering this information were MacDonald and Henderson. Henderson recalled later that Laval had said, "We must know . . . what exactly the situation is. Can the present [German] Government commit itself in the name of the country? Does it represent her? Is there a danger of its being replaced by Hugenberg and Hitler? Is Germany ready to accept our conditions?" Of these questions, the last was clearly the most important, and indeed the last question was the only one to which a weekend visit might conceivably provide an answer. But of these matters, the Foreign Secretary at this time reported only that Laval had urged strongly that Henderson and MacDonald hold to their plan of visiting Berlin, "as it would give us an opportunity of forming our own conclusions as regards the real situation of the German Government." His telegram of July 15 continued: "In view of this emphatic opinion of the French Ministers, I think you will agree that we should not allow our visit to Berlin to be interfered with." [8]

This telegram was not convincing, and we can see now that Henderson had other reasons for wanting to keep to the Berlin visit as scheduled. He still wanted to gain his point on the customs union and Cruiser B, probably all the more so since he had been attacked by the German press and rubbed the wrong way by Neurath. In going to Berlin, his purpose now was not what he told his own government, merely to find out the lay of the land, but rather to try to obtain a German acceptance of various proposals, including the renunciation of the customs union and the cruiser, and also of a new French suggestion, a five-year political moratorium, that is, a moratorium on revision. Such a German acceptance was still to be a "voluntary gesture," but it would serve to provide the "right atmosphere" for an international loan. No

[8] *DBFP*, 2/II, Nos. 193, 194; GFMR, 2548/E300406, E300425: Hoesch to Ministry, July 16, 1931; Memo by Bülow, July 16, 1931. It may be that Henderson said more on the telephone.

doubt the French ministers, in their discussions with Henderson, encouraged him to press hard for these concessions in Berlin.[9]

In the interval since Laval had spoken with Hoesch on Sunday, the French had developed their scheme for a long-term international loan, to be accompanied by safeguards and guarantees such as a lien on German customs receipts and an international supervisory committee. The French seem to have been thinking of the Dawes Plan arrangements, and in some ways their ideas recalled the system imposed on Austria in 1922.[10] And since they now had a plan, there was no longer any reason why they should not also make demands for political concessions. By getting Henderson to press for the concessions, Laval presumably hoped to make the German government feel that they were faced with a united front of the wartime allies.

Meanwhile, on this same Wednesday morning, the German government decided to proceed with the suggestion of a Paris conference, as discussed between Bülow and Hoesch. Because this would involve a postponement of the British visit, Hoesch saw Henderson first, after the latter had had his discussion with the French. Hoesch told Henderson that there had been a slight improvement in the situation, but also that Germany could not master the crisis without help. He outlined the German ideas for a meeting, but Henderson seems to have been too full of his own plans to give the German suggestions much consideration. Henderson informed the German Ambassador of the Anglo-American idea of a London conference, but added that he had found the French not ready for this, their reason supposedly being that French public opinion had to be prepared before a loan could be considered. He did not think that the French government would want to receive a German visit at this time, because it would probably achieve no result, and such a failure would have serious consequences. Laval had urged him three times to go to Berlin,

[9] GFMR, 2548/E300406–8, E300425–6; *FRUS, 1931*, I, 259–260.
[10] *FRUS, 1931*, I, 257–258; GFMR, 2548/E300406–8, E300423: the latter is part of Bülow's memo of July 16.

and he thought that after he had done so and reported the results to the French on July 22, it might then be possible to have a conference with German participation, perhaps in London. Henderson explained (as he had not done to London) the nature of the French loan plan and the guarantees desired by the French. Although Hoesch again expounded the German idea, and warned that the concessions would not be granted, Henderson insisted on his visit to his now-reluctant hosts, and said he planned to take the Nordexpress for Berlin the next day; as Bülow put it in his record of Hoesch's phone call, Henderson was coming "as the representative of France." Of all this discussion, Henderson telegraphed London only that Hoesch had said the German situation was somewhat improved; this message implied that there was plenty of time for a trip to Berlin before any conference.[11]

Stimson had now reached Paris, and a meeting with him at 6:00 P.M. was the next item on Henderson's crowded schedule. When Henderson described his plan of going to Berlin and then reporting to the French, Stimson said that "I thought that was a pretty big order for him to assume and that I myself would not undertake any such responsibility." Stimson warned that the United States would never take part in such a revisionist meeting as Norman had in mind, and Henderson agreed that that was impossible "at this time" and said that "if the French knew any such proposition was even suggested they would have a fit." Henderson said nothing to Stimson about the proposal advanced by Hoesch, and to London he telegraphed only that he had informed Stimson about his conversation with the French.[12]

After seeing Stimson, Henderson went on to a dinner given in his honor at the Colonial Exposition by the Minister of Colonies, Paul Reynaud, and by Marshal Lyautey. Laval was among the French dignitaries present, a circumstance which proved to be most convenient, for while the dinner was going on, a message

[11] GFMR, 2548/E300405–8, E300423–6; *DBFP*, 2/II, No. 194. Henderson may, of course, have said more on the telephone.

[12] Stimson MS. Diary (Deposited at Yale University Library), July 15, 1931; *FRUS, 1931*, I, 257–261; *DBFP*, 2/II, No. 195.

from MacDonald, which had been telegraphed from London by Sir Frederick Leith-Ross, was brought to Henderson.[13] Unfortunately this message is not reproduced in the British published documents, but nevertheless, we can get some clue to its nature from the following :

1) There were sudden heavy withdrawals of funds by French banks on July 15, resulting in gold shipments. MacDonald told Stimson a few days later, "very confidentially, that England had a rather serious financial situation for a day or so after the German crisis on Monday." Actually, this was the beginning of the run on British gold that eventually toppled the Labour government and drove Britain off the gold standard. One cause of withdrawals was probably the publication of the Macmillan Committee's adverse report two days earlier, another was no doubt the knowledge that British lenders had large sums tied up in Germany. Everyone concerned with international finance was now seeking frantically for liquidity, and after Berlin, London was the next most sensitive point.

2) Hugh Dalton, Henderson's Parliamentary Under-Secretary, quotes in his *Memoirs* his diary entry of July 15, which noted that a German moratorium on private payments abroad would force a British moratorium, and added: "I hear later tonight that Norman is in a panic and has demanded an immediate public announcement of a meeting of Ministers in London on Monday, failing which he will demand legislation to be passed on Friday, the day after tomorrow, declaring a moratorium."

3) The message in question was sent on behalf of the Prime Minister by Leith-Ross, who had been a Treasury spokesman for a firm policy with France.

4) Above all, we do have the placating answer to this message, in which Lord Tyrrell reported the results of his investigation for "ascertaining to what degree the heavy withdrawals of 3 and 4½ million sterling mentioned by Sir F. Leith-Ross as having been effected yesterday and today respectively have been occasioned

[13] *DBFP*, 2/II, No. 193.

by French action, and whether such action would have been due to interested motives, political or otherwise." [14]

From this we may surmise that heavy withdrawals on July 15 led Norman and the Treasury to press MacDonald to take prompt action in summoning a conference, lest the meager stock of British gold go the way the German was going. Suspicions of French manipulation for political reasons were apparently aired, and considering this and the patently unsatisfactory reporting from Henderson in Paris, MacDonald presumably authorized Leith-Ross to send a very forceful message. The whole proceeding seems to reflect Norman's "nervous influence," as Stimson was to call it. [15]

The message from London must have been a strong one, as it brought an immediate reversal in Henderson's position. Without leaving the Exposition, the British Foreign Secretary conferred with Laval and Reynaud, pressing Laval to come to London. According to Henderson, Laval resisted the suggestion, proposing that the conference be held in Paris instead, but finally, after an hour's discussion, during which Henderson argued that the British ministers could not leave London while Parliament was sitting, Laval reluctantly agreed that if the French cabinet approved, he would go to London for a conference opening on Tuesday, July 21. He would only do this, however, on condition that the German leaders come to Paris first. It is possible that, if Laval did not

[14] *SIA, 1931*, p. 85; *FRUS, 1931*, I, 272; Hugh Dalton, *Memoirs* (2 vols., London, 1953–7), I, 255; *DBFP*, 2/II, No. 207. It is easy to see how even in 1947 the editors of the *DBFP* might have hesitated to publish a message from a British Prime Minister accusing the French of making a financial attack on Britain for political reasons, especially when the financial attack could be thought to have led to the British cabinet crisis of August 1931, still the subject of bitter debate.

[15] Stimson MS. Diary, July 21, 24, 1931. According to Neurath, MacDonald and even the Foreign Office thought Henderson had probably committed himself too much to the French, "as he had done with the customs union in March." A day later, Neurath said he knew of no ill-feeling between MacDonald and Henderson (GFMR, 2548/E300397, E300440: Memo by Dieckhoff, July 16, 1931; Memo by Plessen, July 17, 1931). Judging by Dalton's *Memoirs*, I, 255–257, Henderson's relations with MacDonald became extremely strained.

already know of the German proposal, Henderson may now have suggested to him that the Germans would willingly accept this arrangement. Henderson still hoped to go to Berlin, returning with Brüning to Paris, and then going on to London. With this understanding Henderson returned to the British Embassy to inform MacDonald.[16]

On reaching the Embassy, Henderson learned that London had called again to inform him that invitations were now being issued for a conference in London at 6:00 P.M. Monday, the twentieth; Henderson and MacDonald would go to Berlin on Friday, bringing Brüning back with them directly to London—a scheme which Dalton described in his diary as "a mad idea." During the night the Foreign Office gave a statement on this plan to the press without waiting to find out the French (or the German) reaction. This procedure must have been a shock to Henderson, and of course it represented a flagrant breach of diplomatic courtesy towards France. Probably the reasons for this abruptness were, first, the pressure from Norman for action, and second, a message from Berlin, indicating that Brüning was ready to go to either Paris or London, and that Hoesch was discussing a Paris conference with Henderson. So far as we know, Henderson had not reported this part of his discussion with Hoesch, and therefore his credit may have been further shaken in MacDonald's eyes. MacDonald was anxious to keep the Germans "out of the hands of the French," fearing that the only conference would be one held in Paris.[17]

Henderson now had to call Laval on the telephone and report this new development. Laval took it calmly, but insisted that the Germans must come to Paris first. Probably the change from Tuesday to Monday night made little difference to him, but the British trip to Berlin would, if carried out as announced, preclude a Paris visit by Brüning. Laval won his point, and it was agreed that the German leaders would pass through the French capital.

[16] *DBFP*, 2/II, No. 193; GFMR, 2548/E300427: Memo by Bülow, July 16, 1931.
[17] *DBFP*, 2/II, Nos. 193, 196, 197; Dalton, *Memoirs*, I, 257; SDP, 462.00R296/4514: Chargé in London to Acting Secretary, July 15, 1931; GFMR, 2548/E300426–7: Memo by Bülow, July 16, 1931.

Hoesch was roused out of bed to see Henderson, and the Ambassador said that the German leaders were still ready to come to Paris. MacDonald was not informed of this arrangement until the next day, or if (as Henderson claimed) he was informed, he had been too sleepy to remember it, and he was highly incensed. Brüning and Neurath had to take some pains in expressing their regret at the abandonment of the original plans for the British visit.[18]

RIVALRY BETWEEN THE PARIS AND LONDON MEETINGS

Two gatherings, one in Paris and one in London, had now been arranged; the London conference had been set for Monday, July 20, and although Henderson had hoped to get the Germans to leave Berlin on Thursday night, Brüning, in view of the problem of Friday's wage payments and the possibility of public disorder, said that he would have to delay his departure until Friday afternoon. It may be that he was happy, now that a conference in London was to follow, to cut short his stay in Paris.[19]

But which conference was to be the more important? The Americans and British agreed that the major meeting should be in London. On the other hand, the Americans agreed with the French that there should be no sweeping review of reparations and war debts. Moreover, the British and Americans agreed that they could not guarantee a loan, and that the Germans should not be forced into concessions as the price for assistance. But if the French could not put over their plan, there was little inducement for them to go to London.

On Thursday, July 16, Flandin explained the details of the French proposal to Stimson and Henderson. The plan was for a

---

[18] *DBFP*, 2/II, Nos. 193, 202; Dalton, *Memoirs*, I, 257; GFMR, 2548/E300472–8, E300385–9, E300440: Memos by Bülow, Dieckhoff, and Plessen, July 16, 17, 1931; SDP, 462.00R296/4578: Chargé in London to Acting Secretary, July 17, 1931.

[19] GFMR, 2548/E300428–9; 1555/D666717: Memos by Bülow, July 16, 1931; *DBFP*, 2/II, Nos. 204, 206. Briand formally extended the French invitation to the German leaders on the evening of the sixteenth (GFMR, 2548/E300381).

$500,000,000 ten-year international loan, issued in Paris, London, and New York. The money was to be deposited at the BIS to the credit, not of the German government, but of the Reichsbank. An international committee was proposed, which would supervise the Reichsbank's use of the fund, preventing the rash extension of credit, or excessive German borrowing abroad. This committee would also have control over customs, similar to that exercised by the Commissioner of Controlled Revenues under the Dawes Plan. Pending the raising of this loan, the central banks might make advances on it. Apparently nothing was said at these meetings about the requirement of any political assurances or political moratorium.[20]

Henderson had now become frightened (at least this was Stimson's opinion), and he hesitated to express any reaction to the French plan. That night, MacDonald telegraphed him that "public opinion" in England would not be ready to guarantee loans for paying reparations to France, and Snowden (who, in Dalton's words, was "as usual, on his crippled hind legs, virulently anti-French") sent a message the next day, ruling out any financial assistance for Germany, either short term or long term; new loans, Snowden said, "would at best relieve the situation temporarily and leave the fundamental defects unsolved, with the result that a further crisis would break out sooner or later. For more than five years Germany has been borrowing abroad in order to pay reparations, and I understand that there is no prospect of getting any further credits from the market here or in America unless some long-term settlement of the debts and reparations can be reached." Norman tried to mobilize the other powers against France; in a passion he called Harrison and poured out his feelings:

Norman says things look very bad; that we are in for a bad week-end; the whole thing is boiling up; [he] has just left the Prime Minister and the Chancellor; the conference the British called for Monday is in danger of being cancelled, if it has not already been cancelled owing

[20] SDP, 462.00R296/4525½: Memo of telephone conversation between President and Secretary, July 16, 1931; *DBFP*, 2/II, Nos. 193, 199, 205; *FRUS, 1931*, I, 261, 265–268; Stimson MS. Diary, July 16, 1931.

to the position of the French; he has just learned within the hour that the French have proposed a huge credit to be guaranteed by the Government, that it is impossible for the British to consider any such thing; that if they did so for Germany, they would have to do it for India, Australia, and so on; no possibility of London even considering it; Henderson is in Paris on disarmament and nothing else; that he knows nothing about the economic situation; that it is entirely up to Snowden and not to Henderson; he mentions it so that he will not have any misunderstanding as to the significance of Henderson's presence in Paris; another reason why the French proposal is impossible is connected with their condition as to customs receipts; it means that the bondholders would take charge of Germany again; would prejudice the Young Loan because it gives another security to a new loan that the Young Loan has not got; no such proposal can be considered; that Norman never heard of it until Snowden just told him; the British are apparently indignant about it. The French are insisting on no change in the fundamental position towards Germany, and it is for that reason the French are trying to break up the conference on Monday. Norman's idea is that Germany does not need long-term money at this moment; what she really needs is the possibility of credit when required; she cannot get this credit, not because she has not got a good basis for credit, but rather because of political obstacles which it was hoped they might dispose of at their conference on Monday; that was the purpose of calling the conference; Norman says that the French are planning to get the Germans into a room tomorrow [*sic:* they would not meet until the day after] and put this huge loan up to them, and that in effect this is sham because they know that they are not going to get Governments to guarantee the loan.

In opposing any loan to Germany, the Governor was no doubt motivated largely by the knowledge that his bank was unable to help; one wonders, however, if he did not also have in mind the idea he had expressed to Luther, of letting the crisis grow worse until the French came to reason.[21]

Norman also called at the German Embassy and voiced his fear that Brüning would arrive at London a French prisoner, with his hands tied behind his back; "if at all possible, the Paris visit should

[21] *FRUS, 1931,* I, 268–269, 316; *DBFP,* 2/II, Nos. 208, 216; Dalton, *Memoirs,* I, 256.

be called off at the last moment." Neurath answered that he shared Norman's concern, but that it was scarcely possible to back out now. Neurath informed Berlin that the King and the Foreign Office had shown the same attitude as Norman. And MacDonald tried to convince the American Chargé in London, Atherton, that the French were trying to jockey the British out of having the conference in London. Norman's desperation suggests that he now half-realized that it would be impossible to bring about early revision, and that he was doubtful about the possibility of any London conference—and perhaps about the possibility of saving the pound.[22]

After he had heard the details of the French plan, Stimson noted in his diary that it was not so bad as he had feared. When he explained to Laval that an American guarantee was impossible, Laval suggested that perhaps there might be different arrangements for the American and French portions. But Stimson faced a difficult problem. To begin with, he soon found out that London was very unbending. In addition, his own countrymen also had ideas directly opposed to those of the French. The Federal Reserve authorities, and with them, President Hoover, held that American participation in a loan would be possible, if at all, only if such a loan had priority in repayment over reparations. And after they had learned more about the French plan, their views hardened further; they now said that an American loan could not be raised without an American guarantee, which was out of the question. But Stimson wanted to hold out the hope of American participation, for otherwise the French might refuse all cooperation, including participation in the London Conference. Moreover, Stimson seems himself to have regarded American financial help as possible and perhaps as essential.[23]

Stimson's attitude was quite apparent to Washington, where the suspicion arose that he was not stating the American objections

---

[22] SDP, 462.00R296/4578: Chargé in London to Secretary, July 17, 1931; GFMR, 2548/E300441–2: Neurath to Ministry, July 17, 1931.

[23] Stimson MS. Diary, July 16, 1931; *FRUS, 1931,* I, 261–263, 268; *DBFP,* 2/II, No. 199.

to the French plan forcefully enough. The President now came
to the conclusion that it would be sufficient if the creditor nations
agreed to have their bankers stabilize credits at their existing
levels; according to Harrison, the New York banks were doing
this already. The administration's thoughts were forwarded to
Stimson on the evening of July 17 with the pointed comment,
"We would like your views on the situation before you give them
to anyone else." On the same night, Thomas Lamont and Russell
Leffingwell of J. P. Morgan and Company cabled their Paris
office, giving a detailed explanation of why it would be impossible
to raise any money in New York at this time, and ending with
instructions to show this explanation to Moret, of the Bank of
France. According to information Consul General Kiep had received, the Morgan firm was the chief obstacle to Germany's
getting a credit from New York without French participation;
Morgan's had always worked closely with the Bank of France,
and Lamont was convinced that Germany could, if she wished,
reach an understanding with the French at any time. Kiep probably exaggerated the readiness of other banks to help, but he
apparently was correct on Lamont's views.[24]

Stimson was furious at the Lamont-Leffingwell intervention,
and he got Hoover to promise to call Lamont. He was now exerting every effort to keep the negotiations from collapsing before
the London Conference. To Hoesch, he stated that he had the
impression that "the French were trying to play fair," and he
argued that "the whole result of the conference depended upon
Brüning and Laval going into this conference and being conciliatory on such questions as they took up." He then told Flandin
what he had said to Hoesch and added that, although the New
York bankers now seemed reluctant to take action, he had often
seen situations before in which the views of the bankers had

---

[24] *FRUS, 1931*, I, 275–278, 279; GFMR, 2548/E300368; 1660/D729761–2:
Kiep to Ministry, July 14, 1931; Prittwitz to Ministry, Sept. 15, 1931. Parker
Gilbert was probably also opposed to lending to Germany; he had attempted
to get the State Department to block an earlier Lee, Higginson–Krueger and
Toll loan in the spring of 1930, but Acting Secretary Cotton, with cabinet
acquiescence, refused to establish a precedent for requiring State Department consent. See SDP, 862.51/2847, 2848, 2848A, 2848B, 2850.

changed. He asked Flandin "whether he was going to London and he said he was. I told him that with a conciliatory spirit on the part of the French as well as the Germans under the guidance of Ramsay MacDonald, who was a very conciliatory element, there would be a great opportunity to make progress. He made a very favorable impression on me by his attitude and he apparently felt the same way." The next morning, Stimson called on Laval and told him he was sure MacDonald would be conciliatory and fair-minded. Later, the Secretary was inclined to think that this call had been "one of the determining elements" in inducing Laval to go to London, and a week later, the French Ambassador in London told Dawes that the French might not have attended the London Conference if Stimson had not been there to bring his common sense to bear.[25]

The spirit shown by Stimson was certainly important, but Laval had not yet finally decided to go to London, and it is likely that for him, the significance of Stimson's attitude was the practical assurance it tended to give that America would help keep the London Conference from going beyond a consideration of the immediate crisis. It may be that Stimson privately gave Laval a specific assurance on this point; Laval said the next day that he had told Stimson that financial aid to Germany would be the sole object of the London Conference, implying that Stimson had agreed. In any case, Hoover had by this time issued a press statement saying that Stimson and Mellon would attend the conference in London, and ending: "It is our understanding that [the] conference is limited entirely to question of present emergency." In a telephone call to London, Stimson had warned MacDonald that if the London Conference tried to go into general European questions, as Norman desired, he would go home. On this matter, the United States stood beside France, the other creditor power.[26]

GERMAN EXPECTATIONS

At the time Stimson was talking to Hoesch and Flandin, Brüning, Curtius, Bülow, and Count Schwerin von Krosigk were

[25] *FRUS, 1931*, I, 274–275, 278–280; SDP, 462.00R296/4760: Ambassador in London to Acting Secretary, July 30, 1931.

[26] *DBFP*, 2/II, Nos. 213, 219; *FRUS, 1931*, I, 272.

on the train for Paris. It was a serious matter to make this trip, since as Brüning remarked at 2:00 A.M. Thursday, when he heard of the Henderson-Hoesch arrangements for a Paris meeting, his absence from Berlin for five days at this time was equivalent to an absence of five months under normal conditions. Before going, Brüning told the cabinet that minor incidents at home should not be taken too seriously, but if there seemed to be organized disorder, "there should be no hesitation about taking energetic action"; a state of emergency could be proclaimed and General Kurt von Hammerstein, Chief of the Army Command of the Reichswehr, would then render every assistance. Brüning also told his cabinet that he would seek no loan from France, and afterwards he told them he had sought none. He likewise maintained before and after that there could be no question of making political concessions. His resolute refusal to seek loans or offer concessions is also reported in the postwar memoirs of Paul Schmidt and Curtius, who have claimed that he did not seek a loan from *any* foreign source. Their version of events only makes one wonder why Brüning bothered to go at all.[27]

Actually, this account of Brüning's intentions and actions is quite deceptive. It is true that Brüning did not ask a loan for the German *government*, like the Lee, Higginson credit, although at one point he did tell the French that he intended to use any credits granted from abroad for consolidating public finances. It is also true that he did not particularly want a long-term loan, which would probably involve some equally long-term controls and commitments. But unquestionably, Brüning wished to secure a credit, and this was what impelled him to go to Paris and London.[28]

[27] GFMR, 1684/D787045-6, D787053, D787114-8, D787120: Cabinet Protocols, July 17, 25, 1931; Paul Schmidt, *Statist auf diplomatischer Bühne* (Bonn, 1949), pp. 218–219; Julius Curtius, *Sechs Jahre Minister der deutschen Republik* (Heidelberg, 1948), pp. 219–220, and *Der Young Plan* (Stuttgart, 1950), p. 121.

[28] GFMR, 1660/D729605: Memo on discussion with French ministers, July 18, 1931; *DBFP*, 2/II, Appendix I (p. 442).

The truth was that Brüning no longer trusted the discretion of his cabinet; in two July cabinet meetings he dwelt on the leakage of government secrets, in one case to the press and in the other to the French.[29] In view of his dependence on Hindenburg and the army, and their strongly nationalist point of view, he naturally wished to avoid any suspicion of "softness" in the matter of seeking foreign support and giving way to foreign pressures. Schmidt and Curtius have continued to follow this line. Yet Brüning was actually anxious to obtain a large new short-term credit for the Reichsbank, while as to concessions, we shall see that he was ready to offer them to France. By July 16, he was telling Rumbold that he might under certain circumstances be able to find a temporary solution for the customs union conflict, by a limited postponement of its completion. And while "a discussion of the cruiser was undiscussable," even here the Chancellor pointed out that he had told Sackett that Cruiser C would not be started, that nine tenths of the funds voted for Cruiser B had already been spent, and that RM50,000,000 were being cut from the expenditures for munitions and naval purposes. It was not really that Brüning would not make any concessions at all, but rather that he would not make any that the German public and army might learn about.[30]

THE PARIS MEETINGS, JULY 18–19, 1931

At 2:05 P.M., Saturday, July 18, Brüning's train steamed into the Gare du Nord. There was some concern as to the public reception he would get, Hoesch having suggested earlier that it might be safer to have the meetings outside Paris. Brüning and

[29] GFMR, 1684/D787044-5, D787115: July 17, 25, 1931.

[30] *DBFP*, 2/II, No. 210. On Friday, July 17, Rumbold reported hearing "from a direct source" that the customs union had been discussed at a cabinet meeting on Thursday night, and that Treviranus, on whom Rumbold had been working, had "strongly advocated that the project be dropped, and was supported on economic grounds by the majority of his colleagues" (*DBFP*, 2/II, No. 215). But the author has found no record of such a cabinet meeting on the sixteenth, and the records of the discussions on the seventeenth and twenty-fifth do not tally with the situation Rumbold describes.

Curtius got ahead of the rest of the German party and disappeared toward the station door, from which, after an interval, a loud noise was heard. Von Krosigk tells us that he asked, "What does this mean?" and Bülow replied, "Now they are probably being hanged." But the Embassy was able to report to Berlin that the mood at the time of arrival was "not unfriendly," with calls of "Vive la paix," "Vive Laval," and "Vive la France," along with some hand-clapping and "a very few whistles." According to Krosigk's memoirs, the German visitors had heard that the French army had moved some divisions to the German frontier, and he says that Hoesch confirmed this information when they arrived.[31]

Brüning met first for an hour with Laval alone; we do not know all that happened at this meeting *à deux*, but from what was said later, Laval apparently told Brüning about the French proposals, and Brüning suggested that a one-year political moratorium might be possible. This was much less than the French wanted, but it was something, and presumably it was offered as a bargaining counter-bid. When the two premiers joined the other ministers, Brüning, at Laval's invitation, described the history of the crisis; he referred to the mistaken dependence on short-term credit, which his government had combatted, stressed the role of the Creditanstalt collapse, and stated that unless foreign assistance was received, Germany would be forced to declare a moratorium on foreign payments. He added (evidently with an eye to appealing to the French interest in Eastern Europe) that Germany had so far sought to avoid this because of the shattering effect it would have on European economic life, especially in the Eastern countries.

Laval answered that any help from abroad, especially from France, would have to be based on a spirit of confidence. "He stated expressly that France did not wish to use Germany's position to make conditions, but on the other hand financial aid, especially a loan, was only possible if it was made on the basis of confidence,

[31] GFMR, 1660/D729554; 2549/E300456: Hoesch to Ministry, July 14, 1931; Fessler and Hoesch to Pünder, July 18, 1931; Lutz, Graf Schwerin von Krosigk, *Es Geschah in Deutschland* (Tübingen and Stuttgart, 1951), pp. 135–136.

for which a German gesture was essential." France was compelled to "take precautions." Flandin then launched into a detailed description of the French plan, similar to that he had given Henderson and Stimson: he proposed a ten-year international loan to the Reichsbank, possibly preceded by a credit from the central banks. The French government would only be able to guarantee the loan, which would be necessary before it could be marketed in France, if there was some special pledge for repayment, such as customs receipts, and if there was some control, possibly through the Bank for International Settlements, over German investment policy. Brüning pointed out that the customs receipts were already pledged under the Young Plan, and that a further assignment from them was impossible unless the other Young Plan signatories agreed.

The French required political as well as financial "precautions." Laval now repeated his earlier remarks about the need for improving the atmosphere. He

mentioned various things which had hitherto disturbed this atmosphere. In this connection he referred repeatedly and expressly to the customs union, the cruiser, the Corridor, the demonstrations of the Stahlhelm, and the attitude of the National Socialists. He could easily see the difficulties which would arise for the French government if there was not a far-reaching improvement of the atmosphere in regard to all these difficult questions. He therefore proposed the idea of a political moratorium, and declared, repeating his idea in various terms, that it was a question of finding a formula which would be bearable for Germany and which for France would make possible the granting of the loan proposed by Flandin. In this connection he referred to the suggestion, made by the *Reichskanzler* in their personal discussion, of having such a moratorium come into effect for one year.

In his reply, the *Reichskanzler* joined in emphasizing the difficulties involved in formulating a declaration that would be acceptable for both sides. He stressed that such a formula must give expression to the possibility and necessity of co-operation and a friendly relationship between the two countries. But he referred to the difficulties which the inclusion of the various questions in this formula could bring. In regard to the customs union he added in particular that the possibility existed of tying it into a larger framework of Franco-German economic relations.

It was agreed that Berthelot would try to draft a formula, which could be taken up, along with more detailed problems, on Sunday afternoon, July 19. The aged Briand added that, despite the impression given by the press, all sections of the French people desired to reach an agreement. Peace in Europe would only be possible on the basis of true Franco-German understanding; if ever it was to come, the hour for that understanding had come now. On the whole, the Germans found the French to be considerate and sympathetic. And while the French and German positions were very far apart, the possibility of agreement on the basis of limited concessions, such as a short-term political moratorium and a wider customs agreement, was by no means excluded at this point.[32]

As Brüning took care to tell Flandin during this meeting, negotiations had already begun for holding existing Anglo-American credits in Germany. Stimson had told Schubert that he understood the Federal Reserve was ready to supply new loans. Messages from Leitner and Kiep had made it appear that almost the only obstacle to a new American loan was J. P. Morgan and Company, and that this problem was being overcome. Financial talks in Berlin on July 18 seemed to give promise of a new Anglo-American credit without French participation and without the necessity of meeting French conditions. But in Washington, the idea was now firmly rooted that with such a standstill on credit withdrawals the need for a new credit might disappear, and Stimson was advised that it was useless to feed more credit into Germany until withdrawals had been stopped. On Saturday night at 10:00 P.M.,

[32] GFMR, 1660/D729601–7, 2549/E300461–3: Memo of conversation with French ministers, July 18, 1931; Bülow and Hoesch to Foreign and Finance Ministries and to Reichskanzlei, July 18, 1931. The Bülow-Hoesch version suggests that Brüning offered more opposition to the proposals for concessions, "using all the well-known arguments." But it agrees that he stated that the customs union could be integrated into the larger framework of Franco-German relations. A very brief summary of the talks was also wired by Curtius (GFMR, 2548/E300458).

Stimson and Mellon met Brüning and, in line with their latest instructions, told him "that we felt that if the $1,400,000,000 of short-term credits held by the banks of various countries (largely by the United States) were held without any present threat to German credit, this should aid greatly in the relief of the German financial situation and would probably make additional loans to Germany unnecessary."[33]

This must have been a great disappointment for Brüning, and one cannot help but admire him at this moment. Perhaps there was something to be said for the idea of picking a leader from the "younger, war-time generation," a former infantry officer, if it produced a man who, after several weeks of crisis, could find the reserves of moral and physical strength to meet this situation. Schmidt has described how Brüning fought off fatigue while trying to make his points in English. The pauses would lengthen as he groped for words, but then he would push himself on. He made a long explanation of why a standstill on existing credits would be insufficient, arguing that "a cash loan of from $400,000,000 to $500,000,000" was required to restore credit and especially to support the Reichsmark. Stimson maintained that no loan would help "unless the holes were plugged," and Brüning "kept insisting that an actual cash loan [was] absolutely necessary —that notwithstanding [Stimson's and Mellon's] frequent reference to the possibility of intergovernmental cooperation to hold the existing acceptances and other credits."[34]

The Americans tried to get Brüning to make an encouraging public statement, and although the discussion wandered off into the question of whether Brüning could promise to resume Young Plan payments later (Brüning felt unable to make such a promise), it appears that what they really wanted was a public acknowledgment from Brüning that a credit standstill would be sufficient.

[33] GFMR, 1660/D729545, D729575-7, D729598; 2548/E300368: Schubert to Ministry, July 14, 1931; Leitner to Ministry, July 17, 1931; Pünder to Fessler (for Brüning in Paris), July 18, 1931; Kiep to Ministry, July 14, 1931; *FRUS, 1931*, I, 275–278, 287.

[34] *FRUS, 1931*, I, 287; P. Schmidt, *Statist*, p. 218. Schmidt passes over the substance of the conversation.

Brüning, however, "clung to his position that, while Germany would do all that it could, an additional loan within 8 or 10 days would be necessary or the situation would be beyond their control." He did succeed in recreating doubts in Stimson's and Mellon's minds on the adequacy of a standstill, and he impressed Stimson as "careful, sincere, and strong," no mean accomplishment under the circumstances.[35] Perhaps he sensed that he was making progress, and perhaps this influenced him when he met with the French the next afternoon.

On Sunday morning, a general meeting took place, attended by the representatives of Germany, France, Great Britain, and the United States, as well as of Italy, Belgium, and Japan (the other signatories of the Young agreements). As Stimson and Henderson had desired, no decisions for resolving the crisis were taken. Brüning again explained the origin of the German difficulties and Germany's need for more foreign exchange, Laval challenged the other powers several times with the claim that France alone had made a definite proposal, and Stimson said that the first thing to be done was to halt the withdrawal of credit: when there was a tub with a hole in it, he stated, it was useless to pour more water in until the hole was stopped up. The chief developments were: (1) a statement from Henderson agreeing that the London Conference should confine itself to the financial situation in Germany; and, (2) partly as a result of this, a tentative indication from Laval that a French delegation would go to London; there would not, however, be a final decision until after the second Franco-German encounter that afternoon. At the end of the morning meeting, Edge approached Laval privately and asked him when he and his associates were going. Laval replied, "At 10 o'clock Monday morning." In order to prevent any possible prolongation of the Paris meetings, MacDonald had told Henderson to return to London on Sunday, and Henderson, Mellon, and Stimson all de-

---

[35] SDP, 462.00R296/4584½: Memo of conversation between Secretary and German Chancellor, July 18, 1931; *FRUS, 1931*, I, 287–288, 317; GFMR, 2549/E300467; Bülow and Hoesch to Foreign, Finance, and Economic Ministries and Reichskanzlei, July 19, 1931.

parted a few hours later. Henderson arrived at Victoria Station that night "looking very tired," and went directly to No. 10 Downing Street, where he had a heated argument with Snowden and the Prime Minister.[36]

At a Friday meeting, Laval had stated that, unless agreement was reached in Paris between the French government and the German ministers, the French would not go to London. This was probably only a reply to the pressure from the British and Americans, and on Sunday morning he all but committed himself to go. But if he had carried out his original threat, Laval would never have left Paris, for the second Franco-German meeting on Sunday afternoon was a failure. This meeting was never expected to produce any final agreements and it mainly involved the preparation of a communiqué on the Franco-German contact in Paris. If, however, that contact was to have any value for the French nation, the communiqué should include German recognition of the *status quo*. Once in London, it would be harder to bring pressure on the German leaders. Two draft communiqués were discussed, one French and one German, but neither was accepted. As the discussion went on, it became clear to the Germans that Laval, and even more, Flandin, considered that a French loan would be impossible unless there was a relaxation of political tension, assured by a political moratorium; further, this moratorium would have to be clearly referred to in the communiqué. According to what Curtius later told the British, the French formula ruled out any appeal to Articles 18 (perhaps an error for 8) and 19 of the League Covenant during the period of

---

[36] GFMR, 2549/E300466: Bülow and Hoesch to Foreign, Finance, and Economic Ministries and Reichskanzlei, July 19, 1931; *DBFP*, 2/II, No. 219; *FRUS*, *1931*, I, 272, 288–295; Dalton, *Memoirs*, I, 256–257. Edge tells us that Laval kept using the word *conférence* in referring to the meeting they were in, and the American interpreter translated this as "conference." At each mention of the *conférence* Henderson, mindful of the British position, interjected the word "consultation," and Laval began to amuse himself by mentioning the *conférence* more and more frequently. Finally, Henderson shook his finger at the interpreter and said, "Young man, if you use the word 'conference' again, I shall leave this meeting." (Walter Edge, *Jerseyman's Journal*, Princeton, 1948, p. 202.)

the moratorium.[37] All the German formulations were rejected by Flandin as not offering enough security to the French lender, or by Laval, as insufficient for getting the French Parliament to approve a guarantee. For several hours the talk went on, centering on the political moratorium, which the French plainly wanted to run for ten years, the length of the loan. Such other matters as the assignment of customs were only touched on. According to Krosigk's memoirs, Brüning suddenly rose when deadlock became obvious, and went over to Laval, saying in French that the tragedy of all attempts to reach a Franco-German understanding was that the French always desired as a precondition for agreement that which might be its consequence. And he added that he felt a personal sadness about this: *"Moi personnellement, j'en suis très triste."* This statement, Krosigk says, made a deep impression. To the French, however, it must have amounted to saying that they should buy a pig in a poke.

The crucial difficulty was not the time period, but the French demand for a *public* statement committing Germany to abide by the Versailles Treaty. For years this treaty had been represented in Germany as a dictated peace, and for years German leaders had avoided any new recognition of its legal validity. The French proposals went right to the heart of Franco-German differences: would the German leaders openly admit that Germany had been and was still a defeated power? When it finally became clear that no agreement could be reached, Laval proposed to confine the communiqué to a general statement on the favorable course of the German visit in Paris, and indicated that he would still go to London; he had no right, he said, to insist on French preconditions when it was not at all certain that a loan could be arranged in London. He maintained a calm bearing throughout, and closed the meeting with a warm declaration of friendship, so that despite the failure, the tone of the Franco-German contacts remained

[37] *DBFP*, 2/II, No. 221. A footnote in the *DBFP* says that the number "18" may be an error. Article 8 was the article on disarmament; Article 19 was the article providing for treaty revision.

cordial.[38] It is likely that at this point, the Germans were still hoping for salvation through an Anglo-American loan, while the French could not isolate themselves by refusing to go to London.

THE QUESTION OF THE POLITICAL MORATORIUM

Laval stated that he was leaving the questions of the loan and the political moratorium open, and the German delegates did not entirely give up hope of devising some agreement which would satisfy the French and open the door to Franco-German "economic cooperation." Curtius attempted on July 22, while in London, to take up the possibility of a modified and extended customs union with Briand, but found Briand too tired to go into details. In response to pressure from Henderson for a political truce, Bülow drafted in London a rather empty treaty or declaration of economic collaboration, but this was dropped when it appeared that Henderson was being restrained by his own government from his search for concessions. And the German records contain an unsigned memorandum, dated July 23, which shows that German officials did consider offering not to appeal to Article 19, the "Revision Article" of the League Covenant. This last idea probably went further than Brüning would ever have dared to go, and to judge by what Curtius told the British, the Germans had in Paris already refused to renounce Article 19. But Brüning and the German Foreign Ministry were clearly more

---

[38] GFMR, 2549/E300476–7, E300509, E300537–8: Curtius to Foreign, Finance, and Economic Ministries and Reichskanzlei, July 20, 1931; Letter, Bülow to Hoesch, July 25, 1931; Letter, Hoesch to Koepke, July 24, 1931; Krosigk, *Es Geschah*, p. 136. See also note 41 below. It appears that Flandin was the more unbending of the French leaders (SDP, 462.00R296/4640: Ambassador in Paris to Acting Secretary, July 21, 1931; GFMR, 2549/E300509). Available information (including, aside from the above, *DBFP*, 2/II, Nos. 221, 238, 266, 267; GFMR, 1684/D787118: Cabinet Protocol, July 25, 1931; André François-Poncet, *Souvenirs d'une ambassade à Berlin*, Paris, 1946, p. 22) indicates that the main French demand, the ten-year moratorium, was the only thing on which they expected a German public statement; in explaining what this would comprise, they seem to have stressed the Corridor and rearmament, while the customs union was only mentioned, if at all, incidentally.

ready to make concessions than they admitted to the German cabinet, and hopes for an agreement did not die for a long time.[39]

The French, too, may have extended further feelers for a political bargain after the Paris meeting. A month later, Brüning told Sir Walter Layton that he had heard since the Paris meetings that "if he would undertake not to raise the question of the disparity between French and German armaments no other political condition of any kind would be raised by the French." Laval in October told Lord Reading, Henderson's successor as Foreign Secretary, that "in his opinion Dr. Brüning personally would not object to [the renewed suggestion of a political moratorium]. Whether the Nationalists could do so was another matter. But Germany like other countries must accept facts if they wished to escape from their present plight. He believed that if Germany secured some material advantage she would accept a [political] moratorium. This was only his personal impression but he felt that Germany could not stand out against the whole world." Laval's calculation was that if he waited, the Germans would be obliged to seek economic assistance and would come to terms, perhaps along the lines of François-Poncet's economic union proposals. While in London in July, the Premier told American newspapermen that in three months the German crisis would have so developed that the Germans would have to accept his conditions, and an informant reported to the Germans that Laval was counting on this with absolute certainty.[40] At the time they went to London neither Laval nor Brüning imagined that Germany could carry on without financial help, by means of a controlled economy.

It was a mistake to suppose, as Norman believed and Ambassador Edge suspected, that the French loan offer was merely a sham, something proposed in the confident expectation that it would founder on British and American reluctance.[41] After all,

[39] GFMR, 2549/E300482–4, E300517–23; 1555/D666724: Unsigned memo, July 23, 1931; Letter, Bülow to Hoesch, July 27, 1931, with enclosed draft texts; Memo by Curtius, July 22, 1931.

[40] *DBFP*, 2/II, Nos. 238, 267; GFMR, 1684/D787115; 2549/E300511: Cabinet Protocol, July 25, 1931; Letter, Bülow to Hoesch, July 25, 1931.

[41] *FRUS, 1931*, I, 269, 295–296. On July 31 Bülow sent the principal German

no German commitments would have been binding in that case. Moreover, this criticism overestimated the propaganda value for the French government of making the loan offer. French opinion was uninterested in helping Germany, and France cared relatively little for that "world opinion" which Americans took so seriously.

There *was* propaganda value, on the other hand, in gaining a new German promise to respect the *status quo*. But even here, France did not (as the Germans claimed) insist on humiliating Germany for the sake of French opinion; she would have been quite happy, perhaps happier, to see the Germans make assurances to the United States or to Henderson on his Berlin visit. More important than a new assurance, we must remember that the idea of a French loan to bind Germany, in connection with some kind of guarantee, was the favorite device of French diplomacy in this period. The basic idea was first tried out in the Young Plan and Young Loan arrangements. We have seen that Berthelot discussed a loan with Hoesch in October 1930 and in February 1931. Coulondre mentioned a loan in May 1931, in connection with François-Poncet's cartel plan, part of the French reply to the Austro-German customs union proposal. And the original French answer to the Hoover moratorium was also largely a scheme for binding Germany with a loan. The loan plan was probably inspired by the permanent officials of the French Foreign Ministry and Ministry of Finance, and the German crisis would have been a pretext for bringing it up again, regardless of the plans of the other powers.

For political as well as financial reasons, the French wished to associate the United States and England with the proposal of a

posts, except London and Paris, a survey of the summer's events which stated that the French ministers had insisted that the American and British portions of a joint loan must be guaranteed—which was constitutionally impossible; moreover, Bülow reported that after agreement was ruled out on the nineteenth, Laval had said frankly that even if all the French conditions had been met, he would have been "in absolutely no position" to extend financial help. Reports prepared at the time do not show that the French made an issue of British and American guarantees, and the alleged Laval statement is unbelievable. Apparently this survey was intended as propaganda guidance for private discussion with foreign officials (GFMR, 4078/L051201–18).

guaranteed loan, and to Paris this may not have seemed impossible, assuming a Franco-German agreement could once be reached. Hoover's moratorium initiative suggested to the French that America was re-entering European politics, and Laval's later trip to Washington seems to have been predicated on the hope that this was so.[42] An American commitment might in turn have brought a British commitment. The French aim was a new Reparations Commission, with American participation. But despite Flandin's repeated statements that Anglo-American participation was essential for any financial assistance, the history of French loan schemes suggests that France might ultimately have lent money alone if (and it was to be sure a big "if") the Berlin government had fully met the French conditions.[43]

THE LONDON CONFERENCE, JULY 20–23, 1931

When Stimson and Mellon arrived in London, they found awaiting them the text of a complete American plan for stabilizing the existing credits in Germany, accompanied by instructions to submit this plan either as Hoover's proposal or as an "American proposal" prepared by Mellon and Stimson themselves. As on

[42] It was apparently the hope that the United States was giving up isolation that made Claudel so enthusiastic when Stimson first told him of the moratorium (*FRUS, 1931*, I, 26–29); on July 30, Claudel, after claiming that the Quai d'Orsay had originally planned a cordial acceptance (which the cabinet had overruled), gave Castle an informal memorandum arguing in favor of a Franco-American consultative pact (SDP, 462.00R296/4910: Memo by Acting Secretary, July 30, 1931). Hoover had also implicitly associated debts with reparations: Briand told Hoesch on July 25 that he himself favored accepting the Hoover proposal "not so much because of the one-year holiday as, much more, because America, once on this road, would not be able to turn back, and because therefore a beginning had been made for a re-examination of the debt problem" (GFMR, 2548/E300087: Hoesch to Ministry, July 25, 1931). On Laval's thoughts on the eve of his departure, see *DBFP*, 2/II, Nos. 266, 267. Laval hoped that the United States would agree to join in economic and financial sanctions in support of the Kellogg-Briand Pact.

[43] On July 7, admittedly before the worst of the German financial crisis, Tyrrell stated that if Germany proved that she would cooperate with France, all the French money that Germany (and Austria) needed would become available (*DBFP*, 2/II, No. 158).

June 20, the President was throwing out a unilateral American plan in the expectation that it would be accepted as a boon by a hither-to unwitting world. Perhaps one aim was to prevent Stimson and Mellon from offering any new financial assistance; almost certainly another aim was to bolster the administration's prestige at home. Stimson was well aware of the reception which any highly touted "New American Plan" was likely to get from France, but for-tunately he now found that MacDonald was also ready to work for a standstill on credits, and this made it possible to play down the American role. Snowden and Norman more or less agreed with Hoover that a stabilization of existing credits was feasible, and that a new credit was not. That they also wanted to sweep away reparations and debts for good was a matter that MacDonald pushed into the background. Since Stimson and MacDonald were now working primarily for stabilization, this became the only solution to Germany's immediate problems that could emerge from the London Conference.[44] With the main outcome practically prejudged, the chief interest of the London meetings lay in Snowden's unsuccessful attempts to obtain a permanent reduction of intergovernmental obligations, and in Brüning's unavailing efforts to get, despite all, a new rediscount credit.

Although Laval declined to give details on the nature of the French political demands, the conference soon established that there had been no agreement between the French and Germans in Paris. Brüning attempted to describe the measures which he thought should be taken, but although he wished to make a case for a new credit, Stimson succeeded by a sort of cross-examination in leading him, Flandin, and Snowden to agree on the importance of first stabilizing existing credits. The finance ministers went into conclave and came up with the following recommendations to be made by the governments to the bankers:

1. That the Central Bank credit of $100,000,000 recently granted to

[44] *FRUS, 1931*, I, 280–282, 283–286, 299–300, 317–318; SDP, 462.00R-296/4606: Chargé in London to Acting Secretary, July 20, 1931; Drew Pearson and Constantine Brown, *The American Diplomatic Game* (Garden City, N.Y., 1935), pp. 236–237; Stimson MS. Diary, July 20, 1931.

the Reichsbank under the auspices of the Bank for International Settlements should be renewed at maturity for a period of 3 months.

2. That the Central Banks should be prepared at the request of the Reichsbank and on conditions to be agreed with it to rediscount internal German commercial bills from the Reichsbank's portfolio.

3. That concerted measures should be taken by the financial institutions in the different countries with a view to maintaining the volume of the credits they have already extended to Germany.

Brüning strongly argued that all three points were essential and that without the second he could not face his country with a hope of success. He did succeed momentarily in winning Stimson and Mellon over to the second point, the rediscount credit. But Hoover, when called, stated that the Federal Reserve Bank (of New York) would not consider that proposition, and that it must be dropped.[45]

Stimson was very disturbed to learn on Tuesday, July 21, that Washington was now publicizing Hoover's plan as a "new American proposal" on stabilization, and he feared the repercussions with the French. He heard that they considered leaving the conference, but they finally decided to stay. Then Snowden took up the cudgels for the British Treasury, after MacDonald had privately told Mellon that he doubted whether Norman could carry on with his bank. Snowden stated that he could not commit British banks to maintaining their existing credits in Germany, and he argued repeatedly that none of the three points went to the root of the German troubles: these were caused by her tremendous foreign obligations which she could not meet from her own resources, and which she had been paying with borrowed money. Snowden held that unless this situation was revised, no permanent solution could be found. But his ideas were no more popular with the Americans than with the French, and he was not supported by MacDonald, who indeed passed a note to Stimson, stating, "I know

---

[45] *DBFP*, 2/II, Appendix I (pp. 435–437); *FRUS, 1931*, I, 298–306; Stimson MS. Diary, July 21, 1931; SDP, 462.00R296/4656A, 4600½: Acting Secretary to Chargé in London; Telephone conversation between Secretary and President, 11:15 P.M., July 21, 1931.

nothing of this." Stimson finally silenced Snowden by using the conference record to show that Snowden had already agreed that stabilization should come first.[46]

In the end, the Conference accepted the first and last points in the draft presented by the finance ministers, extending the rediscount credit and making a standstill in credit withdrawals, but despite Brüning's efforts, the proposal for a rediscount credit was rejected. There was also provision for the establishment of an international committee to examine German credit needs.[47] It seems ironic to reflect that, partly due to the position taken by the Republican President of the United States, Germany was left with no alternative but to adopt a policy of rigid state control of the national economy.

The London Conference was accompanied by other meetings and actions which, on the whole, did little to restore good relations. Curtius had inconclusive talks with Stimson and Henderson about the cruisers, and promised to give each of them a memorandum on Cruiser B. In the Curtius-Henderson discussion, Henderson also tried to find out about the Paris talks, while Curtius kept arguing the necessity for a loan. Henderson finally established that the main difficulty in Paris had been over a political moratorium, and he then took up the cause, suggesting some declaration covering a five-year period. Curtius answered that he had considered a consultative pact, but there could be no agreement involving a renunciation of Germany's remaining rights under the peace treaties. Henderson said that he never suggested the abandonment of rights, but only that certain issues should be left in abeyance for a certain period. Bülow answered that

to leave in abeyance would amount to the same thing and that German

---

[46] SDP, 462.00R296/4600½, 4601½: Conversations between Secretary and President, 11:15 P.M., 11:55 P.M., July 21, 1931; Stimson MS. Diary, July 21, 1931; *FRUS, 1931*, I, 306, 319–320; *DBFP*, 2/II, Appendix I (pp. 458–461); Stimson MS. Papers (Deposited at Yale University Library). The announcement of the "American Plan" was the occasion for a big publicity effort by the American administration: see *New York Times*, July 21, 22, 1931; *Evening Star* (Washington), July 21, 1931.

[47] *DBFP*, 2/II, Appendix I (pp. 457–484).

public opinion would never tolerate any form of words which might even suggest that German rights were to be left in abeyance.

Mr. Henderson replied that that was quite an impossible position to take up for it amounted to nothing else than an attitude of fiddling while Rome was burning.

Dr. Curtius said that he and Chancellor Brüning had done their best to fight against their own public opinion. There was no statesman in Germany less afraid than Dr. Brüning, but Dr. Brüning and he both knew that they had reached the limit beyond which they could not go in the restrictions which they were imposing upon Germany.

Sir R. Vansittart said that if the present conditions were allowed to continue the only result would be two antagonistic choruses leading to a situation which must end civilization.

But these warnings made little impression on the German representatives, who believed Henderson was simply a cat's-paw of the French, or even that he had actually given the French the idea of a political moratorium in the first place. They soon concluded that the British government was reining Henderson in, a view that was probably strengthened by the "jeremiads" (as Stimson called them) of Snowden.[48]

The French government contributed to the difficulties by publishing, on July 22, a long memorandum on its views on disarmament. In essence, it stated that the French forces had been reduced to the lowest point consistent with national security, given the existing circumstances, and that further reductions could only be made if security was somehow increased. This memorandum was only one incident in the long Franco-German contest over disarmament, but there are two points to be noted in relating it to the 1931 crisis. One is that it was not made public with the aim of disturbing the current Franco-German negotiations. The French had been preparing the memorandum as early as the preceding

[48] GMFR, 2549/E300517–8: Letter, Bülow to Hoesch, July 27, 1931; *DBFP*, 2/II, No. 221; SDP, 462.00R296/4671½: Memo of conversation between Secretary and German Foreign Minister, July 21, 1931. The promised German memorandum was given to Stimson in Berlin and a corrected version later substituted (*FRUS, 1931*, I, 517–519).

May, and according to what Briand told Curtius, this paper was a product of the Ministry of War, rather than of his own ministry. Moreover, the publication was originally planned for Friday, July 17; although the French government gave another explanation, the delay was probably due to a desire to avoid antagonizing the German visitors, expected in Paris the next day. The other point is that, contrary to the custom of the disarmament controversy, the German government refrained from making a public reply to this French statement, and made an effort to restrain the German press. The Berlin government's silence may perhaps be attributed to its lingering desire to reach an agreement with France.[49]

The middle period of Brüning's administration, which is the period of this study, brought him little in the way of success, but it did leave him with a reputation for enjoying the confidence of the other powers. On October 9, Rumbold was to report hearing that Brüning's prestige abroad was the only factor making for his retention in office. This reputation, though not unfounded in actual fact, doubtless owed much to the external evidence of his acceptance abroad which was provided by the Chancellor's many meetings with foreign leaders. The creation of this impression had been a primary aim of the British in inviting Brüning and Curtius to come to Chequers. The Paris and London conferences had increased the effect, and they were not the end; Stimson was still to visit Berlin, return visits by the British and French leaders were still to take place, and since a tête-à-tête with Brüning was now becoming one of the hallmarks of great power status, there was also necessarily an exchange of visits with the Italians. None of these later encounters had much real effect on European politics, but the fact of their occurrence undoubtedly helped Brüning in his difficulties at home.[50]

[49] *SIA, 1931,* pp. 283–285; *DBFP,* 2/III, Nos. 212, 213; *FRUS, 1931,* I, 506; GFMR, 1555/D666724; 4507/K240743–4: Memo by Curtius, July 22, 1931; Bülow to Hoesch, July 30, 1931. Grandi did not believe Briand's explanation (GFMR, 1555/D666726: Memo by Curtius, July 23, 1931).
[50] *DBFP,* 2/I, Nos. 350, 354; 2/II, Nos. 235, 269.

THE DEFEAT OF THE BRITISH TREASURY

During July, the British leaders were somewhat concerned to find that although they had, so to speak, been the first to receive Brüning and Curtius into European society, the Germans now seemed to be on almost better terms with the French than with them. At the London Conference of Ministers, MacDonald and Snowden endeavored to find out what had happened between the French and Germans in Paris, but both Laval and Brüning replied with mystifying generalities. Henderson pressed Curtius for an answer, but did not get full satisfaction. When MacDonald and Henderson came to Berlin on July 27–29, the Prime Minister raised the question of "the continued negotiations between France and Germany," and asked:

Did it suit [the German ministers] that these conversations should be continued between the two parties without our intervention, or would they prefer that we intervene? He would remind them that His Majesty's Government were interested politically and it would not do for a settlement to be reached and that His Majesty's Government should be faced with a *fait accompli*. In this connection Mr. Mac-Donald referred to the American-French agreement which had been reached in Paris between M. Laval and Mr. Mellon, which had proved very embarrassing to His Majesty's Government.

Curtius replied to this rather bare-faced overture by saying that, although he did not expect any practical result, he thought Germany must show the French that she was ready for direct negotiations, and that the British should be informed when things were a little more advanced. MacDonald and Henderson pressed further, and Brüning finally agreed "that it was essential that the British should join in the conversations at a point"—whenever that was. MacDonald also tried to woo the German leaders by raising the question of continuing the work of the London Conference; "there was much to be done and it was necessary to take a broad view in regard to the future, since serious problems were involved. There was the question of reparations and war debts." He confided that while Stimson was vacationing in Scotland, he intended to

raise with him the question of what should be done at the end of
the Hoover year. Brüning's response to MacDonald's remarks was
typified by his statement, "What the German Government really
wanted for the time being was help to tide them over the present
year." Although Brüning finally conceded that "the possibility of
the reimposition of the Young Plan would constitute a great
danger for Germany," Curtius suggested that the first step was to
gain time by securing an extension of the Hoover moratorium.
The Germans displayed remarkably little interest in the British
Treasury concept of seeking an immediate revision of intergovernmental obligations.[51]

The British Treasury, in trying to make a fundamental change
in the Versailles system, was racing against time. The aim had long
been to secure a settlement which would give hope for British
export trade and hence for reducing unemployment, balancing the
budget, and saving the pound. Now time was running out, and
the defeat of the Treasury's goals at the London Conference meant
that there could be no external solution to Britain's financial problems. In conversation with Curtius, Norman had described the
result of the London Conference as "nothing." He personally, as
MacDonald told Stimson on July 31, "was now, today, ill, virtually
broken down under the pressure," and on his doctor's orders, the
Governor went for a long sea voyage. When the Experts' Conference resumed after the Ministers' Conference, Snowden tried to
bring about an alteration in the Franco-American agreement of
July 6, especially regarding repayment in a twelve-year period,
but the American government, while prepared to welcome a
change, did not feel that it could openly go back on its agreement
with the French, and the British Treasury failed again to attain its
aims. The abandonment of any hope of revising the July 6 agreement, together with Norman's retirement from the scene, made it
possible for the Bank of England to accept offers of urgently
needed financial assistance from the Bank of France, and although
Snowden caused some delay, being most reluctant to accept help

[51] *DBFP*, 2/II, No. 228; GFMR, 4078/L051223–5: Bülow to London, Paris,
Rome, Moscow, Washington, July 29, 1931.

from that quarter, it was announced on August 1 that the Bank of France and the Federal Reserve Bank of New York had each extended a credit of £25,000,000 to the Bank of England. A German diplomat was told in London that France had been ready to advance the full £50,000,000, "as revenge" for Snowden's and Norman's policy, but the Bank of England refused this until half the sum was obtained in New York.[52]

Perhaps earlier credits would have been more effective, but as it was, the £50,000,000 disappeared rapidly, and were eighty per cent gone by August 26. London was in the position of having to pay out without being able (because of the standstill) to recall its own funds from Germany. Harrison felt unable to make further advances, so that additional financial assistance for England could only be obtained from New York private banks, through J. P. Morgan and Company as banking agents of the British government. Morgan's informed London on August 23 that the New York banks would not lend unless the British budget was balanced to the satisfaction of the Bank of England and the bankers of the City of London. Since the London bankers, and with them Snowden, regarded a reduction in interest on government bonds or a suspension of the Sinking Fund as unthinkable, and since an unbalanced budget was thought likely to lead to an inflation like that in Germany in 1923, the only solution seemed to be a ten per cent cut in the dole. It was true, as Labour was to charge

[52] GFMR, 1660/D729634; 2385/E199426–36: Memo by Curtius, July 24, 1931; Letter, Dufour to Bülow, Aug. 12, 1931; *FRUS, 1931,* I, 164–175, 557; Harold Nicolson, *King George the Fifth* (New York, 1953), p. 455; SDP, 462.00R296/4712, 4760; 841.51/932: Chargé in London to Acting Secretary, July 25, 1931; Ambassador in London to Acting Secretary for President, July 30, 1931; Ambassador in Paris to Acting Secretary, Aug. 4, 1931; *SIA, 1931,* p. 96. As with Stimson, MacDonald told his junior ministers, when breaking to them the news that the Labour government had fallen, "Poor Norman has broken down under the strain." (Dalton, *Memoirs,* I, 272.) There were rumors that French help was subject to conditions regarding financial or political assistance to Germany (see, aside from SDP, 841.51/932, also 841.51/928), but this was denied in Paris, and there is no evidence that the French forced Norman's temporary retirement or British acquiescence in the July 6 agreement by use of financial pressure.

later, that the New York (and for that matter, the London) bankers were lacking in sympathy for those on the dole. But the financiers had more cogent motives than this; the international financial turmoil of the summer was in itself more than enough to explain why the bankers refused to lend without an assurance that the British government placed balancing the budget above any other consideration.[53]

After the formation of the National Government, Stimson called at 10 Downing Street to congratulate MacDonald on the position he had taken, and MacDonald took the occasion to complain of the high interest (four and one-half per cent) and the commission Morgan's was charging. Stimson then deferentially approached the great banker, who was also in London, asking if these charges could not be reduced. Morgan "received the suggestion in the most friendly spirit," but said that the difficulty was that the American banks thought this interest was very low; Britain did not look like a very good risk.[54] It is worth remembering that Germany had paid much higher interest for years, and that Brüning was unable to get further money from New York, no matter how severe his domestic decrees.

Most of the Labour ministers refused, understandably, to assume the onus of a cut in the dole, but since they were unprepared to come forward with an alternative program of braving inflation and throwing the burden on the bondholders and supertax payers, a "National Government" was really the only possibility. Indeed, if a Labour government had somehow remained, the hostility of foreign and domestic capitalists would probably have forced a

---

[53] *SIA, 1931*, p. 98; Nicolson, *George the Fifth*, pp. 455–465.

[54] SDP, 033.1140 Stimson, H. L./155½, 151½: Memos by Secretary of State, Aug. 27, 1931. MacDonald told Stimson that there had been no doubt as to what position he should take, "though he fully expected it ended his public life. He spoke of it being the second time that he had had to take such a step." Stimson also called on Henderson, who said that the ministers had previously agreed on some proposal on which he understood they were all prepared to stand, and suggested that the Prime Minister had been the one to change; Stimson asked if Henderson would still chair the Disarmament Conference, and Henderson indicated that he himself would like to know (SDP, 500.A15A4/356½, Aug. 27, 1931).

series of radical changes, such as a far-reaching currency devaluation, the repudiation of financial obligations, confiscatory taxes, and various draconic measures to halt the flight of capital, and the ultimate result might well have been a dictatorship from Left or Right. That the National Government was able to leave the gold standard in September without serious results does not prove that a Labour government could have taken this step with the same success: the bankers would have regarded such action by such a government as a big step toward revolution. Even the formation of the National Government was only a holding operation, a pledge to Property that its interests would not be damaged more than was absolutely necessary. As with the French "success" in maintaining the principle of unconditional reparations payments, an apparent success really meant only hopelessness, for both the side that lost and the side that won.

Although Hoover's efforts to manipulate popular psychology seemed to reflect a superficial approach to the depression, as well as a lack of flair for international politics, the world did indeed face a major psychological problem, which can best be described as a loss of faith. Dr. Emile Coué's doctrine was peculiarly apt for the 1920's; individuals and nations earnestly wanted to believe that every day, in every way, everything was getting better and better —for, after 1914, they were no longer quite sure. In the first year or so of the depression, people still talked about "adjustment" and looked expectantly around the corner. They still turned to men like Schacht and Young, MacDonald and Hoover, hoping that these men would lead the way to a better world. But in 1931 the masters seemed visibly to lose their touch. A thin plaster of international finance and Locarno ambiguities had covered the cracks left by the Great War, but now the plaster flaked off. Each nation, in its own way, had hoped to retain, regain, or improve a privileged position, and these hopes were now all disappointed. The London Conference in particular seemed to demonstrate an incapacity to reach positive international solutions. As Professor Toynbee wrote: "The London Conference resembled nothing so much as a gathering of fashionable physicians, all anxious above all things to preserve their professional reputations, round the bed-side of a prominent patient whose malady they have no genuine hope of curing. In these embarrassing circumstances the doctors sign a perfunctory report, write out a harmless but ineffective prescription, and slip discreetly away—leaving their patient to suffer a hideous prolongation of his agonies." [55] As the gold standard failed, all the countries were thrown back on their own resources, moral as well as material. In the West, this meant a defensive nationalism, a Maginot Line, Imperial Preference, and in two years, President Roosevelt's 1933 refusal to discuss currency stabilization. In Germany, where there was more anger than self-criticism, the immediate result was an increase in aggressive nationalism. Brüning's crisis decrees laid the foundation for Nazi autarchy, while the army took the first steps toward *Umbau* —not rearmament but a reorganization which would permit rapid expansion and rearmament later. [56]

[55] *SIA, 1931,* p. 87.
[56] Georges Castellan, *Le Réarmament clandestin du Reich* (Paris, 1954), pp. 530–531.

IX

The End of the Story

THE END of the summer of 1931 brought two developments which, although Laval did not recognize it, gave the quietus to whatever hope had existed for a genuine Franco-German accord. These developments were, first, the prompt revival of the question of a permanent reduction or elimination of reparations, and, second, the withdrawal of the Austro-German customs union under French pressure, a circumstance which left a feeling of bitterness and increased suspicion in Germany. The first development might have been regarded as a gain for Germany, but it was not a gain for which Brüning could easily claim public credit. The second development, on the other hand, was a defeat for the Brüning cabinet's plan of winning popularity through an active foreign policy, and recovery from the blow was made only with difficulty and with the sacrifice of Dr. Curtius.

THE "BANKERS' COMMITTEE"

In retrospect, the most important action of the London Conference of Ministers was not the approval of a standstill in credits (which was already being undertaken privately) or the extension of the $100,000,000 credit (which had already been extended for three weeks) but a recommendation that the Bank for International Settlements should "set up without delay a committee of representatives nominated by the Governors of the Central Banks interested to inquire into the immediate further credit needs of Germany and to study the possibilities of converting a portion of

the short-term credits into long-term credits." This recommendation, originating in a suggestion from Washington, led to the
formation of what was called the "Basel Committee," because it
met at the seat of the BIS, or the "International Bankers' Committee," from its composition.

At the London Conference, the main question in regard to
establishing this committee had been whether it should be nomi-
nated by the BIS, as the French preferred, or by the governors of
the central banks, as Brüning desired. Brüning was anxious to
avoid drawing in the BIS, partly because, as he told the Conference, that institution was unpopular in Germany for having failed
to transfer its last meeting, at Luther's request, to Berlin. But he
had other, stronger objections, which he did not mention. One
consideration was that the BIS was ill-regarded in Germany, not
so much for the minor incident just mentioned, but because
Germans considered it a vestige of the post-Versailles Reparations
Commission and of the Dawes Plan Control Committee. An investigation by a committee from the BIS might lead to loud protests
that the bad old days of Poincaré and Parker Gilbert had returned.
The German delegation also believed that a BIS-appointed committee would tend to side against Germany in its decisions.
Brüning wanted a small group of men who would recommend
the short-term rediscount credit he had been seeking; he did not
want a group which would be, through the BIS, under French
leadership, and which would recommend a long-term loan. That
would bring him back again face to face with the French political
conditions. The German documents consulted by the author do
not reflect any thought of using the committee to support a
demand for revision.[1]

The London Conference recommendation was framed as a

---

[1] *DBFP*, 2/II, Appendix I (p. 479); GFMR, 2549/E300529–30; 1684/D-
787116: Letter, Hoesch to Koepke, July 28, 1931; Cabinet Protocol, July 25,
1931. Brüning may have also suspected that France would regard any use
of the BIS, a child of the Hague agreements, as a recognition of the Young
system; France might even claim that the appointees constituted a Special
Advisory Committee. But this objection is not specifically mentioned in the
source material.

compromise, and seemed to lean to the German side of the question. Germany also seemed likely to benefit from the fact that the committee, when named, included the heads of some private banks heavily committed in Germany, although the Germans actually were concerned lest the fears of such bankers for their frozen credits would make them support the French program. The American nominee was Albert Wiggin of the Chase National Bank, one of the institutions most deeply involved. He was elected chairman of the committee. Germany's representative was Dr. Carl Melchior, who had participated in international economic conferences ever since Versailles, and the French appointee was Emile Moreau, a former President of the Bank of France. Norman's nominee, and a very astute choice, was Sir Walter Layton (later Lord Layton), editor of the *Economist*. Since all the other members were bankers, Layton as a writer was uniquely qualified to draft the report, and his wider experience gave him considerable influence in committee decisions. In June he had worked closely with the German representative in the Committee of Economic Experts, a group organized to advise the League's Commission of Inquiry for European Union, and the Germans congratulated themselves that they had won him over to their views on the subject of customs unions. They had in fact been cultivating Layton, and it will be recalled that he was entertained in Berlin on the morrow of Hoover's moratorium announcement. But it would be wrong to suppose that Layton's statements did not represent his own well-considered convictions, particularly on reparations and war debts.[2] In this question he was in truth only one leader of the main body of British economic opinion, which supported the elimination of intergovernmental payments;

[2] GFMR, 2549/E300530–1: Letter, Hoesch to Koepke, July 28, 1931. When the Special Advisory Committee met at the end of the year, the French did not again choose a banker, but rather an economist with an able pen, Professor Charles Rist; the result was the "Layton-Rist Report." For Layton's views expressed in the Committee of Economic Experts, see GFMR, 1659/D729272–4, D729304–5, D729343–4: Memos on telephone calls from Lammers, June 26, 27, 29, 1931. From the start, Layton's journal had shown itself ready to be convinced of the economic benefits of the customs union, although it recognized the political problem: see the *Economist*, 112:659–660, 673 (1931).

this line of thought is strongly evident, among other places, in Toynbee's *Survey of International Affairs* for 1931.

When the committee convened in Basel on August 8, the French seemed, after all, to be uninterested in discussing a long-term loan; they reportedly considered the idea academic at this point. It appears that there had been, throughout, some divergence of view between the French Government and the Bank of France, the Bank being much less interested in risking a loan.[3] And perhaps Paris preferred to plan renewing its offer more privately and at a later time, when Berlin would have come to reason. In any case, the French wished to limit the committee's discussion to the immediate crisis, which could hardly be done if a long-term loan was to be considered. Thus neither the French nor the Germans meant to use the committee to discuss long-range goals.

But with the bankers' committee composed as it was, it proved impossible to restrict the discussion; the bankers would hardly get their money back unless long-term loans were extended, and most of them came to believe that reparations were an obstacle to loans. On August 11, Wiggin suggested that the BIS should convene the Special Advisory Committee as provided under the Young Plan. This idea was dropped, largely owing to German opposition, but alternative proposals were made, to the effect that the question might be referred back again to the governments, or else that the powers might be asked to extend the terms of reference of the bankers' committee. By August 16, a report, drafted by Layton, was under discussion. Brüning informed his cabinet that, according to Dr. Melchior, Wiggin was willing to propose extending his committee's terms of reference, permitting a mention of reparations in the concluding paragraph of the report. The German cabinet agreed that Melchior should be asked to support such a final paragraph, or alternatively, to suggest that the report recommend that the governments or a new committee take up the reparations problem.[4]

---

[3] *FRUS, 1931*, I, 272, 314; SDP, 462.00R296/4615: Ambassador in Paris to Acting Secretary, July 20, 1931.

[4] SDP, 462.00R296/4923, 4931: Consul in Basel to Acting Secretary, Aug. 12, 13, 1931; GFMR, 1684/D787530–1: Cabinet Protocol, Aug. 16, 1931.

The report, usually called the "Layton-Wiggin Report," was signed on August 18 and published a few days later. In a few pages, it made a masterly description of the vicious circle of past German indebtedness, reported (somewhat prematurely) the conclusion of comprehensive six-month standstill arrangements, and considered and dismissed the possibility that Germany might replace her lost capital by selling foreign assets or increasing exports. The report judged that some of the funds recently lost would have to be replaced, and it went on to state that new short-term credits would only lead to a worse situation when the six-month standstill ended. It therefore seemed essential that long-term loans should be arranged.

The problem of raising long-term loans led the Layton-Wiggin Report inexorably into politics. Although the German economy was basically sound, two fundamental difficulties were preventing a restoration of confidence:

The first is the political risk involved. Until the relations between Germany and other European Powers are firmly established on a basis of sympathetic co-operation and mutual confidence and an important source of internal political difficulty for Germany thereby removed, there can be no assurance of continued and peaceful economic progress. This is the first and most fundamental condition of credit-worthiness. The second relates to the external obligations of Germany. So long as these obligations, both private and public, are such as to involve either a continuous increase in a snowball fashion of the foreign debt of Germany, or, alternatively, a disproportion between her imports and exports on such a scale as to threaten the economic prosperity of other countries, the investor is unlikely to regard the situation as stable or permanent. Until the existing or potential creditors of Germany are in a position to foresee what her future situation is likely to be in these respects a most serious obstacle exists either to the extension or even the renewal of short-term credits, or to the raising of a long-term loan.

By halting credit withdrawals, time had been gained during which German credit might be restored. "But time is short. The body of the world's commerce—whose vitality is already low—has suffered a severe shock in one of its chief members. This has resulted in a partial paralysis which can only be cured by restoring the free circulation of money and goods. We believe that this can be accomplished; but only if the Governments of the world will realize the responsibility that rests upon them and will take prompt measures to re-establish confidence. Their action alone can restore it." International relations must be "established on a basis of mutual confidence," and German foreign payments must "not be such as to imperil the maintenance of her financial stability." The Layton-Wiggin Report disclaimed any intention of offering suggestions of a political character, but stated that, nevertheless, "action which lies outside our province must first be taken before any long-term German bonds, however well secured, can be sold. We therefore conclude by urging most earnestly upon all Governments concerned that they lose no time in taking the necessary measures for bringing about such conditions as will allow financial operations to bring to Germany—and thereby to the world—sorely needed assistance." [5]

Thus a blow was struck for the policy of revision, and the responsibility was once more passed back to the governments. Incidentally, despite the divergence between British and French views, the report was so written that it could be used to support French policy almost as well as British. If this had not been the case, presumably Moreau would not have signed it. One thing it definitely did not support was a large short-term credit, and henceforth little more was heard on that subject. Indeed, with this report before the public, the only possible course for the German government was to push for revision. This was evidently recognized by Melchior as soon as he learned of Wiggin's attitude, as he did not ask for a short-term credit, even though this had originally been the German intention. As we have seen, Melchior also opposed the solution of convening the Special Advisory Committee; the German government would have preferred to avoid using this committee, a part of the Young apparatus. Yet, something would have to be done before the Hoover year was

[5] *DBFP*, 2/II, Appendix II.

over. When in October a Franco-American agreement made use of the Young machinery unavoidable, the Germans did all they could to ensure that the Special Advisory Committee's authority would not be confined to advising measures to be taken "in regard to the application of the [Young] plan." But these negotiations belong to the story of the Lausanne Conference, rather than to that of the 1931 crisis.

It is not suggested here that Brüning ever intended to abandon reparations revision. But he and his colleagues seem to have received something of a fright when the Danat Bank failed, and for a time the campaign against reparations became secondary to trying to check the financial crisis. Brüning was conventional in matters of finance, and he himself had no conception of the possibilities of a directed economy in peacetime; after all, no one had tried it before, except in Russia. When the foreign credit he sought so desperately was delayed and then finally placed out of reach, he had no alternative but to pile decree on decree, shut his eyes, and hope for the best. After the July crisis was over and the dust had settled, it turned out that there still was a German economy in operation, even though it could hardly be described as operating smoothly. Still, any operation at all was almost more than Brüning, according to his own lights, had a right to expect.

The experiences of the summer must have also increased Brüning's respect for French power. Hoover's method was not Brüning's, and the Germans had made a point of informing the French (on June 15) of their intention to seek a Young moratorium. But the importance of offering some satisfaction to French feelings was made clearer than ever by the French delay in accepting the Hoover proposal. Bülow wrote a survey of the summer's events which was highly critical of France, but he drew the logical conclusion: "Without a wide-ranging political understanding with France, this goal [reparations revision] cannot be reached." On August 22–23, after the bankers' committee had made its report, Brüning hinted in conversations with Sir Walter Layton that a moderate reparations payment to France for a short period might be possible "if associated with steps by France to bring about a real *rapprochement*." [6] Brüning seems to have been still thinking of making a special agreement with France. Actually, however, the survival of the German government without a loan removed the main incentive for seeking a *rapprochement*.

It is sometimes said that reparations revision was Brüning's achievement, and that Papen should not have had the credit for Lausanne, such as it was.[7] This is not the place to weigh Papen's and Brüning's relative merits, although it may be suggested that the two men had more in common than is usually supposed. But should reparations revision be attributed to any German? It is obvious from our story that the German government was only one of three which ended reparations. Certainly the German government wished to end them, even more for political than for economic reasons, and it was not particular about the methods employed, whether propaganda among American bankers, or the credit-shattering manifesto issued during the Chequers conference. But the manifesto of June 6 was the only German act that contributed directly to wiping the slate. Hoover's moratorium proposal, which was by no means solely due to German activities in creating fears for American credits, must be considered the major slate-wiping action. And the role of the British, especially MacDonald's influence on Stimson in June, and Layton's work in drafting the Layton-Wiggin Report, was very important. It was Norman and Snowden, not Brüning and Curtius, who argued for immediate revision in July—one might say, heedless of cost.

No attempt has been made in this study to answer the question of whether reparations were right or wrong, expedient or inexpedient. To go into the matter thoroughly would involve going back to the Armistice, and pursuing an extremely complicated discussion of politics and economics. The justice of reparations depended, among other things, on the responsibility for starting the war, an issue unresolved even today, while the feasibility of

[6] *DBFP*, 2/II, No. 238; GFMR, 4078/L051217: Circular Dispatch by Bülow, July 31, 1931.
[7] For example, in Otto Meissner, *Staatssekretär unter Ebert-Hindenburg-Hitler* (Hamburg, 1950), p. 205.

reparations depended, among other things, on the possibility of exporting goods into the creditor countries, particularly the United States. It was indeed impractical to pay reparations (or debts) in gold, but on the other hand, payment in goods was never given a really serious trial, and the blame for this does not by any means rest entirely on the creditors. It would be difficult to arrive at a just balance between economic and political considerations, and the balance is important because an economic approach certainly tends to make reparations seem wrong, while a political approach may, at least from one point of view, make them seem right. Nevertheless, if we limit ourselves to the problem of revising an existing reparations settlement, certain conclusions suggest themselves.

This study started with the assertion that the First World War did not end in an overwhelming victory for the Allies, a term which here includes an "Associated Power," the United States. It was well for the Allies to end it, but given the German unreadiness to recognize defeat, the peace should, for the Allies, have been the occasion for attempts to change the German mind by other means. Such means might be conciliation or firmness, or a combination of both. Probably conciliation would have been wiser. But wherever a firm course was adopted, as in the case of reparations, its relaxation was a matter of great delicacy, in which the Allies should have acted in concert, and for which they should have required some earnest of future cooperation. Hoover's bombshell procedure and Norman's Francophobia measure badly by this standard; Henderson's and Castle's attempts to secure a German gesture and Stimson's mediating efforts at Paris measure well. Hoover had his internal political problems, and Norman had his financial difficulties, but these troubles could not be mended by doing violence to inter-Allied relations. Treaties cannot be graven in stone, but they should not be treated as scraps of paper, either.

It may be objected that it is unhistorical to regard the United States in this period as an Allied power. Legally she certainly had never been an Ally, and in the eyes of most Americans she was not concerned with Europe after Wilson's return home. But in interest and responsibility, America was allied with the Western

European powers. Like them, she had a stake in preventing war and in encouraging the gradual evolution of the rest of the world along the same path the West had followed. Liberal democracy, or, if one prefers, bourgeois parliamentarianism, reached its greatest geographical extent in 1919, but the West European bearers of this tradition were weaker than before, so that more of the responsibility fell to the United States. Once the world was made safe for democracy, it was necessary to keep it that way. The heavens did not fall when, under Hoover, the United States vacillated between isolation and what Hans Morgenthau has called "diplomacy by storm." Nevertheless, she was showing a lack of responsibility (if an understandable one), and responsibility shirked or overlooked does not cease to exist—the bill is presented again later, with compound interest.

THE END OF THE CUSTOMS UNION

The Austro-German venture into active diplomacy was now to reach its conclusion. When Schober told Sir Eric Phipps on June 16 that it seemed to him that there could be no question of executing the customs union plan, he was no doubt speaking under the stress of the immediate Austrian crisis, which was eased later in the day by Norman's extension of credit. But Norman's action only postponed Austrian financial problems, it did not solve them. The Bank of England had to renew its credit every week, and in view of the known weakness of that bank, it was very uncertain how long the renewals might continue. After the Hoover proposal the skies momentarily brightened, but rumors soon came to Vienna about the pressure on Germany to abandon the customs union. Although the German government stressed to Vienna that it was resisting this pressure, doubts must have arisen in Austrian minds as to how long this resistance could continue. In any case, Berlin was obviously in no position to offer important financial help.[8]

Schober later told Curtius that the French, having decided that

---

[8] *DBFP*, 2/II, No. 59; GFMR, 1660/D729632–3; 2548/E300259–60, E300270; 4617/K272165: Memo by Curtius, July 24, 1931; Memo of conversation with Austrian Minister, July 6, 1931; Curtius to Rieth, July 6, 1931; Memo on *Chefbesprechung,* June 17, 1931.

their June demands were too arbitrary, dropped, on July 16, their demand that Austria must agree to a League Council investigation and accept the Council's recommendations in advance; the French also (according to Schober) now left it more to the Austrians to choose their own form of renouncing the customs union. It appears that Schober may have indicated that such a modified French suggestion would meet with a favorable response, and although he told Curtius he did not answer the French directly, he lost no time in turning to the League (and thus indirectly to the French) for financial assistance, advising the Secretary General on July 16 that he wished to obtain an international loan.[9]

Curtius seems to have received his first inkling of this on July 23, while he and Brüning were in London. The Austrian Minister there, George von Franckenstein, told the German Foreign Minister in general terms that Austria was seeking a long-term or middle-term credit to pay off the Bank of England; Franckenstein let Curtius infer that the government in Vienna was ready to accept political conditions for the sake of this assistance. Curtius then talked with Norman, who said he would continue to renew his credit from week to week, but also expressed the belief that within a few months Austria would have to turn to the League for help. Two days later, word came to Berlin from Geneva that the Austrians had inquired of the French how they might receive help through the League, and on July 28 the Austrian Minister in Berlin confirmed that a new credit was being sought; the Minister also communicated a copy of Schober's letter to the Secretary General. Curtius recorded later that on this occasion "the Austrian duplicity became clear to me for the first time." [10]

---

[9] GFMR, 2521/E285292–5; 2549/E300515–6; 2382/E197433; 1685/D788403: Dispatch, Curtius to Rieth, Aug. 1, 1931; Memo by Wiehl, July 25, 1931; Memo by Curtius, Aug. 31, 1931; Cabinet Protocol, Oct. 3, 1931.

[10] GFMR, 1660/D729632–3; 2549/E300515–6; 2521/E285292–3; 3620/K-005616: Memo by Curtius, July 24, 1931; Memo by Wiehl, July 25, 1931; Dispatch, Curtius to Rieth, Aug. 1, 1931; Curtius retrospective comment. Koepke protested that Curtius' charge of duplicity was unjustified and should not be placed in the file (GFMR, 5426/K294602–3).

It must have been even harder for Norman than for most Englishmen to admit that the Bank of England had lost its old power, and when he implied to Curtius that he would continue his credit for several months, he was exaggerating the strength of his institution. In the last three weeks of July, the Bank of England had lost £32,501,283 in gold, half of it in the last week. On August 2, the American Consul in Basel reported that the Bank of England would have to withdraw certain of its own credits from Austria and Hungary within a few days, and Schober later told Curtius he had first learned on August 8 that the British were recalling their loan. On the tenth, the Austrian government announced that it had approached the League for help in raising money with which to repay the British credit. Austrian dependence on League assistance was now thoroughly confirmed. Three members of the League Secretariat visited Vienna from August 16 to 21 in order to survey the situation.[11]

All this was naturally very unpleasant for Curtius. Nevertheless, he seemed for a time to have a chance of saving face and perhaps even of making some political profit out of the situation. Departing from its original attitude, the German government had been thinking since June of removing the curse of *Anschluss* from its proposal by stressing the possibility of a larger European customs union. Sir Walter Layton was very interested in this wider plan, and he helped Clemens Lammers, his German colleague in the European Committee of Economic Experts, to draft a report advocating a European customs union organization. As we have seen, the Germans had hinted to the French during the Paris-London meetings that the customs union proposal might be given a broader, more international character. By this change of direction, the critics of the original proposal might be pacified, an untenable position could be more or less gracefully abandoned, and perhaps some credit might even be won at home and abroad for German

[11] SDP, 462.00R296/4783: Consul in Basel to Acting Secretary, Aug. 2, 1931; *SIA, 1931,* pp. 96, 102; GFMR, 2382/E197432: Memo by Curtius, Aug. 31, 1931. See also GFMR, 2382/E197395: Memo by Curtius, Aug. 12, 1931.

constructive economic leadership. And this new emphasis fitted in very well with the idea of developing positive economic and political relations with France.[12]

Curtius proposed to Vienna that Germany and Austria make a statement in the Commission of Inquiry for European Union that they were prepared to postpone their plan as such in order to attempt to realize their goal on a broader European basis. The Austrians had always wanted a broader plan, anyway, and now they were happy to find the Germans willing to collaborate in creating the proper atmosphere for their loan request.[13] On August 17 the discussions were held in Berlin with the Austrian Counselor of Legation, Theodor Hornbostel, and the following formulation was agreed on as expressing the common line to be followed: "The two governments do not intend, under the present circumstances, to pursue further the realization of their plan; they desire instead to make an attempt to achieve their aims on a broader European basis." Hornbostel then reported back to Schober personally; later, he shocked the dedicated members of the German Legation in Vienna by relating that he had gotten the impression that

the leading people in Berlin were decided under all circumstances to prevent the question of the customs union from making any difficulties

[12] GFMR, 1659/D729272–4, D729304–5, D729343–4; 2521/E285313–29, E285393–8: Memos on telephone calls from Lammers, June 26, 27, 29, 1931; Layton-Lammers proposals, Aug. 1931 (including official text). Curtius feared that the customs union might come up during his and Brüning's visit in Rome (Aug. 7–9); there was also some concern lest a political moratorium be proposed again. But neither of these topics was discussed, and Mussolini expressed himself as in favor of further Hoover years; the chief impression the guests received was that Mussolini was extraordinarily concerned about the power and influence of Weygand and the French General Staff: see GFMR, 1555/D666749, D666767–76; 1660/D729668–78; 1684/D787509–11. Mussolini always raised the specter of French European hegemony when speaking with Germans.

[13] GFMR, 2521/E285298–301, E285287, E285316: Dispatch, Curtius to Rieth, Aug. 1, 1931; Rieth to Ministry, Aug. 3, 1931; Dispatch, Rieth to Ministry, Aug. 14, 1931. The Austrians themselves had repeated in July the suggestion of a wider proposal.

for the solution of political and financial questions between Germany and France. Therefore it was only a question of giving the customs union an honorable burial. Hornbostel also had the impression the people in Berlin were ready under certain conditions to alter the formula agreed on, if France would not declare herself satisfied with it. Hornbostel added that people in Vienna could understand that Germany had greater and more urgent cares at the present moment than the renunciation of the customs union, although in this connection it was necessary for internal political reasons to avoid so far as possible the open expression of the word "renunciation."

As the German Legation reported, it appeared from this that Austria might justify her own departure from a pro-German policy by saying that Germany herself had dropped the customs union. But Hornbostel had touched a sensitive nerve. The Legation asked to be informed to what extent Hornbostel had correctly reported German policy; the author has found no reply to this request.[14]

Unfortunately for the German government, the plan of making a graceful withdrawal depended upon three preconditions, two of which were not, as it turned out, fulfilled. Berlin hoped (1) that the Court of International Justice would render a favorable verdict, and (2) that it would render it before the League Council met on September 1, so that the Austro-German statement could be made thereafter as a "generous gesture." Berlin also hoped (3) that discussion in the Council itself could be avoided, and the statement made, in an economic context, in the Commission of Inquiry, which met September 3. But it was learned that the Court's verdict would not be announced until September 5; efforts were made to hasten it, but without success. Delaying tactics might prevent the Council from taking up the matter for two days, but hardly for four. Under these circumstances, unless the statement was made in the Commission of Inquiry as soon as it opened, the customs union would probably come up in the League Council before September 5, and its renunciation would be de-

---

[14] GFMR, 2521/E285334-5, E285337: Unsigned memo on conversation with Hornbostel, Aug. 17, 1931; Letter [Rieth?] to Gaus, Aug. 31, 1931.

manded under open political pressure. This, then, was one reason why the announcement of withdrawal was finally made on September 3 in the Commission.[15]

Another reason was French pressure on Schober. The French Minister in Vienna informed the American Legation that Schober, before leaving for Geneva, had said that Austria was abandoning the idea of a customs union. François-Poncet had a hand in drafting Schober's statement of renunciation, and according to Curtius, it was only possible to eliminate from it the worst features, such as an admission of guilt, a statement that Austria was inseparably tied with Europe, and another statement that the project should be deferred regardless of the opinion of the Hague Tribunal. France (like Germany) was probably uncertain of the decision of the Court, and wished to preclude any possible change of Schober's mind at the last moment, such as a verdict in favor of the Austro-German position might conceivably have brought about. As late as September 1, Schober, in what Curtius calls "an inconceivable interview" with the press, had ruled out renunciation as "a moral surrender" and had prophesied that "any pressure on Austria under the banner of creating confidence would lead to a fiasco." Presumably this incident influenced the French to bring further pressure to bear, in order to make an end to the ambiguous attitude of the Austrian leader. Schober had been thinking of using the customs union for blackmailing other countries, but by now this possibility no longer existed. Austria's need was too great.[16]

When Schober came to make his speech before the European

[15] See GFMR, 2521/E285293–301, E285303–8, E285331–6: Dispatch, Curtius to Rieth, Aug. 1, 1931; Dispatch, Rieth to Ministry, Aug. 14, 1931; Discussion with Hornbostel, Aug. 17, 1931.

[16] *FRUS, 1931*, I, 590; GFMR, 2381/E197438; 1685/D788404: Memo by Curtius, Sept. 2, 1931; Cabinet Protocol, Oct. 3, 1931; Julius Curtius, *Sechs Jahre Minister der deutschen Republik* (Heidelberg, 1948), p. 203; *Berliner Tageblatt*, Sept. 3, 1931 (A.M.). Schober's interview was reported to have appeared in the *Neues Wiener Tagblatt*, which the author has been unable to check, but reference was made to the story in the *New York Times*, Sept. 2, 1931, and *Neues Wiener Journal*, Sept. 2, 1931. On the use of the customs union as a threat: GFMR, 2521/E285304: Dispatch, Rieth to Ministry, Aug. 14, 1931.

Commission, he did not renounce a customs union with Germany for all time, but, contrary to Curtius' wish, he did insist on stressing that it had been clear from the start that a customs union could only be achieved if other states came in. When Curtius spoke on the report of the Committee of Economic Experts, he said that his government agreed with the Austrians in not intending "to pursue the plan they originally contemplated." Curtius says in his memoirs that Brüning tried to get him to let Austria make the renunciation alone, but he, Curtius, regarded this as unworthy, and felt obliged to make his speech match Schober's to the extent of saying that the Austro-German customs union had been intended as the point of departure for far-reaching European economic agreements. Curtius was not just trying to back up Schober; indeed, by this time the German Foreign Minister had no confidence in Austria. But Curtius hoped that this idea of a wider customs union would cover the retreat and fit in with a better relationship with France. He seems to have been surprised by the tone of the press reports and the strength of the adverse reaction at home, where all rationalization in terms of wider agreements was almost completely overlooked, and the only fact recognized was that Austria and Germany had renounced their project under pressure. A campaign for Curtius' dismissal quickly got under way.[17]

On September 5 the Hague Tribunal ruled, eight to seven, that the customs union was incompatible with the Geneva Protocol No. 1, although, by a shift of one of the judges, the Court held that there was no conflict with the Treaty of St. Germain. After the decisions were known, those, like Curtius, who wished to defend the German government argued that, because of the closeness of the vote, the decision of the non-Latin judges for the German side, and the different decisions on the two legal questions, Germany and Austria had really won a moral victory. But this argumentation only interested those who wished to search for solace, and it seems to have made little impression on the German

[17] GFMR, 1685/D788404–5; *SIA, 1931,* pp. 320–321; Curtius, *Sechs Jahre,* pp. 203–204; *Berliner Tageblatt,* Sept. 5 (P.M.), 8 (A.M.), 1931; *Deutsche Allgemeine Zeitung* (Berlin), Sept. 4, 6, 1931.

public, just as the moderate behavior of Flandin in welcoming the Austro-German renunciation made little impression.[18]

Certainly Brüning was dissatisfied with Curtius. On October 1, he indicated to Sackett that Curtius had been "most unfortunate in his action at Geneva over the customs union"; Curtius, he felt, should have announced that in view of the probability of an understanding among a wider group of nations, Germany and Austria would willingly postpone for a time the institution of a customs union. And years afterward, Brüning stated again that he (as opposed to Curtius) had wanted to leave the door open for reviving the project later with other countries; he also seemed to think that Curtius had been too softhearted with Schober when Schober was obliged to give up the customs union, and that some *quid pro quo* should have been exacted for walking the stony path of renunciation with Austria. Brüning's criticism seems unfair, since Curtius had tried to draw on the expectation of wider agreements. The real trouble was, no doubt, that Curtius had developed this scheme, it had failed, and now the whole cabinet was blamed for the failure.[19] When the question was discussed in the cabinet on October 3, the Chancellor thanked Curtius for his explanation and for carrying out the difficult task, and he refrained from direct criticism of the Foreign Minister. But he plainly regarded the plan as a misfortune from beginning to end:

He observed that the proposal of an Austro-German customs union had begun with a very unfavorable start, due to indiscretions immediately after its conclusion. It had not even been submitted to the cabinet at that point. A gradual preparation of the powers had therefore been impossible. Since then all efforts to gain a more favorable position, including at Chequers and in agreement with Sir Walter Layton, had broken down. When renunciation then became necessary, the news sent from Geneva to Berlin about the Foreign Minister had unfortunately had an unfavorable effect. It had brought about a

[18] Curtius, *Sechs Jahre*, pp. 204–207; *SIA, 1931*, pp. 321–322; *FRUS, 1931*, I, 592–593; GFMR, 2521/E285446; 1685/D788403–4: Circular Dispatch from Bülow, Sept. 23, 1931; Cabinet Protocol, Oct. 3, 1931.

[19] *FRUS, 1931*, I, 329; Interview with Dr. Brüning, Jan. 31, 1951.

mobilization of public opinion in Berlin, where the agitation had really been extraordinary.

In judging the situation, the vital point was that one simply could not rely on Austria. The Chancellor reported a communication which had just come to the *Staatssekretär* in the Reichskanzlei [Pünder], according to which Schober had meanwhile been negotiating for a customs union with the Czechs. Already during the trip to Dover, François-Poncet likewise indicated that a customs union of the Danube States was desirable. The Chancellor asked for special care in keeping this information secret, and also that the Foreign Ministry should check into it.[20]

It had been very unfortunate for Germany that the question of the Austro-German customs union had kept coming up at fixed intervals before the League of Nations. It would have been better for Germany if this question could have been handled outside the League within the framework of international politics as a whole.

In slight contrast with his friend and chief, Treviranus said that it would be foolish to make reproaches against Austria, which had been helpless. Then Treviranus added, "What had so upset German public opinion, and also especially his party friends in the Christian-Socialist faction,[21] had been the appearance of voluntariness in the Geneva declaration, and it was being asked again and again whether the whole cabinet had to bear responsibility for this formulation, which must naturally be declined." Thus Treviranus had his revenge for the criticism he had suffered in the summer of 1930.[22]

Curtius resigned the same day, and on October 7 he made a handsome farewell statement to the other ministers, asking them, for the sake of German foreign relations, to use all their influence to keep Brüning at the helm. "The confidence which the present

---

[20] The Legation in Vienna was asked about the rumor of an Austro-Czech customs union, and reported that this was unlikely, although financial pressure was still a danger (GFMR, 2535/E244027-35). The German Minister, Rieth, had already on August 22 discounted a rumor that Schober was about to hold a secret meeting with Beneš (GFMR, 2385/E199595-600).

[21] Treviranus was referring to a section of the dissident German Nationalists, not to the Austrian Christian Socialists.

[22] GFMR, 1685/D788405-7: Cabinet Protocol.

Reich government enjoyed abroad was extremely great, thanks above all to the personality of the *Reichskanzler*, Dr. Brüning. This confidence must be maintained for the new cabinet." From Curtius' letter of resignation and from his own memoirs, it appears that he had informed Brüning of his intention to resign when he returned from Geneva. Sir Horace Rumbold concluded that it had been obviously impossible for Curtius to leave office before the return visit of Laval and Briand to Berlin from September 27 to 29, and Curtius himself attributes the delay to the French visit. By prior agreement, the discussions with the French ministers dealt with nothing more significant than the establishment of a Franco-German economic commission, and the chief interest of the occasion lies in the appalling security problem it presented to the German authorities. It is no wonder that, as part of the effort to minimize Franco-German differences, and to avoid any public unpleasantness, the resignation of Curtius should have been postponed.[23]

Brüning's Problems

While Brüning does not appear in a very favorable light in connection with the dropping of the customs union and of Curtius, it should be borne in mind that he was under terrible strain in this period. He implies in a 1947 letter to the *Deutsche Rundschau* that Hindenburg had a mental breakdown in September, making it very difficult to secure his indispensable support, although this is contested by Otto Meissner. Brüning adds that, after some difficulty, he (with the help of Groener and Schleicher) obtained

[23] *DBFP*, 2/II, No. 262; Curtius, *Sechs Jahre*, pp. 207–208; GFMR, 4617/K272187: Extract from Cabinet Protocol, Oct. 7, 1931. On the Laval-Briand visit, see Curtius, *Sechs Jahre*, pp. 225–227; André François-Poncet, *Souvenirs d'une ambassade à Berlin* (Paris, 1946), pp. 26–29; Paul Schmidt, *Statist auf diplomatischer Bühne* (Bonn, 1949), pp. 228–229; *DBFP*, 2/II, Nos. 243, 254–257, 267; *FRUS, 1931*, I, 326–327; GFMR, 2549/E300617–8, E300720–1, E300726–60: Aug. 14–Sept. 24, 1931. When the visit was discussed in the cabinet (GFMR, 1685/D788236–9: Sept. 26, 1931), Groener, who usually had nothing to say on foreign policy, uttered a strong warning against "throwing oneself around the necks of the French"; behind the French government stood Weygand who represented the policy which had "aimed at the destruction of Germany."

Hindenburg's continued backing for his government and policy, the only sacrifice required being that of Curtius and Wirth. (On October 7, 1931, Curtius also told the cabinet that he had urged Hindenburg to keep Brüning on.)[24] Even if, as Meissner says, Hindenburg only had a touch of the grippe, Brüning still had serious problems. The two parties on the Right, the Nationalists and Nazis, seemed to be showing signs of coming closer together, at least for opposition purposes, and they held a common rally at Harzburg on October 11, in which Schacht participated. The day before, Brüning completed the formation of a new cabinet, the composition of which, as Rumbold reported, showed that he had "publicly failed to secure the support of leading persons, notably in industry." Efforts at wage reduction and the failure to reduce prices caused Socialist and labor union dissatisfaction, and the internal financial situation gave rise to anxiety and tended to alienate the industrialists. Despite the standstill agreements, foreign exchange continued to leak out, and savings bank deposits were being withdrawn and sewn into mattresses. A local election at Hamburg indicated a continuation of the drift to the radical Right and Left. A year of "active" foreign policy had borne little fruit. If it had not been for support from Generals Groener and Schleicher, the Chancellor's position would have been completely impossible. Groener became Minister of Interior as well as of Defense, in order, as he wrote Alarich von Gleich, to "cover Brüning's rear at home, so that he has freedom for negotiation abroad." Brüning himself took on the duties of Minister for Foreign Affairs. Groener understood that Hindenburg had wanted Neurath for Foreign Minister, but that Brüning feared that things might go with him as with Curtius, "only with the omens reversed"; Brüning believed that he could bring it off by himself.[25]

[24] Heinrich Brüning, "Ein Brief," *Deutsche Rundschau*, 8:7–9 (1947); Meissner, *Staatssekretär*, pp. 213–214; GFMR, 4617/K272187. Brüning's statement on Hindenburg is also disputed in Franz von Papen, *Die Wahrheit eine Gasse* (München, 1952), pp. 168–169.

[25] *DBFP*, 2/II, Nos. 265, 272; *FRUS, 1931*, I, 327, 329; Reginald H. Phelps, "Aus den Groener Dokumenten," *Deutsche Rundschau*, 76:1016 (1950); 77:19 (1951).

Dr. Brüning is said to have told a group of American students, "One should not let either one's contemporaries or posterity see the ultimate motives of one's policies." In a way, this statement merely expresses the actual practice of all political leaders. A comparison of their memoirs with archival material serves to remind us of how often statesmen edit the truth to preserve their reputations. Considering the modern gulf between public opinion and governmental action, and the rapid shift in public values, this may be inevitable. Brüning seems to have supposed that he could bridge over real differences with ambiguous formulas: witness his discussions with Sackett in December 1930, and with Laval in July 1931. The whole conduct of German diplomacy under him was characterized by an attempt to appear nationalist at home and conciliatory abroad. Although Brüning was not so responsible as Curtius for it, the customs union was a classic example of this ambiguity.

Still, it is difficult for any leader to be straightforward and statesmanlike when the income from taxes drops off forty per cent, the discount rate rises to fifteen per cent, and the numbers of the unemployed approach a tenth of the total population. Some allowance should be made for this when judging Brüning's actions. Although this study contains much that is critical of Heinrich Brüning, the author would like to place on record his admiration for Brüning's firmness in the face of his domestic enemies, his stamina, and his sense of responsibility toward his people. It was his fate, by establishing a presidential dictatorship, unintentionally to pave the way for the Nazi seizure of power. But no one can accuse him of sympathy for the Nazis, and unlike Papen and Schleicher, he did not delude himself that he could use them. Brüning exemplified the same conscientious conservatism and self-less courage—if also the same reliance on intrigue and manipulation at the top—that characterized the best of the July 1944 conspirators.

CONCLUSION

It is often suggested that the Western powers could have saved the Weimar Republic (or at least, moderate government in Germany) by making concessions to Brüning's government. Those who take this view contend that such action would have given Brüning the popularity he needed to maintain his position in 1932, while weakening the appeal of Nazism to the German masses. "Recognition" and "equality," it is said, would have made Germany a real member of the international community, instead of leaving her an outsider, in opposition. Today, the circumstance that West Germany has been, within the NATO framework, a country of "good Europeans" seems to give further support to this idea, and even those who (like the author) are somewhat skeptical of the claim that Weimar might have been saved, may concede at least that the Western powers get along with West Germany today, not just because the Germans have learned a hard lesson, or because they and the West face a common enemy now, but also because the West has given the Federal Republic its friendship and trust.

Of course, whether a different policy towards Brüning's Germany would have led to different results is a very speculative question. Some of the problems involved lie in the area of German internal politics: for example, whether Brüning could ever have attained popularity while the depression persisted, or whether his reported intention to effect a monarchist restoration[26] might not have provoked Nazi and Communist uprisings. One might ask whether he even seriously desired a wider circle of supporters than that comprising Hindenburg and the Reichswehr; there were advantages to a presidential cabinet that no leader could hope to enjoy while relying on a patchwork majority in the Reichstag. These and some of the external imponderables, such as whether a reconciliation could have been effected without the sacrifice of Poland, could form the basis of endless armchair theorizing, and such is not the purpose of a historical study.

Nevertheless, certain conclusions relevant to this question can be reached on the basis of an examination of the diplomacy of the 1930–1931 period:

1) The German government did not seek an undertanding with

[26] John W. Wheeler-Bennett, *The Nemesis of Power: The German Army in Politics, 1918–1945* (London, 1953), pp. 230–231.

the West as an end; at best, it regarded Western friendship only as a means by which various measures of revision could be achieved. This obviously was the case with the cultivation of America through Sackett or by Schacht; the United States did not ordinarily participate in European politics, and American friendship was scarcely important to Germany in those days except as a means of achieving reparations revision, or for securing private credit. But with England and France, too, the Chequers and Paris visits were for Brüning merely opportunities for broaching the reparations question or getting a loan; all the secret talk of friendship with France was hardly more than an effort to induce the French to grant a credit, or possibly to entice them into accepting a part of the German program. Admittedly, all nations tend to follow a policy of self-interest, but some at least have been willing at times simply to cultivate good relations, in the hope of realizing greater advantages later. While Bismarck recognized the need for friends abroad, his imitators have been curiously blind to this essential element in his policy.

2) As a corollary to the above, Germany was unwilling to offer any genuine *quid pro quo*, even to achieve revisionary aims. This reluctance was a striking feature of Brüning's "grand design" as outlined to Sackett in December 1930, and it was also evident when the British and Americans proposed "gestures" on the customs union and Cruiser B. It would not have been easy for Brüning to make concessions, and we must remember that the politically significant elements in Germany were opposed to making any detectable sacrifice. But if Germany offered the other powers nothing concrete, and if she set no store by their friendship, what lasting result could they expect to accomplish by making concessions to her?

3) Possibly the answer to this last question would be that they might at least have secured the continuation of a moderate government. But concessions to Germany did not necessarily assist the German government in its internal difficulties. The Hoover moratorium was an economic boon to Germany, but of little political value to Brüning, since he could not claim that he had brought it

about. Policies of mutual understanding had become suspect in Germany, so that Bülow's message to Curtius on the morrow of the September 1930 elections emphasized that he should make no recognition of the policy of fulfillment. Indeed, the only kind of foreign policy that was likely to win acclaim in Germany was one that wrested successes from a reluctant world. It may be suspected, though it cannot be proved, that one reason why the customs union proposal was first developed in the way it was, with no prior soundings with any of the other powers, was to avoid publicly contaminating this Austro-German scheme with foreign support.

4) What can be proved is that German policy was permeated with a doctrine of activism—that is, with the belief that taking action is desirable in itself.[27] In the cabinet discussions at the end of the 1930 election campaign, in Curtius' report of Hoesch's preliminary evaluation of the prospects for the customs union, in Bülow's talk with Rumbold on May 6, we find the same emphasis on the need for doing something, simply for the sake of doing. Throughout the German documents on the customs union, the plan is described as a *diplomatische Aktion*, not as a proposal or an undertaking. Trendelenburg thought that even if the customs union failed, a clarification of the situation was desirable. And when Pünder wrote his letter to Bülow, although he advanced reasons why reparations relief was essential, his stress on Brüning's insistence *that* some plan for revision should be advanced seems to reflect the same activist spirit. A defender of German diplomacy might argue that such a state of mind was inevitable, since the whole existing situation was unsatisfactory to Germany. Still, if that was the case, could the Western powers hope to satisfy the Reich's demands and yet maintain their own existence? It would seem that any concessions made would have left the German desire to follow an active course undiminished.

5) Finally, we must remember that some of the Western powers did make gestures to Germany. Aside from the Hoover moratorium, there was the British invitation to Chequers, specifi-

[27] Compare Gordon A. Craig, *Bismarck to Adenauer: Aspects of German Statecraft* (Baltimore, 1958), pp. 84–85, 85 note 56.

cally intended to give Brüning such recognition abroad as would help him with his domestic problems. It does not matter that Hoover and Henderson also had other aims in view; these aims should not have lessened the support afforded to Brüning. For his pains, Henderson was immediately rewarded with the customs union announcement, and when the Chequers visit did take place, it was punctuated with the bombshell manifesto from Berlin. This did not in itself upset the British for long, as they also wanted to end reparations, but the springing of this surprise was scarcely a courtesy to the host government. As for Hoover, although he was amply thanked by Brüning and Curtius, the German refusal to make a "gesture," together with Luther's loan-seeking expedition, helped to defeat the American effort to maintain German credit.

These conclusions do not tell the whole story. France failed to offer Germany any voluntary concession and insisted on her reparations privileges. She tried to use her financial strength to coerce other countries, and displayed a monomania of her own, an almost blind veneration for the Versailles *status quo*. France and Germany seemed to be haunted, in different ways, by the contrast between their respective positions as laid down in the treaties, and their respective economic and miltary potentials. It appeared that the treaties represented an unrealistic effort to establish an artificial French superiority.

But the peace settlement had been the result of a real victory, even though a close one. It was a victory of the Allies, not France alone, and reflected the preponderance of Allied over Austro-German power. Ultimately the peace as laid down could only be maintained if all the Allies supported it. But some of the Allies, principally Britain and the United States, did not do this, and it was largely their irresponsibility which left France in a state of nervous anxiety and exposed Germany to delusions of potential grandeur. As was said before, it did not help the cause of peace when Hoover declared his moratorium without consulting France, or when Norman went "all out" for reparations revision. In the Second World War, Britain and the United States recognized anew their responsibility in maintaining the Western position; it was unfortunate that they had not recognized it in the years of peace. We now have the evidence of the German documents, which reveal a government seeking single-mindedly to reverse an existing order. Yet the Allies had evidence then, too—in the attachés' reports, in the speeches in the Reichstag, in the German press. It was not that there was an absence of evidence, but rather that there was a failure to perceive its importance.

A case can be made that this lack of perception resulted from a lack of political education and a distrust of politics. The leaders of England and the United States had grown up in a world in which the balance of forces was taken for granted. Most of these men did not realize that this balance was maintained by the power politics and "secret diplomacy" which were becoming so much despised. There had been nothing such as conscription to delay a young man's entry into a private career. War, in the days between Appomattox and the retreat from Mons, might be an adventure (Norman had a good Boer War record) or morally repugnant (Hoover was a Quaker, MacDonald a pacifist on principle), but at all events, it and politics in general were something one could either take or leave alone. Most people preferred to leave politics alone; the constant scheming and the impossibility of finishing the job were distasteful to respectable men who had their private affairs to manage. Those who, either as members of an old ruling caste or as precinct leaders, made politics their profession were discredited and suspect by the 1920's, while Hoover's lack of political background was a positive asset in the 1928 campaign. Actually, Hoover had had some negotiating experience, as chief of the Commission for the Relief of Belgium and afterwards, but his forte was administration—telling subordinates what to do and seeing that they do it—and for that, the arts of negotiation are not necessarily required. A patrician like Stimson, who had campaigned in New York City, or an "old Party Secretary" like Henderson, with trade union experience, was better equipped, and we may note that Stimson and Henderson both saw, in the main, the need to concert with France. Expert knowledge, great energy, and high moral conviction are desirable qualities, but political leadership seems to require other abilities, such as the ability to gauge the intentions of people not under one's thumb. Two prerequisites for the maker of foreign policy would seem to be the ability to distinguish an ingratiating aggressor from a petulant victim, and the moral resolve to support the latter in spite of his petulance.

Hoover was quite aware that international relations were in serious trouble, and it is misleading, though not entirely mistaken, to think of him as an isolationist, for he certainly did not hide his head in the sand. Despite everything, the Hoover moratorium was an act of unusual political courage, and a victory over selfish nationalism; the tragedy was that it was fatally marred because France, unlike Britain, was not consulted. This tactical error arose from a failure to perceive the need for equilibrium, and a failure to identify those who were upsetting it. Similarly, Norman was correct in regarding debts and reparations as an incubus to economic normalcy, but economic normalcy also depended on stable political relationships, and on the sanctity of political as well as business contracts. Both Hoover and Norman were heavily influenced by personal antipathy to what seemed to be pettiness on the part of the French. But irritating as French tactics sometimes were, it was France, not Germany, that needed help.

Appendixes
Bibliographical Essay
Index

Appendix I

FRENCH FINANCIAL DIPLOMACY

IN THE question of whether the French deliberately used financial pressure for political ends, and if so, how they did it, it is difficult to find proof. The reliability on these points of many of the accusers, such as Paul Einzig, who spoke for the interests of the Bank of England, or German politicians and officials, who were oversuspicious of France, is open to doubt. Apologists for France can always point to the skittishness of French lenders, based on long experience, and say that dramatic withdrawals were motivated only by fears, all too justified, that their loans might go sour. However, it seems worth while to list the following evidence in one place where it may be examined together.

1) René Massigli told Craigie on December 22, 1930, that, in regard to Italian naval plans and desires for a loan, "France had only to wait a little and Italy would come on hands and knees and beg France for a loan at almost any price." [1] On January 13, 1931, Berthelot said to Lord Tyrrell that "France had no wish to exploit Italy's difficulties, but she could hardly be expected to lend to Italy money which would be spent on enabling her to build up to naval parity with France." [2]

2) On January 14, 1931, Governor Moret of the Bank of France told an informant of the German Embassy that the French Finance Ministry had offered the British a loan "under certain

[1] *DBFP*, 2/I, No. 271.
[2] *DBFP*, 2/I, No. 279.

circumstances and conditions"; the British had turned down the proposal "on grounds of prestige." [3] On February 23, Berthelot replied to a question from Hoesch as to whether other subjects of negotiation were tied in with the current financial discussions: "Berthelot, after some hesitation, answered with a definite 'Yes,' naturally without going into further details." [4]

3) On June 17 and 18, Robert Lacour-Gayet of the Bank of France told Mellon that the French action "concerning the terms upon which France would come to the financial assistance of Austria was taken in full discussion in the Cabinet. The action was unanimous." [5] On June 22, Ambassador de Fleuriau told Vansittart "that he thought Austria would in any case have to address herself to the League; that the question of a new loan would arise and that would be an occasion for his government to renew the conditions they had laid down as to renunciation of the customs union; but that the condition might be put in a milder and more tactful form." [6]

4) At a meeting at Castle's residence during the Franco-American negotiations in the last days of June 1931, Monick, the new Financial Attaché at the French Embassy, told Ogden Mills that if the United States did not accept the French point of view on the Hoover proposal, France would immediately withdraw seven to eight million dollars in gold from the United States. Mills did not hear the remark, but when Castle told him later, Mills said that the next time he saw Monick he would say that if the French wanted to do this, he would give them every assistance. The story came to the ears of the Italian Ambassador, apparently through a leak by Monick. [7]

[3] GFMR, 1776/D808289: Hoesch to Ministry, Jan. 14, 1931.
[4] GFMR, 1554/D666472-3: Hoesch to Ministry, Feb. 23, 1931.
[5] *FRUS, 1931*, I, 25.
[6] *DBFP*, 2/II, No. 76.
[7] SDP, 462.00R296/5038: Memo of conversation between Acting Secretary and Italian Ambassador, June 30, 1931. See also Drew Pearson and Constantine Brown, *The American Diplomatic Game* (Garden City, N.Y., 1935), which states that Mills threatened to debase the French franc, and Monick replied by suggesting a possible withdrawal of French deposits in New York; "Mills changed the conversation."

Appendix II

FILMS of German Foreign Ministry papers are filed in the National Archives, Washington, D.C., by *container* (that is, reel) numbers, and these numbers are used in references in this study. Such numbers must be used in requesting films from the Archives. The team that did the filming in England, however, assigned other numbers, *serial* numbers, to each of the original files, and it is apparently by these that the Public Records Office has filed its photostatic copies of the films. To facilitate the finding of references by scholars using British records, the following table lists the serial numbers corresponding to container numbers referred to in this study.

Container No.	Serial No.	Container No.	Serial No.
913	1598H	1684	3575H
913	1599H	1685	3575H
1484	3086H	1707	3575H
1492	3087H	1776	3642H
1493	3087H	2347	4576H
1553	3147H	2371	4602H
1554	3154H	2374	4606H
1555	3154H	2375	4606H
1657	3243H	2376	4607H
1659	3243H	2381	4618H
1660	3243H	2382	4619H
1683	3575H	2384	4620H

Container No.	Serial No.	Container No.	Serial No.
2385	4620H	3621	K49
2389	4622H	3693	K59
2520	5002H	4078	L176
2521	5002H	4506	K936
2535	5101H	4507	K936
2548	5138H	4617	K1063
2549	5138H	4631	K1090
2640	5648H	5385	K1977
3620	K49	5426	K1148

Bibliographical Essay

1. Archives

An important event of recent diplomatic historiography, comparable to the publication of *Die grosse Politik der europäischen Kabinette* in the twenties, is surely the microfilming for British and American archives of the captured records of the German Foreign Ministry, or Auswärtiges Amt. (The original documents have been returned to the Bonn government.) A mountain of information on German and world diplomacy, this source makes almost everything previously written on German policy in the Weimar era out of date. Users should consult the *Index of Microfilmed Records of the German Foreign Ministry and the Reich's Chancellory Covering the Weimar Period* (Washington, 1958), prepared by the Committee on War Documents of the American Historical Association, and issued by the National Archives, where the American copies of the films are kept. This *Index* is not complete, however, as it does not include the final filming done at Whaddon Hall, England, nor films falling partly within the period covered by the published documentary series (1933–1945). As the *Index* title shows, the films also contain information from the Reichskanzlei, including cabinet protocols of great interest for the light they shed on internal as well as external politics. Scholars may order copies of the films from the Exhibitions and Publications Branch, National Archives, Washington 25, D.C. It may be noted, however, that Brüning's economy drive seems to have extended to ribbon and carbon paper, so that even the Archives' own films of the documents are sometimes illegible.

Access to the American State Department records for the twelve-year period after January 1, 1930, now also at the National Archives, is restricted, which means that the Department authorities must approve the purpose for which their papers are to be used, and must review all notes taken. This control is exercised for the purpose of protecting individuals still living, and out of respect for the trust placed in the Department by other governments, rather than from any intention of suppressing information on past American policy. Since many of these papers have been published in the State Department's continuing series, *Papers Relating to the Foreign Relations of the United States*, these American records do not have the same unique importance as the German microfilms. The *Foreign Relations*, however, is necessarily selective (see below), and the unpublished records should be consulted by anyone wishing to make a thorough study of American policy.

The British and French archives are, of course, closed for the period of this study.

2. Published Documents

As already stated, the State Department publishes a continuing series of volumes, the *Papers Relating to the Foreign Relations of the United States*. (The first 1931 volume, used here, was published in Washington, 1946.) These books remind one of George Kennan's comment that the old State Department had the atmosphere of an old-fashioned law office; often the documents seem to have been chosen with a view to recording precedents for any possible minor international dispute, rather than for documenting major American policies. This may be justified, since the volumes thus serve the Department better in its everyday work, but it is frustrating for the historian, to whom the reporting from the Berlin Embassy before May 1931 would be more important than the problems created by the smelter at Trail, British Columbia. Brüning has suggested that important documents were omitted from this publication, and he is right, though there is not so much in the files from Sackett as he supposes; there seems to be no record of the letter sent in December 1930, bearing the proposal for an international conference. And in any case there is no indication that the editors have tried to conceal any information because it might be embarrassing to the United States —and that is high praise for an official publication.

The *Documents on British Foreign Policy* (London, 1946–), edited by Sir Llewellyn Woodward, Rohan Butler, and latterly also J. P. T. Bury, is more readable, and more explicitly designed as a record of major policies. At the same time, the volumes on 1930–1 evidently omit some significant matter, and indeed the editors had to skate lightly over some rather difficult subjects: Anglo-French friction, the question of foreign influence in the formation of the National Government in 1931, the dropping of the gold standard, and the conflicts between the Foreign Office on the one hand and the Prime Minister and Treasury on the other. Admittedly, there is the difficulty that "sensational" items assume a disproportionate and awkward significance when they are included in an official publication; one partial answer would be to open the archives simultaneously. Students of the interwar period will bear in mind that much of British foreign policy was not conducted by the Foreign Office; material thus omitted would probably look less appealing today than that recorded in these *Documents*. But after all is said, this is an extremely valuable source. If only we had as much from France!

Mention should also be made of the *Documents on German Foreign Policy* (Washington, 1949–), in this country published by the Department of State; this was to have covered the Weimar period, but now apparently will go no earlier than 1933. (A German edition is now planned for the earlier period.) The volumes contain information helpful to users of the pre-1933 microfilms. And there are, of course, such contemporaneously published documents as those in the League of Nations *Official Journal* and the British *Parliamentary Papers* and *British and Foreign State Papers*.

3. Diaries and Private Papers

Those who have been privileged to use Henry L. Stimson's unpublished diary, deposited at the Yale University Library in New Haven, will agree that it is a most important source for international affairs in this period. A portion of the material in it has also appeared in Henry L. Stimson and McGeorge Bundy, *On Active Service in Peace and War* (New York, 1948), and in the *Foreign Relations of the United States,* but there is much more in this manuscript. On the other hand, Stimson's private papers are, in this period, of more potential use to biographers than to students of diplomacy. Charles G. Dawes, *Journal as Ambassador to Great Britain* (New York, 1939), is very frank and revealing, though Dawes was more important to this study as a personal adviser to Hoover than as an ambassador. *Ambassador Dodd's Diary* (New York, 1941), edited by his son, William E. Dodd, Jr., and more well-known daughter, Martha, includes references to Sackett and George Gordon. Reginald H. Phelps, "Aus den Groener Dokumenten," *Deutsche Rundschau,* 76: 530–541, 616–625, 735–744, 830–840, 915–922, 1013–22 (1950); 77: 19–31 (1951), gives some interesting items from Groener's personal correspondence, as does also Dorothea Groener-Geyer, *General Groener: Soldat und Staatsmann* (Frankfurt a.M., 1955).

4. Memoirs

Memoir sources for this period are relatively abundant, particularly from Germany, where the urge to justify their conduct in the last years before Hitler has led almost all the surviving *Prominente* to put pen to paper. One of the few exceptions is Brüning, who still has produced no major memoirs, although he did write a letter which was published in 1947–"Ein Brief," *Deutsche Rundschau,* 70: 1–22 (1947). Brüning also made a controversial speech before the Rhein-Ruhr Klub, published in *Die Vereinigten Staaten und Europa* (Stuttgart, 1954), which includes some historical sidelights, and he earlier contributed a cryptic "Foreword" to Dawes's other diary publication, *Journal of Reparations* (London, 1939). Curtius' memoirs, *Sechs Jahre Minister der deutschen Republik* (Heidelberg, 1948), were largely written during the 1930's, though not published until after the Nazi regime. They are frankly apologetic and often inaccurate, but valuable, nevertheless. Curtius' reports on the customs union (*Bemühung um Oesterreich: Das Scheitern des Zollunionplans von 1931*, Heidelberg, 1947) and on reparations (*Der Young Plan*, Stuttgart, 1950) contain mostly material also appearing in *Sechs Jahre*. Hjalmar Schacht has been a most active memoir-writer. His *The End of Reparations* (New York, 1931), partly a description of the then recent Young negotiations, caused a sensation when it appeared. After Nuremberg, Schacht produced *Account Settled* (London, 1949), another partisan account, defending his past activities. His most recent effort, *76 Jahre meines Lebens* (Bad Wörishofen, 1953), translated as *Confessions of "the Old Wizard"* (Boston, 1956), is a somewhat different affair; more dispassionate, it is a remarkably straightforward and complete autobiography. Lutz, Graf Schwerin von Krosigk's *Es Geschah in Deutschland* (Tübingen and Stuttgart, 1951) is also quite good; less an apologia than most memoirs, it contains vivid sketches of leading personalities. Otto Meissner, *Staatssekretär unter Ebert-Hindenburg-Hitler* (Hamburg, 1950) and Franz von Papen, *Die Wahrheit eine Gasse* (München, 1952), translated as *Memoirs* (New York, 1953), defend themselves and Hindenburg. Some German memoirs, like Erich Kordt's *Nicht aus den Akten* (Stuttgart, 1950) and Ernst Heinrich, Freiherr von Weizsäcker's *Erinnerungen* (München, 1950), translated as *Memoirs* (Chicago, 1951), make only brief reference to the Brüning era, before passing on to the Third Reich. If an Austrian memoir may be included with the German, Sir George Franckenstein, *Facts and Features of My Life* (London, 1939) records aspects of earlier Austrian loan negotiations, but nothing on the 1931 crisis. Moritz J. Bonn, *Wandering Scholar* (London, 1949) is by a professor who was closely associated with Schacht, and acquainted with Bernhard von Bülow. Otto Braun, *Von Weimar zu Hitler* (New York, 1941) offers little on foreign policy, and Friedrich Wilhelm von Prittwitz und Gaffron, *Zwischen Petersburg und Wash-*

ington: Ein Diplomatenleben (München, 1952) is colorless and sparse on the 1931 crisis. Perhaps it might be said that the most valuable memoirs come not from gentlemen with spotless political reputations, but instead from those more or less under a cloud; the latter must come to grips with some of the more embarrassing facts.

British memoirs in this period center around the formation of the National Government, rather than any issue of foreign affairs, and are therefore somewhat less useful. The earliest in the field was Viscount Snowden, *An Autobiography* (2 vols., London, 1934), in which the pictures of MacDonald and Henderson are etched with the acid of its author's bitterness; Montagu Norman, however, receives a rare bouquet. Hugh Dalton's *Memoirs* (2 vols., London, 1953–7) include extracts from Dalton's diaries. L. S. Amery, *My Political Life* (3 vols., London, 1953–5), Viscount Samuel, *Memoirs* (London, 1945), and Viscount Templewood (once Sir Samuel Hoare), *Nine Troubled Years* (London, 1954) are almost entirely devoted to domestic politics in this period. Lord Vansittart's memoirs are an unusual and fascinating series of allusions and recollections, although occasionally the style seems to get in the way of the narrative. Vansittart was not quite so consistently anti-German and pro-French as his book (*The Mist Procession*, London, 1958) and the public stereotype would suggest.

French memoirs, like other French sources for 1930–1931, are disappointing. André François-Poncet, *Souvenirs d'une ambassade à Berlin, Septembre 1931–Octobre 1938* (Paris, 1946), translated as *The Fateful Years: Memoirs of a French Ambassador in Berlin* (New York, 1948), includes some sidelights on Brüning and the Paris and Berlin meetings, but does not mention the author's cartel plan. Edouard Herriot, *Jadis* (2 vols., Paris, 1948–52) and Pierre-Etienne Flandin, *Politique française, 1919–1940* (Paris, 1947) are worthless for the purpose of this study. Raffaele Guariglia, *Ricordi: 1922–1946* (Napoli, 1950), by the permanent chief of the Italian Foreign Ministry, contains little relevant detail.

A list of American memoirs naturally begins with Herbert

Hoover, *The Memoirs of Herbert Hoover* (3 vols., New York, 1951–2), in which the President's forceful personality emerges clearly. It is unfortunate that Hoover was not content to tell the unadorned story, which is not, after all, discreditable. His *The Ordeal of Woodrow Wilson* (New York, 1958) is on another period, but it is largely about Hoover himself, and illuminates his diplomatic attitudes and experience. Walter E. Edge, *A Jersey-man's Journal* (Princeton, 1948) supplements the State Department documents on the June–July negotiations in Paris. Stimson's and Bundy's *On Active Service in Peace and War*, already mentioned, is an important source; in this period, it is largely based on the diary, though some retrospective comments are added. Bernard M. Baruch's memoirs, *Baruch* (2 vols., New York, 1957–60) are self-serving and add little.

5. Secondary Studies

Secondary material on this period seems to fall into several categories. To begin with, there are magazine articles, often strongly partisan, written shortly after the events took place, while public interest was still warm. Most of this voluminous material has now been outdated by the documents and memoirs appearing since World War II. Some items, however, are still worth examination: Lawrence Dennis, "Sold on Foreign Bonds," *New Republic*, 65: 8–11, 38–41, 65–68, 93–97, 131–134 (1930), was a good early critique of American foreign investment; Rudolf Kircher, "The German-Austrian Pact," *Nineteenth Century*, 109: 549–556 (1931), stated the basic German point of view; G. Lechartier, "Proposition Hoover et la diplomatie nouvelle," *Esprit International*, 5: 558–577 (1931), gave a telling French criticism; Romulus, "I colloqui di Chequers," *Nuova Antologia*, 277: 509–531 (1931), contained some clever guesswork; and Mark Sullivan, "President Hoover and the World Depression," *Saturday Evening Post*, 1933, March 11, pp. 3–5, 28, 31, 34; March 18, pp. 10–11, 79–84, was written by a newspaperman close to Hoover, and defended him. Sullivan evidently used official documents in preparing these articles, and there are signs that Hoover in turn used the articles when writing his memoirs years later. Like Hoover's memoirs, they are silent on the President's fears for the short-term loans of the New York banks. By way of contrast with Sullivan's story, mention may be made here of Drew Pearson and Constantine Brown, *The American Diplomatic Game* (Garden City, N.Y., 1935) and Pearson and Robert S. Allen, *The Washington Merry-Go-Round* (New York, 1931), unfriendly to the Hoover administration; these books are often surprisingly accurate, though largely based on rumor and guesswork.

Another category of secondary matter is that of early studies by scholars, economists, and specialists in international affairs or international law. Some are doctoral dissertations: Alceste Antonucci, *Le Bilan des réparations et la crise mondiale* (Paris, 1935) and Mary Margaret Ball, *Die deutsch-österreichische Anschlussbewegung vom völkerrechtlichen Standpunkt* (Emsdetten, 1934), which adopt the French and German standpoints respectively. A revision of the latter appeared later in English: *Post-War German-Austrian Relations* (Stanford, 1937). Other analyses include: H. F. Armstrong, "France and the Hoover Plan," *Foreign Affairs*, 10: 23–33 (1931–2); G. P. Auld, "The Dawes and Young Plans: Then and Now," *Foreign Affairs*, 13: 6–25 (1934–5); R. C. Binkley, "Europe Faces the Customs Union," *Virginia Quarterly Review*, 7: 321–329 (1931); F. W. Foerster, "Germany and Austria: A European Crisis," *Foreign Affairs*, 9: 617–623 (1930–1); Adolf Grabowsky, "Der deutsch-österreichische Wirtschaftsplan," *Zeitschrift für Politik*, 21: 1–12 (1931); John W. Davis, "The World Court Settles the Question," *Atlantic Monthly*, 149: 119–130 (1932); J. C. DeWilde, "French Financial Policy," *Foreign Policy Reports*, 8: 232–240 (1932); Mary Agnes Hamilton, "J. Ramsay MacDonald," *Atlantic Monthly*, 161: 452–462 (1938); and P. H. Emden, "Story of the Vienna Creditanstalt," *Menorah Journal*, 28: 86–98 (Jan. 1940). Walther Federn, "Der Zusammenbruch der österreichischen Kreditanstalt," *Archiv für Sozialwissenschaft und Sozialpolitik*, 67: 403–435 (1932), is still the best available treatment of this subject. W. C. Langsam,

"United States and British Press Opinion of the Proposed Austro-German Customs Union of 1931," *Journal of Central European Affairs*, 2: 377–383 (1943), reveals the success of the Germans with the Anglo-American press. Paul Einzig wrote a number of books in the early thirties, including *The Fight for Financial Supremacy* (London, 1931), *Behind the Scenes of International Finance* (London, 1932), and *Montagu Norman: A Study in Financial Statesmanship* (London, 1932); Einzig attacked French financial diplomacy and defended Norman. In a class by itself is Herbert O. Yardley, *The American Black Chamber* (New York, 1931); Secretary Stimson was responsible for the ending of Yardley's code-cracking activities and in revenge, Yardley described them, and the weakness of State Department ciphers, in this book.

There have been many wholly or partly relevant studies by economists. C. R. S. Harris, *Germany's Foreign Indebtedness* (Oxford, 1935) is an excellent survey of the German private debt problem for the layman. Howard S. Ellis, "German Exchange Control, 1931–1939: From an Emergency Measure to a Totalitarian Institution," *Quarterly Journal of Economics*, 54: 158 (1940, Supplement), is a thorough study, which will probably stand for some time as the best coverage of its subject. Achille Dauphin-Meunier, *La Banque, 1919–1935: Allemagne-Angleterre-France* (Paris, 1936) is a helpful comparative survey of the trends in banking practice. Eleanor Lansing Dulles, *The Bank for International Settlements at Work* (New York, 1932) probably was written too early; it is uncritical and overlooks political problems. H. W. Arndt, *Economic Lessons of the Nineteen-Thirties* (London, 1944) was published by the Royal Institute of International Affairs, as was *The Problem of International Investment* (London, 1937), written by a study group of that body; Arndt's book is especially valuable to the student of this period. Solomon Wolff, *Frankreich und sein Geld* (Frankfurt, 1933) is surprisingly dispassionate; evidently it was written before the *Machtübernahme*. Margaret G. Myers, *Paris as a Financial Center* (New York, 1936) sees no evidence of French financial pressure for political ends, and Willard Hurst, "Holland, Switzerland and Belgium and the English Gold Crisis of 1931," *Journal of Political Economy*, 40: 638–660 (1932), also absolves the French, but more convincingly. Andreas Predöhl, "Die Epochenbedeutung der Weltwirtschaftskrise von 1929 bis 1931," *Vierteljahrshefte für Zeitgeschichte*, 1: 97–118 (1953), is a thought-provoking comment on the significance of the end of the gold standard. Finally, Roy Harrod's *Life of John Maynard Keynes* (New York, 1951) is an indispensable guide to noneconomists, such as the present writer.

Most of the biographic literature in this period, aside from Harrod's *Life of Keynes*, just cited, and Harold Nicolson, *King George the Fifth* (New York, 1953), is not overly impressive. Mary Agnes Hamilton's *Arthur Henderson* (London, 1938) is a sympathetic and laudatory treatment by a former coworker; it is superior to Edwin A. Jenkins, *From Foundry to Foreign Office: The Romantic Life Story of the Right Honourable Arthur Henderson, M.P.* (London, 1933). L. MacNiell Weir, *The Tragedy of Ramsay MacDonald: A Political Biography* (London, 1938) is a hostile treatment which has no doubt contributed to the current public image of its subject; Vansittart was probably right to deprecate it. Benjamin Sacks, *J. Ramsay MacDonald in Thought and Action* (Albuquerque, New Mexico, 1952) is a topical study of MacDonald's ideas and policies; it is of little use in connection with the 1931 crisis, when MacDonald was (perhaps rightly) following principles other than those he had always expounded. Elting E. Morison, *Turmoil and Tradition: A Study of the Life and Times of Henry L. Stimson* (Boston, 1960), contains an excellent summary of Stimson's activity in the summer of 1931. Herbert Hoover will probably not be the subject of a good biography until the Hoover papers become freely available to students. Louis P. Lochner, *Herbert Hoover and Germany* (New York, 1960), was written with access to the Hoover Institute papers. Georges Suarez, *Briand: Sa vie, son oeuvre, avec son journal et des nombreux documents inédits* (6 vols., Paris, 1938–52) is disappointing on events in 1930–1. Laval has had his attackers, such as Henry Torrès, *Pierre Laval* (New

York, 1941), and his defenders, including Jacques Baraduc, *Dans la Cellule de Pierre Laval: Documents inédits* (Paris, 1948); the best study the present writer has seen is Alfred Mallet, *Pierre Laval* (2 vols., Paris, 1955).

Two older books are worth mentioning as background: Friedrich Naumann, *Mitteleuropa* (*Volksausgabe*, with *Bulgarien und Mitteleuropa*) (Berlin, 1916) and Gustav Gratz and Richard Schüller, *Die äussere Wirtschaftspolitik Österreich-Ungarns: Mitteleuropäische Pläne* (Wien, 1925), translated as *The Economic Policy of Austria-Hungary During the War in its External Relations* (New Haven and London, 1928); the latter, published by the Carnegie Endowment for International Peace, gives firsthand information on the Salzburg agreements.

Some most valuable studies have been written since 1945. Karl Dietrich Bracher, *Die Auflösung der weimarer Republik* (Stuttgart and Düsseldorf, 1957) is the most careful survey available on German domestic affairs under the Brüning, Papen, and Schleicher governments, and a heartening proof of the revival of German scholarship. Another excellent study, covering a wider range, but with more attention to foreign policy, is Erich Eyck, *Geschichte der weimarer Republik* (2 vols., Zürich, 1954–6). Of less interest is Ludwig Zimmermann, *Deutsche Aussenpolitik in der Ära der weimarer Republik* (Göttingen, 1958); during the Nazi period Zimmermann had access to the files of the *Auswärtiges Amt*, but does not seem to have used them for Brüning's chancellorship. Heinrich Benedikt, *Geschichte der Republik Österreich* (Wien, 1954) is a good survey of Austrian history, politics, economics, and traditions from 1918 to 1945. In France, Georges Castellan, *Le Réarmament clandestin du Reich, 1930–1935* (Paris, 1954), has proved the perhaps not too startling point that the French military attachés in Berlin sent warnings of German rearmament; more interesting is the attempt to pinpoint the time when the German Army really began to expand. In England, R. S. Bassett, *1931: Political Crisis* (London, 1958) has made a thorough re-examination of that domestic crisis, putting MacDonald, Henderson, and Snowden into what seems to be a fairer perspective; see, however, the criticism of Bassett in Hugh Dalton, "1931," *Political Quarterly*, 29: 356–365 (1958). Further, John W. Wheeler-Bennett has brought his German recollections up to date in *The Nemesis of Power: The German Army in Politics* (London, 1953). Wheeler-Bennett is very sympathetic toward Brüner and Groener, with both of whom he was acquainted. And in America, Gordon A. Craig has pioneered in re-examining Brüning's diplomacy, making an apt and incisive critique in a series of lectures given at Johns Hopkins University, published as *From Bismarck to Adenauer: Aspects of German Statecraft* (Baltimore, 1958). Craig's *The Politics of the Prussian Army, 1640–1945* (New York, 1956) is a useful complement to Wheeler-Bennett's *Nemesis*. Hans W. Gatzke, *Stresemann and the Rearmament of Germany* (Baltimore, 1954), like Annelise Thimme, *Gustav Stresemann: Eine politische Biographie zur Geschichte der weimarer Republik* (Hannover and Frankfurt a. M., 1957), demonstrates the nationalist character of Stresemann's policy, using the microfilmed *Nachlass*. Craig and Felix Gilbert have also edited *The Diplomats* (Princeton, 1953), containing articles on interwar diplomacy: especially valuable for the 1930–1 period are Craig's "The British Foreign Office from Grey to Austen Chamberlain"; Hajo Holborn, "Diplomats and Diplomacy in the Early Weimar Republic"; Henry R. Winkler, "Arthur Henderson"; and Franklin L. Ford, "Three Observers in Berlin: Rumbold, Dodd, and François-Poncet." Henry Cord Meyer, *Mitteleuropa in German Thought and Action* (The Hague, 1955) provides interesting background, but says little on the 1931 customs union proposal. Robert H. Ferrell, *American Diplomacy in the Great Depression* (New Haven, 1957) is highly readable and contains an outstanding bibliography, but its treatment of the Hoover moratorium is somewhat cursory.

Two recent specialized studies are: Jan Krulis-Randa, *Das deutsch-österreichische Zollunionsprojekt von 1931* (Zürich, 1955), and Oswald Hauser, "Der Plan einer deutsch-österreichischen Zollunion von 1931 und die europäische Foederation," *Historische Zeitschrift*, 179: 45–93 (1955). Krulis-Randa's somewhat uninspired juridical study concludes that the customs union was not political in intent, even while admitting that there would have been no immediate economic benefits, particularly for Austria. Hauser sees the customs union as a forerunner of European union. More interesting and suggestive is the article by Wolfgang J. Helbich, a German student at Princeton: "Between Stresemann and Hitler: The Foreign Policy of the Brüning Government," *World Politics*, 12: 24–44 (1959). Helbich, however, attributes too much skill and calculation to Brüning's diplomacy. More recently, F. G. Stambrook, who worked on the microfilming of the German documents, has turned this experience to excellent account by describing the diplomatic preparation for the customs union announcement in "The German-Austrian Customs Union Project of 1931: A Study of German Methods and Motives," *Journal of Central European Affairs*, 21: 15–44 (1961). Other postwar books include Paul Seabury, *The Wilhelmstrasse* (Berkeley, California, 1954), which shows the conservative, nationalist, and aristocratic character of the German Foreign Office; S. William Halperin, *Germany Tried Democracy* (New York, 1946), a useful survey of Weimar history; and Robert S. Shaplen, *Kreuger: Genius and Swindler* (New York, 1960), much of which was first published in *The New Yorker*, and which describes some of the financial maneuvers of the period.

Finally, no bibliography of a study of the 1931 crisis would be complete without a grateful reference to *The Survey of International Affairs, 1931* (London, 1932), a volume, edited and largely written by Arnold J. Toynbee, in the still-continuing series issued by the Royal Institute for International Affairs. Toynbee's own survey, "Annus Terribilis 1931," introduces the work with 161 pages filled with the year's misfortunes. This is followed by a useful article by H. V. Hodson, "Nemesis: The Financial Outcome of the Post-War Years," and other Toynbean chapters on "Disarmament and Security," "The Anglo-Franco-Italian Naval Problem," and "The Project for an Austro-German Customs Union," not to mention other subjects less relevant to the present study. The book is extremely valuable, not only as a summary of what was publicly known at the time, but also as an index to the upsetting effect of the year's events on the British public, whose attitudes Toynbee reflected.

6. Newspapers

Berliner Morgenpost, March 1931.
Berliner Tageblatt, 1930–1931.
Chicago Herald and Examiner, June 1931.
Chicago Tribune, June 1931.
Daily Herald (London), 1931.
Deutsche Allgemeine Zeitung (Berlin), 1930–1931.
The Evening Star (Washington), June–July 1931.
Figaro (Paris), October 1930.
Frankfurter Zeitung, 1931.
Il Giornale d'Italia (Rome), June 1931.
Journal des Débats (Paris), 1930–1931.
Manchester Guardian, 1931.
Neue Freie Presse (Vienna), 1931.
Neues Wiener Journal, 1931.
New York Times, 1930–1931.
New York World-Telegram, June 1931.
Pester Lloyd (Budapest), March 1931.
Le Temps (Paris), March 1931.
The Times (London), 1931.
Vorwärts (Berlin), March 1931.
Vossische Zeitung (Berlin), March 1931.

Index

HARVARD HISTORICAL MONOGRAPHS

16. The Huancavelica Mercury Mine: A Contribution to the History of the Bourbon Renaissance in the Spanish Empire. By A. P. Whitaker. 1941.

17. The Palace School of Muhammad the Conqueror. By Barnette Miller. 1941.*

18. A Cistercian Nunnery in Mediaeval Italy: The Story of Rifreddo in Saluzzo, 1220–1300. By Catherine E. Boyd. 1943.*

19. Vassi and Fideles in the Carolingian Empire. By C. E. Odegaard. 1945.*

20. Judgment by Peers. By Barnaby C. Keeney. 1949.

21. The Election to the Russian Constituent Assembly of 1917. By O. H. Radkey. 1950.

22. Conversion and the Poll Tax in Early Islam. By Daniel C. Dennett. 1950.*

23. Albert Gallatin and the Oregon Problem. By Frederick Merk. 1950.*

24. The Incidence of the Emigration during the French Revolution. By Donald Greer. 1951.

25. Alterations of the Words of Jesus as Quoted in the Literature of the Second Century. By Leon E. Wright. 1952.*

26. Liang Ch'i Ch'ao and the Mind of Modern China. By Joseph R. Levenson. 1953.

27. The Japanese and Sun Yat-sen. By Marius B. Jansen. 1954.

28. English Politics in the Early Eighteenth Century. By Robert Walcott, Jr. 1956.

29. The Founding of the French Socialist Party (1893–1905). By Aaron Noland. 1956.

30. British Labour and the Russian Revolution, 1917–1924. By Stephen Richards Graubard. 1956.

31. RKFDV: German Resettlement and Population Policy, 1939–1945. By Robert L. Koehl. 1957.

32. Disarmament and Peace in British Politics, 1914–1919. By Gerda Richards Crosby. 1957.

33. Concordia Mundi: The Career and Thought of Guillaume Postel (1510–1581). By W. J. Bouwsma. 1957.

34. Bureaucracy, Aristocracy, and Autocracy: The Prussian Experience, 1660–1815. By Hans Rosenberg. 1958.

35. Exeter, 1540–1640: The Growth of an English County Town. By Wallace T. MacCaffrey. 1958.

36. Historical Pessimism in the French Enlightenment. By Henry Vyverberg. 1958.

37. The Renaissance Idea of Wisdom. By Eugene F. Rice, Jr. 1958.

38. The First Professional Revolutionist: Filippo Michele Buonarroti (1761–1837). By Elizabeth L. Eisenstein. 1959.

39. The Formation of the Baltic States: A Study of the Effects of

Great Power Politics upon the Emergence of Lithuania, Latvia, and Estonia. By Stanley W. Page. 1959.*

40. Conservation and the Gospel of Efficiency: The Progressive Conservation Movement, 1890–1920. By Samuel P. Hays. 1959.

41. The Urban Frontier: The Rise of Western Cities, 1790–1830. By Richard C. Wade. 1959.

42. New Zealand, 1769–1840: Early Years of Western Contact. By Harrison M. Wright. 1959.

43. Ottoman Imperialism and German Protestantism, 1521–1555. By Stephen A. Fischer-Galati. 1959.

44. Foch versus Clemenceau: France and German Dismemberment, 1918–1919. By Jere Clemens King. 1960.

45. Steelworkers in America: The Nonunion Era. By David Brody. 1960.

46. Carroll Wright and Labor Reform: The Origin of Labor Statistics. By James Leiby. 1960.

47. Chōshū in the Meiji Restoration. By Albert M. Craig. 1961.

48. John Fiske: The Evolution of a Popularizer. By Milton Berman. 1961.

49. John Jewel and the Problem of Doctrinal Authority. By W. M. Southgate. 1962.

50. Germany and the Diplomacy of the Financial Crisis, 1931. By Edward W. Bennett. 1962.

* Out of print.